UNDERSTANDING 'CLASSICAL' ECONOMICS

The 'classical' approach to economic problems, which can be traced back to Adam Smith and David Ricardo, has seen a remarkable revival in recent years. The essays in this collection argue that this classical approach holds the key to an explanation of important present-day economic phenomena. Focusing on the analytical potentialities of classical economics, the contributors illustrate how an important element of understanding its approach consists of developing and using its explanatory power.

The study opens with a clarification of what is meant by 'classical' economics; modern methods of economic analysis are related to the works of the classical economists. Then follow chapters dealing with the problem of economic growth and foreign trade. Both the von Neumann growth model and the 'new' theories of endogenous growth are shown to belong firmly to the classical tradition. The contributors examine the contribution of Piero Sraffa and clarify some of the more difficult aspects of his analysis. The (un)importance of the labour theory of value in classical thinking is expounded. The work closes with some observations on the critique of neo-classical theory.

Heinz D. Kurz is Professor of Economics at the University of Graz, Austria. The author or editor of twelve other books, including *Theory of Production* (co-authored with Neri Salvadori), he is a managing editor of *The European Journal of the History of Economic Thought* and serves on the editorial board of six other professional journals. Professor Kurz has taught at the Universities of Bremen, Kiel, and the New School for Social Research.

Neri Salvadori is Professor of Economics at the University of Pisa, Italy. The author or editor of four other books, he serves on the editorial boards of *Metroeconomica* and *The European Journal of the History of Economic Thought*. Professor Salvadori has also taught at the Universities of Naples, Catania and Denver and at the Maritime University Institute, Naples.

ROUTLEDGE STUDIES IN THE HISTORY OF ECONOMICS

1 ECONOMICS AS LITERATURE
Willie Henderson

2 SOCIALISM AND MARGINALISM IN ECONOMICS 1870–1930
Edited by *Ian Steedman*

3 HAYEK'S POLITICAL ECONOMY
The Socio-economics of Order
Steve Fleetwood

4 ON THE ORIGINS OF CLASSICAL ECONOMICS
Distribution and Value from Willam Petty to Adam Smith
Tony Aspromourgos

5 THE ECONOMICS OF JOAN ROBINSON
Edited by *Maria Christina Marcuzzo, Luigi Pasinetti and Alesandro Roncaglia*

6 THE EVOLUTIONIST ECONOMICS OF LÉON WALRAS
Albert Jolink

7 KEYNES AND THE 'CLASSICS'
A Study in Language, Epistemology and Mistaken Identities
Michel Verdon

8 THE HISTORY OF GAME THEORY, VOL 1
From the Beginnings to 1945
Robert W. and Mary Ann Dimand

9 THE ECONOMICS OF W. S. JEVONS
Sandra Peart

10 GANDHI'S ECONOMIC THOUGHT
Ajit K Dasgupta

11 EQUILIBRIUM AND ECONOMIC THEORY
Edited by *Giovanni Caravale*

12 AUSTRIAN ECONOMICS IN DEBATE
Edited by *Willem Keizer, Bert Tieben and Rudy van Zijp*

13 ANCIENT ECONOMIC THOUGHT
B. B. Price

14 THE POLITICAL ECONOMY OF SOCIAL CREDIT AND GUILD SOCIALISM
Frances Hutchinson & Brian Burkitt

15 ECONOMIC CAREERS
Economics and Economists in Britain 1930–1970
Edited by *Keith Tribe*

16 UNDERSTANDING 'CLASSICAL' ECONOMICS: STUDIES IN LONG-PERIOD THEORY
Heinz D. Kurz and Neri Salvadori

17 HISTORY OF ENVIRONMENTAL ECONOMIC THOUGHT
E. Kula

UNDERSTANDING 'CLASSICAL' ECONOMICS

Studies in long-period theory

Heinz D. Kurz and Neri Salvadori

ROUTLEDGE

London and New York

First published 1998
by Routledge
11 New Fetter Lane, London EC4P 4EE

Simultaneously published in the USA and Canada
by Routledge
29 West 35th Street, New York, NY 10001

Typeset in Garamond by J&L Composition Ltd, Filey, North Yorkshire
Printed and bound in Great Britain by T J International Ltd,
Padstow, Cornwall

British Library Cataloguing in Publication Data
A catalogue record for this book is available from the British Library

Library of Congress Cataloging in Publication Data
Understanding classical economics: studies in long-period theory/
Heinz D. Kurz and Neri Salvadori.
p. cm.
Includes bibliographical references and index.
1. Classical school of economics. I. Kurz, Heinz-Dieter.
II. Salvadori, Neri.
HB94.U53 1998
330.15′3–dc21 97–18644
CIP

ISBN 0-415-15871-0

CONTENTS

Acknowledgements vii

1 UNDERSTANDING ‘CLASSICAL’ ECONOMICS
An introduction 1

Part I ‘Classical’ economics and modern theory

2 VON NEUMANN’S GROWTH MODEL AND THE ‘CLASSICAL’ TRADITION
Heinz D. Kurz and Neri Salvadori 25

3 ADAM SMITH ON FOREIGN TRADE
A note on the ‘vent for surplus’ argument
Heinz D. Kurz 57

4 ‘ENDOGENOUS’ GROWTH MODELS AND THE ‘CLASSICAL’ TRADITION
Heinz D. Kurz and Neri Salvadori 66

5 THE NON-SUBSTITUTION THEOREM
Making good a lacuna
Heinz D. Kurz and Neri Salvadori 90

Part II On Sraffa’s contribution

6 SRAFFA, MARSHALL AND THE PROBLEM OF RETURNS
Carlo Panico and Neri Salvadori 103

7 THE ‘STANDARD COMMODITY’ AND RICARDO’S SEARCH FOR AN ‘INVARIABLE MEASURE OF VALUE’
Heinz D. Kurz and Neri Salvadori 123

8 MORISHIMA ON RICARDO
Heinz D. Kurz and Neri Salvadori 148

9 PEACH ON RICARDO
Heinz D. Kurz 176

Part III On the labour theory of value

10 KARL MARX ON PHYSIOCRACY
Christian Gehrke and Heinz D. Kurz 187

11 NO RESWITCHING? NO SWITCHING!
Neri Salvadori and Ian Steedman 226

Part IV On the critique of neoclassical theory

12 ON CRITICS AND PROTECTIVE BELTS
Heinz D. Kurz and Neri Salvadori 235

13 'PRODUCTIVITY CURVES' IN *THE ACCUMULATION OF CAPITAL*
Neri Salvadori 259

Name index 277
Subject index 281

ACKNOWLEDGEMENTS

The essays collected in this volume bear the stamp of the influence of many people; for their encouragement, support and criticism over several years we should like to thank especially the following friends: the late Krishna Bharadwaj, Christian Bidard, Antonio D'Agata, Giuseppe Freni, Pierangelo Garegnani, Christian Gehrke, Harvey Gram, Augusto Graziani, Harald Hagemann, Geoffrey Harcourt, Albert Jeck, Bruno Jossa, Peter Kalmbach, Ulrich Krause, Christian Lager, Lynn Mainwaring, Gary Mongiovi, Takashi Negishi, Edward J. Nell, Carlo Panico, Sergio Parrinello, Alessandro Roncaglia, Paul A. Samuelson, Bertram Schefold, and Ian Steedman. We should also like to thank Routledge for their interest in our work and Ray Offord and Kate Chenevix Trench for the fine processing of the material. Those chapters of the book which were first published elsewhere appeared as follows. Our grateful thanks go to the publishers concerned for permission to reprint them here.

2 'Von Neumann's growth model and the "classical" tradition', *European Journal of the History of Economic Thought* 1 (1993): 129–60.

3 'Adam Smith on foreign trade', *Economica* 59 (1992): 475–81.

5 'The non-substitution theorem', *Journal of Economics* 59 (1994): 97–103.

6 'Sraffa, Marshall and the problem of returns', *European Journal of the History of Economic Thought* 1 (1994): 323–43.

7 'The "Standard commodity" and Ricardo's search for an "invariable measure of value"', in M. Baranzini and G. C. Harcourt (eds), *The Dynamics of the Wealth of Nations*, London: Macmillan (1993).

8 'Morishima on Ricardo', *Cambridge Journal of Economics* 16 (1992): 227–47.

9 'Peach on Ricardo', *European Journal of the History of Economic Thought* 1 (1994): 411–20.

10 'Karl Marx on physiocracy', *European Journal of the History of Economic Thought* 2 (1995): 55–92.

11 'No reswitching? No switching!' *Cambridge Journal of Economics* 12 (1988): 481–6.

12 'On critics and protective belts', in A. Salanti and E. Screpanti (eds), *Pluralism in Economics*, Aldershot: Edward Elgar.

13 '"Productivity curves" in *The Accumulation of Capital*', in C. Marcuzzo, L. L. Pasinetti and A. Roncaglia (eds), *The Economics of Joan Robinson*, London and New York: Routledge.

H. D. K.
N. S.

1

UNDERSTANDING 'CLASSICAL' ECONOMICS

An introduction

Ludwig Wittgenstein once remarked, 'The classifications made by philosophers and psychologists are as if one were to try to classify clouds by their shape.' We do not pretend, of course, to know whether this is a fair assessment of the situation in the disciplines mentioned. We rather ask whether it would be true if it were applied to economics. More particularly, we ask whether classifying economic ideas in distinct analytical approaches to certain economic problems and even in different schools of economic thought is a futile enterprise. The title of this book implies that we think that it is not. We are especially convinced that there is a thing that may, for good reasons, be called 'classical' economics, which is distinct from other kinds of economics, in particular 'neoclassical' economics.

This view could immediately be challenged in terms of the indisputable heterogeneity and multi-layeredness of the writings of authors in the two groups. Moreover, whilst with regard to some aspects an author might be classified in one group, with regard to some other aspects he or she might be classified in the other group. Therefore, it should be made clear from the outset that we are not so much concerned with elaborating a classification of authors, which in some cases would be an extremely difficult, if not impossible, task. We are concerned rather with classifying various analytical approaches to dealing with certain economic problems, especially the problem of relative prices and income distribution. What we have in mind is a particular rational reconstruction of 'classical' economics which, in our view, is useful both for an understanding of certain important arguments found in several classical authors and for the development of these arguments. Our interest in these approaches is thus not purely and not even predominantly historical; we consider them rather as containing the key to a better explanation of important economic phenomena. Our concern with classical economics is therefore first and foremost a concern with its analytical potentialities which in our view have not yet been fully explored. If we were of the opinion that they had already been exhausted our interest in classical economics would be moderate. Hence an important element of 'understanding' classical economics, as we conceive it, consists of developing and using its explanatory power.

In this chapter an attempt will be made to specify what we mean by classical economics and to show that it is not an evanescent concept. We begin, in the next section (pp. 3–6), with a brief discussion of the complexity of most economic problems and of economic theory as an attempt to come to grips with that complexity. This leads us to the identification of a first characteristic feature of classical economics: its *long-period* method. As we shall see in the following section (pp. 6–7), a version of this method was also shared by all major marginalist authors until the late 1920s. However, the similarity of the methods adopted by two theories must not be mistaken for a similarity in the content of the theories. This aspect is dealt with in the subsequent two sections. The first (pp. 7–9) turns to the scope and content of traditional classical economics, whereas the second (pp. 9–13) is devoted to traditional neoclassical economics. The emphasis is on the sets of data, or independent variables, on the basis of which these theories attempt to explain the respective unknowns, or dependent variables, under consideration. It will be seen that in this regard classical economics differs markedly from neoclassical economics, the main difference being the way in which income distribution is determined. These two sections also raise the question of whether the sets of data contemplated by the theories are compatible with the long-period method or whether there exist tensions and contradictions between the method and content of a theory. It is argued that, whilst traditional classical theory can be formulated in a consistent way, traditional neoclassical theory faces insurmountable difficulties in this regard. The latter come to the fore in the shape of inconsistencies that undermine the logical foundation of the approach to the problem of income distribution in terms of the demand for and the supply of the factors of production collaborating in the generation of the social product, when there are produced means of production, i.e. 'capital', among these factors. The following section (p. 14) turns to the attempts of neoclassical authors from the late 1920s onwards to remedy this defect and at the same time render the theory more 'realistic', and indeed 'dynamic', in terms of models of temporary and intertemporal equilibria. It can be argued, however, that these alternatives are beset by a number of methodological difficulties and do not escape the problem of capital, the stumbling block of earlier, i.e. long-period, neoclassical theory. The final section deals with some more recent attempts to come to grips with economic change; some approaches belonging to the classical and some approaches belonging to the neoclassical tradition will be summarized. It is shown that long-period reasoning is flourishing in contemporary economics and that there is no reason to believe that it will be abandoned soon.

ECONOMIC SYSTEMS IN MOTION AND THE LONG-PERIOD METHOD IN THE CLASSICAL AUTHORS

As is well known, the concern of the classical economists from Adam Smith to David Ricardo was the laws governing the emerging capitalist economy, characterized by wage labour, an increasingly sophisticated division of labour, the co-ordination of economic activity via a system of interdependent markets in which transactions are mediated through money, and rapid technical, organizational and institutional change. In short, they were concerned with an economic system in motion. The attention focused on the factors affecting the pace at which capital accumulates and the economy expands and how the growing social product is shared out between the different classes of society: workers, capitalists and landowners.

How to analyse such a highly complex system characterized by a dense network of interdependences and feedbacks, *vis-à-vis* which the observer might easily get lost in a myriad of facts and considerations, failing to see the wood for the trees? The ingenious device of the classical authors to see through these complexities and intricacies consisted of distinguishing between the *market* or *actual* values of the relevant variables, in particular the prices of commodities and the rates of remuneration of primary inputs (labour and land), on the one hand, and *natural* or *normal* values on the other. The former were taken to reflect all kinds of influences, many of an accidental and temporary nature, whereas the latter were conceived of as expressing the persistent, non-accidental and non-temporary forces governing the economic system. The classical authors did not consider the 'normal' values of the variables as purely ideal or theoretical; they saw them rather as 'centres of gravitation', or 'attractors', of actual or market values. This assumed gravitation of market values towards their natural levels was seen to be the result of the self-seeking behaviour of agents and especially of the profit-seeking actions of producers. In conditions of *free competition*, that is, the absence of significant and lasting barriers to entry in and exit from all markets – the case with which the classical authors were primarily concerned – profit seeking involves *cost minimization*. This was well understood by the authors under consideration, hence their attention focused on what may be called *cost-minimizing systems of production*.

The method of analysis adopted by the classical economists is known as the *long-period method* or the method of *long-period positions* of the economy. Any such position is nothing but the situation towards which the system is taken to gravitate, given the fundamental forces at work in the particular situation under consideration. A discussion of how the classical economists conceptualized these forces, or determining factors, is deferred to a later section. Here it deserves to be mentioned that in conditions of free competition the resulting long-period position is characterized by a *uniform rate of profits* (subject perhaps to persistent inter-industry differentials), *uniform rates of remuneration* for each particular kind of primary input in the production process (such as different kinds of labour and natural resources), and prices that are assumed not to change between the beginning of the uniform period of production and its end, that is, *static prices*. Such a situation is to be understood as reflecting the salient features of a competitive capitalist economy in an ideal way: it expresses the pure logic of the relationship between relative prices and income distribution in such an economic system. The prices are taken to fulfil the condition of *reproduction*: they allow producers to just cover costs of production at the normal levels of the distributive variables, including profits at the ordinary rate. These prices have aptly been called also *prices of production* (Torrens, Ricardo). We might also talk of 'prices of *re*production'.

A frequent misunderstanding of the notion of the long-period position should be mentioned. According to it the classical economists' view was 'static': they dealt with a given and immutable economic world and were able to say nothing useful either about how that world had come into being or about how it would develop. In short, they are said to have been concerned exclusively with analysing a *given* system of production, turning a blind eye both to the question of the genesis of that system and the path it would take in the future. In this view classical economics is static, not dynamic. Such an interpretation overlooks, first, a very special property the classical economists attributed to a long-period position, i.e. that the actual system *gravitates* around such a position. This is a property which is most certainly obtained on the assumption that the dynamic process of the actual system converges to the long-period position at a speed that is sufficiently large compared with the rate at which technological change tends to upset any such position. However, the classical economists did not ask for *convergence* of the actual system to the long-period position. They were indeed less demanding: in their view gravitation means market values of prices and the distributive variables never moving 'too far away' from natural levels. Second, the classical economists were not concerned only with studying the properties of a given system of production. They were also interested in which system would emerge as a result of the choices of profit-seeking entrepreneurs from a set of technical alternatives at their disposal, where this set was taken to reflect the technological knowledge available at a given time and place. For example, with new methods of production becoming available alongside the growth in technological knowledge, the economic system was envisaged as gravitating towards a new long-period position, characterized by a new set of relative prices and new levels of the distributive variables. That is, it was assumed that the new long-period position would make itself felt immediately: the short-run adjustment processes triggered would propel the economy towards that position.

Analysing economic change and development in these terms involves, as indicated, a short cut. The adjustment process to any such position is simply taken for granted. This is perhaps expressed too strongly, because the classical economists put forward an argument in support of the supposed gravitation of market values to their natural levels. The discussion of this problem in Smith and the authors following him is based on essentially two propositions. First, the market price of a commodity depends on the difference between current supply and 'effectual demand' for that commodity, where the latter is defined as 'the demand of those who are willing to pay the natural price of the commodity' (Smith, *WN* I.vii.8). If the difference is positive, negative, or zero, the market price is taken to be lower, higher, or equal to the natural price. A positive (negative) deviation of the market price from the natural price is reflected in a deviation of the actual levels of the distributive variables from their normal levels and especially in a positive (negative) deviation of actual profits obtained in the industry from normal profits. Second, this latter deviation provides an incentive to profit-seeking producers to reallocate their capital. Profit rate differentials trigger movements of capital (and labour) and, as a consequence, adjustments in the composition of production: the output of a commodity increases (decreases) if the market price is above (below) the natural price. These movements tend to annihilate the deviations and (re)establish a uniform rate of return on the capital invested in the various industries of the economy. Accordingly, in a long-period position actual outputs equal 'effectual demands' and actual prices are at their normal levels.

The above argument in support of the assumed gravitation process cannot, of course, replace a proper dynamic theory, not least because there are particular difficulties the earlier authors were not aware of. For example, it cannot be presumed that a positive (negative) difference between market and natural price is equivalent to an above (below) normal rate of profit, since the positive (negative) difference between the respective prices of the inputs entering into the production of the commodity under consideration may be even larger (cf. Steedman 1984). The question at issue is whether such a possibility does not prevent the ultimate tendency of the market price to gravitate towards the natural level, by causing the output of the commodity to decrease, thereby raising the market price even more.[1]

Ever since the advent of systematic economic analysis in the seventeenth and eighteenth centuries economists have aspired to elaborate a proper dynamic theory, and many ingenious and hard-working people have made great efforts in this regard. However, given the complexity of the object of their analyses – a socio-economic system incessantly in travail – they realized that the long-period method was the best they had. The latter indeed quickly proved to be a powerful tool in studying certain properties of complex interdependent systems, that is, systems which would be extremely difficult to model and analyse in a dynamic framework even with the advanced tools of modern mathematical economics. Moreover, the classicals themselves occasionally ventured probing steps in the direction of such a dynamic analysis. Think, for example, of David Ricardo's discussion of the introduction and diffusion of improved machinery in the additional chapter 'On machinery' in the third edition of his *Principles*, published in 1821. However, a general dynamic analysis of the highly complex system under consideration was regarded as impossible at the time. The analytical tools available did not allow of such a dynamic theory, paying due attention to all relevant interdependences. The long-period method was seen as the best available in order to come to grips, however imperfectly, with an ever-changing world characterized by on-going technical progress, the depletion of natural resources, a changing distribution of income, etc. Long-period analysis was devised precisely to overcome the *impasse* in which the social scientist found himself, confronted with a reality which, at first sight, looked impenetrable, made up of a myriad of relationships between people and natural objects. The long-period method introduced some transparency to the complex object of study and allowed the theorist to derive a large number of interesting insights into the functioning (and the sources of malfunction) of the economic system. Because of its fecundity the long-period method was almost universally adopted in political economy until the 1930s.

This does not mean that there was no interest among economists in short-run problems; there was, of course. However, the important point is that the short-period analyses elaborated by the majority of authors dealing with such problems had – as their backbone, so to speak – fully specified long-period theories. In other words, the long-period theory was considered the core of economic analysis, from which there derived several short-period analyses designed to tackle special problems of a short-run nature, such as the implications of a capital stock not fully adjusted to the other data of the system or a sudden increase of the quantity of money in circulation.

THE ADOPTION OF THE LONG-PERIOD METHOD IN TRADITIONAL NEOCLASSICAL THEORY

The appeal exerted by the long-period method can be inferred from the fact that all early major marginalist authors, including William Stanley Jevons, Léon Walras, Eugen von Böhm-Bawerk, Alfred Marshall, Knut Wicksell and John Bates Clark, fundamentally adopted it. Like the classical economists and Marx they were concerned with explaining the normal rate of profits and normal prices: the concept of long-period 'equilibrium' is the neoclassical adaptation of the classical concept of normal positions. For example, in Marshall’s *Principles of Economics* it is stated:

> The actual value at any time, the market value as it is often called, is often more influenced by passing events, and by causes whose action is fitful and short-lived, than by those which work persistently. But in long periods these fitful and irregular causes in large measure efface one another’s influence so that in the long run persistent causes dominate value completely.
>
> (Marshall [1890] 1977: 291)

And Böhm-Bawerk, agreeing with the classical authors, suggested that the investigation of the permanent effects of changes in what are considered the dominant forces shaping the economy should be carried out by means of comparisons between long-period equilibria. Such comparisons are taken to express the ‘principal movement’ entailed by a variation in the basic data of the economic system (cf. Böhm-Bawerk [1889] 1959 II: 380). This view was shared by Ludwig von Mises, one of the most radical subjectivists of the Austrian school of economic thought, who advocated the long-period method, or, as he preferred to call it, the ‘static method’, in the following terms:

> One must not commit the error of believing that the static method can be used only to explain the stationary state of an economy, which, by the way, does not and never can exist in real life; and that the moving and changing economy can be dealt with only in terms of a dynamic theory. *The static method is a method which is aimed at studying changes;* it is designed to investigate the consequences of a change in *one* datum in an otherwise unchanged system. This is a procedure which we cannot dispense with.
>
> (von Mises, 1933: 117; emphasis added)

However, the adoption of the long-period method was not, of itself, prejudicial as to the *content* of the theory. In order to see this we have to turn to the forces which the classical approach on the one hand and the traditional neoclassical approach on the other conceptualized in order to determine normal income distribution and the corresponding system of relative prices. The emphasis is on the respective sets of data, or independent variables, from which the two types of theory start. We begin with a brief discussion of the classical approach.

THE TRADITIONAL CLASSICAL APPROACH

It is a first characteristic feature of the classical economists’ approach to the problem of value and distribution that the data contemplated all refer to magnitudes that can, in principle, be observed, measured or calculated.

This point of view, which may be called 'objectivist' or 'naturalistic', is present, for example, in William Petty's *Political Arithmetick*, in François Quesnay's *Tableau économique* and in the writings of Adam Smith and David Ricardo.[2] These authors refrained from having recourse to any non-observable, non-measurable or non-calculable magnitudes, or metaphysical concepts, in determining the general rate of profits and relative prices.[3]

Second, the many differences between different authors notwithstanding, the contributions to the theory of value and distribution of 'classical' derivation typically start from the same set of data. In general, the data concern:

(i) The set of technical alternatives from which cost-minimizing producers can choose.
(ii) The size and composition of the social product, reflecting the needs and wants of the members of the different classes of society and the requirements of reproduction and capital accumulation.
(iii) The ruling real wage rate(s) (or, alternatively, the rate of profits).
(iv) The quantities of different qualities of land available and the known stocks of depletable resources, such as mineral deposits.

The treatment of wages (or alternatively, in some theories, the rate of profits) as an independent variable and of the other distributive variables, the rate of profits (the wage rate) in particular, as dependent residuals exhibits a fundamental *asymmetry* in the classical approach to the theory of value and distribution. In correspondence with the underlying long-period competitive position of the economy the capital stock is assumed to be fully adjusted to these data, especially to the given levels of output. Hence the 'normal' desired pattern of utilization of plant and equipment would be realized and a uniform rate of return on its supply price obtained. Prices of production are considered the means of distributing the social surplus in the form of profits between different sectors of the economy and hence different employments of capital and, with scarce natural resources, in the form of differential rents of land and mines.

It deserves to be emphasized that these data, or independent variables, are sufficient to determine the unknowns, or dependent variables, that is, the rate of profits (the wage rate), the rent rates, and the set of relative prices supporting the cost-minimizing system of producing the given levels of output. No other data, such as, for example, demand functions for commodities and factors of production, are needed. The classical approach allows the consistent determination of the variables under consideration: it accomplishes the task it sets itself. It does so by separating the determination of income distribution and prices from that of quantities, taken as given in (ii) above. The latter were considered as determined in another part of the theory, that is, the analysis of capital accumulation, structural change and socio-economic development.

It is frequently claimed that an integral part of classical economics is the *labour theory of value*. According to that theory relative normal prices are proportional to the quantities of labour needed directly and indirectly in the production of the various commodities. Classical economics is said to stand or fall by the correctness or otherwise of that theory. Although it is true that the labour theory of value was adopted by several classical authors, and played an important role in the course of the development of classical economics, the latter does not depend on it. Relative prices (and the dependent distributive variables) may consistently be determined on the basis of data (i)–(iv) and will only in very special cases be proportional to the relative quantities of labour 'embodied' in the different commodities. Hence, while in some earlier authors, most notably Ricardo, the labour theory of value was elaborated as a simplifying device to see through the complexities of the system under investigation, once a satisfactory and logically coherent theory of value and distribution had been developed, the labour theory of value was dispensable. From the higher standpoint of the advanced theory, the labour theory of value turned out to be untenable in general. However, the fact that it applies in some special circumstances may be taken as a sign of sound intuition on the part of authors like Ricardo who adopted it and were able with its help to derive several interesting results.[4]

The abandonment of the classical approach and the development of a fundamentally different one, which came to predominate in the wake of the so-called 'marginalist revolution' in the later nineteenth century, was motivated by the deficiencies of the received analysis. The main targets of criticism were the labour theory of value and the failure of Ricardo and his followers to develop 'a unified general theory to determine the prices of all productive services in the same way' (Walras [1874] 1954: 416). Walras contended that such a unified general theory can be elaborated by generalizing the principle of *scarcity*, which the classical economists had limited to natural resources only, to *all* factors of production, including 'capital'. Let us take a closer look at how the neoclassical authors sought to effectuate this generalization.

THE TRADITIONAL NEOCLASSICAL APPROACH

Since the new theory was to be an alternative to the classical theory, it had to be an alternative theory about the same thing, in particular the normal rate of profits and normal prices. However, the set of data in terms of which the neoclassical approach attempted to determine these variables exhibits some striking differences with respect to the classical approach. First, it introduced independent variables, that is, explanatory factors, that were not directly observable, such as agents' preferences. Second, it took as given not only the amounts of natural resources available but also the economy's 'initial endowments' of labour and 'capital'. The data from which neoclassical theory typically begins its reasoning are:

(i) The set of technical alternatives from which cost-minimizing producers can choose.
(ii) The preferences of consumers.
(iii) The initial endowments of the economy with all 'factors of production', including 'capital', and the distribution of property rights among individual agents.

The basic novelty of the new theory consisted of the following. While the received classical approach conceived the real wage as determined prior to profits and rents, in the neoclassical approach all kinds of income were explained simultaneously and *symmetrically* in terms of the forces of supply and demand with regard to the services of the respective factors of production: labour, 'capital' and land. It was the seemingly coherent foundation of these notions in terms of *functional relationships* between the price of a service (or good) and the quantity supplied or demanded elaborated by the neoclassical theory that greatly contributed to the latter's rapid success in economics.

As has already been indicated, historically long-period neoclassical theory derives from a generalization of the theory of rent in terms of land of uniform quality and 'intensive' margins to all factors of production, including 'capital' (see Bharadwaj 1978). This generalization presupposes a strict analogy between land, labour and 'capital'. On this premiss the principle of scarcity rent, which the classical economists had limited to natural resources in given supply, was thought to be applicable also in explaining the incomes of labour and 'capital', that is, wages and profits. However, in order to be able to conceive of the rate of profits as some kind of index expressing the relative scarcity of a factor called 'capital', that factor had to be assumed to be available in a given 'quantity'. The degree of (relative) scarcity of the given 'quantity of capital', which was taken to be reflected in the level of the rate of profits, was then envisaged as the result of the interplay of data (i)–(iii). The smaller the overall amount of capital at the disposal of producers, other things being equal, the greater in general the relative scarcity of that factor and the higher the rate of profits, and vice versa.

As regards the conceptualization of the 'capital' endowment of the economy, the advocates of the 'marginalist revolution', with the exception of Walras (at least until the fourth edition of the *Eléments*), were aware of the following fact. Whereas different kinds of labour and land can be measured in terms of their own physical units, 'capital', conceived of as a bundle of heterogeneous produced means of production, had to be expressed in terms of a *single magnitude*, related in a known way to the *value* of capital goods, allowing 'capital' to assume the physical composition or 'form' best suited to the other data of the system. For, if the capital endowment were to be given in kind, only a short-period equilibrium, characterized by differential rates of return on the supply prices of the various capital goods, could be established by the forces constituting demand and supply. Such an equilibrium could not, however, be considered a 'full equilibrium' (Hicks 1932: 20). Whereas differential wage and rent rates for different qualities of labour and land are perfectly compatible with a long-period competitive equilibrium, differential profit rates are not: competition would enforce a tendency towards a uniform rate of profits.

To define 'capital' as an amount of value required the specification of the standard of value in which it was to be measured. The common procedure was to express capital in terms of consumption goods or, more precisely, to conceive of it as a 'subsistence fund' in support of the 'original' factors of production, labour and land, during the period of production extending from the initial expenditure of the services of these factors to the completion of consumption goods. This notion corresponded to the view that capital resulted from the investment of past savings, which, in turn, implied 'abstention' from consumption. Thus it appeared to be natural to measure 'capital' in terms of some composite unit of consumption goods.

Now the formidable problem for the neoclassical approach in attempting the determination of the general rate of profits consisted in the necessity of establishing the notion of a market for 'capital', the quantity of which could be expressed independently of the 'price of its service', i.e. the rate of profits. If such a market could be conceptualized in a coherent way, profits could be explained analogously to rent (and other distributive variables), and a theoretical edifice could be erected on the universal applicability of the principle of demand and supply.

The plausibility of the supply and demand approach to the problem of distribution was felt to hinge upon the demonstration of the existence of a unique and stable equilibrium in the market for 'capital'.[5] With the 'quantity of capital' in given supply, this, in turn, implied that a monotonically decreasing demand function for capital in terms of the rate of profits had to be established (see Figure 1.1). This inverse relationship was arrived at by the neoclassical theorists through the introduction of two kinds of substitutability between 'capital' and labour (and land, which is ignored for the sake of simplicity): substitutability in consumption and in production. According to the former concept a rise in the rate of profits would increase the price of those commodities whose production was relatively 'capital-intensive', compared with those in which relatively little 'capital' per worker was employed. This would generally prompt consumers to shift their demand in favour of a higher proportion of the cheapened commodities, i.e. the 'labour-intensive' ones. According to the latter concept a rise in the rate of interest (and thus profits) relative to wages would make cost-minimizing entrepreneurs in the different

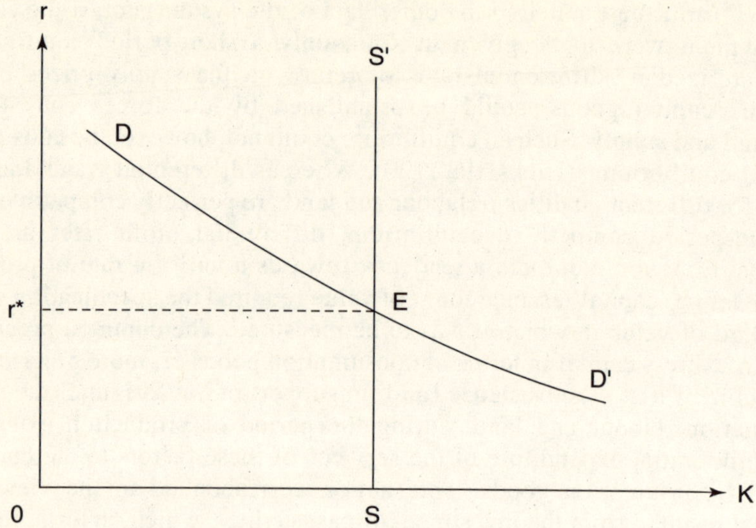

Figure 1.1 Rate of profit determined by demand and supply.

industries of the economy employ more of the relatively cheapened factor of production, i.e. labour. Hence, through both routes ‘capital’ would become substitutable for labour, and for any given quantity of labour employed a decreasing demand schedule for capital would obtain. In Figure 1.1 the demand schedule DD' corresponding to the full employment level of labour L^* (determined simultaneously in the labour market) together with the supply schedule SS' would ensure a unique and stable equilibrium E with an equilibrium rate of profits r^*. Accordingly, the division of the product between wages and profits is expressed in terms of the relative scarcities of the factors of production, including ‘capital’ (conceived as a value magnitude) that is considered *independent* of the rate of profits.

While this approach to the theory of income distribution and relative prices became quickly adopted in large parts of the economics profession, and, interestingly, is still advocated in significant parts of contemporary mainstream economics, its deficiencies were spotted soon after it had been put forward. Among the older neoclassical economists it was perhaps Wicksell who understood best the difficulties related to the problem of a unified treatment of all factors, including ‘capital’, in terms of the demand and supply approach. Wicksell was particularly critical of attempts to work with the *value* of capital as a factor of production alongside the physically specified factors labour and land in the production function of single commodities. In order to preserve a ‘correspondence’ between the factors, the different elements constituting social capital would have to be measured in 'technical units'. Starting from value capital implied 'arguing in a circle' (Wicksell [1901] 1934: 149), since the value of the capital goods inserted in the production function depends on the rate of interest and will change with it. The different versions in which the theory was put forward were variously criticized both from without and from within the camp of neoclassical economists; see, for example, Friedrich August von Hayek's frontal assault on it in his *Pure Theory of Capital* (1941). The criticism culminated in the so-called Cambridge controversies over the theory of capital, in which the emphasis was on the problem of the choice of technique of cost-minimizing producers. It was shown that the direction of change of 'input proportions' cannot be related unambiguously to changes in so-called factor prices. Thus a fall in the wage rate, accompanied by a rise in the rate of profits, may lead to the adoption of the less 'labour-intensive' (that is, more 'capital-intensive') of two techniques. The discovery of *reverse capital deepening* and of the *reswitching of techniques*, that is, a technique is cost-minimizing at two disconnected ranges of the wage rate and not so in between these ranges, runs counter to the conventional neoclassical view. A central element of the explanation of distribution in terms of supply and demand – the principle of substitution as envisaged by the neoclassical approach – is thus revealed as defective. The theory cannot be sustained other than in singularly special cases.[6]

We may conclude by saying that, in contradistinction to classical theory, long-period neoclassical theory does *not,* as a matter of principle, allow the consistent determination of income distribution and normal prices.

This was well understood by some major protagonists of the demand and supply approach as early as the late 1920s. However, confronted with the alternative of abandoning the demand and supply approach or the long-period method, in terms of which the former had so far been conceptualized, authors such as Friedrich August von Hayek, Erik Lindahl and John Richard Hicks opted for the second alternative. The result of these attempts to overcome the *impasse* in which neoclassical long-period theory found itself was the development of the notions of *intertemporal* and *temporary equilibrium.* In this way the demand and supply approach was meant to be rendered not only consistent but also more 'realistic' (cf. Lindahl [1929] 1939: 271; Hicks [1939] 1946: 116). Indeed, as the protagonists of the new developments kept stressing, economic theory had to be liberated from the straitjacket of 'static' analysis and turned into a proper 'dynamic' analysis. The declared aim was the elaboration of a model capable of portraying, in abstract terms, a 'real' economy moving through time.

TEMPORARY AND INTERTEMPORAL EQUILIBRIUM THEORY

The major novelty of the new theories was the abandonment of concern with a uniform rate of interest and static prices. As Lindahl stressed, in the new framework the concept of a uniform rate of interest was generally devoid of any 'clear and precise content' (Lindahl [1929] 1939: 245); and, as Hayek insisted, the notion of intertemporal equilibrium is not merely 'incompatible with the idea that constant prices are a prerequisite to an undisturbed economic process, but is in the strictest opposition to it' (Hayek 1928: 37; our translation). In contradistinction to traditional neoclassical theory, the capital endowment of the economy was given in terms of a vector of quantities of heterogeneous capital goods which were then treated in full analogy to different kinds of natural resources, that is, as 'rent goods' (Wicksell 1934). As Lindahl pointed out, 'During the initial period in the dynamic process under observation, all existing capital equipment in the community can be regarded as *original*, including any that has actually resulted from the production of earlier periods not covered by the analysis.' Hence 'Produced capital goods have the same significance for price formation as *true original* sources of similar kinds' (Lindahl [1929] 1939: 320–1; emphases added). In this way the problem of capital and interest was thought to be reducible to a special case of the problem of scarce factors of production and the type of income typically associated with them: rent.

It should also be mentioned that temporary equilibrium theory in general and intertemporal equilibrium theory until recently assumed a finite time horizon, which was arbitrarily given from outside. This points to the fact that the new approaches were essentially *short-period*. Intertemporal theory, as is well known, culminated in the so-called Arrow–Debreu model (cf. Arrow and Debreu 1954; see also Debreu 1959).

Here it is not necessary to enter into a detailed discussion of the merits and demerits of the temporary and intertemporal equilibrium models; the interested reader is recommended to consult Kurz and Salvadori (1995: 455–67). Suffice it to say that in our view those models are beset with serious methodological difficulties and, moreover, do not escape the problem of capital. We shall rather focus attention on some more recent developments in economic theory, and especially the theory of economic growth, which illustrate the resounding come-back of long-period analysis.

LONG-PERIOD ANALYSIS AND CONTEMPORARY ECONOMICS

In this introductory chapter we have specified what we mean by 'classical economics' and defined it in terms of method (long period) and content (the data do not include an endowment of 'capital'; instead they include either the real wage rate or the rate of profits). It hardly needs to be stressed that, with this definition of 'classical economics', this school of thought did not vanish with the death of Ricardo or some other early classical economists. It is, rather, possible to point out a large number of cases in the economic literature since Smith and Ricardo and up to our own time where in one way or another scholars have adopted the classical point of view. It is our contention that long-period analysis can be performed in a consistent, formally correct way *only* when based on the 'classical' approach. There is no consistent long-period neoclassical theory other than in exceptionally special cases that are of no economic interest.

Whilst some authors working in the classical tradition were keen to analyse systems displaying the whole set of phenomena for which explanations were sought, including reproducible commodities, especially capital goods, and scarce natural resources, others limited themselves to studying only selected aspects of the multi-faceted problem. The contributions of Piero Sraffa (1951, 1960) belong to the first category, whereas the early writings of Wassily Leontief (cf., for example, Leontief 1928) and the famous model of economic growth by John von Neumann ([1937] 1945) belong to the second.

Because of his unique importance for the revival of classical political economy, Sraffa's contributions figure prominently in this book. His ideas permeate several of the reprinted papers and are at centre stage in Part II. There the emphasis is especially on two aspects of his work which met with serious difficulties of understanding: first, the problem that constant returns are not assumed in his analysis (Chapter 6); and, secondly, the role played by the Standard commodity in it (Chapter 7). Two additional chapters (Chapters 8 and 9) deal with Sraffa's interpretation of Ricardo and recent attacks levelled at it.[7]

In the von Neumann model the problem of scarcity is set aside: this involves specifying datum (iv) on p. 8 above in such a way that, whatever the activity level of the economy, there is always an abundance of natural resources; therefore from an economic point of view these resources may be neglected. Attention focuses instead on the choice of technique problem in the case of universal joint production and constant returns to scale. The real wage rate is given from outside the system and any interest (profit) is taken to be accumulated. On the basis of these givens von Neumann determines a (uniform) rate of interest and the system of relative prices, a (uniform) rate of expansion and the activity levels of the different processes, and shows that the rate of interest equals the rate of growth. The model shares with the classical approach the asymmetrical treatment of income distribution, with the real wage rate given from outside and the rate of interest determined endogenously. For a discussion of the 'classical' character of the von Neumann model see Chapter 2 below.

Von Neumann's model is a *steady-state* model. Yet, as the classical economists were already well aware, there is no reason to presume that the actual economy will ever be in a stationary state or will follow closely a path of equi-proportionate growth. The dynamics of the economic system will generally be complex and can at most be expected to come close to such states during short intervals of time. This was also well understood by several authors working on the von Neumann model after its publication in English in 1945. It is not surprising, then, that their efforts resulted in a number of other results with a classical flavour, such as the so-called 'non-substitution' and 'turnpike' theorems.

The non-substitution theorem states that under certain specified conditions, and taking the rate of profits (rate of interest) as given from outside the system, relative prices are independent of the pattern of final demand. The theorem was received with some astonishment by authors working in the neoclassical tradition, since it seemed to flatly contradict the importance attached to consumer preferences for the determination of relative prices. As Samuelson wrote, 'From technology and the interest rate alone, *and completely without regard to the demand considerations* . . .[,] price relations can be accurately predicted as constants' (1966: 530).

In order for demand to exert an influence on the price of a good the supply function must not be horizontal. Then how do neoclassical models that are subject to constant returns to scale, no joint production and homogeneous labour arrive at an upward sloping supply curve? The upward slope of the supply curve reflects the increase in the relative price of the productive service which is required in a relatively high proportion in the production of the good. For example, if the good under consideration happens to be produced with a relatively high proportion of labour to 'capital', that is, a high 'labour intensity', an increase in the demand for the good, that is, a rightward shift of the demand schedule, would lead to a rise in the relative price of the good due to an increase in the wage rate relative to the rate of profits. This change in the relative prices of productive services is ultimately traced back to changes in the relative scarcity of the factors, labour and 'capital', the endowments of which are assumed to be given.

It is therefore the hypothesis that the rate of profits (or, alternatively, the wage rate) is given and independent of the level and composition of output which account for the theorem. This hypothesis is completely extraneous to the neoclassical approach and in fact assumes away the role played by one set of data from which that analysis commonly begins: given initial endowments. The assumption of a given rate of profits radically transforms the substance of the theory. With the endowment side chopped off, the concept of 'scarcity' of factors of production loses the significance usually attributed to it in neoclassical explanations of relative prices. Hence the demand for goods, and thus preferences, can no longer exert an influence on prices via the derived demand for factor services which are available in given supply: the prices of goods are independent of demand because income distribution is assumed to be independent of demand. It goes without saying that in the framework of classical analysis, with its different approach to the theory of value and distribution, a characteristic feature of which is the non-symmetrical treatment of the distributive variables, there is nothing unusual or exceptional about the non-substitution theorem.[8] A similar argument can be developed with respect to the turnpike theorems.

Until a few decades ago the time horizon in intertemporal general equilibrium theory was assumed to be finite and, therefore, arbitrary. The introduction of an *infinite* horizon turned out to be critical (see also Burgstaller 1994: 43–8). It pushed the analysis inevitably towards the long period. This was clearly spelled out, for instance, by Robert Lucas in a contribution to the 'new' theories of endogeneous growth. Lucas (1988) replaced the 'behaviouristic' approach to the problem of saving in terms of a given saving rate (as in Solow) by assuming that there exists an immortal 'representative' agent concerned with maximizing an intertemporal utility function over an infinite horizon. The utility function is specified in terms of two parameters: the rate of time preference, or discount rate, and the elasticity of substitution between present and future consumption. The production function of the consumption good is specified in terms of human capital and physical capital. There is also a function describing the formation of human capital in terms of human capital and nothing else. Lucas observed that 'for *any* initial capital $K(0) > 0$, the optimal capital–consumption path $(K(t), c(t))$ will converge to the balanced path asymptotically. That is, the balanced path will be a good approximation to any actual path "most" of the time' and that 'this is exactly the reason why the balanced path is interesting to us' (Lucas 1988: 11). Lucas thus advocated a *(re-)switching* from an intertemporal analysis to a long-period steady-state one. Since the balanced path of the intertemporal model is the only path analysed by Lucas, the intertemporal model may be regarded simply as a step towards obtaining a rigorous long-period setting. (Paraphrasing a dictum put forward by Paul Samuelson in a different context, we may say that intertemporal analysis is a *detour* with regard to long-period steady-state analysis.) Moreover, Lucas abandoned one of the characteristic features of all neoclassical theories, that is, income distribution is determined by the demand and supply of factors of production: if we concentrate on the 'balanced path', capital in the initial period *cannot* be taken as given along with other 'initial endowments'. In Chapter 4 below we show that, as regards its basic analytical structure (as opposed to its building blocks), the so-called 'new' growth theory belongs within the realm of what we have called 'classical' economics. In particular, it will be shown that in the free competition versions of this theory (the other versions are not analysed here) the 'technology' to produce 'human capital' (or, alternatively, 'knowledge' in some approaches) plays the same role as the assumption of a given wage rate in 'classical' economics.

We hope that this book will make it clear (i) that the long-period method is an extremely powerful tool of analysis, if handled correctly; and (ii) that a correct long-period analysis cannot take the endowment of 'capital' as given. However, our tribute to long-period analysis of 'classical' derivation must not be mistaken to imply opposition on our part to the development of a proper dynamic analysis. We are convinced, rather, that a correct long-period analysis provides the best ground for starting to elaborate a dynamical analysis. As Edwin Burmeister stressed in a recent review of Kurz and Salvadori (1995), 'It is natural to try to answer the easiest questions first, and it is much easier to study economics in a "long-period equilibrium" than ones in which the rate of profit is not uniform and is changing over time. Very little is known about the properties of such more realistic economies . . . , and even the little that is known usually is only about special and quite unrealistic cases (such as the one-good case). Almost nothing is known about the dynamic behavior of the more complex models', which can be studied within a long-period classical framework (Burmeister 1996: 1345–6).

NOTES

1 Garegnani (1990b) has put forward the following argument in support of 'gravitation'. Taking a system in which each commodity enters (directly or indirectly) into the production of all commodities, when a negative deviation in the market price of a particular commodity is accompanied by a positive deviation in the rate of profit, the same opposition of signs cannot be true for at least one of the means of production that enter directly or indirectly into the production of that commodity. For that means of production both the rate of profit deviation and the market price deviation will have to be negative. Hence the fall in its output will tend to raise its market price, leading directly or indirectly to a fall in the rate of profit of the commodity. This fall in the rate of profit will then reverse 'the initial "perverse" rise in output' (ibid: 331).

2 See also Kurz (1994) and Gehrke and Kurz (1995), reprinted as Chapters 9 and 10 below. Whilst most of the reasoning in this book refers to the case of a closed economy, Chapter 3, which is a reprint of Kurz (1992), is concerned with foreign trade, paying special attention to joint production in Adam Smith's 'vent for surplus' argument.

3 It should be pointed out here that we shall encounter a similar perspective in the writings of later authors who can be reckoned as belonging to the classical tradition, including Vladimir K. Dmitriev, Ladislaus von Bortkiewicz, Georg von Charasoff, Wassily Leontief, Robert Remak, John von Neumann and Piero Sraffa. For some evidence see Kurz and Salvadori (1993), reprinted as Chapter 2 below, and Kurz and Salvadori (1995: Chapter 13).

4 The conditions required for the validity of the labour theory of value with no choice of technique are well known (see, for instance, Kurz and Salvadori 1995: 110–13). Starting from Baldone (1984), Salvadori and Steedman (1988, re-

printed as Chapter 11 below) have investigated some further requirements when a choice of technique is involved and no technique is cost-minimizing at each relevant rate of profit.

5 On the importance of uniqueness and stability see, for example, Marshall ([1890] 1977: 665 n.).

6 For a summary statement of the different versions of the theory and the debates around them see Kurz (1987), Garegnani (1990a) and Kurz and Salvadori (1995: Chapter 14). The debate started with a paper by Joan Robinson (1953), using a description of technology in terms of 'productivity curves'. This description was soon put on one side after the publication of Piero Sraffa's *Production of Commodities by Means of Commodities* (1960). Salvadori (1996, reprinted as Chapter 13 below) provides a mathematical reconstruction of the description of technology introduced by Joan Robinson. This description has the advantage of being more easily accessible to economists with a neoclassical background and an interest in macroeconomics. Kurz and Salvadori (1997, reprinted as Chapter 12 below) put a part of the debate on the theory of capital in a methodological framework and raise the question of how it was possible, despite the fact that the neoclassical authors participating in the debate admitted the difficulty under consideration, for this to have apparently, and surprisingly, gone largely unnoticed in contemporary mainstream economics.

7 For a more detailed discussion of Sraffa's contribution see Kurz and Salvadori (1995, especially Chapter 13).

8 Kurz and Salvadori (1994, reprinted as Chapter 5 below) show that the non-substitution theorem conceived of as a uniqueness theorem does not need to hold if the rate of profits equals its maximum level (implying a zero wage rate) unless a further assumption is introduced. However, even if uniqueness may fail in this case, nevertheless demand plays no role in determining prices.

REFERENCES

Arrow, K. J. and Debreu, G. (1954) 'Existence of an equilibrium for a competitive economy', *Econometrica* 22: 265–90.

Baldone, S. (1984). 'From surrogate to pseudo production function', *Cambridge Journal of Economics* 8: 271–88.

Bharadwaj, K. (1978), *Classical Political Economy and Rise to Dominance of Supply and Demand Theories*, New Delhi: Orient Longman.

Böhm-Bawerk, E. von (1959) *Capital and Interest*, two vols, South Holland, Ill.: Libertarian Press. Translation of the 4th edn of *Kapital und Kapitalzins. Zweite Abteilung: Positive Theorie des Kapitales*, Jena: Fischer, 1921. First edition (1889), Innsbruck: Wagner.

Burgstaller, A. (1994) *Property and Prices. Toward a Unified Theory of Value*, Cambridge: Cambridge University Press.

Burmeister, E. (1996) Review of Kurz and Salvadori (1995), *Journal of Economic Literature* 34: 1344–6.

Debreu, G. (1959) *Theory of Value: an Axiomatic Analysis of Economic Equilibrium*, New York: Wiley.

Garegnani, P. (1990a) 'Quantity of capital', in Eatwell, Milgate and Newman (1990), pp. 1–78.

—— (1990b) 'On some supposed obstacles to the tendency of market prices towards natural prices', in M. Caminati and F. Petri (eds), *Convergence to Long-period Positions*, special issue of *Political Economy. Studies in the Surplus Approach* 6 (1990), pp. 329–59.

Gehrke, C. and Kurz, H. D. (1995) 'Karl Marx on physiocracy', *European Journal of the History of Economic Thought* 2: 55–92.

Hayek, F. A. von (1928) 'Das intertemporale Gleichgewichtssystem der Preise und die Bewegungen des "Geldwertes"', *Weltwirtschaftliches Archiv* 2: 33–76. Translated as 'Intertemporal price equilibrium and movements in the value of money', in Hayek, *Money, Capital and Fluctuations,* ed. R. McCloughry, London: Routledge, 1984.

—— (1941) *The Pure Theory of Capital*, London: Routledge.

Hicks, J. R. (1932) *The Theory of Wages*, London: Macmillan.

—— (1946) *Value and Capital*, 1st edn 1939, Oxford: Clarendon Press.

Kurz, H. D. (1987) 'Capital theory: debates', in *The New Palgrave: a Dictionary of Economics* I, ed. J. Eatwell, M. Milgate and P. Newman, London: Macmillan, pp. 357–63.

—— (1992) 'Adam Smith on foreign trade: a note on his "vent for surplus" argument', *Economica* 59: 475–81.

—— (1994) 'Peach on Ricardo: a review article', *European Journal of the History of Economic Thought* 1: 411–20.

Kurz, H. D. and Salvadori, N. (1993) 'Von Neumann's growth model and the "classical" tradition', *European Journal of the History of Economic Thought* 1: 129–60.

—— (1994) 'The non-substitution theorem: making good a lacuna', *Journal of Economics – Zeitschrift für Nationalaökonomie* 59: 97–103.

—— (1995) *Theory of Production: a Long-period Analysis*, Cambridge, Melbourne and New York: Cambridge University Press.

—— (1997) 'On critics and protective belts', in A. Salanti and E. Screpanti (eds), *Pluralism in Economics: New Perspectives in History and Methodology*, Cheltenham: Edward Elgar, pp. 232–55.

Leontief, W. (1928) 'Die Wirtschaft als Kreislauf', *Archiv für Sozialwissenschaft und Sozialpolitik* 60: 577–623.

Lindahl, E. (1929) 'Prisbildningsproblemets uppläggning från kapitalteorisk synpunkt', *Ekonomisk Tidskrift*. Translated as 'The place of capital in the theory of price' and reprinted as Part III of Lindahl (1939).

—— (1939) *Studies in the Theory of Money and Capital*, London: Allen & Unwin.

Lucas, R. E. (1988) 'On the mechanics of economic development', *Journal of Monetary Economics* 22: 3–42.

Marshall, A. (1977) *Principles of Economics*, London: Macmillan. Reprint, reset, of the 8th edn (1920), 1st edn 1890.

Mises, L. von (1933) 'Intervention', in L. von Mises and A. Spiethoff (eds), *Probleme der Wertlehre* II, *Schriften des Vereins für Socialpolitik* 183/II, Munich and Leipzig: Duncker & Humblot.

Neumann, J. von (1945) 'A model of general economic equilibrium', *Review of Economic Studies* 13: 1–9. English translation of 'Über ein ökonomisches Gleichungssystem und eine Verallgemeinerung des Brouwerschen Fixpunktsatzes', *Ergebnisse eines mathematischen Kolloquiums* 8 (1937), pp. 73–83.

Ricardo, D. (1951 *ssq.*) *The Works and Correspondence of David Ricardo*, 11 vols, ed. P. Sraffa in collaboration with M. H. Dobb, Cambridge: Cambridge University Press. In the text referred to as *Works*, volume number and page number.

Robinson, J. V. (1953) 'The production function and the theory of capital', *Review of Economic Studies* 21: 81–106.

Salvadori, N. (1996) '"Productivity curves" in *The Accumulation of Capital*', in C. Marcuzzo, L. L. Pasinettti and A. Roncaglia (eds), *The Economics of Joan Robinson*, London and New York: Routledge.

Salvadori, N. and Steedman, I. (1988) 'No reswitching? No switching', *Cambridge Journal of Economics* 12: 481–6.

Samuelson, P. A. (1966) *The Collected Scientific Papers of P. A. Samuelson* I, ed. J. E. Stiglitz, Cambridge, Mass.: MIT Press.

Smith, A. (1976) *An Inquiry into the Nature and Causes of the Wealth of Nations*, 1st edn 1776. Vol. II of *The Glasgow Edition of the Works and Correspondence of Adam Smith*, ed. R. H. Campbell, A. S. Skinner and W. B. Todd, London: Oxford University Press. In the text quoted as *WN*, book number, chapter number, section number, paragraph number.

Sraffa, P. (1951) 'Introduction', in Ricardo (1951 *ssq.*), *Works* I, pp. xiii–lxii.

—— (1960) *Production of Commodities by Means of Commodities: Prelude to a Critique of Economic Theory*, Cambridge: Cambridge University Press.

Steedman, I. (1984) 'Natural prices, differential profit rates and the classical competitive process', *Manchester School* 52: 123–40.

Walras, L. (1954) *Elements of Pure Economics*, ed. W. Jaffé, London: Allen & Unwin. English translation of the definitive edition of Walras, *Eléments d'économie politique pure*, Lausanne: Corbaz, 1874, 5th and definitive edn Paris: Richon, 1924.

Wicksell, K. (1934) *Lectures on Political Economy* I, London: Routledge. Translation by E. Classen, ed. Lionel Robbins, of K. Wicksell, *Föreläsingar i Nationalekonomi* I, Lund: Berlingska Boktrycheriet, 1901.

Part I

'CLASSICAL' ECONOMICS AND MODERN THEORY

2

VON NEUMANN'S GROWTH MODEL AND THE 'CLASSICAL' TRADITION

Heinz D. Kurz and Neri Salvadori

'It is obvious to what kind of theoretical models the above assumptions correspond' (von Neumann 1945: 2). With this remark John von Neumann (1903–57) concluded the exposition of the premises underlying his famous growth model, which was first published in German in 1937 and then translated into English and published in 1945 (see von Neumann 1937, 1945). What was obvious to him need no longer be obvious to us. However, scrutinizing the contemporary literature on the von Neumann model shows that there exists a clearly dominant view as to the nature and theoretical affiliation of von Neumann's contribution. This dominant view is well expressed by Kenneth Arrow, who, in a contribution to a volume celebrating the fiftieth anniversary of the publication of the growth model, wrote, 'Though von Neumann makes no reference . . . , it seems very clear that he took Cassel's work as a starting point' (Arrow 1989: 17). This interpretation is shared by the editors of that volume, who maintained that the Cassellian system 'forms the backdrop to the model expounded in his 1937 paper' (Dore *et al.* 1989: 2; see also Weintraub 1985: 77). And Lionel McKenzie in his entry 'General equilibrium' in *The New Palgrave* contended that Cassel's model 'was generalized to allow joint production in a special context by von Neumann' (1987: 500). The reference is to Gustav Cassel's *Theoretische Sozialökonomie*, published in 1918, which contains a considerably simplified version of Walras's theory (see Cassel 1918).[1] It is known as the 'Walras–Cassel model', a name coined by Robert Dorfman, Paul Anthony Samuelson and Robert Solow (1958: 346).

This chapter examines the conventional interpretation of the von Neumann model and confronts it with an alternative interpretation. The idea of writing this chapter was born while we were working on a book manuscript dedicated to the theory of production from a von Neumann–Sraffa point of view (see Kurz and Salvadori 1995). Since one concern of the book is with tracing the historical origins of the concepts used, we studied the literature on the two proximate originators of the approach adopted by us, only to find out that their contributions are frequently regarded as belonging to vastly different or even diametrically opposed traditions in economic thought. Hence our view as to the compatibility of the two approaches was questioned.

Delving deeper into the matter amplified our doubts about the conventional interpretation of the von Neumann model. These doubts concern both the circumstantial evidence put forward in support of a 'Walras-Cassel connection' of von Neumann's growth model and, much more important, the possibility of reconciling characteristic features of the latter with neoclassical (long-period) theory. Since from our point of view the conventional interpretation does not stand up to examination, the question was close at hand whether a different interpretation could be tried which is both plausible and not in conflict with the facts known to us. We think that we can offer elements of such an interpretation, in which the von Neumann model emerges as belonging to the 'classical' tradition of economic thought. It deserves to be stressed that for this interpretation it is of no importance whether von Neumann was familiar with the writings of the classical economists or those working in that tradition; in all probability he was not and did not care whether his analysis was 'classical', 'neoclassical' or anything else. What matters is the similarity of the structure of the respective approaches. Interestingly, though, von Neumann may well have come across pieces of economic analysis of classical derivation while he was a *Privatdozent* at the University of Berlin from 1927 to 1929. However, since we lack direct evidence in favour of the interpretation put forward here, either from von Neumann himself or from the group around him, it would be presumptuous of us to demand more than that our interpretation be heard together with the traditional one. It is up to the reader to decide which of the two, if either, is more convincing.

For the purpose of this chapter we shall adopt the following distinction between the 'classical' and the 'neoclassical' approach to the theory of distribution and relative prices in conditions of free competition, i.e. in the absence of substantial barriers to entry or exit. The 'classical' tradition focuses attention on goods that are reproducible. Production is conceived as a circular flow: commodities are produced by means of commodities. The wage rate(s) are assumed to be given from outside the system of production, determined by social conditions. The means of production are divided into scarce and reproducible: scarce means of production, such as land, yield their owners a (differential) rent, whereas reproducible means of production, i.e. capital goods, yield their owners a uniform rate of profit on the value of the capital invested. Hence, there is a fundamental *asymmetry* in the classical theory of distribution.

In contradistinction, in the 'neoclassical' tradition all prices, including the prices of 'factor services', are conceived as indexes of scarcity. Wages, profits and rents are determined *symmetrically* in terms of supply and demand. This requires that supply and demand are conceived as schedules relating price and quantity, where either the supply or the demand curve or both incorporate some substitutability between factor services or goods such that the two curves intersect. The point of intersection gives the equilibrium price and quantity. In the *long-period* versions of neoclassical analysis, with which we shall be exclusively concerned in this chapter, the economy is assumed to be in a self-replacing state, which means that the prices of the newly produced means of production are exactly the same as those of the means of production that entered as inputs at the beginning of the production process, and that a uniform rate of profits (or interest) is obtained on the supply price of capital goods.[2]

The structure of the chapter is as follows. In the first part, comprising the next three sections, the conventional interpretation of the von Neumann model will be scrutinized. Pages 27–9 summarize that interpretation; pp. 29–31 sketch the von Neumann model; and pp. 31–3 point out the difficulties in the conventional view. In the second part, pp. 33–46, the von Neumann model will be compared with major contributions to the 'classical' tradition preceding von Neumann. On pp. 33–41 central concepts employed by him are traced back to classical authors and authors working in that tradition. Pages 41–5 provide a summary statement of a contribution by Robert Remak, who was a colleague of von Neumann's at the University of Berlin. Pages 45–6 argue that von Neumann's paper can be read as containing, among other things, an implicit answer to the paper by his fellow mathematician. The final section draws some conclusions.

ON THE CONVENTIONAL INTERPRETATION OF THE VON NEUMANN MODEL

The essential reasons given in the literature in support of the 'neoclassical' interpretation are as follows. First, in 1936 von Neumann gave his paper in Karl Menger's famous Mathematical Colloquium at the University of Vienna; the paper was then for the first time published in the proceedings of the colloquium, *Ergebnisse eines mathematischen Kolloquiums* (von Neumann 1937). Since the earlier contributions to the colloquium dedicated to economics dealt with the problem of the existence of an equilibrium solution of the 'Walras–Cassel model', it is concluded that von Neumann was concerned with essentially the same problem, adopting the same (neoclassical) perspective.[3]

While circumstantial evidence of this kind is not without interest, it cannot of course replace a proper demonstration of the 'family resemblance' of the analyses under consideration. Such a demonstration is all the more needed since we know from von Neumann that he had read his paper for the first time in the winter of 1932 at the Mathematical Seminar of Princeton University (cf. von Neumann 1945: 1), i.e. more than one year before Schlesinger and Wald gave their papers at Menger's colloquium on 19 March 1934.[4] Such a family resemblance could be shown to exist if in terms of scope, method and content the analyses were similar. According to some authors there is clear evidence that this is the case (see, for example, Weintraub 1985; Punzo 1989, 1991).

In terms of *scope*, von Neumann is said to share Cassel's concern with equi-proportionate growth in the production of all commodities (e.g. Weintraub 1985: 77). Cassel presents two models, one of a 'continuous stationary society' (Cassel 1932: 144), the other of an economy growing along a steady-state path. In his first model it is assumed that *n* commodities are produced by using *m* primary resources, or factors of production, in given supply, employing a single fixed coefficients technology. This provides the basis for his second model, which is sketched only verbally. He introduces it in the following terms: 'We must now take into consideration the society which is progressing at a uniform rate. In it, the quantities of the factors of production which are available in each period . . . are subject to a uniform increase' (ibid.: 152). The *exogenously* given uniform and constant rate of growth of the various endowments also gives the rate of expansion of the economy as a whole. In Cassel's view this 'generalization' of the previous model does not cause substantial problems: the original set of equations giving the supply and demand for goods and factors is easily adapted to the new case, 'so that the whole pricing problem is solved' (ibid.: 153).

As regards the *method* used, we may distinguish between several aspects. In terms of the notion of equilibrium adopted, Cassel, the Viennese economists and von Neumann are all concerned with long-run competitive equilibria characterized by the absence of extra profits. Yet there appear to exist two even more important aspects which account for the close link seen by many interpreters between the von Neumann model and neoclassical general equilibrium analysis. First, it is pointed out that von Neumann on the one hand and Schlesinger and Wald on the other 'share one essential outlook, that of emphasizing inequalities rather than equalities as the true characterization of economic equilibrium' (Arrow 1989: 18). It is indeed a widespread opinion that the original novelty of the contributions to Menger's seminar consisted in the introduction of complementary slackness conditions, and that von Neumann in his paper simply made use of the same device.[5] Second, interpreting 'method' in the technical sense of the mathematical technique used to prove the existence of an equilibrium, the tool developed by von Neumann, i.e. a generalization of Brouwer's fixed point theorem, soon became *the* basic tool of neoclassical general equilibrium theory.

Finally, it is pointed out that in terms of *content* the Rule of Free Goods is employed by Schlesinger, Wald and von Neumann. This rule is taken to express the neoclassical view that a good that is in excess supply assumes a zero price. In a controversy with Kaldor, Solow claimed that 'the pricing side of von Neumann's model contained assumptions which took us back to Menger, Walras and the marginal productivity theory' (see Lutz and Hague 1961: 297).

Hence, on all three counts, the conventional interpretation appears to be well founded. Moreover, there is some evidence that von Neumann was familiar with the writings of major marginalist authors. Kaldor, who knew von Neumann from Budapest, their home town, and who was on friendly terms with him, recalls that 'One day he expressed an interest in economics and he asked me whether I could suggest a short book which gives a formal mathematical exposition of prevailing economic theory.' Kaldor suggested Wicksell's *Über Wert, Kapital und Rente* (1893). 'He read it in a very short time and expressed some scepticism of the "marginalist" approach on the grounds that it gives too much emphasis to substitutability and too little to the forces which make for mutually conditioned expansion.' According to Kaldor, von Neumann subsequently had a look at the original Walrasian equations (cf. Walras [1874] 1954). 'He told me afterwards that they provide no genuine solution, since the equations can result in negative prices (or quantities) just as well as positive ones' (Kaldor 1989: viii).

Thus, while the works of Wicksell and Walras appear to have been a source of inspiration to von Neumann, according to Kaldor's recollection he was dissatisfied not only with the fact that no proper existence proof of equilibrium was provided but also with the economic substance of the argument put forward. The following summary statement of von Neumann's model provides the basis of the ensuing critical discussion of the dominant interpretation of that model.

THE VON NEUMANN GROWTH MODEL

Von Neumann assumes that there are *n* goods which can be produced by *m* constant returns to scale production processes. The problem is to establish which processes will actually be used and which will not, being 'unprofitable'.[6] Von Neumann takes the real wage rate, consisting of the 'necessities of life', to be given and paid at the beginning of the (uniform) production period. In addition he assumes 'that all income in excess of necessities of life will be reinvested' (1945: 2). The characteristic features of the model include: (i) 'Goods are produced not only from "natural factors of production", but in the first place from each other. These processes of production may be circular' (ibid.: 1); (ii) the processes of production 'can describe the special case where good G_j can be produced only jointly with certain others, viz. its permanent joint products' (ibid.: 2); (iii) both circulating and fixed capital can be dealt with: 'wear and tear of capital goods are to be described by introducing different stages of wear as different goods, using a separate P_i [process $_i$] for each of these' (ibid.: 2).

These assumptions are coupled with the Rule of Free Goods: 'if there is excess production of G_j, G_j becomes a free good and its price $[p_j] = 0$' (ibid.: 3).

Von Neumann's approach can be summarized as follows. Let **A** and **B** be the $m \times n$ input and output matrices, respectively, where **A** includes the means of subsistence in the support of workers; and let **q** be the m-dimensional vector of activity levels and **p** the n-dimensional price vector. $\alpha = 1 + g$ is the expansion factor, where g is the expansion or growth rate; $\beta = 1 + r$ is the interest factor, where r is the rate of interest (or rate of profits). The model is subject to the following axioms.

$$\mathbf{q}^T\mathbf{B} \geqq \alpha\mathbf{q}^T\mathbf{A} \tag{1}$$

$$\mathbf{Bp} \leqq \beta\mathbf{Ap} \tag{2}$$

$$\mathbf{q}^T(\mathbf{B} - \alpha\mathbf{A})\mathbf{p} = 0 \tag{3}$$

$$\mathbf{q}^T(\mathbf{B} - \beta\mathbf{A})\mathbf{p} = 0 \tag{4}$$

$$\mathbf{q} \geq \mathbf{0} \text{ and } \mathbf{p} \geq \mathbf{0} \tag{5}$$

Axiom (1) implies that α times the inputs for a given period are not larger than the outputs of the previous period. (2) is the no extra profits condition. (3) states the free disposal assumption. (4) implies that processes which incur extra costs will not be operated. Finally, (5) requires that both the intensity and the price vector are semi-positive. In order to demonstrate that for any pair of non-negative matrices **A** and **B** there exist solutions for **q** and **p** and for α, $\alpha \geq 0$, and β, $\beta \geq 0$, von Neumann in addition assumes:

$$\mathbf{A} + \mathbf{B} > \mathbf{0} \tag{6}$$

which implies that every process requires as an input or produces as an output some positive amount of every good.

On the basis of these givens von Neumann determines (i) which processes will be operated; (ii) at what rate the economic system will grow; (iii) what prices will obtain; (iv) what the rate of interest will be. He is able to demonstrate the existence of a solution and that, of necessity, $\alpha = \beta$, i.e. the growth and the interest factor are equal.

The stimulation to publish an English version of the paper came from Nicholas Kaldor, then chairman of the editorial committee of *The Review of Economic Studies*. Kaldor arranged also for the translation of the paper and was concerned with rendering the mathematically demanding paper attractive to an audience of economists. A first step in the pursuit of this goal appears to have been the adaptation of the paper's title (cf. Kaldor 1989: x), a literal translation of the original German version of which would have been 'On an economic system of equations and a generalization of Brouwer's fixed point theorem'. The second part of the title, which reflects von Neumann's assessment that the main achievement of the paper consisted in the generalization of a mathematical theorem, was dropped entirely, and the neutral term 'economic system of equations' was replaced by the not so neutral term 'model of general economic equilibrium'.

The second step consisted in asking David Champernowne, 'the most mathematically-minded economist I knew, to write an explanatory paper *ad usum delphini*, for the use of the semi-numerates, to appear alongside it in the *Review of Economic Studies*' (ibid.: x).[7] In a footnote to the introduction of his paper, Champernowne thanks Nicholas Kaldor for help with economic ideas, and Piero Sraffa and a Mr Crum for 'instruction in subjects discussed in this article' (Champernowne 1945: 10 n. 1). Interestingly, in Champernowne's interpretation von Neumann's model emerges as one characterized by essentially 'classical' features. Before we deal with the classical tradition and von Neumann's paper, a critical discussion of the now conventional view will be provided.

SOME DIFFICULTIES IN THE CONVENTIONAL INTERPRETATION

It is a characteristic feature of neoclassical theory of whichever variety that it attempts to explain all prices and quantities, including the prices of productive services and the employment levels of these services, in terms of demand and supply. The data or independent variables from which the theory starts are the following. It takes as given:

(i) Initial endowments of the economy and who owns them.
(ii) Preferences of consumers.
(iii) The set of available techniques.

On the basis of these data the theory tries to find an 'equilibrium' price vector that simultaneously clears all markets for goods and services. In some representations of the theory demand and supply functions, or correspondences, are constructed for each good and each service. The intersection between a demand and the corresponding supply function then gives the equilibrium values of the quantity traded and the price ruling in the respective market.

Those who claim that von Neumann's model can be given a neoclassical interpretation would have to demonstrate that the former starts from the same set of data (i)–(iii) and centres around the same theoretical concepts: 'demand' and 'supply'. Such a demonstration is still lacking, and the following discussion shows why.

In von Neumann's model there are no initial endowments that could constrain productive activity and economic expansion: it is explicitly assumed that primary factors are available in abundance and that there is no historically given endowment of the economy with physical or value capital.[8,9]

This observation leads to the following one. As mentioned on pp. 26–7, the neoclassical economists explain all distributive variables, including profits, symmetrically in terms of supply and demand in regard to the respective factors of production, including a factor called 'capital'. This *necessitates* that one starts from a given 'quantity of capital', the 'scarcity' of which is seen to be reflected in the level of the rate of profits, or rate of interest.[10] In contradistinction – and this concerns a crucial difference – in the von Neumann model we encounter exactly the same asymmetry in the theory of distribution that is characteristic of classical analysis: the real wage rate is given from outside the system and profits are conceived as a residual magnitude. As Kaldor stressed at the 1958 Corfu conference on the theory of capital, there is no reason to presume 'that von Neumann's model was merely Wicksell, Marshall or the whole neoclassical school in a new disguise' (cf. Lutz and Hague 1961: 296–7).

Finally, it deserves to be mentioned that in the von Neumann model the (long-term) rate of growth is determined *endogenously* rather than exogenously, as in Cassel's neoclassical analysis, which takes as given the rates of growth of all primary factors and assumes their continuous full employment. No such assumption is to be found in von Neumann.

In von Neumann's model preferences can at most be said to play a rather concealed role: the only route through which they could exert some influence on the equilibrium solution is via the so-called 'necessities of life', which are taken into account in the (augmented) input matrix **A** (see p. 30 above). If the necessities of life reflect consumers' choice to some extent, as is argued by Samuelson (1989), it might be said that tastes play a role in the determination of relative prices and income distribution. For, with a different vector of wage goods reflecting workers' needs, even with given available methods, the method(s) chosen, the product(s) that have zero prices and the rate of interest may be different (see the numerical example in Steedman 1977: 186–91).

Samuelson is, of course, right in stressing that a change in the real wage rate may, and generally will, result in a change in the equilibrium solution of a von Neumann model. Yet in von Neumann's analysis the vector of goods constituting the means of subsistence of workers does not depend on relative prices. Hence, while it is perhaps an exaggeration to maintain that the von Neumann model is characterized by 'a complete omission of final demand' (Arrow 1989: 22), it is of course true that 'In contrast to Walras's formulae . . . , no direct marginalistic connection between prices and quantities is assumed' (Menger 1973: 56).[11]

As regards the assumption of a given set of alternative processes of production from which producers can choose, there is no material difference between the neoclassical (with the Walras–Cassel model as a special case) and the von Neumann model.[12] However, as has already been noted, there are important differences in the way in which the latter and the Walras–Cassel model conceptualize production. While in the Walras–Cassel model production is conceived as the instantaneous transformation of the services of the original factors of production into final goods, in the von Neumann model it is assumed that production takes time and that commodities are produced by means of commodities: the outputs of a process are available one time unit later than the inputs enter it. While the Walras–Cassel model sets aside capital goods, the von Neumann model takes into account both circulating and fixed capital.

Hence salient features of any type of (long-period) neoclassical model, including the Walras–Cassel variant of it, are absent in von Neumann's formulation. We may therefore conclude that the conventional interpretation of the latter is in serious trouble. We have also suggested that there exist some striking parallels between the approach chosen by von Neumann and that of the old classical economists. The following section will scrutinize the relationship between the two in greater detail. In the course of tracing back major concepts used in von Neumann's model in the history of economic thought we shall also take the opportunity to question some received opinions regarding the originality of ideas.

THE 'CLASSICAL' TRADITION

Several authors have emphasized the 'classical' nature of von Neumann's model. The first to point out that characteristic features of it are difficult to reconcile with 'the more traditional [i.e. neoclassical] approach' was David Champernowne (1945). These features include: society is assumed to be stratified in two classes, 'workers' and 'the propertied class'; 'workers spend all their income and capitalists save theirs' (ibid.: 16 n. 1); emphasis is on 'the circular nature of the production process' (ibid.: 12); prices 'depend on supply conditions alone and not on the tastes of consumers. This emphasis is important because the orthodox analysis has distributed attention evenly between marginal utility and conditions of supply' (ibid.: 12; similarly 17); 'the rate of interest is not determined as the supply price of waiting, abstinence or saving', no reference is made 'to marginal products or to the marginal efficiency of capital' or to the (Austrian) concept of the 'period of production' (ibid.: 12). Similarly, in his contribution to the 1958 Corfu conference Kaldor called the von Neumann model 'a variant of the classical approach of Ricardo and Marx' (Kaldor 1961: 181; see also Lutz and Hague 1961: 295); and Michio Morishima stressed that 'Marx's theory contains in itself a way to the von Neumann Revolution' (1973: 3; see also Walsh and Gram 1980; Goodwin 1986).

In what follows we shall deal briefly with the historical roots of the concept of production as a circular flow; the notion of a uniformly expanding economy; the Rule of Free Goods as applied to original factors of production and produced goods; and the use of inequalities in the formal analysis of the existence of a cost-minimizing system of production.

Production as a circular flow and the concept of a uniformly expanding economy

Profits and growth

The concept of 'the circular nature of the production process' emphasized by von Neumann can be traced back to the very beginnings of classical political economy.[13] It is present as early as in the works of William Petty and Richard Cantillon and was given a clear two-sectoral expression in the *Tableau Économique* of François Quesnay. The concept of circular flow surfaces in the writings of Adam Smith; it is put into sharp relief in David Ricardo's *Essay on Profits* (cf. Ricardo, *Works* VI) and in the second edition of Robert Torrens's *Essay on the External Corn Trade* (cf. Torrens 1820).[14] In that essay Torrens lays down, 'as a general principle', that the agricultural rate of profit is determined in physical terms and takes the exchange value of manufactured goods relative to corn to be so adjusted that the same rate of profit obtains in manufacturing (cf. ibid.: 361).[15] And in his *Essay on the Production of Wealth*, published in 1821, he shows that the applicability of that principle is not limited to the case in which there is only one sector which is in the special position of not using the products of other sectors while all the others must use its product as capital. However, the case of uniform input proportions put forward by him to illustrate the argument (cf. Torrens 1821: 372–3) is hardly less special.[16]

Further important contributions based on the concept of production as a circular flow were put forward, among others, by Karl Marx (1956, Part III; 1959, Part II); Ladislaus von Bortkiewicz (1906–7; 1907), who elaborated on the formalization of Ricardo's theory of value and distribution by Vladimir K. Dmitriev (1974); and the Russian mathematical economist Georg von Charasoff (1910).[17] Von Charasoff built on the foundations laid by his fellow-countrymen in an attempt to reformulate Marx's theory in a way that is logically unassailable. He deserves the credit for discussing prices and the rate of profits on the one hand and quantities and the rate of growth on the other within the framework of a physically fully specified input–output system, and for pointing out the remarkable symmetry of the two sets of variables.[18]

Anticipating 'duality'

Von Charasoff develops his main argument within the framework of an interdependent model of (single) production, which exhibits all the properties of the later input–output model. The central concept of his analysis is that of a 'series of production' (*Produktionsreihe*): it consists of a sequence, starting with any (semi-positive) net output vector (where net output is defined exclusive of wage goods), followed by the vector of the means of production and the means of subsistence in the support of workers needed to produce this net output vector, then the vector of the means of production and the means of subsistence needed to produce the previous vector of inputs, and so on. Von Charasoff calls the first input vector 'capital of the first degree' (*Kapital erster Ordnung*), the second 'capital of the second degree' (*Kapital zweiter Ordnung*), etc. This series 'has the remarkable property that each element of it is both the product of the following and the capital of the preceding element; its investigation is indispensable to the study of all the theoretical questions in political economy' (Charasoff 1910: 120).

The series under consideration is obviously closely related to the expanded Leontief inverse. In the case of circular production it is infinite. Tracing it backwards, first all commodities that are 'luxury goods' disappear from the picture, next all commodities that are specific means of production needed to produce the luxury goods, then the specific means of production needed in the production of these means of production, etc. On the implicit assumption that none of the commodities mentioned so far enters in its own production,

> it is clear that from a certain finite point onward no further exclusions have to be made, and all the remaining elements of the series of production will always be made up of the selfsame means of production, which in the final instance are indispensable in the production of all the different products and which therefore will be called *basic products* (*Grundprodukte*).

Von Charasoff adds:

> The whole problem of price boils down . . . to the determination of the prices of these basic products. Once they are known, the prices of the means of production used in the production of luxuries and finally also the prices of the latter can be derived.
>
> (ibid.: 120–1)

A further property of the 'series of production' deserves to be stressed: the capital of the second degree is obtained by multiplying the capital of the first degree by the augmented input matrix.

> Yet since the physical composition of a sum of capitals is obviously always a medium between the physical compositions of the summands, it follows that capitals of the second degree deviate from one another to a smaller extent than is the case with capitals of the first degree.
>
> (ibid.: 123)

The further one goes back in the 'series of production' the more equal the compositions of the capitals become, i.e. capitals of a sufficiently high degree 'may practically be seen as different quantities of one and the same capital: the *original* or *prime capital* (*Urkapital*)'. As Charasoff observes,

> this original type, to which all capitals of lower degree converge, possesses the property of growing in the course of the process of production without any qualitative change, and that the rate of its growth gives the general rate of profits.
>
> (ibid.: 124)

The rate of profits can thus be ascertained in terms of a comparison of two quantities of the same composite commodity: the 'original capital'. Von Charasoff emphasizes, 'The original capital expresses the idea of a surplus-value yielding, growing capital in its purest form, and the rate of its growth appears in fact as the general capitalist profit rate' (ibid.: 112).[19] In the hypothetical case in which all profits are accumulated, the proportions of the different sectors equal the proportions of the original capital. In that case the actual rate of growth equals the rate of profits: the system expands along a von Neumann ray.

These considerations provide the key to a solution of the problem of price. For, if the various capitals can be conceived 'as different amounts of the selfsame capital . . . , then prices must be proportional to the dimensions of these, and the problem of price thus finds its solution in this relationship based on law' (ibid.: 123). The solution to the price problem can therefore be cast in a form in which 'the notion of labour is almost entirely by-passed' (ibid.: 112). Implicit in this reasoning is the abandonment of the labour theory of value as a basis for the theory of relative prices and the rate of profits: taking the technical conditions of production and the real wage rate as given, prices of all commodities and the general profit rate can be determined without having recourse to labour values.

Von Charasoff was perhaps the first author to note clearly what von Neumann more than two decades later was to call 'the remarkable duality (symmetry) of the monetary variables (prices p_j, interest factor β) and the technical variables (intensities of production q_i, coefficient of expansion of the economy α' (von Neumann 1945: 1).[20]

The rule of free goods

As we have seen (pp. 28–9), it is widely held that the original novelty of the contributions to Menger's colloquium consisted in the use of inequalities in economic analysis. Whether a productive resource in fixed supply is scarce or not is no longer taken as given from outside, as in previous theory, but is decided endogenously and is thus a part of the solution of the system.[21]

While there can be no doubt that the introduction of complementary slackness conditions represents an achievement, it is questionable whether the underlying idea is really new. In what follows we shall distinguish between the application of the Rule of Free Goods to 'original' factors of production – in particular, different qualities of land on the one hand and (one or several qualities of) labour on the other, and to produced commodities.

The notion that in conditions of free competition the services of certain factors of production, such as some qualities of land, which are in excess supply assume a zero price was a standard element in classical rent theory from James Anderson to David Ricardo. See, for example, the following statement by Ricardo in which reference is to land available in abundant quantity: 'no rent could be paid for such land, for the reason stated why nothing is given for the use of air and water, or for any of the gifts of nature which exist in boundless quantity' (*Works*: 69; see also Sraffa 1960: 75). At most, one could say that there is old wine in new bottles. What *is* new is that the applicability of the Rule of Free Goods is defined differently. In classical economics that rule was *not* applied to labour; see, for example, Ricardo's discussion of the labour-displacing effects of the introduction of machinery: the presence of unemployed labourers does not drive the wage to zero (cf. *Works* I: chapter 31). In contradistinction, in early contributions to neoclassical general equilibrium theory the rule is taken to be indiscriminately applicable to *all* primary inputs, including labour. Hence the 'reservation price' for all primary inputs is taken to be zero, whereas in classical economics that for labour is positive.

Interestingly, von Neumann applied the Rule of Free Goods in the same way as the classics. While he assumed 'That the natural factors of production, including labour, can be expanded in unlimited quantities' (1945: 2), that did not make him treat all these factors alike. Rather, he singled out labour as the only factor that is exempt from that rule; all other primary factors, although needed in production, 'disappear' from the scene because they are taken to be non-scarce.[22] Labour is assumed to receive an exogenously given wage bundle which is independent of the degree of unemployment.[23]

By contrast, von Neumann rather generalized the Rule of Free Goods to products. This is possible because unlike the Viennese economists (and Walras), who assumed single production, he allowed joint production: with single production no produced commodity can be a free good, other than in the ultra-short period. Interestingly, the Rule of Free Goods as applied to products can likewise be traced back to the writings of the classical economists. Adam Smith pointed out that with joint production the proportions in which the products can be produced need not coincide with those in which they are wanted. Hence some products may be overproduced, with the consequence that 'the greater part of them would be thrown away as things of no value' (see Smith, *WN* I.xi.c.4; see also Kurz 1986).[24]

These considerations show how misleading it can be to try to infer the economic content of a model from the analytical tools or 'method' used. The way in which von Neumann used the inequality method appears to preclude the possibility of interpreting his model in a straightforward manner as belonging to the neoclassical tradition. At the same time the use he made of that method does not seem to be in conflict in any simple or obvious way with a classical interpretation of his model.

The choice of technique problem and the use of inequalities

The classical approach

Ever since the inception of systematic economic analysis the problem of the choice of technique has played an important role. Scrutiny shows that the classical economists proceeded in two steps. They first analysed an economy using a *given* system of production. Thus, in the chapter 'On value' of the *Principles*, Ricardo is concerned with investigating the relationship between relative prices and the level of the rate of profits for a given system of production. It is only subsequently that the problem of the choice of technique is addressed.

This latter problem can be divided into two sub-problems: (i) Which methods of production should be chosen from a given set of alternative methods? (ii) Should a newly available method of production be adopted? Problem (i) is investigated, for example, in the second chapter of Ricardo's *Principles*, 'On rent'. Emphasis is on which kinds of land (or methods of production) will be used in order to produce given outputs. With free competition the choice of technique problem consists in finding, given the real wage rate, a cost-minimizing system of production, including the cultivation of land, for which commodity prices, rents and the rate of profits are non-negative and no process yields extra profits. Problem (ii) – in modern parlance, whether an invention will become an innovation – is investigated in chapter 31, 'On machinery'. There Ricardo also provides, albeit in a rudimentary form, an analysis of the transition of the economy from one long-period position to another. Initially the capitalist 'who made the discovery of the machine, or who first usefully applied it, [would make] . . . great profits for a time' (*Works* I: 387), i.e. would pocket 'extra' or 'surplus' profits. Competition would then bring about a fall in prices to costs of production and force other capitalists to adopt the superior method of production. The adjustment process would eventually establish a new long-period position characterized by a new system of production and the associated new levels of the rate of profits, of real wages, and of prices (similarly Smith, *WN* I.x.b.43). Ricardo was thus also concerned with investigating the logical generation of a long-period position of the economy.[25]

Inequalities

Only a few years after the publication of the third edition of Ricardo's *Principles* (1821) a group around William Whewell at the University of Cambridge applied 'symbolic language . . . to the solution of some problems in Political Economy' (Tozer 1838: 507).[26] This included the treatment of the choice of technique problem in algebraic terms, employing *in*equalities. Whewell (1831) investigates the case where a given amount of commodities can be produced either by direct labour alone, without the assistance of machinery, i.e. what Ricardo called 'unassisted labour', or by labour operating a machine that lasts for only a year and is itself the product of a series of labour inputs. He demonstrates that 'the machine can be employed without loss' if (in Whewell's notation)

$$l + l' + l'' + \&\text{c.} < L$$

(Whewell 1831: 20), where the left-hand side of the inequality gives the direct and indirect amount of labour needed to produce the given output by means of the machine, while the right-hand side gives the amount of unassisted labour required with the alternative method of production. Thus, Whewell adds, 'when machinery is employed, it has always cost less labour than would obtain the same produce without machinery' (ibid.). John Edward Tozer, whose algebraic formulation is more sophisticated, follows Whewell in using inequalities in the discussion of the choice of technique problem. Summarizing his argument in terms of p and p_1, i.e. the price of produce before and after the introduction of machinery, he writes: 'It may be observed that p_1 cannot be $> p$; if it were, more than the ordinary profit would arise from employing labour, and the machine would be superseded' (1838: 512).

The classical approach to the problem of the choice of technique in terms of extra profits and extra costs was also adopted by Karl Marx. His discussion of the falling tendency of the rate of profits in volume III of *Capital* starts from the premiss: 'No capitalist ever voluntarily introduces a new method of production, no matter how much more productive it may be, . . . so long as it reduces the rate of profit' (Marx 1959: 264). Yet if no capitalist ever 'voluntarily' does so, how is it possible that the general rate of profits declines? Marx's answer reads as follows. While a capitalist who first employs a new method of production that allows him to produce at lower costs per unit of output will reap extra profits, competition will eventually lead to the general adoption of the new method and bring about a fall in prices. It is this fall in prices which, according to Marx, is the proximate reason why the general rate of profits is bound to fall in consequence of the gradual replacement of an old method of production by a new one.

Marx's analysis is of particular interest since it was the focus of a criticism elaborated by Ladislaus von Bortkiewicz in the final part of his tripartite treatise 'Wertrechnung und Preisrechnung im Marxschen System' (von Bortkiewicz 1906–7), in which another formalization of the choice of technique problem in terms of inequalities is provided. Since we are not aware of any evidence showing that von Bortkiewicz was familiar with the writings of Whewell or Tozer, we may credit him with the independent introduction of a new tool in economic analysis. Compared with the discussions of his precursors, von Bortkiewicz's is economically more interesting.

Von Bortkiewicz accuses Marx of having committed the elementary error of not taking into account that the price changes 'affect the product in the same measure as the capitalist's advances' (1906–7 III: 458). He then demonstrates in terms of some simple models of production that the introduction and generalization of a new method of production can never reduce the rate of profits, given the real wage rate, and will raise it if the new method contributes directly or indirectly to a cheapening of wage goods (cf. ibid.: 454–68).[27] The comparison of two methods by means of which a commodity can be produced is carried out on the premiss 'that prices (and thus also the price expression of the commodity bundle constituting the real wage) are still the old ones' (ibid.: 457). The criterion adopted is whether a method incurs extra costs or yields extra profits: if it incurs extra costs it will not be adopted; if it yields extra profits it will be introduced and will gradually replace the old method.

Hence there is a striking parallel between the analyses of the choice of technique problem of early authors working in the classical tradition and von Neumann, which is also expressed formally in the use of inequalities. Moreover, taking together the contributions of von Bortkiewicz and Charasoff, we have, *in nuce*, a combination of some of the constituent elements of the von Neumann model. What is missing are the assumptions of (i) joint production, and (ii) the Rule of Free Goods, which however, as we have seen, are not extraneous to the classical approach. Hence von Neumann's approach can be said to have been anticipated in all important material aspects by authors whose contributions can be strictly located within the classical tradition. It goes without saying that this characterization is not meant to play down the importance of von Neumann's contribution. After all, it was he who provided a comprehensive and general formulation of what other authors were able to put forward only partially and with respect to special cases, and it was he who was able to prove the existence of a solution.

Next we turn to Robert Remak, a colleague of von Neumann's while a *Privatdozent* at the Berlin Institute of Mathematics. Interestingly, in contributions to the history of general equilibrium analysis, in which von Neumann's model generally features prominently, Robert Remak is hardly paid any attention at all.[28] This neglect is particularly harmful since a potentially important link with the von Neumann model is lost.

REMAK ON 'SUPERPOSED PRICE SYSTEMS'

Robert Remak was a student of Georg Frobenius and H. A. Schwarz. In 1929 he acquired the *venia legendi* in mathematics at the University of Berlin and was a *Privatdozent* there until 1933.[29] John von Neumann had become a *Privatdozent* at the same university in 1927; he held the position until 1929 (see Ulam 1958).

According to the information gathered by Wittmann from some of Remak's former friends and colleagues, Remak was in all probability stimulated by a group of economists around von Bortkiewicz to study the problem of the conditions under which positive solutions of systems of linear equations obtain (cf. Wittmann 1967: 401). His 1929 paper was a result of those studies (see Remak 1929). Unfortunately, of Remak's paper only the greater part of the third section dealing with the existence problem of price equilibrium is available in English (cf. Baumol and Goldfeld 1968: 271–7). Hence the motivation of his paper and its economic reasoning are largely unknown in the English-speaking world. In what follows we shall briefly summarize the main argument.[30]

Methodological issues

Remak begins his paper with a definition of what he means by an exact science, which bears a close resemblance to Leontief's 'naturalistic' point of view (cf. Leontief 1928): an exact science regards as 'exactly correct' only what can be ascertained by physical observation, counting or calculation (1929: 703). He then applies this definition to 'economics', which he tends to equate with Marshallian demand and supply analysis;[31] his concern is particularly with the demand side. He argues:

> All existing approaches in theoretical economics always start from these [demand] functions, which characterize the buyer's behaviour at different prices. However, since this behaviour can be neither experimentally nor theoretically ascertained quantitatively, there is no way to get from these theories to practical calculations. We will therefore take into consideration approaches which result in quantitative calculations that can also be carried out practically.
>
> (ibid.: 711–12; similarly Leontief 1928: 622)[32]

The alternative Remak suggests is what he calls 'superposed price systems' (*superponierte Preissysteme*): 'A superposed price system has nothing to do with values. It only satisfies the condition that each price covers the prices of the things required in production, and the consumption of the producer on the assumption that it is both just and feasible' (ibid.: 712).[33] Its calculation obviously requires a detailed knowledge of the socio-technical relations of production, i.e. the methods of production in use and the needs and wants of producers (ibid.: 712–13).

For most of the paper, and particularly in its third part, which formalizes the argument, Remak assumes (implicitly) a stationary economy. Yet he makes it clear that this is but a first step towards an analysis of a dynamic economic system, i.e. one evolving over time: while a stationary economy can be represented by a single point in what Remak calls the 'economic phase space' made up of a finite number of economic co-ordinates, a developing economy involves 'a moving point which in the phase space describes a curve' (ibid.: 717).

'Superposed prices'

Remak then constructs 'superposed prices' for an economic system in which there are as many single-product processes of production as there are products, and each process or product is represented by a different 'person'.[34] It would not affect the logic of the argument if the term 'person' were to be replaced by the term 'industry' or 'activity' (see also Wittman 1967: 404). The amounts of the different commodities acquired by a person over 'a certain period of time, e.g. a year', in exchange for his own product, are of course the amounts needed as means of production to produce this product, given the technical conditions of production, and the amounts of consumption goods in support of the person (and his family), given the levels of sustenance. With an appropriate choice of units, the resulting system of 'superposed prices' can be written (using matrix notation).

$$\mathbf{p} = \mathbf{A}\mathbf{p} \tag{7}$$

where **A** is the augmented matrix of inputs (means of production and consumption) per unit of output, and **p** is the vector of exchange ratios. Remak then discusses system (7) and arrives at the conclusion that there exists a solution to it which is semi-positive and unique except for a scale factor.[35]

Socialism vs. capitalism

Model (7) refers to a kind of ideal economy with independent producers, no wage labour and hence no profits; it thus bears a close resemblance to Marx's concept of 'simple commodity production'. However, it could also be interpreted as reflecting a socialist economic system.[36] Although Remak does not refer to Marx or to any socialist author, it is clear that his paper is intended to contribute to the then politically heated debate on socialism vs. capitalism. As Remak stresses in the introductory section of his paper:

> The question of whether or not an exact economics is possible is not of a purely theoretical interest, but is of fundamental practical importance. The socialist doctrine maintains the possibility of another, a better economic order which utilizes the given technical possibilities much more effectively to the benefit of the population. Diametrically opposed to this is the capitalist economic doctrine, which claims that through the free play of forces, which includes monopolies and other phenomena, the economic optimum will already be realised, and that any other regulation of economic life, by preventing this free play, would entail a smaller produce. . . . *The main task of an exact economics would consist in deciding between these two views by means of exact instruments of calculation.*
>
> (1929: 704; emphasis added)

In Remak's view there are two problems to be solved here. The first concerns the question whether an appropriate price system for a socialist economy can be found. Without being able to demonstrate that a system of '"reasonable" prices' actually exists, the socialist alternative would be deprived of its rational basis: 'These prices . . . represent a "necessary" condition in the mathematical sense for an efficient economy exempt from unemployment and crises to exist' (1933: 840). Remak takes pride in having shown with his concept of 'superposed prices' that such a solution in fact exists and how it can be determined. Towards the end of his article he also expresses the conviction that the technical problem of numerically solving large systems of linear equations can be expected to be overcome soon, given the progress made in the development of electric calculating machines (cf. ibid.: 735).

The second and much more difficult problem concerns the comparative assessment of the economic efficiency of capitalism and socialism, respectively. Remak does not pretend to be possessed of a definite answer to this intricate question. He indicates, however, the direction in which an answer should be sought. In his view the problem boils down to the question of whether the modern capitalist economy is 'extremal', that is, whether it fully uses its productive potential or forgoes production possibilities. In view of unemployment and idle plant and equipment Remak sees reason to conjecture that it fails on that account (ibid.: 706, 721–2). How can this failure be explained?

On the 'non-extremality' of capitalism

Although Remak's discussion is occasionally rather cloudy, two closely connected causes are singled out as responsible for the malfunctioning of the capitalist economy: first, the role money plays in the system, and second, the distribution of income and thus purchasing power between capital owners and workers. Scrutiny shows that Remak advocates some kind of underconsumption-cum-miscalculation explanation of effective demand failures. In one place he writes:

> Today wages are reckoned as a part of the commodity; the latter on its way to completion is subject to several high percent mark ups, so that the worker eventually buys only a fractional part of his own daily work. It does not follow, however, that he gives the remaining part of his work to capitalism, since it is clearly conceivable that a wrong method of calculation gives rise to a lack of sales and thus prevents the realisation of a technically feasible additional production.
>
> (ibid.: 733–4)[37]

Remak does not provide a formalization of his view of the determination of prices in a capitalist economy. The price system he appears to have in mind can, however, easily be constructed, following the hints he gives. There are two kinds of mark-up: a general mark-up for the economy as a whole, i.e. the rate of interest (ibid.: 713), and a mark-up specific to an industry (or a firm). On the same technological premisses as those underlying the construction of system (7) (single production, no choice of technique, etc.) the system of prices would now be given by

$$\mathbf{p}_c = (\mathbf{I} + \mathbf{M})[(1 + r)\mathbf{C}\mathbf{p}_c], \tag{8}$$

where $\mathbf{I}$ is the identity matrix, $\mathbf{M}$ is the diagonal matrix of the sectoral mark-ups $m_i \geq 0$, $i = 1, 2, \ldots, n$, r is the rate of interest, $\mathbf{p}_c$ is the vector of 'capitalist' prices and $\mathbf{C}$ is the matrix of material inputs, $\mathbf{N}$, plus wage goods per unit of output, i.e.

$$\mathbf{C} = \mathbf{N} + \mathbf{l}\mathbf{w}^T \tag{9}$$

$\mathbf{l}$ being the vector of labour inputs and $\mathbf{w}^T = (w_1, w_2, \ldots, w_n)$ the real wage bundle per unit of labour.[38] System (8) is sketched only verbally by Remak; no discussion of its mathematical properties is provided.

As we have seen, in Remak's opinion there are reasons to suppose that the problem of underutilization of productive resources in modern capitalism is closely related to the general levels and the structure of the m_i's and the level of r. The question is close at hand whether a transition from price system (8) to the system of 'reasonable' prices (7) would remedy the idleness of labour and capital. Remak's answer is cautiously in the affirmative. The investigation of system (7) is taken to serve the purpose of finding out whether 'an economy which is perceived to be both just and efficient (*zweckmäßig*) can be brought about by appropriate directions regulating the formation of prices of all commodites' (ibid.: 724). In his second article, which was written under the impact of the Great Depression, Remak concludes that it can be surmised 'that the system of "reasonable" prices would allow merchants to apply only much lower mark-ups than the usual ones, which would lead in effect to putting a severe curb on profits' (1933: 841).

VON NEUMANN AND REMAK

Wittmann (1967: 407–8) points out that Remak gave his paper at a meeting of the Berlin Mathematical Society and that his ideas were discussed at the Institute of Mathematics in Berlin. He also conjectures that von Neumann was familiar with Remak's ideas. According to Wittmann's sources most of Remak's colleagues 'derided' the conclusions of his paper.

It is possible that von Neumann was among those colleagues who took a critical position towards Remak's contribution. We may even consider the possibility that von Neumann's paper contains, *inter alia*, an implicit answer to his colleague. Since we do not know of any statement to that effect by von Neumann himself, the only evidence on which such an interpretation could possibly rest has to derive from a careful textual comparison of the papers of the two authors. Such a comparison leads in fact to some remarkable observations.

Both authors are concerned with the efficiency, or lack thereof, of what von Neumann calls 'the normal price mechanism' of a capitalist economy (von Neumann 1945: 1). While Remak contended that the way prices are formed in a capitalist economy is partly responsible for the fact that the system is statically (and dynamically) non-'extremal', i.e. inefficient, a main result of von Neumann's paper reads: 'the normal price mechanism brings about . . . the technically most efficient intensities of production' (1945: 1).[39] The other factor mentioned by Remak as potentially detrimental to efficiency, money, is also touched upon by von Neumann. The passage just quoted is followed by the adjunct: 'This seems not unreasonable since we have eliminated monetary complications' (ibid.: 1).

In Remak's paper scarce natural resources, such as land, play no significant role. He rather focuses attention on systems of production that are in a self-replacing state and in which there are at most three types of income: wages, interest and profits. By implication, none of the natural resources utilized is scarce and therefore yields its owner a rent. In accordance with the capitalism vs. socialism debate Remak is interested in, emphasis is on the conflict between workers and capital owners over the distribution of the product. Interestingly, the total neglect of the problem of scarcity is also a characteristic feature of von Neumann's model. If his concern had been with generalizing the 'Walras–Cassel model', as is maintained by the conventional interpretation, this neglect would be totally incomprehensible, whereas it can easily be understood if one of his implicit aims was refuting Remak's view.

Just like Remak, von Neumann adopts a circular notion of production and considers the means of subsistence an integral part of the advances at the beginning of the uniform period of production. However, in every respect von Neumann's model is more general than Remak's. Repeatedly one gets the impression that where Remak drops an idea or poses a question that is beyond the scope of his own model, von Neumann offers a conceptualization and provides an answer. While Remak emphasizes that what is at stake is the question of the dynamic (in)efficiency of an economy, but then restricts his discussion essentially to the case of a stationary system, von Neumann adopts a dynamic framework of analysis, albeit limited to the case of steady-state growth. While Remak is aware of the fact that an important aspect of the efficiency issue is how the problem of the choice of technique is decided, von Neumann tackles the problem head-on. While Remak notes incidentally that production and consumption activities may generate 'waste' which has to be disposed of,[40] von Neumann starts directly from the assumption of general joint production coupled with the assumption of free disposal of all superfluous products. While Remak discusses mark-up pricing without, however, addressing the problem of the mutual consistency of the mark-ups, including the rate of interest, the given real wage rate(s) and the given technical conditions of production, von Neumann demonstrates that the rate of interest, i.e. the general mark-up across all processes of production, is uniquely determined by the technical alternatives, given the real wage rate(s).

Circumstantial evidence and a detailed textual comparison seem to support the conjecture that von Neumann's model contained, among other things, an answer to his mathematical colleague. Compared with the widespread opinion that von Neumann's model was meant to provide a solution to a problem posed by Cassel, that of uniform growth, and not dealt with by the Viennese mathematical economists, this interpretation appears to us to be more plausible. Indeed, in our view there are too many elements in the analyses of von Neumann and the Viennese that are difficult to reconcile (see, in particular, pp. 31–3 above), while we are not aware of any aspect contradicting our interpretation. It goes without saying that we cannot prove that we are right: *se non è vero, è ben trovato*.

CONCLUSION

This chapter has shown that the conventional interpretation of von Neumann's growth model is difficult to sustain. Most important, in von Neumann there is no endowment of the economy with a given (physical or value) 'quantity of capital' that constrains productive capacity and provides the basis, in terms of its relative 'scarcity', for a determination of the rate of interest. It is a characteristic feature of the von Neumann model that the distributive variables, the wage rate and the rate of interest, are not determined in the conventional symmetrical way in terms of the demand for and supply of the respective factors of production, labour and 'capital'. Moreover, whereas in the growth model of Cassel the (long-term) rate of growth of the system is given from outside by a 'natural' rate of growth, assuming the full employment of all primary factors, in von Neumann the rate of growth is endogenously determined and full employment of labour (or natural resources) is not assumed.

While the structure of the von Neumann model is difficult to reconcile with the neoclassical point of view, it is fully compatible with the classical one. This concerns in particular the asymmetrical treatment of the wage rate, the independent variable, and the rate of interest, the dependent one. It is shown that von Neumann's approach has been anticipated in all relevant aspects by authors whose contributions can be strictly located within the classical tradition. These aspects concern: (i) the concept of production as a circular flow; (ii) the notion of a uniformly expanding economy in which the rate of expansion is endogenously determined, i.e. a 'quasi-stationary system'; (iii) the concept of duality of the relationship between relative quantities and the rate of growth on the one hand and that between relative prices and the rate of interest (rate of profits) on the other; (iv) the use of inequalities in the discussion of the problem of the choice of technique; and (v) the way the Rule of Free Goods is applied to primary factors of production and to products, respectively. The authors referred to include, among others, Smith, Ricardo, Torrens, Whewell, von Bortkiewicz and Charasoff.

Next it is argued that von Neumann's model may be interpreted as containing, *inter alia*, an answer to the ideas laid out in a paper by his fellow mathematician Robert Remak. Both circumstantial evidence and, more important, a careful textual comparison of Remak's paper on 'superposed price systems' and von Neumann's analysis support this interpretation. In contradistinction to Cassel and the Viennese economists Schlesinger and Wald, and in accordance with Remak, von Neumann set aside scarce natural resources and adopted a circular flow concept of production which differs from the neoclassical concept of a one-way avenue that leads from primary factors of production to consumption goods. It is argued that von Neumann was particularly concerned with refuting Remak's opinion that the 'normal price mechanism' in a capitalist economy is inefficient. It is concluded that there are too many elements in the analyses of von Neumann and the Viennese economists that are difficult to reconcile, while there appears to be none contradicting the interpretation put forward in this chapter.

NOTES

1 Cassel's book was published in English as *The Theory of Social Economy* in 1923; a revised translation of the fifth German edition was published in 1932 (see Cassel 1932).

2 It would of course be quite inappropriate, indeed pointless, to compare the von Neumann model, which is long-period, with any short-period neoclassical model. In the latter the endowment of the economy with 'capital' is specified in terms of an arbitrarily given vector of heterogeneous capital goods. Therefore, in these models, flukes apart, an equilibrium is characterized by differential rates of return on the supply prices of the various capital goods.

3 In reading about Menger's colloquium one occasionally gets the impression that it was concerned with little else than the above problem. However, in the period of its existence, 1932–7, only two people other than von Neumann, the banker and economist Karl Schlesinger and the mathematician Abraham Wald, read altogether four papers on economic problems at the seminar, three of which were also published in the *Ergebnisse* (see Schlesinger 1935; Wald 1935, 1936). Another paper by Wald could not be published, first 'owing to lack of space' (*Ergebnisse* 8: 84) and then because of the colloquium's untimely termination due to the pending *Anschluß* of Austria to Hitler's Germany in 1938. Wald, who fled Europe with the arrival of the Nazis, seems to have lost the paper on his way to the United States; on the history of Wald's paper see Chipman (1965: 720 n. 18). In what follows we refer to Schlesinger and Wald as the 'Viennese economists'.

4 As Karl Menger recalled, 'Wald's paper on the equations concerning production greatly interested von Neumann, as he told me when passing through Vienna soon after its publication. It reminded him of equations he had formulated and solved in 1932 and now offered to present in our Colloquium' (Menger 1973: 55). See also Hicks (1960: 676 n. 1) and the story told by Jacob Marschak to Axel Leijonhufvud and Earlene Craver, as reported by Weintraub (1985: 74 n.) and Arrow (1989: 25). Although there is some uncertainty as to the year in which the event at the Kaiser Wilhelm Institut in Berlin took place, Marschak's story provides further evidence that von Neumann had developed his ideas several years before he gave his talk at Menger's colloquium. Weintraub comments on this: 'This story . . . suggests that the genesis of von Neumann's *Ergebnisse* paper was quite specific and roughly contemporary with von Neumann's [1928] paper on game theory. The min–max idea, the duality ideas, and the strategy of proof to be used later for the fixed-point theorem are found in each paper. The papers appear, then, to be naturally related not only by content, but also by place of origin' (ibid.). With regard to the last observation it would appear to be natural to pay special attention to the Berlin scientific community around the time when von Neumann was there as a lecturer and researcher. However, von Neumann's 'Berlin connection' is not dealt with by Weintraub. In his book neither von Neumann's fellow mathematician Robert Remak nor Ladislaus von Bortkiewicz, Berlin's eminent Professor of Statistics and Political Economy, are mentioned. On the possible implications of this omission see below.

5 Although it is not clearly stated, this seems to be the implication of the following passage in Arrow (1989: 23): 'Von Neumann makes no reference to the papers of Schlesinger and Wald, though he is publishing in the same journal two years later. He does state that the paper had been delivered to the Princeton Mathematical Club in 1932, so that it may be taken to be independent of Wald and Schlesinger.' Then follows the remarkable adjunct: 'Wald must have been very self-effacing; he was one of the editors of the volume of the *Ergebnisse* in which von Neumann's paper appeared.'

6 Brody (1989: 141) has put forward the interesting conjecture that the new tools employed by von Neumann, i.e. the use of inequalities rather than equations and the adoption of max–min criteria for the existence of equilibrium, may have

come to his attention while studying chemistry in Berlin under W. Ostwald. Ostwald had translated J. W. Gibb's *On the Equilibrium of Heterogeneous Substances* (1875–8), who had used these tools to describe chemical processes. This interpretation may throw light on the parallel drawn by von Neumann between the function ϕ (X, Y) in his analysis and that of 'thermodynamic potentials in phenomenological thermodynamics' (von Neumann 1945: 1).

7 It is interesting to note that in the title of Champernowne's paper (see Champernowne 1945) the title of the English version of von Neumann's paper is referred to incompletely: the adjective 'general' is left out.

8 It is true, though, that both in von Neumann and in those long-period versions of neoclassical theory that start from a given endowment of the economy with value capital, the *proportions* in which the different capital goods are needed are fully adjusted to the data, or independent variables, of the respective approaches. Hence these proportions are taken to be a part of the solution of the system rather than a given (as in neoclassical short-period analysis). However, in contradistinction to neoclassical long-period models, in von Neumann the aggregate value or 'quantity' of the capital stock is not among the data of the problem.

9 This is one of the reasons why Koopmans considered von Neumann's paper 'not very good economics' (Koopmans 1974). The assumption of a given initial endowment of the economy with capital goods was only subsequently appended to von Neumann's growth model, e.g. in Dorfman *et al.* (1958). This, together with the assumption of a given terminal endowment with capital goods, has led to the development of 'turnpike theorems'. Another reason for this harsh judgement was the treatment of the consumption of workers, which, in Champernowne's interpretation, reduced 'the role of the worker-consumer to that of a farm animal' (Champernowne 1945: 12).

10 Since 'capital' is set aside in the formulations of the Viennese economists, it is not surprising that the concept of the rate of interest (or rate of profits) makes no appearance.

11 In another place Arrow writes, 'Why von Neumann discarded the whole apparatus of demand functions, we cannot know' (1989: 25). See, however, Kaldor's recollection quoted in this chapter (p. 29).

12 It should be noted, though, that the Viennese economists, following Cassel's basic model, assumed that there is only one fixed-coefficients method of production for each commodity, i.e. there is no choice of technique.

13 For a brief account of the classical concept of production see Kurz and Salvadori (1995: chapter 1).

14 On Torrens's contribution see also Schefold (1981: section 4) and de Vivo (1985, 1986).

15 Torrens acknowledges his indebtedness to Ricardo's 'original and profound inquiry into the laws by which the rate of profits is determined' (ibid.: xix).

16 Torrens also indicates that if the entire 'surplus' or 'profit' were to be accumulated, the rate of expansion of the economy would be equal to the rate of profits. Hence Torrens may be said to have anticipated, in embryonic form, what Champernowne (1945: 10) in his interpretation of the von Neumann model called a 'quasi-stationary state'.

17 Dmitriev published his essay on Ricardo in Russian in 1898. This essay together with two others, one on Cournot's theory of competition, the other on marginal utility theory, was reprinted in 1904. A French translation of the three essays was edited by A. Zauberman in 1968 (see Dmitriev 1968), an English translation by D. M. Nuti in 1974 (see Dmitriev 1974). (According to

Nuti (cf. Dmitriev 1974: 30), the only copy of Dmitriev's 1904 book available in the West was in the possession of Piero Sraffa.) Both von Bortkiewicz and Charasoff published in German. Charasoff, who was born in Tiflis in 1877, obtained a doctorate in mathematics in 1901 at the University of Heidelberg.

18 Charasoff's contributions have only recently been rediscovered by Egidi and Gilibert (1984); see also Duffner and Huth (1988). For a summary statement of his main argument see Kurz (1989: 44–6).

19 The family resemblance with Sraffa's notion of the 'Standard system' in which the rate of profits 'appears as a ratio between quantities of commodities irrespective of their prices' (Sraffa 1960: 22) is close at hand.

20 As is well known, the concept of production as a circular flow figures prominently also in Leontief's 1928 Ph.D. thesis, written under the supervision of von Bortkiewicz at the University of Berlin (see Leontief 1928), and in his subsequent formulation of input–output analysis. Owing to lack of space we cannot enter into a proper discussion of his works; see, however, the brief remarks on Leontief on p. 41.

21 Prior to the Viennese economists the Danish economist F. Zeuthen (1933) had argued that Cassel's resource constraints ought to be written as inequalities. In a review article published in Swedish only one year after Cassel's *Theoretische Sozialökonomie* Knut Wicksell had already pointed out that the Cassellian system may possess no solution or may have solutions where some factor prices are zero because there is an excess supply of the respective factors (cf. Wicksell 1934: appendix 1, p. 228). (This reference may help to answer a query by Baumol and Goldfeld 1968: 268 n.)

22 Assuming that natural resources are non-scarce is, of course, not the same thing as assuming that there are no natural resources at all. Von Neumann's model is frequently misinterpreted in the latter sense. In this context it deserves to be noted that von Neumann does not define goods in the same way as Debreu (1959: 32): he does not consider a particular plot of land in a particular location as a special good. However, with the system growing for ever, the point will surely come where some natural resource(s) will become scarce. Surprisingly, von Neumann does not seem to have seen this point. As Professor Samuelson has pointed out to us in private correspondence, 'More by inadvertence than conscious intention, v.N. failed to emphasize the *basic classical* notion of land resources as unproducible or diminishable.' The total neglect of the problem of scarce primary resources such as land distinguishes his analysis in fact from the analyses of both the classical and the neoclassical economists. For a possible explanation of this neglect see p. 45 below.

23 'At most, one could say that a "Rule of Zero 'Excess' Wages" is applied because labour is less than fully employed' (Steedman 1987: 419). The interpretation given by Dore of von Neumann's use (or rather non-use) of the Rule of Free Goods is difficult to sustain: according to Dore (1989: 83), in the von Neumann model 'Cassel's "principle of scarcity" . . . is given an extreme binary interpretation whereby a resource has either a positive economic value if it is fully utilized, or its value is zero. . . . Unless every single man and woman is fully employed, the social value of labour is zero; this is indeed extreme. Why did von Neumann resort to this formulation?' The answer to this question is: he did not.

24 Thus Varri's contention (1982: 10–11) that the Rule of Free Goods is 'completely extraneous' to the theory of value of 'classical derivation' does not stand up to examination – unless, of course, Adam Smith is declared non-classical.

25 Therefore, it is seriously misleading to characterize the classical approach as one which is exclusively concerned with 'a fixed economic universe' and thus 'cannot account for the generation of an equilibrium because it refers to an empirically unique observed economy' (Punzo 1991: 15).

26 On Whewell and the group of mathematical economists see Campanelli (1982) and Henderson (1985).

27 This finding anticipates the essence of the Okishio theorem (see Okishio 1963).

28 For example, there is no reference to Remak's contribution in Weintraub (1985), Punzo (1989, 1991) or Dore *et al.* (1989). See, however, Gilibert (1991: 396), who deserves the credit for having drawn attention to the importance of Remak's paper in his attempt to reconstruct the history of mathematical economics at the beginning of this century.

29 Remak died in the concentration camp at Auschwitz.

30 It is interesting to note that the papers by Remak (1929) and Leontief (1928) have several elements in common. These include: (i) the general methodological position adopted; (ii) the concept of price put forward; and (iii) the description of the economic process in terms of what Sraffa (1960: 3) was to call 'the methods of production and productive consumption'.

31 Marshall's *Principles of Economics* is the only book referred to in the entire paper (cf. ibid.: 709 n.). Therefore the foundation of the view conveyed by Baumol and Goldfeld (1968: 267) that Remak aimed at pointing out 'a serious gap in Walras's argument' is unclear.

32 See also Kaldor's recollection (cf. p. 29 above) of the reservations expressed by von Neumann with regard to the marginalist theory of demand.

33 In an addendum to his paper published in 1933, Remak stresses: 'A price does not emerge from supply and demand, it is rather a number which has to satisfy certain conditions. The price of a commodity must cover the prices of the expenses contained in it, including the cost of living, which may be taken to be known, of the people participating in its production. This leads to the superposed price systems' (1933: 840). Remak also talks of '"reasonable" prices' ('*vernünftige*' *Preise*). See also Leontief (1928: 598), who stresses that the concept of value adopted by him has nothing to do with any intrinsic property of goods as judged by the consumer; it rather refers to the 'exchange relation' deduced from the 'relations of production'.

34 The somewhat unfortunate phrasing of the problem by Remak may have been the source of the misconception that his concern was with a pure exchange economy; for this interpretation see Gale (1960: 290) and Newman (1962: 60).

35 It should be mentioned that Remak does not make use of the mathematical tools provided by Perron and his own former teacher Frobenius.

36 The view that system (7) is open to alternative interpretations is especially emphasized by Remak in his second paper (1933: 840).

37 While most of Remak's argument refers to an economy with a given productive capacity, he touches also upon the dynamic features of a capitalist economy. In his view there is the danger that the innovative potential of such an economy will not be fully exploited: 'Today's economy allows increases in value in consequence of technological change in favour of capital only. These increases can, however, be utilized only partially, since the producer will not find the buyers of all the goods he could produce if it were not for the limited sales possibilities' (1929: 708; see also p. 722). As seen by Remak, the modern capitalist economy is neither statically nor dynamically efficient, or 'extremal'.

38 In the case in which there is a single uniform mark-up, m, throughout the economy, equation (8) would simplify to

$$\mathbf{p}_c^* = (1 + R)\mathbf{C}\mathbf{p}_c^* \tag{10}$$

where $(1 + R) = (1 + m)(1 + r)$ and $\mathbf{p}_c^*$ is the corresponding price vector.

39 In the German original von Neumann uses the expression 'die rein technisch *zweckmäßigste* Verteilung der Produktionsintensitäten'. He thus uses the same terminology as Remak. More important, the conception of efficiency adopted by the two authors appears to be the same. Interestingly, Champernowne in his commentary on the von Neumann model remarks on the above passage, 'This may immediately suggest an argument in favour of free enterprise in the real world' (Champernowne 1945: 16).

40 Remak even mentions the possibility of 'negative prices' in this context (1929: 726) and points out that the negativity of the price of a substance that has to be removed corresponds with the positivity of the price of the respective disposal service.

REFERENCES

Arrow, K. J. (1989) 'Von Neumann and the existence theorem for general equilibrium', in Dore, Chakravarty and Goodwin (1989): 15–28.

Baumol, W. J. and Goldfeld, S. M. (eds) (1968) *Precursors in Mathematical Economics*, LSE Series of Reprints of Scarce Works on Political Economy 19, London: London School of Economics.

Bortkiewicz, L. von (1906–7) 'Wertrechnung und Preisrechnung im Marxschen System', *Archiv für Sozialwissenschaft und Sozialpolitik* 23 (1906): 1–50, 25 (1907): 10–51, 445–88; quoted as 1906–7 I, II and III.

—— (1907) 'Zur Berichtigung der grundlegenden theoretischen Konstruktion von Marx im 3. Band des "Kapital"', *Jahrbücher für Nationalökonomie und Statistik* 34: 319–35.

Brody, A. (1989) 'Economics and thermodynamics', in Dore, Chakravarty and Goodwin (1989): 141–8.

Campanelli, G. (1982) 'W. Whewell's contribution to economic analysis: the first mathematical formulation of fixed capital in Ricardo's system', *Manchester School* 50: 248–65.

Cassel, G. (1918) *Theoretische Sozialökonomie*, Leipzig: Deichert.

—— (1932) *The Theory of Social Economy*, revised English translation of the 5th German edn of Cassel (1918) by L. Barron, New York: Harcourt Brace. Reprinted (1967) New York: Augustus M. Kelley.

Champernowne, D. G. (1945) 'A note on J. von Neumann's article on "A model of economic equilibrium"', *Review of Economic Studies* 13: 10–18.

Charasoff, G. von (1910) *Das System des Marxismus. Darstellung und Kritik*, Berlin: Bondy.

Chipman, J. S. (1965) 'A survey of the theory of international trade' 2, *Econometrica* 33: 685–760.

Debreu, G. (1959) *Theory of Value*, New York: Wiley.

De Vivo, G. (1985) 'Robert Torrens and Ricardo's "corn ratio" theory of profits', *Cambridge Journal of Economics* 9: 89–92.

—— (1986) 'Torrens on value and distribution', *Contributions to Political Economy* 5: 23–36.

Dmitriev, V. K. (1968) *Essais Economiques: esquisse de synthèse organique de la théorie de la valeur-travail et de la théorie du l'utilité marginale*, ed. A. Zauberman, Paris: Editions du Centre national de la récherche scientifique.

—— (1974) *Economic Essays on Value, Competition and Utility*, ed. D. M. Nuti, Cambridge: Cambridge University Press.

Dore, M. (1989) 'The legacy of von Neumann', in Dore, Chakravarty and Goodwin (1989): 82–99.

Dore, M., Chakravarty, S. and Goodwin, R. (eds) (1989) *John von Neumann and Modern Economics*, Oxford: Clarendon Press.

Dorfman, R., Samuelson, P. A. and Solow, R. M. (1958) *Linear Programming and Economic Analysis*, New York, Toronto and London: McGraw-Hill.

Duffner, H. and Huth, T. (1988) 'Georg Charasoff's theory of value, capital and prices of production', University of Bremen (mimeo).

Egidi, M. and Gilibert, G. (1984) 'La teoria oggettiva dei prezzi', *Economia Politica* 1: 43–61. In English: 'The objective theory of prices', *Political Economy: Studies in the Surplus Approach* 5 (1989): 59–74.

Ergebnisse eines mathematischen Kolloquiums (1931–7) ed. K. Menger in collaboration with K. Gödel and G. Nöbeling, 6 (1935), 7 (1936), 8 (1937), Leipzig and Vienna: Deuticke.

Gale, D. (1960) *The Theory of Linear Economic Models*, New York: McGraw-Hill.

Gilibert, G. (1991) 'La scuola russo-tedesca di economia matematica e la dottrina del flusso circolare', in G. Beccatini (ed.), *Le scuole economiche*, Turin: Utet, pp. 387–402.

Goodwin, R. M. (1986) 'Swinging along the turnpike with von Neumann and Sraffa', *Cambridge Journal of Economics* 10: 203–10.

Henderson, J. P. (1985) 'The Whewell group of mathematical economists', *Manchester School* 53: 404–31.

Hicks, J. R. (1960) 'Linear theory', *Economic Journal* 70: 671–709.

Kaldor, N. (1961) 'Capital accumulation and economic growth', in Lutz and Hague (1961): 177–222.

—— (1989) 'John von Neumann: a personal recollection'. Foreword in Dore, Chakravarty and Goodwin (1989): vii–xi.

Koopmans, T. C. (1974) Contribution to 'General discussion on past and future of the von Neumann model', in Los and Los (eds), *Mathematical Models of Economic Growth*, Amsterdam: North-Holland, pp. 3–4.

Kurz, H. D. (1986) 'Classical and early neoclassical economists on joint production', *Metroeconomica* 38: 1–37. Reprinted in Salvadori and Steedman (1990).

—— (1989) 'Die deutsche theoretische Nationalökonomie zu Beginn des 20. Jahrhunderts zwischen Klassik and Neoklassik', in B. Schefold (ed.) *Studien zur Entwicklung der ökonomischen Theorie* VIII, Berlin: Duncker & Humblot, pp. 11–61.

Kurz, H. D. and Salvadori, N. (1995) *Theory of Production: A Long-period Analysis*, Cambridge: Cambridge University Press.

Leontief, W. (1928) 'Die Wirtschaft als Kreislauf', *Archiv für Sozialwissenschaft und Sozialpolitik* 60: 577–623. An English translation of parts of this paper was published, with an introduction by P. A. Samuelson, as 'The economy as a circular flow', in *Structural Change and Economic Dynamics* 2 (1991): 177–212.

Lutz, F. A. and Hague, D. C. (eds) (1961) *The Theory of Capital*, London: Macmillan.

Marx, K. (1956) *Capital* II, Moscow: Progress Publishers. English translation of *Das Kapital* II, ed. F. Engels, Hamburg (1885): Meissner.

—— (1959) *Capital* III, Moscow: Progress Publishers. English translation of *Das Kapital* III, ed. F. Engels, Hamburg (1894): Meissner.

McKenzie, L. W. (1987) 'General equilibrium', in J. Eatwell, M. Milgate and

P. Newman (eds), *The New Palgrave* 2, London and Basingstoke: Macmillan, pp. 498–512.

Menger, K. (1973) 'Austrian marginalism and mathematical economics', in J. R. Hicks and W. Weber (eds), *Carl Menger and the Austrian School of Economics*, Oxford: Clarendon Press, pp. 38–60.

Morishima, M. (1973) *Marx's Economics: A Dual Theory of Value and Growth*, Cambridge: Cambridge University Press.

Neumann, J. von (1928) 'Zur Theorie der Gesellschaftsspiele', *Mathematische Annalen* 100: 295–320.

—— (1937) 'Über ein ökonomisches Gleichungssystem und eine Verallgemeinerung des Brouwerschen Fixpunktsatzes', *Ergebnisse eines mathematischen Kolloquiums* 8: 73–83.

—— (1945) 'A model of general economic equilibrium', *Review of Economic Studies* 13: 1–9. English translation of von Neumann (1937).

Newman, P. (1962) 'Production of commodities by means of commodities', *Schweizerische Zeitschrift für Volkswirtschaft und Statistik* 98: 58–75.

Okishio, N. (1963) 'A mathematical note on Marxian theorems', *Weltwirtschaftliches Archiv* 91: 287–99.

Punzo, L. F. (1989) 'Von Neumann and Karl Menger's mathematical colloquium', in Dore, Chakravarty and Goodwin (1989): 29–65.

—— (1991) 'The school of mathematical formalism and the Viennese circle of mathematical economists', *Journal of the History of Economic Thought* 13: 1–18.

Remak, R. (1929) 'Kann die Volkswirtschaftslehre eine exakte Wissenschaft werden?' *Jahrbücher für Nationalökonomie und Statistik* 131: 703–35.

—— (1933) 'Können superponierte Preissysteme praktisch berechnet werden?' *Jahrbücher für Nationalökonomie und Statistik* 138: 839–42.

Ricardo, D. (1951 *ssq.*) *The Works and Correspondence of David Ricardo*, ed. P. Sraffa in collaboration with M. H. Dobb, Cambridge: Cambridge University Press. In the text referred to as *Works*, volume number and page number.

Samuelson, P. A. (1989) 'A revisionist view of von Neumann's growth model', in Dore, Chakravarty and Goodwin (1989): 100–22.

Schefold, B. (1981) 'Nachfrage und Zufuhr in der klassischen Ökonomie', in F. Neumark (ed.), *Studien zur Entwicklung der ökonomischen Theorie* I, Berlin: Duncker & Humblot, pp. 53–91.

Schlesinger, K. (1935) 'Über die Produktionsgleichungen der ökonomischen Wertlehre', *Ergebnisse eines mathematischen Kolloquiums* 6: 10–11.

Smith, A. (1976) *An Inquiry into the Nature and Causes of the Wealth of Nations*. Volume II of *The Glasgow Edition of the Works and Correspondence of Adam Smith*, ed. R. H. Campbell, A. S. Skinner and W. B. Todd, Oxford: Oxford University Press. In the text quoted as *WN*, book number, chapter number, section number, paragraph number.

Sraffa, P. (1960) *Production of Commodities by Means of Commodities: Prelude to a Critique of Economic Theory*, Cambridge: Cambridge University Press.

Steedman, I. (1977) *Marx after Sraffa*, London: NLB.

—— (1987) 'Free Goods', in J. Eatwell, M. Milgate and P. Newman (eds), *The New Palgrave* 2, London and Basingstoke: Macmillan, pp. 419–20.

Torrens, R. (1820) *An Essay on the Influence of the External Corn Trade upon the Production and Distribution of National Wealth*, 2nd edn, London: Hatchard.

—— (1821) *An Essay on the Production of Wealth*, London: Longman. Reprint (1965), ed. J. Dorfman, New York: Augustus M. Kelley.

Tozer, J. E. (1838) 'Mathematical investigation of the effect of machinery on the wealth of a community in which it is employed, and on the fund for the payment of wages', *Transactions of the Cambridge Philosophical Society* VI, part III, Cambridge: Pitt Press, pp. 507–22. Reprinted (1968) New York: Augustus M. Kelley.

Ulam, S. (1958) 'John von Neumann, 1903–57', *Bulletin of the American Economic Society* 64: 1–49.

Varri, P. (ed.) (1982) *I prodotti congiunti*, Milan: Vita e Pensiero.

Wald, A. (1935) 'Über die eindeutige positive Lösbarkeit der neuen Produktionsgleichungen', *Ergebnisse eines mathematischen Kolloquiums* 6: 12–18. Comments by Schams and Menger, pp. 18–20.

—— (1936) 'Über die Produktionsgleichungen der ökonomischen Wertlehre' II, *Ergebnisse eines mathematischen Kolloquiums* 7: 1–6. Comment by Gödel, p. 6.

Walras, L. (1954) *Elements of Pure Economics*, London: Allen & Unwin. English translation of the definitive edition of Walras's *Eléments d'économie politique pure* (first published 1874) by W. Jaffé.

Walsh, V. and Gram, H. (1980) *Classical and Neoclassical Theories of General Equilibrium: Historical Origins and Mathematical Structure*, New York and Oxford: Oxford University Press.

Weintraub, E. R. (1985) *General Equilibrium Analysis: Studies in Appraisal*, Cambridge: Cambridge University Press.

Whewell, W. (1831) 'Mathematical exposition of some of the leading doctrines in Mr. Ricardo's "Principles of political economy and taxation"', *Transactions of the Cambridge Philosophical Society*, pp. 1–44. Reprinted in Whewell (1971).

—— (1971) *Mathematical Exposition of some Doctrines of Political Economy*. Reprint of four papers published by Whewell in 1829, 1831 and 1850, New York: Augustus M. Kelley.

Wicksell, K. (1893) *Über Wert, Kapital und Rente nach den neueren nationalökonomischen Theorien*, Jena: Fischer. English translation (1954) *Value, Capital and Rent*, London: Allen & Unwin.

—— (1934) *Lectures on Political Economy* I, *General Theory*. Trans. from Swedish by E. Classen and ed., with introduction, by Lionel Robbins. London: Routledge & Sons.

Wittmann, W. (1967) 'Die extremale Wirtschaft. Robert Remak – ein Vorläufer der Aktivitätsanalyse', *Jahrbücher für Nationalökonomie und Statistik* 180: 397–409.

Zeuthen, F. (1933) 'Das Prinzip der Knappheit, technische Kombination und ökonomische Qualität', *Zeitschrift für Nationalökonomie*, 4: 1–24.

ACKNOWLEDGEMENTS

We should like to thank the participants at a session of the conference on 'Istituzioni, distribuzione e crescita economica' in Catania, Italy, in February, at a session at the Eastern Economic Association meeting in New York in March, at seminars in the Istituto di ricerca sulla Dinamica dei Sistemi Economici (IDSE), Milan, in March, and the University of Graz in May and at a session at the International Economic Association meeting in Moscow in August 1992 for helpful comments. We are particularly grateful to Giorgio Gilibert, Pier Luigi Porta, Lionello Punzo and Ian Steedman, who served as commentators on our paper, and to Christian Bidard, Stephan Böhm, Andras Brody, Gilbert Faccarello, Pierangelo Garegnani,

Christian Gehrke, Geoff Harcourt, Peter Kalmbach, Ulrich Krause, Gary Mongiovi, Paul Anthony Samuelson, Bertram Schefold and especially Ian Steedman, who gave us detailed comments on a previous version of this chapter. Last but not least we should like to express our indebtedness to Giorgio Gilibert, whose works on the history of the concept of circular flow were of great help in shaping our own opinion on the matter. It goes without saying that any remaining misconceptions are our responsibility. Neri Salvadori thanks also the MURST (the Italian Ministry of University and Technological and Scientific Research) and the CNR (the Italian National Research Council) for financial support.

3

ADAM SMITH ON FOREIGN TRADE

A note on the 'vent for surplus' argument

Heinz D. Kurz

Adam Smith is generally considered an important, perhaps even *the* most important, advocate of free trade. At the same time, he is commonly given little credit as a trade theorist. Viner (1937: 108–9) suggests that all significant aspects of Smith's free-trade doctrine are already to be found in the earlier English literature. Robbins (1971: 191) argues that Smith's contribution lacks analytical rigour. Hollander (1973: chapter 9) views Smith's treatment of the issue as unclear, contradictory and in parts incompatible with the rest of his analysis. The main criticism put forward against him is that he failed to elaborate the principle of comparative costs and based his explanation of the benefits from trade on absolute cost differences only.

A rather different picture of Smith's contribution is painted by authors such as Bloomfield (1975), Myint (1958, 1977) and Negishi (1985: chapter 2). In their view, Smith's great merit is to be seen in the fact that his investigation is not restricted to static gains from trade arising from the reallocation of given resources, but is also concerned with the gains from trade in terms of economic development, i.e. the benefits derived from the international division of labour arising from increasing returns, induced innovations, the transfer of technology, etc. Reference is to what Myint (1977) called Smith's '"productivity" doctrine'.

It was also Myint who reappraised yet another element of Smith's theory of international trade which has generally met with fierce criticism: his 'vent for surplus' argument. Myint arrived at the cautious conclusion that 'Smith's "vent-for-surplus" theory does not seem to conflict in any simple or obvious way with the allocative-efficiency interpretation of his trade theory' (1977: 245).

This chapter is concerned exclusively with one aspect of Smith's 'vent for surplus' argument which seems to have escaped both friend and foe. To the extent that his analysis involves the aspect under consideration, it can be shown to be both clear and consistent and immune to the objections raised against it. This aspect concerns the fact that in much of his respective reasoning Smith refers to *joint* production rather than to single production, as is implicitly assumed in all contributions dealing with his trade theory.

The structure of this chapter is as follows. The next section will briefly summarize Smith's 'vent for surplus' argument and the criticism put forward against it. In the following section it will be shown that Smith was well aware of the case of joint production and clearly saw that with joint production the proportions in which the products are produced need not coincide with those in which they are wanted domestically. Hence there will be an excess supply of some of the joint products. The subsequent section (pp. 60–2) argues that Smith's 'vent for surplus' argument can be given a clear and unambiguous interpretation in the case under consideration: in the absence of foreign trade the overproduced amounts of certain joint products would be discarded, while with foreign trade there is the possibility of exchanging them for commodities produced abroad for which there is a demand at home. The final section contains some concluding remarks.

SMITH'S 'VENT FOR SURPLUS' ARGUMENT

The 'vent for surplus' argument recurs in various places in *The Wealth of Nations* (henceforth *WN*). In chapter V of Book II, 'Of the different employment of capitals', Smith writes:

> When the produce of any particular branch of industry exceeds what the demand of the country requires, the surplus must be sent abroad, and exchanged for something for which there is a demand at home. Without such exportation, a part of the productive labour of the country must cease, and the value of its annual produce diminish. The land and labour of Great Britain produce generally more corn, woollens, and hard ware, than the demand of the home market requires. The surplus part of them, therefore, must be sent abroad, and exchanged for something for which there is a demand at home. It is only by means of such exportation, that this surplus can acquire a value sufficient to compensate the labour and expense of producing it
>
> (*WN* II.v.33)

and in the first chapter of Book IV, 'Of the principle of the commercial, or mercantile system', Smith argues:

> The importation of gold and silver is not the principal, much less the sole benefit which a nation derives from its foreign trade. Between whatever places foreign trade is carried on, they all of them derive two distinct benefits from it. *It carries out that surplus part of the produce*

> *of their land and labour for which there is no demand among them*, and brings back in return for it something else for which there is a demand. *It gives a value to their superfluities*, by exchanging them for something else, which may satisfy a part of their wants, and increase their enjoyments. By means of it, the narrowness of the home market does not hinder the division of labour in any particular branch of art or manufacture from being carried to the highest perfection. By opening a more extensive market for whatever part of the produce of their labour may exceed the home consumption, it encourages them to improve its productive powers, and to augment its annual produce to the utmost, and thereby to increase the real revenue and wealth of the society.
>
> (*WN* IV.i.31; emphasis added)[1]

While the 'productivity' argument in the second part of the above passage met with approval, the 'vent for surplus' argument in the first part was generally rejected. Ricardo, in chapter XXI of the *Principles*, 'Effects of accumulation on profits and interest', comments on the latter as follows. He first gives Smith the credit for anticipating Say's law in all important respects: 'No writer has more satisfactorily and ably shown than Dr Smith, the tendency of capital to move from employments in which the goods produced do not repay by their price the whole expenses, including the ordinary profits, of producing and bringing them to market' (Ricardo [1817] 1951 I: 291 n.). Hence any glut of particular commodities will be only temporary: it will be overcome by an appropriate reallocation of capital and labour. Ricardo concludes that Smith's 'vent for surplus' doctrine 'is at variance with all his general doctrines on this subject' (p. 295).

Essentially the same objection recurs in the subsequent literature. Smith's respective view is generally regarded as a somewhat puzzling remnant of the mercantile doctrine which, as is well known, he was keen to refute. Because the 'vent for surplus' argument seemingly does not fit in with the rest of his doctrine, various attempts were made to play down its importance. According to Hollander (1973: 276), Smith does not appear to have been clear about the subject and 'mere lip service' was paid by him to the 'vent for surplus' doctrine. In Bloomfield's opinion 'there still remains something of a mystery as to the exact meaning of Smith's "surplus-produce" argument . . . It is probable that more may have been read into this argument than Smith in fact intended' (1975: 472).

While it cannot be claimed that the following argument is capable of fully clearing up the 'mystery' Bloomfield spoke of, it does provide some hints as to the circumstances under which Smith's argument is both perfectly reasonable and exempt from the criticism that it represents a left-over of the (infamous) mercantile doctrine. In order to see this, we have to take a closer look at Smith's analysis of production.

JOINT PRODUCTION AND THE RULE OF 'FREE' GOODS IN SMITH[2]

In most of the literature on Smith's approach to the theory of production and distribution of the wealth of a nation, it is implicitly assumed that his reasoning is in terms of single-product processes of production. This is understandable, given the fact that many of his examples in Book I refer to cases that are seemingly characterized by the absence of joint production. Thus, in chapter VI of Book I, 'Of the component parts of the price of commodities', Smith appears to hold, at least for one page of his book, a pure labour cost theory of value:

> In that early and rude state of society which precedes both the accumulation of stock and the appropriation of land, the proportion between the quantities of labour necessary for acquiring different *objects* seems to be the only circumstance which can afford any rule for exchanging them for one another.
>
> (*WN* I.vi.1; emphasis added)

This passage is immediately followed by the famous deer and beaver example, which describes the specific rule of barter for this hypothetical economy. Smith's argument has generally been interpreted as being concerned with the exchange relationships in a system in which each process of production produces a single commodity only (see, e.g., Hollander 1973: chapter 4; Samuelson 1977). This interpretation is obvious, since nowhere in this chapter does Smith mention joint production. The careful reader will have noticed, however, that in the passage quoted Smith does not speak of 'commodities', as in the chapter title, but rather refers to 'objects'. Although it cannot be excluded that this choice of words is purely accidental, it is possible to try an interpretation that suggests that it is not, i.e. that Smith, the Scottish teacher of rhetoric, used the term 'object' on purpose.

For Smith, beavers and deer may be desired to satisfy several needs. In a society of hunters (and in most other societies as well) animals are the 'source' of a multitude of use values: they provide different kinds of meat, furs, hides, bones, tendons, etc., some or all of which can be used either directly or indirectly to satisfy various wants. Each 'object' thus represents a *compositum mixtum* of different use values or 'goods' (and in addition possibly some 'bads'), which accrue as joint products in the separation process.

Adam Smith was well aware of this. Yet he presupposes a patient reader with a good memory, for it is not until chapter XI of Book I, 'Of the rent of land', that the issue is taken up again:

> The skins of the larger animals were the original materials of clothing. Among nations of hunters and shepherds, therefore, whose food con-

> sists chiefly in the flesh of those animals, every man, by providing himself with food, provides himself with the materials of more clothing than he can wear. *If there was no foreign commerce, the greater part of them would be thrown away as things of no value.* This was probably the case among the hunting nations of North America before their country was discovered by the Europeans, with whom they now exchange their surplus peltry for blankets, fire-arms, and brandy, which gives it some value.
>
> (*WN* I.xi.c.4; emphasis added)

This passage is interesting for several reasons. First, it attests to Smith's clear perception of the existence of joint-product processes of production. Second, it shows his awareness of the possibility that with joint production the proportions in which the products are produced need not coincide with those in which they are wanted. Third, in it we encounter, possibly for the first time in the history of economic thought, the rule of 'free' goods, which implies that a good that is in excess supply obtains a zero price. Finally, it holds the key to an understanding of at least one aspect of Smith's 'vent for surplus' doctrine. In fact, trade may prove beneficial to a country because it allows the counry to dispose of a part of its joint output, which would otherwise have been 'thrown away' as superfluous, in exchange for useful things produced abroad.

In the section 'Third sort' of chapter XI of Book I, Smith stresses that whether or not some of the joint products will be in excess supply depends on 'the extent of their respective markets', which in turn depends on the level of 'improvement' attained by society (cf. *WN* I.xi.m.1–6). To give an example, whereas in Smith's time, i.e. prior to the introduction of freezing and canning/bottling techniques, the market for meat was almost everywhere confined to the producing country, the markets for the joint products wool and raw hides were much larger. For, Smith notes, these products 'can easily be transported to distant countries, wool without any preparation, and raw hides with very little: and as they are the materials of many manufactures, *other countries may occasion a demand for them*, though that of the industry of the country which produces them might not occasion any' (*WN* I.xi.m.5; emphasis added). Therefore, in the 'rude beginnings' there will be a tendency to an excess supply of meat arising from an insufficient domestic demand and no foreign demand at all, combined with a relatively large foreign demand and a small domestic demand for the joint products wool and hides. In the course of a country's development, however, the domestic demand for meat will rise in consequence of the growth in population and, other things being equal, thus will gradually reduce the superabundance of meat. In fact it cannot be excluded that at some stage the role of a 'free good' is passed on from meat to one (or several) of its joint products.[3]

The discussion of joint production in *The Wealth of Nations* is clearly dominated by animal-rearing, yet it is not confined to it. Smith discusses numerous examples of multiple-product processes of production, mostly from agriculture, fishing and mining but some even from manufacturing. The impression remains that in his view cases of joint production, far from being exceptional, are rather common, and deserve to be studied carefully; the primary sector of the economy appears in fact to be characterized by universal joint production.[4] He illustrates his investigation by means of historical material from Spain, Latin and North America, England, Ireland and Scotland. He reports some long-run trends of relative prices of various joint products and tries to assess the impact of tariffs, exports and import restrictions and other regulations concerning a particular product on the prices and quantities traded of its joint products (cf. *WN* I.xi.m.2–14).[5]

SMITH AND AFTER

Smith's discussion of joint production seems to have left little impression on his contemporaries and successors.[6] This is also reflected in the fact that, in textbooks on the history of economic thought, John Stuart Mill is generally given the credit for having pioneered the study of joint production and joint costs in chapter XVI of Book III of his *Principles*, 'Of some peculiar cases of value'.[7] Interestingly, Mill, in the very next chapter, 'Of international trade', launches an attack on Smith's 'vent for surplus' doctrine, which he calls 'a surviving relic of the Mercantile Theory' (Mill, *Principles* III.xvii.s.4.2). It should be noticed, however, that in neither chapter is Smith's contribution to an analysis of joint production or the importance attached to this case by him, not least with respect to his 'vent for surplus' argument, mentioned. Hence Mill and the subsequent authors who followed him appear to have missed a crucial element in Smith's analysis. Given the lukewarm reception of the latter, it comes as no surprise that the 'vent for surplus' argument met with serious difficulties of interpretation and even misunderstandings.

Myint, who more recently made an important effort to vindicate Smith's argument, came perhaps closest to the answer given in the present chapter. He correctly pointed out that what Smith has to say on foreign trade is not confined to the chapters on the mercantile system and the colonies in Book IV, but is scattered throughout *The Wealth of Nations*. He added, 'For instance, important elements of Smith's foreign trade theory may be found in the chapter on rent' (1977: 233–4). However, when Myint later in his paper scrutinizes the chapter (cf. pp. 243–5), it is in one place only, and rather incidentally, that he mentions a (relatively insignificant) case of joint products: the feeding of pigs and poultry 'on kitchen scraps or "the offals of the barn and stables"' (p. 244). This case is taken to substantiate Smith's opinion that there exists a substantial surplus productive capacity in agriculture, for, if the waste mentioned were to be used more effectively and 'unimproved wilds' were to be employed to raise cattle and sheep, then the domestic production of meat could be increased without taking land away from corn-growing. The much more direct and obvious cases dealt with by Smith in the relevant chapter, in which after the opening of trade the overproduced amounts of certain joint products are channelled into exports, are apparently overlooked by Myint.

'If there was no foreign commerce,' we heard in the chapter on rent, 'the greater part of them would be thrown away as things of no value' (*WN* I.xi.c.4). 'It gives value to their superfluities' (*WN* IV.i.31); this is echoed in the chapter on the mercantile system.

CONCLUSION

With few exceptions, Smith's 'vent for surplus' argument has been rejected as inconclusive and contradicting the rest of his doctrine, in particular his version of what was later to become known as 'Say's law of markets'. However, both advocates and critics of his argument seem to have overlooked the fact that much of Smith's respective argument *explicitly* refers to the case of joint production: with the relatively fixed proportions in which different products are produced, it cannot be presumed that these proportions match those in which the products are domestically required for use. Hence without foreign trade some of the joint products tend to be overproduced; superfluous amounts of these products are assumed by Smith to be disposed of freely. With the opening of trade, at least some of the products that are available in excess supply may be exchanged for goods produced abroad for which there is a domestic demand. Foreign trade is thus directly beneficial to a nation, since it gives value to some of its products which would otherwise be subject to the rule of 'free' goods. To the extent that Smith's argument is actually based on the situation just described, it appears to be perfectly sensible. Hence it should be concluded that there is a case for which Smith's 'vent for surplus' doctrine can be given a clear and consistent interpretation.

NOTES

1 The 'vent for surplus' argument is also to be found in *WN* III.i.1 and 7, *WN* IV.iii.c.4 and *WN* IV.vii.c.4–9. As the passages referred to show, Smith applies the argument equally to trade between town and country, trade between sovereign nations and trade between colony and motherland.

2 For a discussion of classical and early neoclassical economists on joint production see Kurz (1986, 1991).

3 Smith's above observation is also interesting because it questions the rather common presupposition in much of the literature on the subject that the joint products of a process can generally be divided into a 'main product', whose

acquisition is desired and because of which the productive activity is called forth, and one or several 'by-products', which may or may not be useful and which, at any rate, are of secondary economic interest. Smith's discussion makes it clear that what is the 'main product' of a joint production process cannot be ascertained *a priori*.

4 Cases of joint production are mentioned, for example, in *WN* I.xi.b.3, 32; c.4–5, 7, 21, 28; 1.9–11; m.2 *et seq*.

5 The continuing relevance of Adam Smith's 'vent for surplus' argument is well documented by the controversy about the draft conclusions to the Uruguay Round of international trade talks; see the *Financial Times* of 13 and 20 January 1992. A major theme of these reports is the EC's opposition to the impending increase of imports from the United States of cereal substitutes, especially oilseeds. According to German newspapers, it was particularly the proposed liberalization of trade in corn-gluten feed, a by-product of whiskey production, that was fiercely criticized by representatives of European agricultural interest groups.

6 The fact that hardly any of the early authors who wrote about joint production acknowledged Smith's contribution does not imply, of course, that they were not inspired or influenced by what Smith had to say on the subject in *The Wealth of Nations*.

7 See e.g. Stigler (1965: 8), Blaug (1968: 198), O'Brien (1975: 45, 95–6) and Ekelund and Hebert (1983: 154). For a critical discussion of this widespread view see Kurz (1986).

REFERENCES

Blaug, M. (1968) *Economic Theory in Retrospect*, Homewood, Ill.: Irwin.

Bloomfield, A. I. (1975) 'Adam Smith and the theory of international trade', in A. S. Skinner and T. Wilson (eds), *Essays on Adam Smith*, Oxford: Clarendon Press, pp. 455–81.

Ekelund, R. B. and Hebert, R. F. (1983) *A History of Economic Theory and Method*, New York: McGraw-Hill.

Hollander, S. (1973) *The Economics of Adam Smith*, Toronto and Buffalo: University of Toronto Press.

Kurz, H. D. (1986) 'Classical and early neoclassical economists on joint production', *Metroeconomica* 38: 1–37. Reprinted in N. Salvadori and Ian Steedman (eds), *Joint Production of Commodities*, Aldershot: Edward Elgar, 1990.

—— (1991) 'Adam Smith, die Regel der freien Güter und die 'vent for surplus' Begründung des Außenhandels', in H. D. Kurz (ed.), *Adam Smith (1723–1790). Ein Werk und seine Wirkungsgeschichte*, 2nd edn, Marburg: Metropolis, pp. 235–58 (first published 1990).

Mill, J. S. (1848) *Principles of Political Economy, with some of their Applications to Social Philosophy*, vols. II and III of *The Collected Works of John Stuart Mill*, ed. V. W. Bladen and J. M. Robson, London: Routledge, 1965.

Myint, H. (1958) 'The "classical theory" of international trade and the underdeveloped countries', *Economic Journal* 68: 317–37.

—— (1977) 'Adam Smith's theory of international trade in the perspective of economic development', *Economica* 44: 231–48.

Negishi, T. (1985) *Economic Theories in a non-Walrasian Tradition*, Cambridge: Cambridge University Press.

O'Brien, D. P. (1975) *The Classical Economists*, Oxford: Clarendon Press.

Ricardo, D. (1817) *On the Principles of Political Economy, and Taxation*, vol. I of

The Works and Correspondence of David Ricardo, ed. P. Sraffa with M. H. Dobb, Cambridge: Cambridge University Press, 1951.
Robbins, L. (1971) *Money, Trade, and International Relations*, London: Macmillan.
Samuelson, P. A. (1977) 'A modern theorist's vindication of Adam Smith', *American Economic Review, Papers and Proceedings* 67: 42–9.
—— (1980) 'Noise and signal in debates among classical economists: a reply', *Journal of Economic Literature* 21: 575–8.
Smith, A. (1776) *An Inquiry into the Nature and Causes of the Wealth of Nations*, vol. I of the *Glasgow Edition of the Works and Correspondence of Adam Smith*, ed. R. H. Campbell, A. S. Skinner and D. D. Raphael, Oxford: Oxford University Press, 1976.
Stigler, G. J. (1965) *Essays in the History of Economics*, Chicago: University of Chicago Press.
Viner, J. (1937) *Studies in the Theory of International Trade*, New York: Harper.

ACKNOWLEDGEMENTS

I should like to thank an anonymous referee of *Economica* for his useful suggestions and Christian Gehrke for his assistance in preparing the final version of the chapter. It goes without saying that the responsibility for any errors and misconceptions rests entirely with myself.

4

'ENDOGENOUS' GROWTH MODELS AND THE 'CLASSICAL' TRADITION

Heinz D. Kurz and Neri Salvadori

> Profits do not necessarily fall with the increase of the quantity of capital because the demand for capital is infinite and is governed by the same law as population itself. They are both checked by the rise in the price of food, and the consequent increase in the price of labour. If there were no such rise, what could prevent population and capital from increasing without limit?
>
> (Ricardo [1817] 1951 VI: 301)

Growth theory, like several other subjects in economics, has had remarkable ups and downs in the history of our subject. It was a major focus of attention of the classical economists from Adam Smith to David Ricardo, and then of Karl Marx. Afterwards the problem of economic growth was almost completely lost sight of at the time of the so-called 'marginal revolution', championed by William Stanley Jevons, Carl Menger and Léon Walras. While there were notable exceptions to the rule, around the turn of the century economists were predominantly concerned with the problem of value. The interest in the problem of economic growth was reignited by a contribution of John von Neumann in the 1930s. However, a greater direct impact on the profession as a whole came from the attempts to generalize Keynes's principle of effective demand to the long run. It was particularly Roy Harrod's 1937 contribution that gave rise to a large literature devoted to the study of economic growth and business cycles. The 'instability principle' enunciated by Harrod with regard to the process of capital accumulation was countered, in the mid 1950s, by the neoclassical economists Trevor Swan and Robert Solow, who showed that on the basis of sufficiently strong assumptions the economic system would gravitate towards a steady state, with the rate of expansion equal to some exogenously given 'natural' rate of growth. In these models Say's law was assumed to hold, implying the full employment of labour and full capacity utilization. At the same time Nicholas Kaldor put forward the post-Keynesian model of growth and distribution, which also started from the assumption of full employment and full capacity utilization. With the rate of growth of the labour supply and the rate of growth of labour productivity given from outside on one hand and the growth rate of investment given by the 'animal spirits of the investors' on the other, both neoclassical theory and post-Keynesian theory ascertained, via different routes, the distribution of income between wages and profits compatible with the given long-term growth rate. While the former assumed a given overall saving rate and a flexible capital–output ratio (via changing proportions of capital and labour by means of which a unit of social output could be produced), the latter assumed *prima facie* a flexible overall saving rate (via a changing distribution of income and different propensities to save out of wages and profits) and a fixed capital–output ratio.

The 1960s could be seen as the 'golden age' of Solovian growth economics: they brought a host of theoretical and empirical studies. However, in the 1970s and early 1980s growth economics as a whole was marginalized. The situation changed dramatically in the mid 1980s, when growth economics started to boom again, following the lead of Paul Romer and Robert Lucas. A formidable industry of theoretical and empirical research into economic growth sprang up like a mushroom. Also described as 'new' growth theory (NGT) to indicate the claim to originality, some advocates are quite explicit in their view that NGT will revolutionize the way economists think about certain problems (see Grossman and Helpman 1994: 42). The emphasis is on 'endogenous' mechanisms generating economic growth, that is, long-term growth is determined 'within the model, rather than by some exogenously growing variables like unexplained technological progress' (Barro and Sala-i-Martin 1995: 38). This is considered the main distinguishing feature between NGT and old, Solovian, growth theory. Other characteristic features of NGT are said to be the incorporation of economies of scale in the model and of providing a solid microfoundation of saving (alias investment) behaviour.

In this chapter an attempt will be made to relate some of the most prominent models of the NGT literature to the 'classical' tradition of economic thought. It will indeed be argued that in a very precise sense the NGT can be said to involve a *return* to modes of thought and the method of analysis characteristic of the classical authors. In terms of method, the NGT is *long-period* theory, advocated by Adam Smith and developed by David Ricardo. In terms of content, many of the models of the 'new' growth theory (NGMs) dispense with the traditional neoclassical determination of the rate of profit in terms of the supply of and demand for 'capital'. The following discussion attempts to clarify this fact.

Scrutiny shows that the contributions to the theory of value and distribution of 'classical' derivation, notwithstanding the many differences between different authors, share a common feature: in investigating the relationship between the system of relative prices and income distribution they start from the same set of *data*. These data concern:

(i) The technical conditions of production of the various commodities.
(ii) The size and composition of the social product.
(iii) One of the distributive variables: either the ruling wage rate(s) or the ruling rate of profit.
(iv) The quantities of available natural resources.

In correspondence with the underlying long-period competitive position of the economy the capital stock is assumed to be fully adjusted to these data. Hence the 'normal' desired pattern of utilization of plant and equipment would be realized and a uniform rate of return on its supply price obtained. The data or independent variables from which neoclassical theories typically start are the following. They take as given

(a) The set of technical alternatives from which cost-minimizing producers can choose.
(b) The preferences of consumers.
(c) The initial endowments of the economy and the distribution of property rights among individual agents.

It is easily checked that the given (a) is not very different from the given (i), whereas the given (ii) could be thought of as determined by the given (b). What makes the two theories really different are the data (iii) and (c). However, in the special case in which there is no labour in the economy – and therefore the given (iii) is automatically deleted, because the rate of profit would be endogenously determined and could not be given from outside the system – the given (c) is not very different from the given (iv). It will be shown that it is a characteristic feature of some of the most prominent contributions to the modern literature on endogeneous growth that they eliminate labour from the picture and put in its stead 'human capital' or 'knowledge', that is, something that a twentieth century audience can accept as a producible (and accumulable) factor of production. However, the conditions of production of this surrogate of 'labour' play exactly the same role played in the classical analysis by the assumption of a given real wage rate. This chapter is devoted to a clear statement of this fact.

In this chapter we focus attention on the *analytical structure* of the theory. That does not mean that we are unaware of the fact that there are other elements in the NGT with a decidedly classical flavour. The insistence on increasing returns, for example, bears a close resemblance to Adam Smith's treatment of the division of labour. It was indeed Smith's contention that the accumulation of capital is a prerequisite of the emergence of new, and the growth of many of the existing, markets which is intimately intertwined with an ever more sophisticated division of labour, and which in turn is seen to be the main source of a continual increase in labour productivity. In Smith's view the division of labour leads to the discovery of new methods and means of production – new machines – and new goods and is generally associated, at least temporarily, with forms of monopolistic competition which allow the successful innovators to reap extra profits for some time (see, for example, Smith, *WN* I.x.b.43; see also Young 1928). Hence in Smith the endogeneity of the rate of growth is the result not so much of the features of some *given* technology as of the continuous *revolution* of the technological, organizational and institutional conditions of production, that is, a process of the development of the 'productive powers of society'. Whilst we are aware of the similarities between this view and some of the ideas developed in more recent contributions to NGT,[1] our main concern in this chapter is not with them but with showing that the set of data from which the majority of NGMs start is that typical of the classical and not that of the neoclassical approach.

The next section shows that Ricardo consistently conceptualized economic growth as endogenous. In addition, it is shown that the usual Ricardian model can be transformed into one or the other of the conventional NGMs, either by eliminating the scarcity of land or by limiting the effect of the scarcity of land on the rate of profit by means of a backstop technology or by means of increasing returns to scale effects connected with the division of labour. The typology elaborated is used in the following section in order to analyse and classify some of the more recent NGMs. It is shown that the models under consideration replicate the behaviour of the Ricardesque models investigated in the next section. The final section draws some conclusions.

ENDOGENOUS GROWTH IN THE 'CLASSICAL' ECONOMISTS

Accumulation *vis-à-vis* diminishing returns in agriculture

The problem of economic growth and income distribution was a major concern of Adam Smith and David Ricardo. Ricardo's argument about what he called the 'natural' course of the economy contemplated an economic system in which capital accumulates, the population grows, but there is no technical progress: the latter is set aside. Hence the argument is based on the (implicit) assumption that the set of (constant returns to scale) methods of production from which cost-minimizing producers can choose is given and constant. Assuming the real wage rate of workers to be given and constant, the rate of profit is bound to fall: due to extensive and intensive diminishing returns on land, 'with every increased portion of capital employed on it, there will be a decreased rate of production'

(Ricardo [1817] 1951: 98). Profits are viewed as a residual income based on the surplus product left after the used-up means of production and the wage goods in the support of workers have been deducted from the social product (net of rents). The 'decreased rate of production' thus involves a decrease in profitability. On the premiss that there are only negligible savings out of wages and rents, a falling rate of profit involves a falling rate of capital accumulation. Hence, as regards the dynamism of the economy, attention should focus on profitability. Assuming that the marginal propensity to accumulate out of profits, s, is given and constant, a 'classical' accumulation function can be formulated:

$$g = \begin{cases} s(r - r_{\min}) & \text{if } r \geq r_{\min} \\ 0 & \text{if } r \leq r_{\min} \end{cases}$$

where $r_{\min} \geq 0$ is the minimum level of profitability which, if reached, will arrest accumulation (cf. ibid.: 120). Ricardo's 'natural' course will necessarily end up in a stationary state.[2]

Clearly, in Ricardo the rate of accumulation is endogenously determined. The demand for labour is governed by the pace at which capital accumulates, whereas the long-term supply of labour is regulated by the 'Malthusian law of population'.[3]

Assuming for simplicity a given and constant real wage rate, Ricardo's view of the long-run relationship between profitability and accumulation and thus growth can be illustrated in terms of Figure 4.1, which is a diagram used by Kaldor (1956). The curve CEGH is the marginal productivity of labour-cum-capital; it is decreasing, since land is scarce: when labour-cum-capital increases, either less fertile qualities of land must be cultivated or the same qualities of land must be cultivated with processes

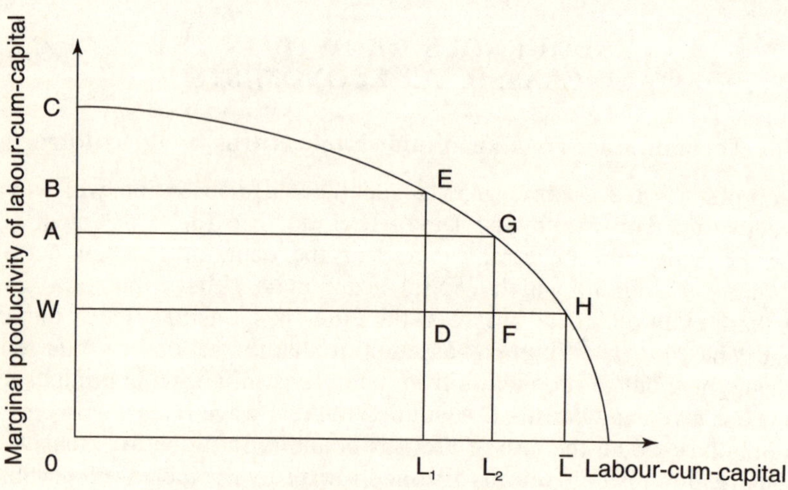

Figure 4.1 Land as an indispensable resource

which require less land per unit of product but are more costly in terms of labour-cum-capital. Let the real wage rate equal OW. Then, if the amount of labour-cum-capital applied is L_1, the area $OCEL_1$ gives the product, $OWDL_1$ gives total capital employed, and BCE total rent. Profit is determined as a residual and corresponds to the rectangular WBED. As a consequence, the *rate* of profit can be determined as the ratio of the areas of two rectangulars which have the same basis and therefore it equals the ratio WB/OW. Let us now consider the case in which the amount of labour-cum-capital is larger, that is, L_2. Then $OCGL_2$ gives the product, $OWFL_2$ the capital, ACG the rent, and WAGF profits. The rate of profit has fallen to WA/OW. Obviously, if a positive profit rate implies a positive growth rate (i.e. $r_{min} = 0$), the economy will expand until labour-cum-capital has reached the level $\bar{L}$. At that point the profit rate is equal to zero and so is the growth rate. The system has arrived at a stationary state. Growth has come to an end because profitability has.

The required size of the work force is considered essentially generated by the accumulation process itself. In other words, labour power is treated as a kind of producible commodity. It differs from other commodities in that it is not produced in a capitalistic way by a special industry on a par with other industries but is a result of the interplay between the generative behaviour of the working population and socio-economic conditions. In the most simple conceptualization possible, labour power is seen to be in elastic supply at a given real wage basket. Increasing the number of baskets available in support of workers involves a proportional increase of the work force. In this view the rate of growth of the labour supply adjusts to any given rate of growth of labour demand without necessitating a variation in the real wage rate.[4] Labour can thus set no limit on growth because it is 'generated' within the growth process. The only limit on growth can come from other non-accumulable factors of production: as Ricardo and others made clear, these factors are natural resources in general and land in particular. In other words, there is only endogenous growth in the classical economists. This growth is bound to lose momentum as the scarcity of natural factors of production makes itself felt in terms of extensive and intensive diminishing returns. (Technical change is, of course, envisaged as counteracting these tendencies.)

Production with land as a free good

For the sake of the argument let us try to think about Ricardian theory without the problem of land. Setting aside land in Ricardo's doctrine may strike the reader as somewhat akin to Hamlet without the prince. However, the only purpose of this thought experiment is to prepare the ground for a discussion of the NGMs on pp. 75–85. If there were no land – or, rather, if land of the best quality were available in abundance, that is, a free good –

then the curve of the graph showing the marginal productivity of labour-cum-capital would be a horizontal line and the rate of profit would be constant whatever the amount of labour-cum-capital. This case is illustrated in Figure 4.2. As a consequence, the growth rate would also be constant: the system could grow for ever at a rate that equals the given rate of profit times the propensity to accumulate. As the passage from Ricardo's *Works* at the opening of this chapter shows, Ricardo was perfectly aware of the implication.

Production with a 'backstop technology'

However, to assume that there is no land at all or that it is available in given quality and unlimited quantity is unnecessarily restrictive. With the system growing for ever, a point will surely come where land of the best quality gets scarce. This brings us to another situation in which the rate of profit need not vanish as capital accumulates. The situation in question bears a close resemblance to a case discussed in the economics of 'exhaustible' resources, that is, the case in which there is an ultimate 'backstop technology'. For example, some exhaustible resources are used to produce energy. In addition, there is solar energy, which may be considered an undepletable resource. A technology based on the use of solar energy defines the backstop technology mentioned. Let us translate this assumption into the context of a Ricardian model with land.

The case under consideration would correspond to a situation in which 'land', although useful in production, is not indispensable. In other words, there is a technology which allows the production of the commodity with-

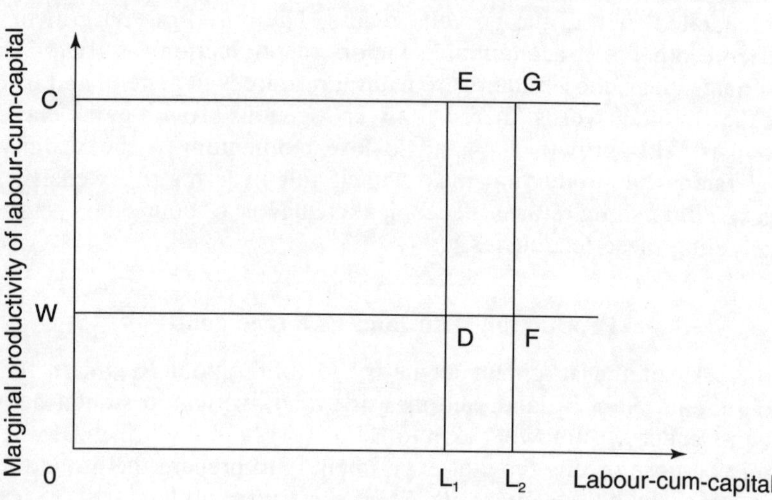

Figure 4.2 Land as a free good

out any 'land' input; this is the backstop technology. With continuous substitutability between labour-cum-capital and land, the marginal productivity of labour-cum-capital would be continuously decreasing, but it would be bounded from below. This case is illustrated in Figure 4.3, with the dashed line giving the lower boundary. In this case the profit rate and thus the growth rate would be falling, but they could never fall below certain levels, which are positive. The system would grow indefinitely at a rate which would asymptotically approach the product of the given saving rate times the value of the (lower) boundary of the profit rate. In Figure 4.3 the latter is given by WR/OW.

Increasing returns to capital-cum-labour

Finally, we may illustrate the case of increasing returns to labour-cum-capital (see Figure 4.4), as it was discussed, following Adam Smith's analysis of the division of labour, by authors such as Allyn Young (1928) and Nicholas Kaldor (1957). For the sake of simplicity, taking the wage rate as given and constant, the rate of profit and the rate of growth are bound to rise as more labour-cum-capital is employed. (In Figure 4.4 it is assumed that there is an upper boundary to the rise in output per unit of labour-cum-capital given by OR.) In order to be able to preserve the notion of a uniform rate of profit, it has to be assumed that the increasing returns are *external* to the firm and exclusively connected with the expansion of the market as a whole and the social division of labour. This implies that, whereas in the case of decreasing returns due to the scarcity of land (cf. Figures 4.1 and 4.3) the product was given by the area

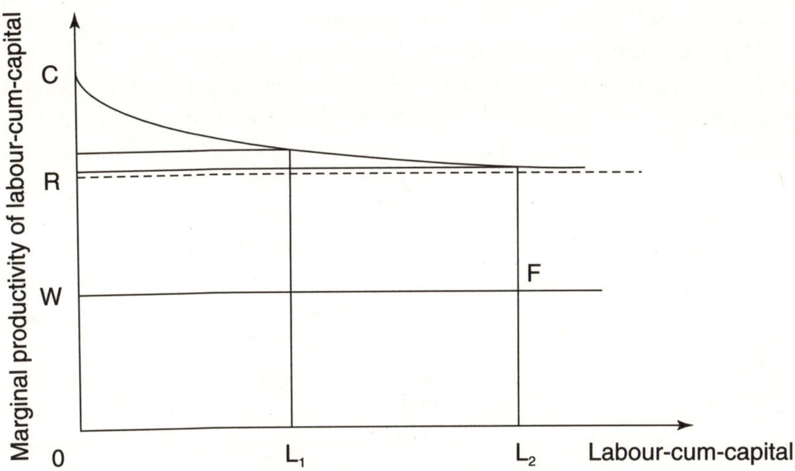

Figure 4.3 A backstop technology

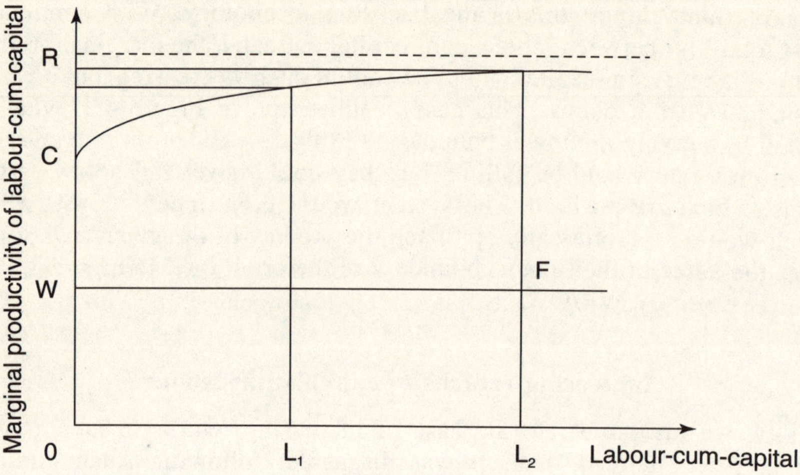

Figure 4.4 Increasing returns

under the marginal productivity curve, now the product associated with any given amount of labour-cum-capital is larger than or equal to that amount times the corresponding level of output per unit of labour-cum-capital. It is larger if there is still scarce land; it is equal to it if there is not. In any case, the sum of profits and wages equals the product of the given amount of labour-cum-capital times the corresponding level of output per unit of labour-cum-capital.[5] Hence, in the case in which labour-cum-capital is L_2, the product is given by the corresponding rectangular. In consequence, the product is larger than the area under the marginal productivity curve. The cases of decreasing and increasing returns are therefore not symmetrical. It goes without saying that in that case a rising real wage rate need not involve a falling general rate of profit.

To conclude, it is to be stressed again that the 'Ricardesque' patterns of endogenous growth illustrated in Figures 4.1–4 are intimately related to the fact that labour is envisaged as a commodity which is in some sense 'produced' by using corn and nothing else. The real wage rate is considered 'on the same footing as the fuel for the engines or the feed for the cattle'. The straight line WF in Figures 4.1–4 can indeed be interpreted as the 'marginal cost function' related to the 'production' of labour. If the wage rate were to depend on the amount of labour employed, the marginal cost function would not be a straight line, but substantially the same argument would apply. To put it in a nutshell, the 'secret' of the endogeneity of growth in the classical authors consisted of the assumption of a 'technology' producing labour. We shall see in the next section that essentially the same secret is at the heart of the NGT.

There is, however, another way of interpreting the diagrams. In order for this alternative interpretation to hold, we have to remove labour from the scene. If that is done, a picture emerges in which corn is produced by using only corn (including corn used as real wage rate) and, eventually, land. The curve that was previously interpreted as the marginal productivity of labour-cum-capital can now be interpreted as the marginal productivity of corn (as an input); the straight line WF would therefore be located at a distance from the horizontal axis of exactly one unit (WO = 1). All the other elements of the argument developed above would remain exactly the same. We shall see in the next section that this interpretation provides a key to understanding an important aspect of the NGT.

THE 'NEW' GROWTH MODELS

As we have seen, the concept of 'endogeneity' employed in the NGMs as specified by Barro and Sala-i-Martin implies that long-run growth is determined 'within the model' rather than by some exogenously growing variables. They add, 'The key property of endogenous-growth models is the absence of diminishing returns to capital' (1995: 39). Therefore the mechanism by means of which diminishing returns to capital are avoided provides a criterion to classify the NGMs (see also Kurz and Salvadori 1997a). We may distinguish between the following types of models:

(i) 'Linear models' or '*AK* models' (Rebelo 1991; King and Rebelo 1990).
(ii) Models in which returns to capital are bounded from below (Jones and Manuelli 1990).
(iii) The model by Lucas (1988), which focuses attention on the accumulation of human capital.
(iv) The model by Romer (1986), which emphasizes the generation of new knowledge in the research and development activities of firms.

We shall deal with these different models in turn.

Linear or '*AK*' models

First, there are models which set aside all *non-accumulable* factors of production such as labour and land and assume that all inputs in production are accumulable, that is, 'capital' of some kind. The simplest version of this class of models is the so-called '*AK* model', which assumes that there is a linear relationship between total output, *Y*, and a single factor, capital, *K*, both consisting of the *same* commodity:

$$Y = AK \tag{1}$$

where $1/A$ is the amount of that commodity required to produce one unit of itself. Because of the linear form of the aggregate production function, these models are also known as 'linear models'. The rate of return on capital, r, is given by

$$r + \delta = \frac{Y}{K} = A \tag{2}$$

where δ is the exogenously given rate of depreciation. The saving–investment mechanism jointly with the assumption of a uniform rate of growth, that is, a steady-state equilibrium, then determines a relationship between the growth rate, g, and the rate of profit, r. Rebelo (1991: 504, 506) obtains either

$$g = \frac{A - \delta - \rho}{\sigma} = \frac{r - \rho}{\sigma} \tag{3}$$

or

$$g = (A - \delta)\, s = sr \tag{4}$$

Equation (3) is obtained when savings are determined on the assumption that there is an immortal representative agent maximizing the following intertemporal utility function:

$$\int_0^\infty e^{-\rho t} \frac{1}{1 - \sigma} \left[c(t)^{1-\sigma} - 1\right] \mathrm{d}t \tag{5}$$

subject to constraint (1), where ρ is the discount rate, or rate of time preference, and $1/\sigma$ is the elasticity of substitution between present and future consumption ($1 \neq \sigma > 0$), and where $Y = c(t) + \dot{K}$, where $\dot{K}$ is the derivative of K with respect to time, i.e. investment. Equation (4) is obtained when the average propensity to save, s, is given. Hence in this model the rate of profit is determined by technology alone and the saving–investment mechanism determines the growth rate.

This model is immediately recognized as the model dealt with on pp. 71–2, in which labour was set aside, on the assumption that the technology to produce corn is that illustrated in Figure 4.2. Even the saving–investment mechanism is essentially the same: in the case of equation (3) $\sigma = 1/s$ and $\rho = r_{\min}$ (provided that $r > r_{\min}$); in the case of equation (4) $r_{\min} = 0$. Hence the version of the 'new' growth theory under consideration is but the most elementary of all classical models. No classical economist can be accused of having taken that model too seriously.

A slightly different avenue was followed by King and Rebelo (1990). Instead of one kind of 'capital' they assumed that there are two kinds, real capital and human capital, both of which are accumulable. There are two lines of production, one for the social product and the real capital, which consist of quantities of the same commodity, and one for human capital. The production functions relating to the two kinds of capital are assumed to be homogeneous of degree one and strictly concave. There are no diminishing returns to (composite) capital, for the reason that there is no non-accumulable factor such as simple or unskilled labour that enters into the production of the accumulable factors, investment goods and human capital.[6] The production functions relating to the two kinds of capital are given by

$$H = H(H_H, K_H) \tag{6.1}$$

and

$$K = K(H_K, K_K) \tag{6.2}$$

As in Rebelo's model the rate of profit is uniquely determined by the technology (and the maximization of profits, which implies that only one technique can be used in the long run); the growth rate of the system is then endogenously determined by the saving–investment equation. Maximization of profits implies that:

$$\frac{\partial H}{\partial H_H} = r \tag{7.1}$$

$$\frac{\partial H}{\partial K_H} = \frac{r}{p} \tag{7.2}$$

$$\frac{\partial K}{\partial H_K} = rp \tag{7.3}$$

$$\frac{\partial K}{\partial K_K} = r \tag{7.4}$$

where r is the rate of profit and p is the price of human capital in terms of the commodity which is consumed or accumulated as physical capital (δ has been set equal to 0 in order to simplify the notation). Since functions (6.1–2) are homogeneous of degree one, their first derivatives are homogeneous of degree zero, and hence the four equations (7.1–4) are enough to determine the four unknowns r, p, H_H/K_H, H_K/K_K.[7] This is nothing other than the non-substitution theorem,[8] which, as is well known, implies that only one technique can be used in the long run. The growth rate of the system is then endogenously determined by the saving–investment equation. The larger the propensity to accumulate human and physical capital the larger is the growth rate.

Comparing the latter model with the classical theory, we can draw the following conclusion: the role played by 'labour' in the classical authors is assumed by 'human capital' in King and Rebelo (1990). Both factors of production are taken to be producible; with constant returns to scale, as in King and Rebelo (1990) and in the case depicted in Figure 4.2, the rate of profit and, therefore, the rate of growth are determined and constant over time. The linear NGMs thus simply replicate in elementary terms the logic of the classical approach to the theory of distribution and growth.

Returns to capital bounded from below

Next there are models which preserve the dualism of accumulable and non-accumulable factors but restrict the impact of an accumulation of the former on their returns by a modification of the aggregate production function. Jones and Manuelli (1990), for example, allow for both labour and capital and even assume a convex technology, as does the Solow model (cf. Solow 1956). However, a convex technology requires only that the marginal product of capital is a decreasing function of its stock, not that it vanishes as the amount of capital per worker tends to infinity. Jones and Manuelli assume that:

$$h(k) \geq bk \qquad \text{each } k \geq 0$$

where $h(k)$ is the *per capita* production function and b is a positive constant. The special case contemplated by them is:

$$h(k) = f(k) + bk \tag{8}$$

where $f(k)$ is the conventional Solovian production function. As capital accumulates and the capital–labour ratio rises, the marginal product of capital will fall, asymptotically approaching b – its lower boundary. With a given propensity to save, s, and assuming capital to be everlasting, the steady-state growth rate, g, is endogenously determined: $g = sb$. Assuming, on the contrary, intertemporal utility maximization, the rate of growth is positive provided the technical parameter b is larger than the rate of time preference ρ. In the case in which it is, the steady-state rate of growth is given by (3) with $r = b$.

It is not difficult to recognize that the difference between the model of Jones and Manuelli (1990) and that of Rebelo (1991) is the same as the one existing between the cases illustrated by Figures 4.3 and 4.2 above.

Finally, there is a large class of models which contemplate various factors counteracting any diminishing tendency in returns to capital. The models can be grouped into two types. In both kinds of model *positive external effects* play an important part: they offset any fall in the marginal product of capital.

Human capital formation and its externalities

Models of the first group attempt to formalize the role of human capital formation in the process of growth. Elaborating on some ideas of Uzawa (1965), Lucas (1988) assumed that agents have a choice between two ways of spending their (non-leisure) time: to contribute to current production or to accumulate human capital. It is essentially the allocation of time between the two alternatives contemplated that decides the growth rate of the system. For example, a decrease in the time spent producing goods involves a reduction in current output; at the same time it speeds up the formation of human capital and thereby increases output growth. With the accumulation of human capital there is said to be associated an externality: the more human capital society as a whole has accumulated, the more productive each single member will be. This is reflected in the following macroeconomic production function:

$$Y = AK^{\beta}(uhN)^{1-\beta}h^{*\gamma} \tag{9}$$

where the labour input consists of the number of workers, N, times the fraction of time spent working, u, times h, which gives the labour input in efficiency units. Finally, there is the term h^*. This is designed to represent the externality. The single agent takes h^* as a parameter in his or her optimizing by choice of consumption c and u. However, for society as a whole the accumulation of human capital increases output both directly and indirectly, that is, through the externality. Here we are confronted with a variant of a *public good* problem, which may be expressed as follows. The individual optimizing agent faces constant returns to scale in production: the sum of the partial elasticities of production of the factors he or she can control, that is, his or her physical and human capital, is unity. Yet for society as a whole the partial elasticity of production of human capital is not $1 - \beta$ but $1 - \beta + \gamma$.

Lucas's conceptualization of the process by means of which human capital is built up is the following:

$$\dot{h} = \upsilon h(1 - u) \tag{10}$$

where υ is a positive constant. (Note that equation (10) can be interpreted as a 'production function' of human capital by means of human capital: the average product is constant and equals υ.)

Interestingly, it can be shown that if there is *not* the above-mentioned externality, i.e. if γ in equation (9) equals zero, and therefore returns to scale are constant and, as a consequence, the non-substitution theorem holds, endogenous growth in Lucas's model is obtained in essentially the same way as in the models of Rebelo (1991) and King and Rebelo (1990): the rate of profit is determined by technology and profit maximization alone; and for the predetermined level of the rate of profit the saving–investment mechanism determines the rate of growth. Hence, as Lucas himself pointed out, the endogenous growth is positive *independently* of the fact that there is the above-mentioned externality, that is, independently of the fact that γ is positive.

With the 'production functions' (9) and (10), and $\gamma = 0$, profits are maximized when

$$w_e = p\upsilon \tag{11.1}$$

$$r = \beta A \left(\frac{K}{uhN}\right)^{\beta - 1} \tag{11.2}$$

$$w_e = (1 - \beta)A \left(\frac{K}{uhN}\right)^{\beta} \tag{11.3}$$

where w_e is the wage per efficiency unit of labour (if w_h is the hourly wage of a worker of skill h, then $w_h = w_e h$), p is the price of human capital in terms of the single commodity that is consumed or accumulated as physical capital, and r is the rate of profit. In conditions of free competition the rate of profit tends to be uniform across the two sectors. This implies that the existing human capital times the rate of profit equals the income obtained from that human capital, that is,

$$rNhp = w_e uNh + \dot{N}hp + N\dot{h}p + Nh\dot{p} \tag{12}$$

Since the non-substitution theorem holds, p and w_e are uniquely determined in the long run and, therefore, in steady states $\dot{p} = 0$. Then, from equations (10), (11.1) and (12) we obtain

$$r = \upsilon + \lambda$$

where λ is the *exogenous* rate of growth of population. There is only one meaning that can be attributed to the dependence of r on λ: it is a consequence of the remarkable fact that in Lucas's model the growth of 'population' means simply that the immortal consumer grows 'bigger' at rate λ. (Otherwise one would have to assume the existence of another type of externality: costless cultural transmission, that is, to new generations the existing knowledge is a free good.) Thus, as in Rebelo's model, the rate of profit is determined by technology (and profit maximization) alone. Equations (11.2) and (11.3) determine the technique utilized in the commodity – producing sector and the wage rate:

$$\frac{K}{uhN} = \left(\frac{\upsilon + \lambda}{\beta A}\right)^{(\beta - 1)^{-1}}$$

$$w_e = (1 - \beta)A \left(\frac{\upsilon + \lambda}{\beta A}\right)^{\beta(\beta - 1)^{-1}}$$

Hence, if u is constant over time, and K, h, and N grow at rates that are also constant over time, that is, the economy is in a steady state, then:

$$\frac{\dot{K}}{K} = \frac{\dot{h}}{h} + \frac{\dot{N}}{N}$$

Finally, as in the models of Rebelo (1991) and King and Rebelo (1990), the behaviour of consumers (and investors) reflected in the saving–investment equation determines a relationship between the rate of profit and the rate of growth, and since the profit rate is determined by technology (and the choice of technique), the growth rate is *endogenously* fixed. With Lucas's assumptions about saving

$$\frac{\dot{h}}{h} = \frac{r - \rho}{\sigma} \tag{13}$$

that is

$$\frac{\dot{h}}{h} = \frac{\upsilon + \lambda - \rho}{\sigma}$$

which implies that

$$u = \frac{\upsilon(\sigma - 1) + \rho - \lambda}{\upsilon\sigma}$$

and since $0 \leq u \leq 1$

$$0 \leq \frac{\upsilon + \lambda - \rho}{\sigma} \leq \upsilon$$

Let us now assume a positive γ (but lower than $(1 - \beta)\sigma$). In this case returns to scale are not constant. Hence the non-substitution theorem does not apply, and this is the reason why neither the profit-maximizing technique, nor w_e, nor p is determined by technology and profit maximization alone. As a consequence r is not so determined, either. The simple 'recursive' structure of the model is thereby lost. Nevertheless, technology and profit maximization still determine, in steady states, a *relationship* between the rate of profit and the rate of growth. This relationship, together with the relationship between the same rates, obtained from the saving–investment equation, determines both variables. Thus, although the analysis is more complex, essentially the same mechanism applies.

In fact, if $\gamma > 0$, equations (11.1–3) become:

$$w_e = p\upsilon \tag{14.1}$$

$$r = \beta A h^{\gamma}\left(\frac{K}{uhN}\right)^{\beta - 1} \tag{14.2}$$

$$w_e = (1 - \beta)Ah^\gamma \left(\frac{K}{uhN}\right)^\beta \tag{14.3}$$

From equations (14.1) and (14.3) we obtain

$$\frac{\dot{w}_e}{w_e} = \frac{\dot{p}}{p}$$

$$\frac{\dot{w}_e}{w_e} = (\gamma - \beta)\frac{\dot{h}}{h} + \beta\left(\frac{\dot{K}}{K} - \lambda\right)$$

From the production function (9) we obtain that in steady states

$$\frac{\dot{Y}}{Y} = \frac{\dot{K}}{K} = \frac{1 - \beta + \gamma}{1 - \beta}\frac{\dot{h}}{h} + \lambda$$

Hence

$$\frac{\dot{p}}{p} = \frac{\dot{w}_e}{w_e} = \frac{\gamma}{1 - \beta}\frac{\dot{h}}{h}$$

which, substituted in equation (12), and taking account of equations (10) and (14.1), gives

$$r = \upsilon + \lambda + \frac{\gamma}{1 - \beta}\frac{\dot{h}}{h}$$

which jointly with equation (13) determines both the growth rate and the rate of profit:

$$r = \frac{(1 - \beta)\sigma(\upsilon + \lambda) - \gamma\rho}{(1 - \beta)\sigma - \gamma}$$

$$\frac{\dot{h}}{h} = \frac{(1 - \beta)(\upsilon + \lambda - \rho)}{(1 - \beta)\sigma - \gamma}$$

Thus, although the analysis is more complex, essentially the same mechanism applies as in the models dealt with on pp. 75–8. Once again the concept of 'human capital' has assumed a role equivalent to the role of the concept of 'labour' in classical economics. However, while most contemporary economists would presumably be hostile to the idea that 'labour' could be treated as a produced factor of production, they appear to have had no difficulty in accepting the idea that there is a technology producing 'human capital'.[9]

We want to stress that the results obtained in this section are no different from those Lucas (1988) obtained by using his procedure of maximizing the functional (5) subject to the constraints (9) and (10) and then assuming that the available amounts of human capital and physical capital are those which allow the steady state. However, we arrived at the results much more easily since our analysis was a long-period one from the beginning, and that gave us directly equations (11) and (12) in the case of constant returns to scale (and (14) and (12) in the case of increasing returns to scale). The results are obtained when these equations are put together with equation (13) – an equation that Lucas obtained by the assumption of an everlasting consumer, but which can also be obtained otherwise. This should clarify the *detour* aspect of the intertemporal analysis with respect to the long-period one, when we are interested in the 'balanced path', considered 'as a good approximation to any actual path "most" of the time' (ibid.: 11).

Endogenous technical change

Models of the second group attempt to portray technical change as generated endogenously. The proximate starting point of this kind of model was Arrow's paper on 'learning by doing' (Arrow, 1962). In Romer (1986) attention focuses on the role of a single state variable called 'knowledge' or 'information'. It is assumed that the information contained in inventions and discoveries has the property of being available to anybody to make use of at the same time. In other words, information is considered essentially a non-rival good. However, it need not be totally non-excludable, that is, it can be monopolized at least for some time. It is around the two different aspects of publicness (non-rivalry and non-excludability) that the argument revolves. Discoveries are made in research and development departments of firms. This requires resources to be withheld from producing current output. The basic idea of Romer's model is 'that there is a trade-off between consumption today and knowledge that can be used to produce more consumption tomorrow' (ibid.: 1015). He formalizes this idea in terms of a 'research technology' that produces 'knowledge' from forgone consumption. Knowledge is assumed to be cardinally measurable and not to depreciate: it is like perennial capital.

Romer stipulates a research technology that is concave and homogeneous of degree one,

$$\dot{k}_i = G(I_i, k_i) \tag{15}$$

where I_i is an amount of forgone consumption in research by firm i and k_i is the firm's current stock of knowledge. (Note that equation (15) can be interpreted as a production function describing the production of 'knowledge' by means of 'knowledge' and the forgone consumption good.) The production function of the consumption good relative to firm i is

$$Y_i = F(k_i, K, \mathbf{x}_i) \tag{16}$$

where K is the accumulated stock of knowledge in the economy as a whole and $\mathbf{x}_i$ is a vector of inputs different from knowledge. Romer assumes that 'factors other than knowledge are in fixed supply' (ibid.: 1019). This implies that 'knowledge' is the only capital good utilized in the production of the consumption good. (The forgone consumption good is a capital good used in the production of knowledge.) Spill-overs from private research and development activities increase the public stock of knowledge K. It is assumed that the function is homogeneous of degree one in k_i and $\mathbf{x}_i$ and homogeneous of a degree greater than one in k_i and K.

Assuming, contrary to Romer, that the above production function (16) is homogeneous of degree one in k_i and K involves constant returns: the diminishing returns to k_i are exactly offset by the external improvements in technology associated with capital accumulation. In this case it can be shown that, as in the models previously dealt with, the rate of profit is determined by technology and profit maximization alone, provided, as is assumed by Romer, that the ratio K/k_i equals the (given) number of firms.

In fact, profit maximization requires that

$$p\frac{\partial G}{\partial I_i} = r \tag{17.1}$$

$$\frac{\partial G}{\partial k_i} = r \tag{17.2}$$

$$\frac{\partial F}{\partial k_i} = rp \tag{17.3}$$

$$\frac{\partial F}{\partial x_{ij}} = w_j \tag{18}$$

where p is the price of 'knowledge' in terms of the consumption good and w_j is the rental of the j-th fixed factor. The derivative of $F(k_i, K, \mathbf{x}_i)$ with respect to k_i is homogeneous of degree zero in k_i and K. Then it depends only on the given vector $\mathbf{x}_i$ and the ratio K/k_i, which, since all firms are taken to be equal to one another, coincides with the (given) number of firms S. That is, since $\mathbf{x}_i$ is a given vector and since function (15) is homogeneous of degree one, the three equations (17) involve only three unknowns: r, p, I_i/k_i. As in the models previously dealt with, the rate of profit is determined by technology and profit maximization alone, so that the saving–investment relation can determine the growth rate *endogenously*. (Equation (18) just determines the rentals of the fixed factors.)

Once again endogenous growth does not depend on an assumption about increasing returns with regard to accumulable factors. Growth would not be 'more endogenous' if increasing returns were to be assumed. Such an assumption renders the analysis a good deal more complicated. In particular, a steady-state equilibrium does not exist unless the marginal product of capital is taken to be bounded from above. This is done by Romer in terms of an *ad hoc* assumption regarding equation (15) (ibid.: 1019). This assumption is not different from the one used in drawing Figure 4.4 above, where the marginal product of labour-cum-capital is shown to be increasing with the scale of production but is bounded from above.

CONCLUDING REMARKS

The chapter has shown how in some of the best-known NGMs endogenous growth is generated. Notwithstanding their many differences, it is a striking common feature of these models that the rate of profit is determined by technology alone, or, if there is a choice of technique, by the profit-maximizing behaviour of producers. With the rate of profit determined in this way, the task of the saving–investment mechanism is restricted to the determination of the steady-state growth rate. With a given saving rate, the growth rate is simply the profit rate times the saving rate. With intertemporal utility maximization things are slightly more complicated and the saving rate is endogenously determined. It has also been shown that increasing returns are not an indispensable ingredient of endogenous growth. The profit rate is determined by technology because it is assumed that there is a technology producing 'labour'. In order to render this fact acceptable to a twentieth-century audience, the factor has been given new names and enters the stage either as 'human capital' or 'knowledge'. Exactly as in the Ricardian analysis, in this way the profit rate is determined. The readers of *Production of Commodities by Means of Commodities* by Piero Sraffa (1960) will immediately recall that when at the beginning of chapter II (§§ 4–5) wages are regarded as entering the system 'on the same footing as the fuel for the engines or the feed for the cattle', the profit rate and the prices are determined by technology alone. On the contrary, when workers get a part of the surplus, the quantity of labour employed in each industry has to be represented explicitly, and the profit rate and the prices can be determined only if an extra equation determining income distribution is introduced into the analysis. The additional equation generally used by advocates of neoclassical analysis is the equality between demand and supply of 'capital', which requires the homogeneity of this factor.[10] But no extra equation is required in the NGT, since, as in Ricardo and in §§ 4–5 of Sraffa's book, there is a technology producing 'labour'.

Finally, it should be noted that the NGT has revived *long-period* analysis, centred around the concept of a uniform rate of profit. However, the kind of long-period argument put forward in the NGT falls way behind the present state of the art in this field of research. In particular, it appears to us anachronistic to attempt to develop a theory of growth that focuses on product innovations, new 'industrial designs', etc., in terms of a model which preserves several of the disquieting features of the neoclassical growth theory of the 1950s and 1960s, including the setting aside of the diversity of behaviour and the heterogeneity of goods, particularly capital goods. These latter assumptions the NGT shares with Knight's famous Crusonia plant, in particular, a homogeneous capital jelly (cf. Kurz and Salvadori 1997a). There is no need and indeed no justification for continuing to dwell on such fairy tales. First, because the structure of the theory does not require such an assumption, since distribution is *not* determined by the equality of the demand for and supply of 'capital'. Second, because modern long-period theory of 'classical' derivation may offer an alternative that allows a better understanding of the phenomena under consideration.

We hope to have shown that many of the interesting aspects of the NGMs are related to the classical perspective their authors (unwittingly) take on the problem of growth, whereas some of their shortcomings derive from the lack of solutions to the problems of the neoclassical theory of growth which were put into sharp relief during the 1960s.

NOTES

1 See, for example, Yang and Borland (1991), Becker and Murphy (1992), Rodriguez-Clare (1996); see also the so-called neo-Schumpeterian models, e.g. Aghion and Howitt (1992).

2 This path must not, of course, be identified with the *actual* path the economy is taking, because technical progress will repeatedly offset the impact of the 'niggardliness of nature' on the rate of profit.

3 Real wages may rise, that is, the 'market price of labour' may rise above the 'natural' wage rate. This is the case in a situation in which capital accumulates rapidly, leading to an excess demand for labour. As Ricardo put it, 'notwithstanding the tendency of wages to conform to their natural rate, their market rate may, in an improving society, for an indefinite period, be constantly above it' (ibid.: 94–5). If such a situation prevails for some time it is even possible that 'custom renders absolute necessaries' what in the past have been comforts or luxuries. Hence the natural wage is driven upward by persistently high levels of the actual wage rate. Accordingly, the concept of 'natural wage' in Ricardo is a flexible one and must not be mistaken for a physiological minimum of subsistence. For Smith's view on wages and the growth of the work force see Kurz and Salvadori (1995: chapter 15).

4 In the more sophisticated conceptualizations underlying the arguments of Smith and Ricardo, higher rates of growth of the labour supply presuppose higher levels of the real wage rate. But the basic logic remains the same: in normal conditions the pace at which capital accumulates regulates the pace at which labour grows.

5 Let $x = f(L, L^*)$ be the product of the last unit of labour-cum-capital when L represents the amount of labour-cum-capital employed and the division of labour is artificially kept fixed at the level appropriate when the amount of labour-cum-capital employed is L^*. Obviously, $f(L, L^*)$ as a function of L alone is either decreasing as in Figures 4.1 and 4.3 (if land is scarce) or constant, as in Figure 4.2 (if land is not scarce). The product at L^* equals

$$\int_0^{L^*} f(L, L^*)dL$$

that is, the area under the curve $f(L, L^*)$ in the range $[0, L^*]$. If

$$\frac{\partial f}{\partial L^*} > -\frac{\partial f}{\partial L} \quad \text{for } L = L^*$$

then the curve

$$x = f(L, L)$$

which is the curve depicted in Figure 4.4, is increasing, but the product is, as stated in the text, larger than or equal to the sum of profits and wages, which equals the product of the given amount of labour-cum-capital times the corresponding level of output per unit of labour-cum-capital.

6 The assumption that the formation of human capital does not involve any unskilled labour as an input is not convincing: the whole point of education processes is that a person's capacity to perform unskilled labour is gradually transformed into the capacity to perform skilled labour. Adam Smith, for example, was perfectly aware of this. For an analytical treatment of the problem of human capital, taking Smith's discussion as a starting point, see Kurz and Salvadori (1995: chapter 11).

7 It is easily checked that if the production functions (6) are 'well behaved', then there is one and only one solution to system (7).

8 We need a special case of the non-substitution theorem, because no primary factor (or a primary factor with zero remuneration) is assumed; see Kurz and Salvadori (1994), reproduced below as Chapter 5.

9 It is possible to show that the Lucas model can easily be generalized to take into account non-produced means of production. If land, Q, is introduced so that the production function (9) becomes

$$Y = AK^{\beta}(uhN)^{\alpha}Q^{1-\alpha-\beta}h^{*\gamma}$$

by following the above procedure we obtain

$$r = \upsilon + \frac{\alpha}{1-\beta}\lambda + \frac{\alpha+\beta+\gamma-1}{1-\beta}\frac{\dot{h}}{h}$$

Note that if $\alpha + \beta + \gamma = 1$, that is, if returns to scale with respect to accumulable factors are constant, then the rate of profit is determined by technology and profit maximization alone; otherwise technology and profit maximization determine a linear relationship between the rate of profit and the rate of growth.

10 This is the famous critique of that theory put forward in the 1960s; for a review of that critique see Harcourt (1972) and Kurz and Salvadori (1995: chapter 14).

REFERENCES

Aghion, P. and Howitt, P. (1992) 'A model of growth through creative destruction', *Econometrica* 60: 323–51.

Arrow, K. J. (1962) 'The economic implications of learning by doing', *Review of Economic Studies* 29: 155–73.

Barro, R. J. and Sala-i-Martin, X. (1995) *Economic Growth*, New York: McGraw-Hill.

Becker, G. S. and Murphy, K. M. (1992) 'The division of labour, coordination costs, and knowledge', *Quarterly Journal of Economics* 106: 501–26.

Burgstaller, A. (1994) *Property and Prices: Toward a Unified Theory of Value*, Cambridge: Cambridge University Press.

Grossman, G. M. and Helpman, E. (1994) 'Endogenous innovation in the theory of growth', *Journal of Economic Perspectives* 8: 23–44.

Harcourt, G. C. (1972) *Some Cambridge Controversies in the Theory of Capital*, Cambridge: Cambridge University Press.

Jones, L. E. and Manuelli, R. (1990) 'A convex model of equilibrium growth: theory and policy implications', *Journal of Political Economy* 98: 1008–38.

Kaldor, N. (1956) 'Alternative theories of distribution', *Review of Economic Studies* 23: 83–100.

—— (1957) 'A model of economic growth', *Economic Journal* 67: 591–624.

King, R. G. and Rebelo, S. (1990) 'Public policy and economic growth: developing neoclassical implications', *Journal of Political Economy* 98: 126–50.

Kurz, H. D. and Salvadori, N. (1994) 'The non-substitution theorem: making good a lacuna', *Journal of Economics* 59: 97–103.

—— (1995) *Theory of Production: A Long-period Analysis*, Cambridge, Melbourne and New York: Cambridge University Press.

—— (1996) 'In the beginning all the world was Australia . . .', in M. Sawyer (ed.) *Capital Contoversy, Post-Keynesian Economics and the History of Economic Thought. Essays in honour of G. C. Harcourt* II, London: Routledge, pp. 425–43.

—— (1997a) 'What is new in the "new" theories of economic growth? or: Old wine in new goatskins', in F. Coricelli, M. Di Matteo and F. H. Hahn (eds), *Growth and Development: Theories. Empirical Evidence and Policy Issues*, London: Macmillan.

—— (1997b) 'Theories of "Endogenous" Growth in Historical Perspective', paper given at the Eleventh World Congress of the *International Economic Association*, 17–22 December 1995, Tunis, Tunisia. To be published in the conference proceedings.

Lucas, R. E. (1988) 'On the mechanics of economic development', *Journal of Monetary Economics* 22: 3–42.

Rebelo, S. (1991) 'Long run policy analysis and long run growth', *Journal of Political Economy* 99: 500–21.

Ricardo, D. ([1817] 1951) *On the Principles of Political Economy and Taxation*, vol. I of *The Works and Correspondence of David Ricardo*, ed. Piero Sraffa with the collaboration of M. H. Dobb, Cambridge: Cambridge University Press.

Rodriguez-Clare, A. (1996) 'The division of labour and development', *Journal of Development Economics*, pp. 3–32.

Romer, P. M. (1986) 'Increasing returns and long-run growth', *Journal of Political Economy* 94: 1002–37.

Smith, A. (1976) *An Inquiry into the Nature and Causes of the Wealth of Nations*, 1st edn 1776. Vol. II of *The Glasgow Edition of the Works and Correspondence of Adam Smith*, ed. R. H. Campbell, A. S. Skinner and W. B. Todd, Oxford: Oxford University Press. In the text quoted as *WN*, book number, chapter number, section number, paragraph number.

Solow, R. M. (1956) 'A contribution to the theory of economic growth', *Quarterly Journal of Economics* 70: 65–94.

Sraffa, P. (1960) *Production of Commodities by Means of Commodities*, Cambridge: Cambridge University Press.

Uzawa, H. (1965) 'Optimum technical change in an aggregate model of economic growth', *International Economic Review* 6: 18–31.

Yang, X. and Borland, J. (1991) 'A microeconomic mechanism for economic growth', *Journal of Political Economy* 99: 460–82.

Young, A. (1928) 'Increasing returns and economic progress', *Economic Journal* 38: 527–42.

ACKNOWLEDGEMENTS

This chapter uses some of the material contained in some earlier papers by us on the so-called 'new' growth theory; see, in particular, Kurz and Salvadori (1996, 1997a, b). We thank Antonio D'Agata, Christian Gehrke, and Alberto Zazzaro for useful comments. Neri Salvadori gratefully acknowledges financial support from MURST (the Italian Ministry of University and Technological and Scientific Research) and CNR (the Italian National Research Council).

5

THE NON-SUBSTITUTION THEOREM

Making good a lacuna

Heinz D. Kurz and Neri Salvadori

A non-substitution theorem is a uniqueness theorem which asserts that under certain specified conditions an economy has one particular price structure for each admissible value of the rate of interest. The original formulations of the theorem assumed single production and therefore circulating capital only (see Arrow 1951; Georgescu-Roegen 1951; Koopmans 1951; Samuelson 1951).[1] In all these formulations the rate of interest is assumed to be at a level lower than the maximum one, which is obtained at a wage rate equal to zero. The problem of whether the theorem holds good when wages are zero seems never to have been investigated. Although there is no particular economic motivation to study this situation, it is startling that a limiting case of a theorem which has been studied so extensively and is generally accepted in the scientific community has not been analysed. In this chapter the lacuna is made good. We first show in terms of a numerical example that, if wages are zero, then the theorem need not hold. Next we show that if there exists a commodity which is indispensable for the reproduction of all commodities, then the theorem does apply, i.e. uniqueness of prices obtains, even if wages are zero. The proof supplied offers also some insights into the formal structure of the non-substitution theorem.

THE EXAMPLE

Consider an economy with only one primary factor, labour, no joint production, and constant returns to scale, in which two goods, called 'wheat' and 'iron', are produced. Both goods are taken to serve as means of production and as consumption goods. The rate of interest is assumed to be equal to unity, while the growth rate is smaller than unity. There exist two processes to produce wheat and two processes to produce iron; the production conditions of these processes are summarized in Table 5.1.

Table 5.1 The input–output conditions

	Material input				Output	
Process	*Wheat*	*Iron*	*Labour*		*Wheat*	*Iron*
(1)	1	–	2	→	2	–
(2)	3	4	24	→	–	12
(3)	2	1	6	→	6	–
(4)	–	1	2	→	–	2

In standard notation, the price vector **p** and the intensity vector **x** will be determined jointly with the wage rate w by the system

$$[\mathbf{B} - (1 + r)\mathbf{A}]\mathbf{p} \leqq w\mathbf{l} \qquad (1.1)$$

$$\mathbf{x}^T[\mathbf{B} - (1 + r)\mathbf{A}]\mathbf{p} = w\mathbf{x}^T\mathbf{l} \qquad (1.2)$$

$$\mathbf{x}^T[\mathbf{B} - (1 + g)\mathbf{A}] \geqq \mathbf{d}^T \qquad (1.3)$$

$$\mathbf{x}^T[\mathbf{B} - (1 + g)\mathbf{A}]\mathbf{p} = \mathbf{d}^T\mathbf{p} \qquad (1.4)$$

$$\mathbf{p} \geqq \mathbf{0}, \quad \mathbf{x} \geqq \mathbf{0}, \quad w \geq 0, \quad \mathbf{q}^T\mathbf{p} = 1 \qquad (1.5)$$

where **A** is the material input matrix, **l** is the labour input vector, **B** is the output matrix, $\mathbf{d} \geq \mathbf{0}$ is the consumption vector, r is the rate of interest, and g is the uniform rate of growth. Inequality (1.1) implies that no process is able to pay (extra) profits. Equation (1.2) implies, also because of inequalities (1.5), that, if a process is not able to pay the given rate of interest, it is not operated. Inequality (1.3) implies that the total demand (consumption and gross investment) is satisfied.[2] Equation (1.4), also because of inequalities (1.5), is the rule of free goods: overproduced commodities fetch a zero price. Equation (1.5) fixes the numeraire, where **q** is any given semi-positive vector.

If the interest rate equals 1, it is possible to operate alternatively either processes (1, 2), processes (1, 4), or processes (3, 4). In all cases the wage rate is equal to zero. If wheat is chosen as numeraire, i.e. if **q** equals the first unit vector, then the price of iron equals 3/2 in the first alternative, 1 in the third alternative, and can assume any value between 1 and 3/2 in the second alternative. Whichever of the above-mentioned pairs of processes are operated, the determined prices are such that no process is able to pay profits, i.e. inequality (1.1) holds. Moreover, each of the above-mentioned pairs of processes can be operated in such a way as to fulfil demand, whatever is the growth rate $g < r$ and whatever are the proportions in which wheat and iron are consumed (i.e. prices are independent of the rate of growth and of consumption demand whichever technique is chosen). However, prices are not uniquely determined. (If, on the contrary, both processes (2, 3) are operated, then the prices so determined do not satisfy inequality (1.1) and the wage rate is negative.)

THE NON-SUBSTITUTION THEOREM RESTATED

Let $(\mathbf{p}^*, w^*, \mathbf{x}^*)$ and $(\mathbf{p}^\circ, w^\circ, \mathbf{x}^\circ)$ be two solutions to system (1) for a given r. (The two solutions need not be calculated for the same scalar $g \geq 0$ and the same vector $\mathbf{d} > \mathbf{0}$.) The non-substitution theorem asserts that $\mathbf{p}^* = \mathbf{p}^\circ$ and $w^* = w^\circ$. If $\mathbf{d}$ is semi-positive but not positive, the theorem asserts that the prices of commodities that are produced are the same in both solutions. Prices of commodities that are not produced may vary in a range. We need the following definitions.

Let $(\mathbf{A}^*, \mathbf{B}^*, \mathbf{l}^*)$ and $(\mathbf{A}^\circ, \mathbf{B}^\circ, \mathbf{l}^\circ)$ be obtained from $(\mathbf{A}, \mathbf{B}, \mathbf{l})$ by deleting the rows corresponding to zero elements of vectors $\mathbf{x}^*$ and $\mathbf{x}^\circ$, respectively. Since single production holds, each row of matrix $\mathbf{B}$ can be considered a unit vector and therefore we can arrange processes in such a way that $\mathbf{B}^* = \mathbf{B}^\circ = \mathbf{I}$. In the following we will refer to the set of processes defined by matrix $\mathbf{A}^*$ and vector $\mathbf{l}^*$ $(\mathbf{B}^* = \mathbf{I})$ as *technique* $(\mathbf{A}^*, \mathbf{l}^*)$. Similarly for *technique* $(\mathbf{A}^\circ, \mathbf{l}^\circ)$. We say that commodity j *enters directly* into the production of commodity i in technique $(\mathbf{A}^*, \mathbf{l}^*)$ if and only if $\mathbf{e}_i^T \mathbf{A}^*\mathbf{e}_j > 0$. Similarly, we say that commodity j *enters directly or indirectly* into the production of commodity i in technique $(\mathbf{A}^*, \mathbf{l}^*)$ if and only if

$$\mathbf{e}_i^T (\mathbf{A}^* + \mathbf{A}^{*2} + \ . \ . \ . \ + \mathbf{A}^{*n})\mathbf{e}_j > 0$$

where n is the number of commodities involved. A *basic commodity* of technique $(\mathbf{A}^*, \mathbf{l}^*)$ is a commodity which enters directly or indirectly into the production of all commodities in technique $(\mathbf{A}^*, \mathbf{l}^*)$, i.e. commodity j is basic for technique $(\mathbf{A}^*, \mathbf{l}^*)$ if and only if

$$(\mathbf{A}^* + \mathbf{A}^{*2} + \ . \ . \ . \ + \mathbf{A}^{*n})\mathbf{e}_j > \mathbf{0}$$

Similarly, we say that labour enters directly or indirectly into the production of all commodities in technique $(\mathbf{A}^*, \mathbf{l}^*)$ if and only if

$$(\mathbf{I} + \mathbf{A}^* + \ . \ . \ . \ + \mathbf{A}^{*n-1})\mathbf{l}^* > \mathbf{0}$$

Then we can state the following theorem.

Theorem 1. Let $(\mathbf{p}^*, w^*, \mathbf{x}^*)$ and $(\mathbf{p}^\circ, w^\circ, \mathbf{x}^\circ)$ be two solutions to system (1) for a given r and let $(\mathbf{A}^*, \mathbf{l}^*)$ and $(\mathbf{A}^\circ, \mathbf{l}^\circ)$ be the corresponding techniques. If labour enters directly or indirectly into the production of all commodities in both techniques and there is a commodity j which is basic for both techniques, then $w^* = w^\circ$ and $\mathbf{p}^* = \mathbf{p}^\circ$.

Proof. Assume first that $w^* > w^\circ$ (≥ 0). Since

$$\mathbf{p}^* = (1 + r)\mathbf{A}^*\mathbf{p}^* + w^*\mathbf{l}^* = w^*\mathbf{l}^* + w^* (1 + r)\mathbf{A}^*\mathbf{l}^* + (1 + r)^2\mathbf{A}^{*2}\mathbf{p}^*$$

we obtain by iteration that

$$\mathbf{p}^* = w^*[\mathbf{l}^* + (1 + r)\mathbf{A}^*\mathbf{l}^* + (1 + r)^2\mathbf{A}^{*2}\mathbf{l}^* + \ldots + (1 + r)^t\mathbf{A}^{*t}\mathbf{l}^* + \ldots]$$

The above series is increasing and bounded, hence it is convergent. As a consequence

$$\lim_{t\to\infty} (1 + r)^t\mathbf{A}^{*t}\mathbf{l}^* = \mathbf{0} \tag{2}$$

If vector $\mathbf{l}^*$ is positive, then equality (2) implies that

$$\lim_{t\to\infty} (1 + r)^t\mathbf{A}^{*t} = \mathbf{0} \tag{3}$$

If vector $\mathbf{l}^*$ has some zero elements, we obtain from equality (2) that

$$\lim_{t\to\infty} [(1 + r)\mathbf{A}^*]^t\{\mathbf{l}^* + (1 + r)\mathbf{A}^*\mathbf{l}^* + \ldots + [(1 + r)\mathbf{A}^*]^{n-1}\mathbf{l}^*\}$$

$$= n \lim_{t\to\infty} [(1 + r)\mathbf{A}^*]^t\mathbf{l}^* = \mathbf{0}$$

which implies equality (3), since

$$\mathbf{l}^* + (1 + r)\mathbf{A}^*\mathbf{l}^* + \ldots + [(1 + r)\mathbf{A}^*]^{n-1}\mathbf{l}^* > \mathbf{0}$$

Equality (3) ensures that matrix $[\mathbf{I} - (1 + r)\mathbf{A}^*]$ is invertible and that its inverse is semi-positive. Moreover, since $\mathbf{p}^\circ$ and w° satisfy inequality (1.1),

$$[\mathbf{I} - (1 + r)\mathbf{A}^*]\mathbf{p}^\circ \leqq w^\circ\mathbf{l}^*$$

which, premultiplied by $\mathbf{q}^T[\mathbf{I} - (1 + r)\mathbf{A}^*]^{-1} \geq \mathbf{0}^T$, gives

$$1 = \mathbf{q}^T\mathbf{p}^\circ \leq w^\circ\mathbf{q}^T[\mathbf{I} - (1 + r)\mathbf{A}^*]^{-1}\mathbf{l}^* = \frac{w^\circ}{w^*}$$

Hence a contradiction is obtained and therefore $w^* \leq w^\circ$. A similar argument proves that $w^\circ \leq w^*$. Hence

$$w^* = w^\circ \tag{4}$$

With no loss of generality assume that the commodity that is basic for both techniques is commodity 1 (i.e. $j = 1$). Then take the numeraire to consist of commodity 1 only, i.e. $\mathbf{q} = \mathbf{e}_1$, and introduce the following partitions:

$$\mathbf{A}^* = \begin{bmatrix} B^* & \mathbf{C}^* \\ \mathbf{D}^* & \mathbf{F}^* \end{bmatrix}, \mathbf{A}^\circ = \begin{bmatrix} B^\circ & \mathbf{C}^\circ \\ \mathbf{D}^\circ & \mathbf{F}^\circ \end{bmatrix}, \mathbf{p}^* = \begin{bmatrix} 1 \\ \mathbf{y}^* \end{bmatrix}, \mathbf{p}^\circ = \begin{bmatrix} 1 \\ \mathbf{y}^\circ \end{bmatrix}$$

where the B's are scalars, the $\mathbf{C}$'s are row vectors, and the $\mathbf{D}$'s are column vectors. Then

$$[\mathbf{I} - (1 + r)\mathbf{F}^*]\mathbf{y}^\circ \leqq (1 + r)\mathbf{D}^* + w^\circ\mathbf{l}^* \tag{5.1}$$

$$[\mathbf{I} - (1 + r)\mathbf{F}^\circ]\mathbf{y}^* \leqq (1 + r)\mathbf{D}^\circ + w^*\mathbf{l}^\circ \tag{5.2}$$

where

$$[\mathbf{I} - (1 + r)\mathbf{F}^*]\mathbf{y}^* = (1 + r)\mathbf{D}^* + w^*\mathbf{l}^* := \mathbf{m}^* \geq \mathbf{0} \tag{6.1}$$

$$[\mathbf{I} - (1 + r)\mathbf{F}^\circ]\mathbf{y}^\circ = (1 + r)\mathbf{D}^\circ + w^\circ\mathbf{l}^\circ := \mathbf{m}^\circ \geq \mathbf{0} \tag{6.2}$$

Then, by applying to $\mathbf{F}^*$, $\mathbf{y}^*$, $\mathbf{m}^*$ and to $\mathbf{F}^\circ$, $\mathbf{y}^\circ$, $\mathbf{m}^\circ$ the same procedure as applied above to $\mathbf{A}^*$, $\mathbf{p}^*$, $w^*\mathbf{l}^*$, taking into account that $\mathbf{m}^* \geqq (1 + r)\mathbf{D}^*$ and $\mathbf{m}^\circ \geqq (1 + r)\mathbf{D}^\circ$ and therefore

$$\mathbf{m}^* + (1 + r)\mathbf{F}^*\mathbf{m}^* + \ldots + [(1 + r)\mathbf{F}^*]^{n-1}\mathbf{m}^* > \mathbf{0}$$

$$\mathbf{m}^\circ + (1 + r)\mathbf{F}^\circ\mathbf{m}^\circ + \ldots + [(1 + r)\mathbf{F}^\circ]^{n-1}\mathbf{m}^\circ > \mathbf{0}$$

we obtain that matrices $[\mathbf{I} - (1 + r)\mathbf{F}^*]$ and $[\mathbf{I} - (1 + r)\mathbf{F}^\circ]$ are invertible and their inverses are semi-positive. Finally, we obtain from inequalities (5.1–2), taking into account equations (6.1–2) and (4), that

$$\mathbf{y}^* \leqq \mathbf{y}^\circ \leqq \mathbf{y}^*$$

In the example of the previous section the assumption that there exists a commodity that is basic for all competitively viable techniques is not met. In fact, in technique (1, 2) wheat is basic, but iron is not, whereas in technique (3, 4) iron is basic, but wheat is not. Moreover, in technique (1, 4) no commodity is basic.

NOTES

1 For a summary statement on non-substitution theorems without and with fixed capital, in conditions of stationary or quasi-stationary states of the economy, see von Weizsäcker (1971: I, II) and Salvadori (1987).

2 If $\mathbf{x}$ is the vector of the intensities of operation of the different processes at time t, then $(1 + g)\mathbf{x}$ is the vector of the intensities of operation at time $t + 1$.

REFERENCES

Arrow, K. J. (1951) 'Alternative proof of the substitution theorem for Leontief models in the general case', in *Activity Analysis of Production and Allocation*, ed. T. C. Koopmans, New York: Wiley.

Georgescu-Roegen, N. (1951) 'Some properties of a generalized Leontief Model', in *Activity Analysis of Production and Allocation*, ed. T. C. Koopmans, New York: Wiley.

Koopmans, T. C. (1951) 'Alternative proof of the substitution theorem for Leontief models in the case of three industries', in *Activity Analysis of Production and Allocation*, ed. T. C. Koopmans, New York: Wiley.

Salvadori, N. (1987) 'Non-substitution theorems', in *The New Palgrave: a Dictionary of Economics* III, ed. J. Eatwell, M. Milgate and P. Newman, London: Macmillan.

Samuelson, P. A. (1951) 'Abstract of a theorem concerning substitutability in open Leontief models', in *Activity Analysis of Production and Allocation*, ed. T. C. Koopmans, New York: Wiley.

Weizsäcker, C. C. von (1971) *Steady State Capital Theory*, Heidelberg: Springer.

ACKNOWLEDGEMENTS

We are especially grateful to Paul Samuelson for valuable advice, comments, and encouragement; we thank also Harvey Gram, Ian Steedman and anonymous referees of the *Journal of Economics* for useful comments. It goes without saying that the responsibility for any remaining errors rests with the authors. N. Salvadori thanks also the MURST (the Italian Ministry of University and Technological and Scientific Research for financial support).

POSTSCRIPT

Above we have reprinted our paper as it was published in 1994. The results presented there are correct and correctly stated, but there is a small slip in the introduction. Moreover, further work has convinced us that the presentation could have been simpler and more precise if we had been more concerned about the distinction between the following two expressions: 'a commodity (or labour) entering directly or indirectly into the production of all commodities' as opposed to 'a commodity (or labour) indispensable for the reproduction of all commodities'.

With respect to a technology $(\mathbf{A}, \mathbf{I}, \mathbf{l})$ consisting of n processes and involving n commodities (i.e. a *technique*) we say that 'commodity j (labour) enters directly or indirectly into the production of all commodities' if and only if for each i either $a_{ij} > 0$ ($l_i > 0$) or there is a sequence of $z \in \mathbb{N}$ indices i_1 $i_2, \ldots, i_z$ such that

$$a_{ii_1}a_{i_1i_2}\ldots a_{i_zj} > 0 \ (a_{ii_1}a_{i_1i_2}\ldots a_{i_{z-1}z}l_z > 0)$$

It is then proved that it is always possible to assume that $1 \leq z \leq n-1$ and therefore commodity j (labour) enters directly or indirectly into the production of all commodities if and only if

$$(\mathbf{A} + \mathbf{A}^2 + \ldots + \mathbf{A}^n)\mathbf{e}_j > \mathbf{0} \ \ ((\mathbf{I} + \mathbf{A} + \ldots + \mathbf{A}^{n-1})\mathbf{1} > \mathbf{0}) \qquad (7)$$

With respect to a technology $(\mathbf{A}, \mathbf{B}, \mathbf{l})$ consisting of m processes and involving n $(m \geq n)$ commodities all of which are producible ($\mathbf{Be}_j \geq \mathbf{0}$ each j) we say that 'commodity j (labour) is indispensable for the reproduction of all commodities' if and only if

$$(\mathbf{u}^T(\mathbf{B}-\mathbf{A})\geqq\mathbf{0}^T,\ \mathbf{u}\geq\mathbf{0})\Rightarrow\mathbf{u}^T\mathrm{A}\mathrm{e}_j>0 \ \ ((\mathbf{u}^T(\mathbf{B}-\mathbf{A})\geqq\mathbf{0}^T,\ \mathbf{u}\geq\mathbf{0})\Rightarrow\mathbf{u}^T\mathbf{l}>0) \quad (8)$$

Although the two concepts originated in two different pieces of literature (the former was introduced by Sraffa (1960), the latter in connection with the von Neumann growth model), they have often been regarded as substantially amounting to the same thing. But they are different! In fact, implications (8) are satisfied also if there is no vector $\mathbf{u}$ such that

$$\mathbf{u}^T(\mathbf{B} - \mathbf{A}) \geqq \mathbf{0}^T, \mathbf{u} \geq \mathbf{0}$$

That is, implications (8) also hold if the economy is not viable. On the contrary, inequalities (7) depend only on the distribution of zeroes and are totally independent from the viability of the economy.

The paper here reprinted correctly referred to the direct or indirect entering into the production of all commodities in the statements to be proved and in the proofs, but it incorrectly (and inconsistently) referred to the indispensability to reproduction of all commodities in the introduction. Moreover, the direct or indirect entering into the production of all commodities was defined with respect to single techniques, as usual, and not with respect to the whole technology. This drove the authors (and the readers) to some unnecessary complication. We want to take the opportunity of this reprint to clarify all these aspects.

First of all we need a definition of 'a commodity (or labour) entering directly or indirectly into the production of all commodities' which can also be used in reference to a set of processes larger in number than the set of commodities involved. In order to do so let us first prove that the following Proposition 1 holds. Then it will be obvious to define with respect to a technology $(\mathbf{A}, \mathbf{B}, \mathbf{l})$ consisting of m processes and involving n $(m \geq n)$ commodities all of which are producible that 'commodity j (labour) *always* enters directly or indirectly into the production of commodity i' if and only if for each $\varepsilon > 0$.

$$(\mathbf{u}^T(\mathbf{B} - \varepsilon\mathbf{A}) \geqq \mathbf{e}_i^T, \mathbf{u} \geqq \mathbf{0}) \Rightarrow \mathbf{u}^T\mathbf{A}\mathbf{e}_j > 0 \; ((\mathbf{u}^T(\mathbf{B} - \varepsilon\mathbf{A}) \geqq \mathbf{e}_i^T, \mathbf{u} \geqq \mathbf{0}) \Rightarrow \mathbf{u}^T\mathbf{l} > 0)$$

Proposition 1. With respect to a technology $(\mathbf{A}, \mathbf{I}, \mathbf{l})$ consisting of n processes and involving n commodities:

(a) The inequality $\mathbf{e}_i^T(\mathbf{A} + \mathbf{A}^2 + \ldots + \mathbf{A}^n)\mathbf{e}_j > 0$ holds if and only if for each $\varepsilon > 0$

$$(\mathbf{u}^T(\mathbf{I} - \varepsilon\mathbf{A}) \geqq \mathbf{e}_i^T, \mathbf{u} \geqq \mathbf{0}) \Rightarrow \mathbf{u}^T\mathbf{A}\mathbf{e}_j > 0 \tag{9}$$

(b) The inequality $\mathbf{e}_i^T(\mathbf{I} + \mathbf{A} + \ldots + \mathbf{A}^{n-1})\mathbf{l} > 0$ holds if and only if for each $\varepsilon > 0$

$$(\mathbf{u}^T(\mathbf{I} - \varepsilon\mathbf{A}) \geqq \mathbf{e}_i^T, \mathbf{u} \geqq \mathbf{0}) \Rightarrow \mathbf{u}^T\mathbf{l} > 0$$

Proof. If ε is so large that there is no $\mathbf{u}$ such that

$$\mathbf{u}^T(\mathbf{I} - \varepsilon\mathbf{A}) \geqq \mathbf{e}_i^T, \mathbf{u} \geqq \mathbf{0} \tag{10}$$

then implication (9) holds for that ε. In order to prove the 'only if' part of statement (a), let ε be such that inequalities (10) have a solution and let $\mathbf{u}^*$ be one of such solutions. Let ε' be positive, not larger than ε, and in any case so small that the matrix $(\mathbf{I} - \varepsilon'\mathbf{A})$ is invertible and $(\mathbf{I} - \varepsilon'\mathbf{A})^{-1} \geq \mathbf{0}$. Then we have

$$\mathbf{u}^{*T}[\mathbf{I} - (\varepsilon - \varepsilon')\mathbf{A}(\mathbf{I} - \varepsilon'\mathbf{A})^{-1} = \mathbf{u}^{*T}[\mathbf{I} - \varepsilon'\mathbf{A} - (\varepsilon - \varepsilon')\mathbf{A}](\mathbf{I} - \varepsilon'\mathbf{A})^{-1} \geqq \mathbf{e}_i^T(\mathbf{I} - \varepsilon'\mathbf{A})^{-1}$$

Then, taking account of the fact that

$$(\mathbf{I} - \varepsilon'\mathbf{A})^{-1} = \lim_{s\to\infty} \sum_{t=0}^{s} (\varepsilon'\mathbf{A})^t$$

we obtain

$$\mathbf{u}^{*T}\mathbf{A}\mathbf{e}_j \geq \mathbf{e}_i^T((\mathbf{I} - \varepsilon'\mathbf{A})^{-1}\mathbf{A}\mathbf{e}_j \geq \mathbf{e}_i^T \sum_{t=0}^{n-1} (\varepsilon'\mathbf{A})^t\mathbf{A}\mathbf{e}_j > 0$$

This completes the proof of the 'only if' part of statement (a). If implication (9) holds for each $\varepsilon > 0$, than it holds for a positive ε so small that inequalities (10) hold. The $\mathbf{A}\mathbf{e}_j \geq \mathbf{0}$. If $\mathbf{e}_i^T\,\mathbf{A}\mathbf{e}_j > 0$, then

$$\mathbf{e}_i^T(\mathbf{A} + \mathbf{A}^2 + \ldots + \mathbf{A}^n)\mathbf{e}_j > 0 \tag{11}$$

If $\mathbf{e}_i^T\mathbf{A}\mathbf{e}_j = 0$, then by appropriate interchange applied to both rows and columns of matrix $\mathbf{A}$ and to vectors $\mathbf{e}_i$ and $\mathbf{e}_j$, which become matrix $\mathbf{C}$ and vectors $\mathbf{e}_h$ and $\mathbf{e}_k$, respectively, let

$$\mathbf{C}\mathbf{e}_k = \begin{bmatrix} \mathbf{0} \\ \mathbf{y} \end{bmatrix}$$

where $\mathbf{y} > \mathbf{0}$.

$$\begin{bmatrix} \mathbf{u}_1 \\ \mathbf{u}_2 \end{bmatrix}^T \begin{bmatrix} \mathbf{I} - \varepsilon\mathbf{C}_{11} & -\varepsilon\mathbf{C}_{12} \\ -\varepsilon\mathbf{C}_{21} & \mathbf{I} - \varepsilon\mathbf{C}_{22} \end{bmatrix} = \begin{bmatrix} \mathbf{e}_h \\ \mathbf{0} \end{bmatrix}^T$$

Since $\mathbf{u}^T\mathbf{C}\mathbf{e}_k$ need to be positive, $\mathbf{u}_2^T\mathbf{y} > 0$, $\mathbf{u}_2^T \geq \mathbf{0}$ and $\mathbf{C}_{12} \geq \mathbf{0}$. Hence

$(\mathbf{I} + \mathbf{C})\mathbf{C}\mathbf{e}_k$

has a number of positive elements larger than $\mathbf{C}\mathbf{e}_k$, i.e.

$(\mathbf{A} + \mathbf{A}^2)\mathbf{e}_j$

has a number of positive elements larger than $\mathbf{A}\mathbf{e}_j$. If $\mathbf{e}_i^T(\mathbf{A} + \mathbf{A}^2)\mathbf{e}_j > 0$, then inequality (11) holds. If $\mathbf{e}_i^T(\mathbf{A} + \mathbf{A}^2)\mathbf{e}_j = 0$, the same procedure can be applied until we obtain that inequality (11) holds. This completes the proof of the 'if' part of the statement (a). Statement (b) is proved in an analogous way.

Then we can make use of a definition given above, which for simplicity is repeated here: we define with respect to a technology $(\mathbf{A}, \mathbf{B}, \mathbf{l})$ consisting of m processes and involving n ($n \leq m$) commodities all of which are producible that 'commodity j (labour) *always* enters directly or indirectly into the production of all commodities' if and only if for each $\varepsilon > 0$

$$(\mathbf{u}^T(\mathbf{B}-\varepsilon\mathbf{A})\geq\mathbf{0},\ \mathbf{u}\geqq\mathbf{0}) \Rightarrow \mathbf{u}^T\mathbf{A}\mathbf{e}_j>0\ ((\mathbf{u}^T(\mathbf{B}-\varepsilon\mathbf{A})\geq\mathbf{0},\ \mathbf{u}\geqq\mathbf{0}) \Rightarrow \mathbf{u}^T\mathbf{l}>0)$$

Now, theorem 1 above can be stated as

*Theorem 1**. Let ($\mathbf{p}^*$, w^*, $\mathbf{x}^*$) and ($\mathbf{p}^\circ$, w°, $\mathbf{x}^\circ$) be two solutions to system (1) for a given r. If labour always enters directly or indirectly into the production of all commodities and there is a commodity j which always enters directly or indirectly into the production of all commodities, then $w^* = w^\circ$ and $\mathbf{p}^* = \mathbf{p}^\circ$.

The proof of theorem 1* can go as the proof of theorem 1 once some minor obvious changes are carried out. We want just to provide two remarks. The former is an alternative proof of the fact that the square matrix $[\mathbf{I} - (1 + r)\mathbf{A}^*]$ is invertible and its inverse is semi-positive. Let $0 < \varepsilon \leq 1 + r$ be so small that the square matrix $(\mathbf{I} - \varepsilon\mathbf{A}^*)$ is invertible and its inverse is semi-positive. If $\varepsilon < 1 + r$, whatever is i,

$$\mathbf{e}_i^T(\mathbf{I} - \varepsilon\mathbf{A}^*)^{-1} \geqq \mathbf{0}^T$$

and

$$\mathbf{e}_i^T(\mathbf{I} - \varepsilon\mathbf{A}^*)^{-1}(\mathbf{I} - \varepsilon\mathbf{A}^*) \geq \mathbf{0}^T$$

Hence, whatever is i, $\mathbf{e}_i^T(\mathbf{I} - \varepsilon\mathbf{A}^*)^{-1}\mathbf{l}^* > 0$, since labour always enters directly or indirectly into the production of all commodities. Then from the equation

$$\mathbf{p}^* = (1 + r)\mathbf{A}^*\mathbf{p}^* + w^*\mathbf{l}^*$$

we obtain that

$$[\mathbf{I} - (1 + r - \varepsilon)(\mathbf{I} - \varepsilon\mathbf{A}^*)^{-1}\mathbf{A}^*]\mathbf{p}^* = w^*(\mathbf{I} - \varepsilon\mathbf{A}^*)^{-1}\mathbf{l}^* \ (> \mathbf{0})$$

Therefore the square matrix $[\mathbf{I} - (1 + r^* - \varepsilon)(\mathbf{I} - \varepsilon\mathbf{A}^*)^{-1}\mathbf{A}^*]$ is invertible and its inverse is semi-positive because of a well known theorem (see, for instance, Kurz and Salvadori 1995: 510–11, Theorem A.3.1). Finally, since

$$[\mathbf{I} - (1 + r)\mathbf{A}^*] = (\mathbf{I} - \varepsilon\mathbf{A}^*)[\mathbf{I} - (1 + r - \varepsilon)(\mathbf{I} - \varepsilon\mathbf{A}^*)^{-1}\mathbf{A}^*]$$

we obtain that the square matrix $[\mathbf{I} - (1 + r)\mathbf{A}^*]$ is invertible and its inverse is semi-positive.

The second remark concerns the proof of thc fact that if

$$(\mathbf{I} + \mathbf{A}^* + \ldots + \mathbf{A}^{*n-1})\mathbf{A}^*\mathbf{e}_1 > \mathbf{0}$$

then

$$(\mathbf{I} + \mathbf{F}^* + \ldots + \mathbf{F}^{*n-1})\mathbf{D}^* > \mathbf{0}$$

This fact is considered obvious in the reprinted paper, but one reader has privately pointed out to one of us that it is not so obvious. Since other readers may be stopped by this (missing) proof we take the opportunity to remark that this proof is a consequence of the fact that if

$$\mathbf{A}^{*t}\mathbf{e}_1 = \begin{bmatrix} \alpha \\ (\beta_0\mathbf{I} + \beta_1\mathbf{F}^* + \ldots + \beta_{t-1}\mathbf{F}^{*t-1})\mathbf{D}^* \end{bmatrix}$$

where α and the β's are non-negative scalars, then

$$\mathbf{A}^{*t+1}\mathbf{e}_1 = \begin{bmatrix} \gamma \\ (\delta_0\mathbf{I} + \delta_1\mathbf{F}^* + \ldots + \delta_t\mathbf{F}^{*t})\mathbf{D}^* \end{bmatrix}$$

where γ and the δ's are also non-negative scalars.

Part II

ON SRAFFA'S CONTRIBUTION

6

SRAFFA, MARSHALL AND THE PROBLEM OF RETURNS

Carlo Panico and Neri Salvadori

In the preface to *Production of Commodities by Means of Commodities* Sraffa claimed that he had not introduced any assumption on returns in that book since it was not concerned with *changes* either in the *scale of production* or in the *proportions* with which the 'factors of production' are employed. The effects of these changes on the costs of production were instead at the centre of the stage in his 1920s critique of Marshall's supply functions. The objective of his long 1925 essay, published in Italian in *Annali di Economia* and briefly summarized at the start of his 1926 article in the *Economic Journal,*[1] was to examine the ability of Marshall's competitive partial analysis to provide an adequate treatment of the relevant connection between costs and quantities.

The aim of this chapter is to point out the existence of some links between Sraffa's 1920s critique and *Production of Commodities.* It moves along the lines set by those authors who have argued 'that it is necessary to view the latter against the background of the former' (Maneschi 1986: 10 n. 2),[2] and does not intend to deny the 'classical' derivation of Sraffa's theory of value and distribution.[3]

With respect to these authors, this chapter points out the existence of some neglected links between the mentioned contributions published by Sraffa in different periods of his life. It argues that the content of the 1920s critique can justify the lack of reference in 1960 to the analysis of the firm,[4] clarify Sraffa's views on the determinants of variable returns,[5] and explain some origins of the method based on the assumption of 'given quantities' which characterizes *Production of Commodities.*

The chapter is in six sections. The next deals with some aspects of the chronological development of Sraffa's work in the second half of the 1920s. The third section (pp. 105–7) emphasizes that the 1960 choice to examine the costs of the industries at a given level of production, without referring to the cost curves of the representative firms, can be justified on the basis of the 1920s study of the long-period relation between costs and quantities. This chapter shows that to deal with the costs of the industry at different levels of production it is sufficient to indicate how changes in the quantity produced by the industry affect the minimum average costs of the representative firm. The fourth section (pp. 107–13) reconsiders the determinants of variable returns in the 1920s critique, confirming that in *Production of Commodities* Sraffa held the same view on this topic. The fifth (pp. 113–16) deals with the interdependence among sectors, arguing that the method of 'given quantities' originated in the critique of Marshall's approach. Finally, the last section summarizes the chapter and draws some conclusions.

THE CHRONOLOGICAL DEVELOPMENT OF SRAFFA'S WORK IN THE SECOND HALF OF THE 1920s

The time distance between the elaboration of Sraffa's analyses in the 1920s and in his 1960 book cannot be defined by the three decades separating their dates of publication. The actual time is much shorter.[6] Sraffa himself in the preface to *Production of Commodities* recalls

> the disproportionate length of time over which so short a work has been in preparation. Whilst the central propositions had taken shape in the late 1920s, particular points, such as the Standard commodity, joint products and fixed capital, were worked out in the 'thirties and early 'forties. In the period since 1955, while these pages were being put together out of a mass of old notes, little was added, apart from filling gaps which had become apparent in the process.
>
> (Sraffa 1960: vi)

The 'central propositions' of *Production of Commodities* were thus elaborated shortly after writing the article published in December 1926 in the *Economic Journal*. This article was written during summer 1926,[7] while an early draft of *Production of Commodities* was discussed with Keynes shortly after Sraffa's arrival in Cambridge for the academic year 1927–8.[8]

Beside showing that the central propositions of *Production of Commodities* were elaborated before Sraffa's appointment in 1930 as editor of the *Works and Correspondence of David Ricardo*, the available evidence on the chronological development of Sraffa's thought in those years also raises another problem in relation to Sraffa's interpretation of Ricardo's work. In 1925 Sraffa seemed to accept Marshall's idea [9] that for Ricardo the majority of commodities exchanged daily in the market are produced at constant costs.[10] This interpretation is in contrast with the opening sentences of the preface to *Production of Commodities*, where it is stated that the method based on the assumption of 'given quantities' 'is that of the old classical economists from Adam Smith to Ricardo, [which] has been submerged and forgotten since the advent of the ''marginal'' method' (Sraffa 1960: v). On the basis of the available evidence, it is difficult to state *when* Sraffa reached this new position. In this respect, the preface to *Production of Commodities* only clarifies that in the draft of the opening propositions of this book, discussed with Keynes, Sraffa had already avoided 'the temptation to presuppose constant returns' and had based his analysis on the assumption of 'given quantities'.[11]

> The temptation to presuppose constant returns is not entirely fanciful. It was experienced by the author himself when he started on these studies many years ago – and it led him in 1925 into an attempt to argue that only the case of constant returns was generally consistent with the premises of economic theory. And what is more, when in 1928 Lord Keynes read a draft of the opening propositions of this paper, he recommended that, if constant returns were *not* to be assumed, an emphatic warning to that effect should be given.
>
> (Sraffa 1960: vi)

In conclusion, while nothing can presently be said on the chronological development in those years of Sraffa's interpretation of the theory of value of Ricardo and of the classical economists, the limited evidence available makes it possible to state three points. First, Sraffa's last attempt to argue that only constant returns are generally consistent with the premisses of economic theory was made in 1925–6. Second, the central propositions of *Production of Commodities* were elaborated shortly after writing the 1926 article in the *Economic Journal*. Third, the method based on 'given quantities' was introduced in his analysis by the same time, that is, before he was appointed as the editor of the *Works and Correspondence of David Ricardo* in 1930.

THE ANALYSIS OF THE FIRM IN THE 1920s AND IN 1960

In *Production of Commodities* the theory of prices does not move from an analysis of the firm. Price determination is concerned directly with the technical conditions prevailing in the industry at a given level of production and is not derived from an aggregation of firms' behaviour. In this respect the book only assumes that producers' choices are based on minimization of unit costs: 'At any given level of the general rate of profits, the method that produces at a lower price is of course the most profitable . . . for a producer who builds a new plant' (Sraffa 1960: 81).[12] In contrast to this, the 1920s critique of Marshall's supply functions considers the conditions of production of the industry as the result of its firms' behaviour. The passage from individual behaviour to the collective curve is seen as

> the main problem in the study of an industry in conditions of free competition, in which the general equilibrium is the result of the series of individual equilibria which the competitive firms must reach independently of one another. To show clearly these relations between the

> individual and the industrial collectivity, it is necessary to reconstruct the passage from the individual supply curve to the collective curve.
> (Sraffa 1925: 300; ER's translation p. 21)

The analysis moves from the introduction of the average and marginal cost curves of the representative firm. These curves refer to 'the conditions of a single firm only in a given state of the industry' defined by 'the quantity produced collectively' (Sraffa 1925: 313; ER's translation p. 31) from that industry: the position of the average cost curve and its minimum level depend on the quantity produced by the industry and may vary with it.

> This curve presupposes, among its conditions, that the industry as a whole produces a fixed quantity. With the variation of this quantity, the form of the individual curve may be modified, since it is supposed that the conditions of production of the individual firms that compose the industry are not independent of one another.
> (Sraffa 1925: 309; ER's translation pp. 28–9)

In a long-period competitive analysis, it is assumed that 'the firm will simply receive reimbursement of expenses, without any producer's rent being left over' (Sraffa 1925: 311–12; ER's translation p. 30). As a consequence, for each level of production of the industry, the minimum average costs represent for the firms their only long-period equilibrium positions and the only points of their individual cost curves entering the construction of the collective supply curve.

> Under these conditions, the collective supply function must be formed in the following manner. Since each individual curve shows, in general, only one point of possible stable equilibrium for each quantity produced collectively, only these points would figure in the composition of the collective curve. All the others . . . represent conditions that would be realised only with the failure of the assumed perfect competition.
> (Sraffa 1925: 313; ER's translation pp. 32–3)

This analysis of the supply curve can be presented in formal terms by specifying the average cost of the representative firm, ac, as a function of the quantity produced by the firm, q, and of the quantity produced by the industry, x, and by denoting with p the price of the commodity and with $H(x)$ the (collective) supply function of the industry.

$$ac = h\,(q, x)$$

$$p = \min_{q} h(q, x) \equiv H(x)$$

The trend of the supply curve depends on how changes in x influence the minimum average costs of the representative firm. If these costs are constant when x changes, the collective supply curve will be horizontal. If they decrease (rise), the supply curve will be decreasing (rising).

Sraffa (1925) follows explicitly the above procedure for the case of decreasing costs (increasing returns). For the case of increasing costs (decreasing returns) Sraffa focuses instead on the increase in the rent determined by the increase in quantity produced by the isolated industry. This rent is calculated by considering 'the whole industry as a single firm which employs the whole of the "constant factor", and employs successive doses of the other factors in the amounts necessary to bring production to the requested level'[13] (Sraffa 1925: 300; ER's translation p. 21). The emergence of this larger rent causes a shift in the average cost curve of the representative firm in the same way as the emergence of a 'fixed cost' would do. The use of this procedure, which is explicitly recalled by the graphical exposition of Viner (1931), confirms that the minimum average costs of the representative firm are the only points of the individual cost curves entering the construction of the collective supply curve and that the trend of the supply function always depends on how changes in the quantity produced by the industry affect the minimum average cost of the representative firm.

To sum up, the study of the long-period relation between costs and quantities, presented in the 1920s critique of Marshallian supply functions, shows that, in order to deal with the costs of the industry at different levels of production, it is sufficient to indicate how changes in the quantity produced by the industry affect the minimum average costs of the representative firm. This means that in order to analyse the long-period conditions of production of the industry, it is possible to refer to the firm only to recall that average costs are minimized. This conclusion can be seen as that followed in *Production of Commodities*, where the costs of all the industries at given levels of their production are examined by indicating the minimum average costs borne by the 'producer who builds a new plant', without referring to the cost curves of the representative firms.

DETERMINANTS OF VARIABLE RETURNS IN THE 1920s AND IN 1960

A close investigation of the 1920s critique of Marshall's analysis and of *Production of Commodities* clarifies that Sraffa presented in them the same determinants of variable returns.[14] That is, he based his analysis on the same factors as those of the analysis of the relationship between produced quantities and prices,[15] which was in the centre of the stage in the 1920s and is occasionally mentioned in 1960.[16]

The most detailed treatment of this point was presented in the 1925 Italian article in *Annali di Economia*, where he stated that variable returns are determined either by *changes in the scale of production* or by *changes in the proportions* with which 'factors of production' are employed.

The same position was presented in *Production of Commodities* where – precisely in the passage in which he declared his intention to avoid the treatment of variable returns – Sraffa explicitly confirmed that variable returns can be determined either by *changes in the scale of production* or by *changes in the proportions* in which different means of production are employed by an industry.

> Anyone accustomed to think in terms of the equilibrium of demand and supply may be inclined, on reading these pages, to suppose that the argument rests on the tacit assumption of constant returns in all industries. If such a supposition is found helpful, there is no harm in the reader's adopting it as a temporary working hypothesis. In fact, however, no such assumption is made. No *changes in output* and (at any rate in Parts I and II) no *changes in the proportions* in which different means of production are used by an industry are considered, so that no question arises as to the variation or constancy of returns. The investigation is concerned exclusively with such properties of an economic system as do not depend on *changes in the scale of production* or *in the proportion of 'factors'*.
>
> (Sraffa 1960: v; emphasis added)

In 1925 Sraffa presented his analysis by dealing first with the determinants of diminishing returns and increasing costs, arguing that these returns are uniquely determined by the presence of a 'constant factor' and, as a consequence, by *changes in the proportions* with which 'factors of production' are employed in the industry under consideration. He referred to the case of agriculture and was mainly concerned with the occurrence of 'extensive margins', although 'intensive margins' were not neglected. His analysis developed as follows:

> When, having spent an annual sum on the cultivation of a given land, and wishing to spend another thousand lire, reference to the agricultural technology will indicate not only one way but a whole series of different ways, A, B, C, D, . . . in which it is technically possible to spend the additional 1,000 lire . . . , or any combination of these. In addition, the technology will determine that by spending the 1,000 lire on method A a product x_a will be obtained, by spending the 1,000 lire on method B, a product x_b, etc. Beyond this point the farmer will no longer be guided by technology, and he will select, on the economic criterion the method which will give him the largest product from the methods of using the 1,000 lire. This choice is already, in itself, a long way from agricultural technology, and it will be even further from it if x_a, x_b . . . are quantities of heterogeneous products that to be compared

must be reduced to the common standard of their value.

(Sraffa 1925: 289–90; ER's translation p. 12)

The analytical procedure contained in this passage can be described through a diagram, as shown in Figure 6.1, where the value of the *variable factors* is represented on the horizontal axis and the value of the product is represented on the vertical axis.[17] The best choice for the farmer is that relative to alternative B, until it can be utilized. Thereafter, Sraffa continues, some change in the method of production becomes necessary.

> If, subsequently it is decided to spend another 1,000 lire the choice will be restricted. There will no longer be either method B, or those methods among the others that are incompatible with B, that is that can no longer be used when B is used. This will leave the choice, let us say, between methods A, C, D, . . . each of which *in the preceding conditions* (when the 1,000 lire had not yet been spent on B), would have given a product less than, or, at best, equal to that of B. If, in the current conditions, after having spent 1,000 lire on B, the productivity

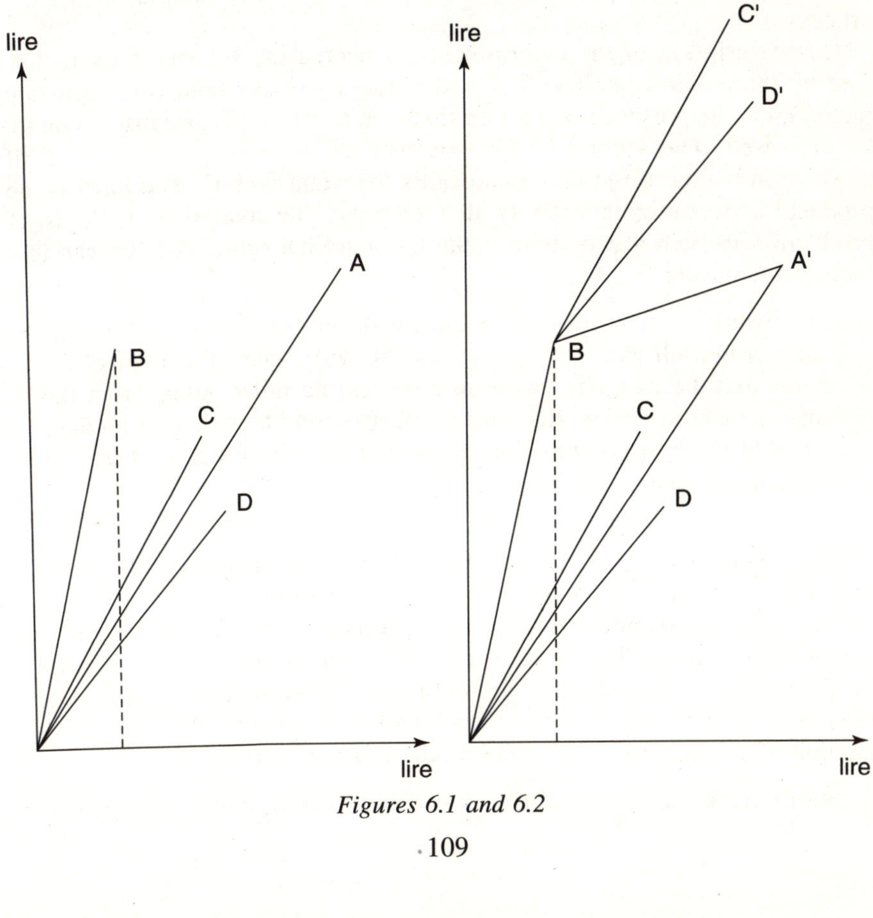

Figures 6.1 and 6.2

> of these methods is unchanged (which is the case when they are perfectly independent of the use of method B), it is clear that the second 1,000 lire will give a product less than the first 1,000 lire, since the producer has chosen and has acted in precisely such a way as to make this happen.
>
> (Sraffa 1925: 290; ER's translation pp. 12–13)

The analytical procedure described in this passage too can be presented through a diagram, as shown in Figure 6.2, where the occurrence of 'intensive margins' is also taken into account. In Figure 6.2 the processes A, C, D move from the point where process B, owing to the scarcity of the quality of land that it uses, is exhausted. New processes C′ and D′ are parallel to the old processes C and D, since they use a quality of land which was not used by process B (extensive margin). These new processes are, therefore, *independent* of the use of B. New process A′, instead, employs the same quality of land as process B. Its use is not *independent* of that of B and can be put in operation only by reducing the latter and making available a corresponding part of that quality of land (intensive margin).[18] Its terminal point in the diagram is consequently the same as that of the old process A.

This description of the determinants of decreasing returns is characterized by three elements. The first is the scarcity of the land (the 'constant factor'), i.e. the presence of a factor that is in short supply because it cannot be increased. The second is the existence of more than one method of production owing to the presence of this 'constant factor'. The third is the producer's maximizing activity that employs the available methods of production in such a way as to make the marginal returns of the variable factors decreasing.

> Diminishing returns must of necessity occur because it will be the producer himself who, for his own benefit, will arrange the doses of the factors and the methods of use in a decreasing order, going from the most favourable ones to the most ineffective, and he will start production with the best combinations, resorting little by little, as these are exhausted, to the worst ones.
>
> (Sraffa 1925: 288; ER's translation p. 11)

Sraffa emphasized this third element by discussing at length Wicksteed's distinction between 'spurious' and 'genuine' margins.[19]

The same treatment of diminishing returns is adopted in *Production of Commodities*, where he referred to *changes in the proportions* in which different means of production are employed by an industry, emphasizing the role played by the scarcity of land, by the emergence of more than one method of production, and by the producer's maximizing activity.

While the scarcity of land thus provides the background from which

> rent arises, the only evidence of this scarcity to be found in the process of production is the duality of methods: if there were no scarcity, only one method, the cheapest, would be used on the land and there could be no rent.
>
> (Sraffa 1960: p. 76)

The treatment of diminishing returns represents the only part of *Production of Commodities* where Sraffa examined variations in the quantities produced and thus the relationship between quantities and prices.[20] In the chapter on land he examined the emergence of 'extensive rent' (section 86), of 'intensive rent' (section 87), and of the problem of multiplicity of agricultural products (section 89) as the result of a process of diminishing returns, showing how, in line with what he had argued in 1925, a *progressive increase of production* on land leads to the gradual introduction of different methods of production. In section 88 the working of this process was described in detail for the case of 'intensive' margins, which he considered 'less obvious' (Sraffa 1960: 76) than the case of 'extensive' margins. Its application to the case of 'extensive' diminishing returns was instead not described, since it can be 'readily recognized' (Sraffa 1960: 76).

> From this standpoint the existence side by side of two methods can be regarded as a phase in the course of *a progressive increase of production* on the land. The increase takes place through the gradual extension of the method that produces more corn at a higher unit cost, at the expense of the method that produces less. As soon as the former method has extended to the whole area, the rent rises to the point where a third method which produces still more corn at a still higher cost can be introduced to take the place of the method that has just been superseded. Thus the stage is set for a new phase of *increase in production* through the gradual extension of the third method at the expense of the intermediate one. In this way *the output may increase continuously*, although the methods of production are changed spasmodically.
>
> (Sraffa 1960: 76, emphasis added)[21]

The analysis of this passage confirms that in his 1960 book Sraffa emphasized the role of the scarcity of the 'constant factor', of the emergence of different methods of production, and of producers' maximizing activities in the analysis of the determinants of diminishing returns. The latter element, besides, was also recalled in the preface to the 1960 book through the reference to Wicksteed's distinction between 'genuine' and 'spurious' margins.

Thus there seems to be sufficient evidence for claiming that in *Production of Commodities* Sraffa examined the determinants of diminishing returns essentially in the same way as in 1925.

In a subsequent section of his 1925 article Sraffa completed the analysis of variable returns by considering the determinants of increasing returns (decreasing costs). In this analysis he stressed the role of economies of scale, arguing that these returns cannot be derived from *changes in the proportions* in which the factors of production are employed in the industry under consideration. The existence of a 'constant factor', that is, of a factor that cannot be increased (but can be reduced), does not generate increasing marginal returns of the 'variable factors' employed in production, unless we also assume that the 'constant factor' is indivisible. The occurrence of increasing marginal returns of the 'variable factors' would imply that the marginal returns of the 'constant factor' are negative, so that 'the best way of using a further dose of [it] would be, precisely, not to use it' (Sraffa 1925: 287, ER's translation p. 9).[22]

For Sraffa (1925), then, increasing returns can only be derived from *changes in the scale of production* of the industry under consideration. Besides, he emphasized that these returns can only be determined by the occurrence of economies of scale *external to the firm*. Economies of scale *internal to the firm* are to be excluded from the determinants of these returns, since their occurrence would make impossible, as Marshall recognized, the maintenance of the assumption of competitive markets.

> It is clear that, if a firm can decrease its costs without limits by increasing production, it would continue to reduce the selling price until it had acquired the whole market. We would then have abandoned the hypothesis of competition. We will, therefore, stop to analyse such cases.
>
> (Sraffa 1925: 303–4, ER's translation p. 24)

In *Production of Commodities* Sraffa made no explicit reference to the determinants of increasing returns or to the distinction between *internal* and *external economies*. Yet, besides referring to *changes in the proportions* in which different means of production are employed by an industry as determinants of decreasing returns, he claimed that variable returns are also determined by *changes in the scale of production*. This statement can be seen as an implicit reference to economies of scale as determinants of increasing returns, economies of scale that are to be considered *external to the firm*, owing to the assumption in *Production of Commodities* of competitive markets and a uniform rate of profits,[23] and owing to the fact that in the analysis of switches in methods of production developed in Part III of his book it is assumed that unit cost minimization by the firms is operated at given *gross* produced quantities by all industries.

Thus, in spite of the limited space devoted to this subject, it is possible to claim that in 1960 Sraffa maintained, on the determinants of both kinds of returns, the same view as that held in his 1920s critique of Marshall's supply functions.

INTERDEPENDENCE AND THE ASSUMPTION OF GIVEN QUANTITIES

In *Production of Commodities* the analysis of interdependence among the costs of production of different sectors is carried out by assuming as given the quantities produced by all industries. Sraffa was very accurate, throughout his book, in maintaining this assumption, even at the cost, on some occasions, of obscuring the exposition. The only exception, as mentioned above, was made in section 88, in the chapter mentioned, on land, where the maintenance of this assumption makes it difficult to perceive the emergence of rent as the result of a process of diminishing returns. To avoid this confusion, Sraffa described the connection 'between the employment of two methods of producing corn on land of a single quality and a process of "intensive" diminishing returns' (Sraffa 1960: 76). He examined the effects on the costs of production of a change in the *gross* quantity produced by the corn industry on land of a single quality, by assuming, at the same time, that the *gross* quantities produced by the other industries and the methods of production used by them are unchanged. The change in the quantity produced by the corn industry implies a more intensive use of land and the occurrence of diminishing returns through the gradual extension of the use of the method that produces more corn at a higher unit cost, 'the cost being calculated at the ruling levels of the rate of profits, wages and prices' (ibid.: 75). The variation in the price of corn (and in the prices of the other commodities, if any, produced on the same quality of land[24]) may in turn feed back, owing to the interdependence with the costs of production of the other industries, on the prices of other commodities, causing further changes in the methods of production used too.[25]

The way Sraffa analysed variable returns in *Production of Commodities* resembles the approach that, according to Joan Robinson (1941), was used by Marshall in his analysis of supply functions. This approach, which Joan Robinson considered 'queer' and 'artificial' (Robinson 1941: 36), was different, according to her, from that adopted by Hicks in *Value and Capital*. It was based on an '*ad hoc*' change in the produced quantities of the different industries, that is, on the assumption that the quantity produced by one industry varies while the quantities produced by all other industries remain constant.

This change, Joan Robinson says, is not the result of a new general equilibrium, generated, for instance, by a variation in consumers' preferences, and is always able by assumption to call forth an increase in the 'factors of production', apart from land, employed in increasing the supply of the commodity under consideration.

> Marshall's analysis . . . seems most often to be discussing the problem of the change in the supply of a particular commodity which occurs . . . [when the] demand for one commodity increases, but the demand for the rest does not decline. The additional factors, apart from land, employed in increasing the supply of the commodity are called into existence by the increase in demand.
>
> (Robinson 1941: 35)

A similar procedure is presented in the 1920s critique of Marshall's supply functions too. This critique essentially regards the legitimacy of the *ceteris paribus* assumption in the treatment of these functions and the failure of this approach to deal adequately with *interdependence* among the costs of production of different sectors. Since a detailed analysis of this point has been provided by one of the authors of the present chapter (Panico 1991), a few remarks will suffice here.

To evaluate up to which point mutual interdependence can be disregarded and the *ceteris paribus* assumption of partial analysis can legitimately be made, Sraffa's 1920s analysis defined a criterion based on a distinction between two ways in which mutual interdependence can operate when a change in the quantity produced by the isolated industry, call it x_j, occurs while the quantities produced by the other industries remain constant. The first way implies that variations in x_j bring about variable returns operating *directly* only on the cost function of the representative firm of the isolated industry. This leads to variations in the price of the isolated commodity, which *in turn* may feed back on the price of other industries and may cause changes in their cost functions, in the technical processes used and in demand.[26] These influences on other sectors are *indirect*, that is, they are induced by previous changes in the price of the isolated commodity. The second way implies that variations in x_j bring about non-constant returns operating *directly* on the cost function of the representative firm of both the isolated and some other industries. This leads to variations in prices, and to further effects on the technical processes used and on demand.

The criterion adopted by Sraffa to evaluate the legitimacy of the *ceteris paribus* assumptions stated that in partial analysis mutual interdependence producing only *indirect* or feedback effects on other industries can be disregarded. On the contrary, that operating *directly* also on the cost function of the representative firm of other industries cannot be neglected. On the basis of this criterion[27] Sraffa pointed out that in Marshall's analysis only two cases of non-constant supply curves are compatible with the *ceteris paribus* assumption.

According to Sraffa (1925: 304–7, 326–7, 1926: 540), decreasing supply functions can be consistently derived on the basis of increasing returns to scale 'external to the firm and internal to the industry', defined by Sraffa as those due to a change in the output of the isolated industry and affecting *only* the cost function of its representative firm.[28] In this case, variations in x_j *directly* affect only the cost functions of the representative firm of the isolated industry, as required by the criterion previously defined. On the other hand, economies of scale 'internal to the firm' are incompatible with perfect competition (1925: 304, 1926: 536–7), while economies of scale 'external to both the firm and the industry' affect in the same *direct* way the cost functions of the representative firm of the isolated and of other industries, making illegitimate the maintenance of the *ceteris paribus* assumption (1925: 326–7, 1926: 540).

A consistent rising supply function can be obtained (1925: 323, 1926: 539) when some primary factors, different from labour and available in a fixed and limited amount, are employed *only* in the isolated industry.[29] In this case, an increase in x_j brings about a more intensive use of these constant factors, diminishing marginal returns, and a rise in the cost functions of the firms of the isolated industry. Mutual interdependence, however, may occur only *indirectly* through feedback effects. No *direct* effects on the cost functions of other industries occur. On the contrary, no rising supply function can be consistently derived in partial analysis if the constant primary factors are also employed in other industries (1925: 323–6, 1926: 539). They too would experience in this case the effects of the more intensive use of the constant factors. Variations in x_j would thus cause the same *direct* effects on the cost functions of the representative firm of other industries, contradicting the criterion established to evaluate the consistence of partial analysis.

The existence of these two consistent cases of a non-constant supply curve was not considered by Sraffa a satisfactory result for Marshall's partial analysis. On the one hand, even if there are cases in which the industry can be defined on the basis of the set of goods employing the same primary factor, this cannot be considered, according to Sraffa, the general rule (1925: 320, 1926: 539). On the other hand, the fact that a consistent derivation of decreasing Marshallian supply functions requires the occurrence of economies of scale external to the firm and internal to the industry cannot be considered a satisfactory result either, given the admittance by Marshall himself of the exceptional occurrence of these kinds of economies (1925: 327, 1926: 540).

Sraffa's conclusion that Marshall's approach fails to deal adequately with the important connection between cost and quantity is thus based on an analysis of interdependence[30] similar to that presented in section 88 of *Production of Commodities*. Like the latter, the 1920s critique follows Marshall's procedure and moves from the assumption of an 'ad hoc' variation in the *gross* produced quantity of an industry, and considers the interdependence between the effects of this variation on the costs of production of that industry as well as of all other industries. This similarity makes it possible to think that some origins of the method based on the assumption of 'given quantities' can also be found in the Marshallian tradition and in the 1920s critique that Sraffa presented against it.

SOME CONCLUSIONS AND IMPLICATIONS

On the basis of what has been said, it seems possible to conclude that some important aspects of the development of *Production of Commodities* find their origin in the Marshallian tradition as well as in the 'classical' one. The content of Sraffa's 1920s articles on the former tradition can justify the lack of reference in the 1960 book to the analysis of the firm. Besides, it can clarify his position on the determinants of variable returns and some origins of the method based on the assumption of 'given quantities' which characterizes *Production of Commodities*.

As has been noted above, the method based on the assumption of 'given quantities' was adopted by Sraffa already in a draft of his 1960 book written before he was appointed as the editor of the *Works and Correspondence of David Ricardo* in 1930. It has been argued that Sraffa was very accurate, throughout his 1960 book, in maintaining the assumption of 'given quantities'. Yet, when the maintenance of this assumption made it difficult to appreciate the content of his analysis, as occurred in the chapter on land, he allowed for variations in the quantities produced, following the approach used by Marshall in his analysis of supply functions. This approach appears compatible with the theories of the classical political economists, since in it, as Joan Robinson (1941: 35–6) also pointed out, the analysis of what causes the variations in the quantities produced is not worked out, while labour and the other 'variable factors' are not necessarily fully employed.

Thus the acceptance of a Marshallian derivation of some developments of *Production of Commodities* does not deny the links of Sraffa's work with the classical authors that the literature has clearly emphasized. It only clarifies some aspects of Sraffa's analysis that seem to have been overlooked up to now, emphasizing that some features of this analysis had been worked out before he focused attention on the reconstruction of the theories of Ricardo and of the other classical economists.

The acceptance of this interpretation may stimulate reflections on other aspects of Sraffa's work related to his position on returns and on the relationship between prices, quantities and distributive variables. It allows one to stress the fact that the adoption of the method based on the assumption of 'given quantities' is not an attempt to play down the role of 'demand' in the determination of prices.[31] On the contrary, it can be seen as an attempt to avoid the problems involved by the treatment of external economies, as suggested by Sylos Labini (1989). The introduction of this method in the draft of his book shown to Keynes soon after his arrival in Cambridge in 1927 can also be seen as an attempt to prevent the reader from misinterpreting his position by stating that certain kinds of returns, and not others, actually prevail in the economy or in some industries. This risk of misinterpretation was recalled by Sraffa himself in a letter to Keynes of 6 June 1926.[32]

> This conclusion has been misunderstood and taken to imply that in actual life constant returns prevail: although I believe that Ricardo's assumption is the best available for a simple theory of competition (viz. a first approximation) of course in reality the connection between cost and quantity produced is obvious. It simply cannot be considered by means of the system of particular equilibria for single commodities in a regime of competition devised by Marshall.

According to what Sraffa claimed in his 1920s critique of Marshall's analysis, this risk was also related to the assumption of variable returns, as can be noticed by reading the literature on supply functions of the early 1920s. The need to attribute a rising or a decreasing supply curve to each particular industry, Sraffa claimed in 1925, led contemporary economists to overlook the fact that the influences of changes in the quantities produced on the minimum average costs of the representative firms do not depend upon 'objective circumstances inherent in the various industries' (Sraffa 1925: 278; ER's translation p. 2). Besides, as he noticed,[33] forces pushing in opposite directions can operate simultaneously, making it difficult to state *a priori* which kinds of returns will prevail in each industry and which kind of correspondence can be established between prices and quantities produced by the different industries.

Further work and evidence are necessary to verify the validity of this explanation of *why* Sraffa adopted the method based on the assumption of 'given quantities' both in the 1927–8 draft and in the final version of *Production of Commodities*.

NOTES

1 The Anglo-Saxon reader may be less acquainted with the content of the 1925 article, which has not been published in English yet. A summary, provided by Maneschi (1986), and a translation, made by John Eatwell and Alessandro Roncaglia, are however available. In this chapter we will refer to the latter as 'ER's translation'.

2 Maneschi (1986) recalls that this position is shared by Talamo (1976), Bharadwaj (1978), Roncaglia (1978) and Harcourt (1983). He summarizes the links between Sraffa's 1920s critique and *Production of Commodities* as follows: '(i) the fact that interdependence among economic sectors . . . makes any type of partial equilibrium both unnecessary and indeed unfeasible, (ii) the absence of demand as a determinant of price, (iii) the lack of any need to classify industries into increasing, decreasing and constant ones . . . (iv) the ability of Sraffa's framework to allow for land or other factors in fixed supply . . . while eschewing any functional Wicksteed-type curves of diminishing marginal product, and (v)

the possibility of incorporating technical progress in the form of reduction of one or more coefficients of production, with possible repercussions on all sectors of the economy, which obviates the need to assume industry-specific external economies' (Maneschi 1986: 11–12).

3 For some detailed analyses of the 'classical' derivation of *Production of Commodities* see Garegnani (1984, 1989) and Roncaglia (1978).

4 Roncaglia (1975: 29) considers Sraffa's 1920s contributions as a critique of the marginalist theory of the firm. He seems to agree with Talamo (1976: 73–4), Maneschi (1986: 11–12) and Sylos Labini (1989: 7–11) on the fact that the problems raised by the treatment of economies to scale within the *static* approach proposed by Marshall helped to persuade Sraffa to look for an analysis, like that of *Production of Commodities*, in which technical progress is incorporated in the form of reduction of one or more coefficients of production, with possible repercussions on all sectors of the economy. Bharadwaj (1989: 58) too has pointed out the existence of these problems. Yet she does not seem to derive from them any consequence for the content of *Production of Commodities*.

5 This has been also pointed out by Talamo (1976: 72–3), whose analysis, however, is less detailed than that proposed here.

6 This has also been noticed by Maneschi (1986: 9).

7 Sraffa's 1925 article, published in Italian in *Annali di Economia*, was appreciated by Edgeworth, editor at the time of the *Economic Journal*. At Edgeworth's request, Keynes invited Sraffa to contribute to the *Economic Journal* another article on Marshall's supply functions. This invitation was accepted by Sraffa in a letter to Keynes, dated 6 June 1926, which is in the Keynes papers, collected in the library of King's College, Cambridge, and is partly reprinted in Roncaglia (1978: 12). The article was handed in a few months later and published in the December issue of that year. For a reconstruction of these events see Roncaglia (1978) and Kaldor (1986).

8 In the preface to *Production of Commodities* Sraffa states that 'in 1928 Lord Keynes read a draft of the opening propositions of this [book]' (Sraffa 1960: vi). Notice too that in a letter to his wife, dated 28 November 1927, Keynes describes 'a long talk with Sraffa about his work. It is very interesting and *original*' (Keynes's emphasis; unpublished writings of J. M. Keynes, copyright the Provost and Scholars of King's College, Cambridge, 1993, King's College library, Cambridge).

9 Roncaglia has noticed that in appendix I of the *Principles* Marshall interpreted Ricardo's theory of value 'as a cost-of-production theory of price determination based on the assumption of constant returns to scale' (Roncaglia 1991: 378).

10 Sraffa quoted Ricardo on this point: 'This must have been Ricardo's opinion, since the commodities that can be produced at constant costs constitute "by far the greatest part of the goods that are daily exchanged on the market"' (Sraffa 1925: 316, ER's translation p. 34). A few lines later he also wrote: 'We must ask ourselves if, in the case we are considering, the mathematical economists have not gone far in correcting this vice, so much so, as to fall into the opposite vice, that is, treating a constant as a variable' (Sraffa 1925: 318, ER's translation pp. 35–6). This statement was, however, amended in 1926, when Sraffa seems to hold a more cautious position: 'the mathematical economists have gone so far in correcting this vice that they can no longer conceive of a constant except as the result of the compensation of two equal and opposite variables' (Sraffa 1926: 541 n.). As to his 1926 writings, two more pieces of evidence concerning the interpretation of Ricardo's view can be quoted. Again in the

1926 article in the *Economic Journal* Sraffa referred to the 'old and now obsolete theory which makes it [i.e., value] dependent on the cost of production alone' (Sraffa 1926: 541). Finally, in the letter to Keynes dated 6 June 1926 (see note 7 above) Sraffa wrote that 'Ricardo's assumption [of constant returns] is the best available for a simple theory of competition (viz, a first approximation)'.

11 The oral tradition claims that the set of propositions shown to Keynes in 1927–8 were derived from Marx's reproduction schemes.

12 This quotation refers to a non-basic commodity. Section 93 extends the same reasoning to basic commodities.

13 This analysis refers to the so-called 'specific-factor case'. Sraffa's reference to the 'specific-factor case' has been overlooked by Samuelson (1987, 1989). This neglect has been noticed by Garegnani (1989), Schefold (1989) and Panico (1991). See also Samuelson (1991) for a rejoinder on his interpretation of Sraffa's 1920s critique of Marshall's analysis.

14 For a similar view see Talamo (1976: 72–3).

15 In the 1920s Sraffa dealt with partial equilibrium and was consequently concerned with the relationship between two variables (the quantity produced of the commodity under consideration and its price). In 1960 he took, instead, into account the relation between changes in at least one produced quantity and changes in all prices. Besides, he allowed the costs of a single process to vary with variations in the rate of profits.

16 For reference to these occasions see below.

17 In Figures 6.1–2 values are used on the axes and each process is described by a straight line segment on the plane cost of variable factors–value of product. The use of values on the axes may be justified by the fact that only partial equilibrium is considered and, therefore, the price of each single factor is considered as given. It would be, of course, better to use doses of capital-and-labour and doses of product, respectively, both measured in physical terms. In any case Sraffa refers to values (*lire*, the Italian currency). The use of the straight lines is justified by the following arguments in Sraffa's treatment. When dealing with the issue of possibility of ranking land plots in order of decreasing fertility Sraffa rejects the definitions of fertility advanced by Marshall, Malthus and J. S. Mill and argues that the order of fertility, i.e. the order of activation of different qualities of land, coincides with the order of the maximum average product available from each quality of land. Moreover, at the beginning of section II the average product has been shown to be constant when the 'constant factor' is not in short supply and a decreasing function of the variable factors afterwards.

18 In 1925 Sraffa was not aware of the possibility of treating 'intensive margins' in the same way as 'extensive margins'. In fact he presented it as 'a case of a "physical law of diminishing returns"' (Sraffa 1925: 290; ER's translation p. 13).

19 See Sraffa (1925: 288–95). Sraffa also referred to Barone's wrong application of extensive margins to firms within an industry (see Sraffa 1925: 298–9) and to the problems related to the definition of the order of fertility of land (see Sraffa 1925: 295–8).

20 For a more detailed consideration of this part see pp. 113–16.

21 There are remarkable similarities between the process of 'intensive' diminishing returns described in this passage and that given in 1925 (pp. 289–91).

22 A formal proof that the marginal product of the 'constant factor' is negative is provided by Allen (1937, § 12.9) under the assumption that the production function is homogeneous of degree one, i.e. on the assumption that if there were

not a 'constant factor', then returns would be constant. Sraffa (1925) refers to a non-mathematical analysis by Carver (1909).

23 See Salvadori (1985), where, however, no reference to external economies is made.

24 See Sraffa (1960: section 89).

25 According to Sraffa 'the change in methods of production, if it concerns a basic product, involves of course a change of Standard system' (Sraffa 1960: 76 n.). This implicitly acknowledges the occurrence of a change in *all* prices.

26 There are cases (one is that pointed out by Samuelson 1971: 12–13) in which any further effects on technical processes and on demand do not occur.

27 The criterion adopted by Sraffa does not identify conditions to be met by the utility functions, nor does it impose on the production function of each sector the same restrictive technological conditions as those imposed by Samuelson (1971).

28 Economies of scale which *also* affect the technical coefficients of other industries are defined by Sraffa as 'external to both the firm and the industry'. It has to be noticed that Sraffa's definition of firm externalities internal to the industry does not coincide with that used by Pigou (1927, 1928). For the latter, all economies of scale due to a change in the output of the isolated industry are 'internal to the industry', independently of whether they affect only the cost functions of the firms of the isolated industry or those of other industries too. Pigou's definition is also used by Samuelson (1976: 476–7). More on this point in Panico (1991).

29 This case, as Schefold (1989) has also noticed, resembled the 'specific-factor case', recalled by Viner (1931) and by Samuelson (1971, 1987, 1989).

30 Pigou (1927, 1928) suggests that Sraffa's critique was based instead on the negligible size in partial analysis of the effects of changes in the quantities produced. Yet in Sraffa's work, the negligible size argument, though existing, plays only a secondary role and can be eliminated without altering the substance of his final result. For a detailed analysis of the limits of Pigou's interpretation, which has been sometimes accepted in the literature, see Panico (1991).

31 As Samuelson (1989) exemplifies, the adoption of this method has been interpreted as an attempt to play down the role of demand in the determination of prices.

32 See note 7 above.

33 '[S]trictly speaking, there is no logical difficulty in supposing that the two groups of causal elements can operate simultaneously. Thus, it is possible that in an industry which uses the totality of the existing quantity of a factor of production, and therefore has a tendency towards increasing costs, the increase in production carries with it an increase in external economies, such as to give rise to an opposite tendency' (Sraffa 1925: 316; ER's translation, p. 34).

REFERENCES

Allen, R. G. D. (1937) *Mathematical Analysis for Economists*, London: Macmillan.

Bharadwaj, K. (1978) *Classical Political Economy and Rise to Dominance of Supply and Demand Theories: 1976 R. C. Dutt Lectures of Political Economy*, Calcutta: Orient Longman.

—— (1989) 'Sraffa's return to classical theory', in Bharadwaj and Schefold (1989): 53–81.

Bharadwaj, K. and Schefold, B. (eds) (1989) *Essays on Piero Sraffa: Critical*

Perspectives on the Revival of Classical Theory, London: Unwin Hyman, reprinted by Routledge.
Carver, T. N. (1909) 'Diminishing returns and value', *Scientia* 2: 331–44.
Garegnani, P. (1984) 'Value and distribution in the classical economists and Marx', *Oxford Economic Papers* 36: 291–325.
—— (1989) 'Professor Samuelson on Sraffa: a comment', in Bharadwaj and Schefold (1989): 283–301.
Harcourt, G. C. (1983) 'On Piero Sraffa's contributions to economics', in P. Groenewegen and J. Halevi (eds), *Italian Economics Past and Present*, Sydney: Frederick May Foundation for Italian Studies.
Kaldor, N. (1986) *Ricordi di un economista*, ed. M. C. Marcuzzo, Milan: Garzanti.
Maneschi, A. (1986) 'A comparative evaluation of Sraffa's "The laws of returns under competitive conditions" and its Italian precursor', *Cambridge Journal of Economics* 10: 1–12.
Panico, C. (1991) 'Some notes on Marshallian supply functions', *Economic Journal* 101: 557–69.
Pigou, A. C. (1927) 'The laws of diminishing and increasing cost', *Economic Journal* 37: 188–97.
—— (1928) 'An analysis of supply', *Economic Journal* 38: 238–57.
Robinson, J. V. (1941) 'Rising supply price', *Economica*, new series 8: 1–8.
Roncaglia, A. (1975) *Sraffa e la teoria dei prezzi*, Bari: Laterza; English translation: Roncaglia (1978).
—— (1978) *Sraffa and the Theory of Prices*, Chichester: Wiley.
—— (1991) 'Sraffa's 1925 article and Marshall's theory', *Quaderni di Storia dell'Economia Politica* 9 (1–2): 373–97.
Salvadori, N. (1985) 'Was Sraffa making no assumption on returns?' *Metroeconomica* 36: 175–86.
Samuelson, P. A. (1971) 'An exact Hume–Ricardo–Marshall model of international trade', *Journal of International Economics* 1: 1–18.
—— (1976) *Economics*, Tokyo: McGraw-Hill Kogakusha, 10th edn.
—— (1987) 'Sraffian economics', in J. Eatwell, M. Milgate and P. Newman (eds), *The New Palgrave 4*, London: Macmillan.
—— (1989) 'Revisionist findings on Sraffa', in Bharadwaj and Schefold (1989): 263–79.
—— (1991) 'Sraffa's other leg', *Economic Journal* 101: 570–4.
Schefold, B. (1989) 'Comment on Samuelson', in Bharadwaj and Schefold (1989): 301–17.
Sraffa, P. (1925) 'Sulle relazioni fra costo e quantità prodotta', *Annali di Economia* 2: 277–328.
—— (1926) 'The laws of returns under competitive conditions', *Economic Journal* 36: 535–50.
—— (1960) *Production of Commodities by Means of Commodities*, Cambridge: Cambridge University Press.
Sylos Labini, P. (1989) 'Sraffa's critique of the Marshallian theory of prices', in Bharadwaj and Schefold (1989): 3–19.
Talamo, O. (1976) 'Piero Sraffa: su alcuni problemi di interpretazione', in M. C. Marcuzzo (ed.), *Problemi e storia delle teorie economiche*, Milan: Mazzotta, pp. 45–93.
Viner, J. (1931) 'Cost curves and supply curves', *Zeitschrift für Nationalökonomie* 3 (September). Reprinted in G. J. Stigler and K. E. Boulding, *Readings in Price Theory*, London: Allen & Unwin, 1953.

ACKNOWLEDGEMENTS

The authors wish to thank P. Garegnani, G. C. Harcourt, H. D. Kurz, A. Roncaglia and I. Steedman for comments on previous versions. The suggestions and useful comments of two anonymous referees are also gratefully acknowledged. Special thanks are due to Giuseppe Freni for frequent and constructive discussions on specific points. Financial support from MURST (the Italian Ministry of University and Technological and Scientific Research) and CNR (the Italian National Research Council) is also gratefully acknowledged. Usual caveats apply.

7

THE 'STANDARD COMMODITY' AND RICARDO'S SEARCH FOR AN 'INVARIABLE MEASURE OF VALUE'

Heinz D. Kurz and Neri Salvadori

Who seeks to find eternal treasure
Must use no guile in weight or measure
(Epigram in the Manchester Cotton Exchange)

Even three decades after the publication of Piero Sraffa's *Production of Commodities by Means of Commodities* (1960) and in spite of extended discussions on the matter there does not yet exist a commonly accepted view as to the meaning of the 'Standard commodity' and the role it plays in Sraffa's analysis. Moreover, it seems to be still unclear what is the relationship between this concept and Ricardo's search for an 'invariable measure of value'.[1]

The present chapter attempts to contribute to a clarification of the questions involved. This makes it necessary, first, to reconstruct, albeit briefly, Ricardo's search for an 'invariable measure of value'; this is done in the second section. Emphasis is laid on Ricardo's concern with intertemporal and interspatial comparisons, on the one hand, and his concern with the impact of changes in distribution on relative prices, on the other. The third section deals with Sraffa's interpretation of Ricardo's analysis of value and distribution and the role the 'invariable measure of value' plays in it. The following section scrutinizes carefully the structure of Part I of Sraffa's book, with special regard to the elaboration of the concept of the Standard commodity. It is argued that Sraffa considers this device essentially an analytical tool capable of simplifying the study of price changes as income distribution changes. It is shown that a few sections in Part I would not be necessary for the general argument, but have been included to pay a tribute to Ricardo's search for an 'invariable measure of value': we know now when this problem is solvable and when it is not, and what is the solution when there is one. However, it is clear that Sraffa refers exclusively to the second aspect of Ricardo's problem mentioned. In the course of this argument many of the opinions found in the literature are shown to be difficult to sustain. The final section contains some concluding remarks.

RICARDO'S SEARCH FOR AN 'INVARIABLE MEASURE OF VALUE'

As has been pointed out by Sraffa in his Introduction to Ricardo's *Works*, the search for an invariable measure of value 'preoccupied Ricardo to the end of his life' (Sraffa 1951: xl). However, in the course of time Ricardo's view as to the function such a standard would have to perform and the characteristic features it would have to exhibit underwent considerable change. Hence in order to be clear about which of Ricardo's conceptualizations of the 'invariable measure of value' may be related to Sraffa's Standard commodity, if any, it is necessary to recapitulate briefly Ricardo's changing views on the matter.

Intertemporal and interspatial comparisons

The first time we encounter in Ricardo's writings the problem of an invariable standard of value is in his contribution to the bullion controversy in 1810 (cf. Marcuzzo and Rosselli 1986). There Ricardo opposed the popular view that the value of a currency should be measured in terms of its purchasing power over the 'mass of commodities' (*Works* III: 59); it should rather be measured by the purchasing power over the commodity which was used as the standard. The choice of a monetary regime would have to comply with the task of keeping the purchasing power of money over the standard fairly constant. Changes in the money prices of commodities (other than the standard) could then be unambiguously traced back to 'real' causes. In *The High Price of Bullion* Ricardo argues:

> Strictly speaking, there can be no permanent measure of value. A measure of value should itself be invariable; but this is not the case with either gold or silver, they being subject to fluctuations as well as other commodities. Experience has indeed taught us, that though the variations in the *value* of gold or silver may be considerable, on a comparison of distant periods, yet for short spaces of time their value is tolerably fixed. It is this property, among their other excellencies, which fits them better than any other commodity for the uses of money. Either gold or silver may therefore, in the point of view in which we are considering them, be called a measure of value.
>
> (*Works* III: 64 n.; Ricardo's emphasis)

Here Ricardo is concerned with a standard which would measure the value of commodities at different times and places, that is, he is interested in *intertemporal* and *interspatial comparisons*, a concern which is closely related to the time-honoured problem of distinguishing between 'value' and 'riches' (cf. *Works* I: chapter XX), which had already worried authors such as Petty and Smith: in this regard Ricardo's contribution is largely in accord with the discussion of his time. While no single commodity can be considered a perfect and thus 'permanent' measure, it is Ricardo's contention that gold and silver are least subject to fluctuations and hence, for comparisons of periods which are not too distant from one another, may reasonably be used as measures of value.

The problem of an invariable measure of value is dealt with in greater detail in Ricardo's *Principles*. In the first two editions he maintained that in order to be invariable in value a commodity should require 'at all times, and under all circumstances, precisely the same quantity of labour to obtain it' (*Works* I: 27 n.). Here again the criterion of invariability is defined in terms of the intertemporal and interspatial constancy of the amount of labour needed to produce one unit of the respective commodity. If such a commodity could be found and were used as a standard of value, any variation in the value of other commodities expressed in terms of this standard would unequivocally point towards changes in the conditions of production of those commodities. Value measured in the invariable standard Ricardo called 'absolute value'. (In the third edition of his *Principles* he also used the term 'real value'.) Ricardo's early approach to the problem under consideration is neatly summarized in the following passage:

> If any one commodity could be found, which now and at all times required precisely the same quantity of labour to produce it, that commodity would be of an unvarying value, and would be eminently useful as a standard by which the variations of other things might be measured.

The passage continues:

> Of such a commodity we have no knowledge, and consequently are unable to fix on any standard of value. It is, however, of considerable use towards attaining a correct theory, to ascertain what the essential qualities of a standard are, that we may know the causes of the variation in the relative value of commodities, and that we may be enabled to calculate the degree in which they are likely to operate.
>
> (*Works* I: 17 n. 3)[2]

Basically the same opinion as to the 'essential qualities' of the invariable measure of value is expressed in several other places. For example, in his *Notes on Mr. Malthus' work*, completed in November 1820, Ricardo emphasized: (i) 'Length can only be measured by length, capacity by capacity, and value by value'; (ii) 'invariability is the essential quality of a measure of value'; and (iii) invariability means 'that precisely the same quantity of labour was required' at different times for the production of the standard (cf. *Works* II: 29–33).

The impact of changes in distribution

Although in the first and second editions Ricardo was clearly aware of the modifications necessary to the labour embodied rule of relative value,[3] he apparently did not think that these modifications rendered obsolete his original definition of the invariable measure of value or his approach to the theory of profit. In the third edition, however, he conceded that the same difficulties encountered in determining relative prices also carried over to his attempt in defining the essential properties of a correct standard. He argued that even if

> the same quantity of labour [would] be always required to obtain the same quantity of gold, still gold would not be a perfect measure of value, by which we could accurately ascertain the variations in all other things, because it would not be produced with precisely the same combinations of fixed and circulating capital as all other things; nor with fixed capital of the same durability; nor would it require precisely the same length of time, before it could be brought to market . . . Neither gold then, nor any other commodity, can ever be a perfect measure of value for all things.
>
> (*Works* I: 44–5)

Whereas in his original approach to the problem of the standard of value Ricardo was exclusively concerned with intertemporal and interspatial comparisons, that is, measurement with respect to *different* technical environments, he is now in addition concerned with the different problem of measurement with respect to the *same* technical environment, but changing distributions of income.[4]

Indeed, Ricardo considered both the problem of interspatial and intertemporal comparisons and the problem of price changes due to changes in distribution as theoretical issues (ibid.: 45). Yet it is a common feature of all approaches to the theory of value and distribution, including Ricardo's, that the socio-technical environment is taken as given. Therefore, the first aspect of Ricardo's concept of an 'invariable measure of value' simply cannot in general be treated within this context.[5]

A similar criticism was put forward by McCulloch in his letter to Ricardo of 11 August 1823:

> There is a radical and essential difference between the circumstances which determine the exchangeable value of commodities, and a measure of that value, which I am afraid is not always kept sufficiently in view. If you are to measure value, you must measure it by the agency

> of some one commodity or other possessed of value . . . ; and as the circumstances under which every commodity is produced must always be liable to vary none can be an invariable measure, though some are certainly much less variable than others and may, therefore, be used as approximations. It is evident, I think, that there neither is nor can be any real and invariable standard of value; and if so it must be very idle to seek for that which can never be found.

McCulloch continues:

> The real inquiry is to ascertain what are the circumstances which determine the exchangeable value of commodities *at any given period.*
>
> (*Works* IX: 344; emphasis added)

And in his reply of 24 August to Ricardo's answer three days earlier McCulloch put his view on what he called 'the *vexata questio* of value' even more succinctly. He expressed anew his conviction that the problem of the invariable measure of value, as stated by Ricardo, 'is quite insoluble' and that he himself did not want to enter 'this transcendental part of Pol. Economy':

> before I attempt to get a measure of the value of cloth and wine in the reign of Augustus and George IV, I must obtain a measure of their value in the same market.
>
> (*Works* IX: 369)

Ricardo in his answer to the first of the two letters insisted that despite their disagreement even McCulloch 'will still contend for the mathematical accuracy of the measure'. He continued:

> I do not see the great difference you mention between the circumstances which determine the exchangeable value of commodities, and the medium of that value . . . Is it not clear . . . that as soon as we are in possession of the knowledge of the circumstances which determine the value of commodities, we are enabled to say what is necessary to give us an invariable measure of value?
>
> (*Works* IX: 358)

A similar passage is to be found in his letter to Trower of 31 August 1823, in which his dispute with McCulloch is touched upon. Ricardo criticizes the latter for not seeing 'that if we were in possession of the knowledge of the law which regulates the exchangeable value of commodities, we should be only one step from the discovery of a measure of absolute value' (*Works* IX: 377). According to Sraffa 'this came close to identifying the problem of a measure with that of the law of value' (1951: xli).

'Absolute Value and Exchangeable Value'

As is well known, two most important documents of Ricardo's search for an invariable measure of value are a complete draft and an unfinished later version of his paper 'Absolute Value and Exchangeable Value', which must have been written shortly before Ricardo fell ill in early September 1823 (cf. Sraffa's note in *Works* IV: 359–60). In the two manuscripts Ricardo attempted to render precise his own concept of the standard of value and confront it with those advocated by Malthus, Torrens, Mill and McCulloch. Here a brief summary of Ricardo's argument must suffice.

To begin with, it is important to notice that Ricardo's main concern was still with intertemporal and interspatial comparisons. This is expressed in various passages, the most emphatic of which is perhaps the following:

> It is a great desideratum in Polit. Econ. to have a perfect measure of absolute value in order to be able to ascertain what relation commodities bear to each other at distant periods. Any thing having value is a good measure of the *comparative value* of all other commodities at the *same time and place*, but will be of no use in indicating the variations in their *absolute value at distant times and in distant places*.
>
> (*Works* IV: 396; emphasis added)

Next it deserves to be mentioned that Ricardo's own efforts were explicitly directed at establishing a straightforward analogy between measurement in natural sciences and in economics. In one place he writes:

> There can be no unerring measure either of length, of weight, of time or of value *unless there be some object in nature* to which the standard itself can be referred and by which we are enabled to ascertain whether it preserves its character of invariability.
>
> (*Works* IV: 401; emphasis added)

Referring implicitly to his earlier views on the subject, he continues:

> It has been said that we are not without a *standard in nature* to which we may refer for the correction of errors and deviations in our measure of value, *in the same way as in the other measures which I have noticed*, and that such a standard is to be found in the *labour of men*.
>
> (Ibid.; emphasis added)

However, this opinion has turned out to be erroneous, the reason being that commodities

> will not vary only on account of the greater or less quantity of labour necessary to produce them but also on account of the greater or less proportion of the finished commodity which may be paid to the work-

man . . . It must then be confessed that *there is no such thing in nature as a perfect measure of value.*

(*Works* IV: 404; emphasis added)[6]

The study of the impact of distribution on relative prices is frequently couched in terms of intertemporal comparisons of situations before and after a change in the real wage rate.[7] However, the real point at issue is not what may cause real wages to rise or fall, but rather that there are *two* circumstances affecting relative value at any point in time, i.e. the technical conditions of production and the division of the product between wages and profits. The impact of the second factor on 'natural' prices is best studied by carrying out some thought experiments. This is what Ricardo does in a couple of simple numerical examples, where he hypothetically varies the wage rate, taking into account that with *given technical conditions of production* the rate of profits is bound to vary in the opposite direction, and then tries to ascertain the involved movement of relative prices (cf., for examples, *Works* IV: 373–8).

After having disposed of the idea that there may exist such a thing as a perfect standard of value, fulfilling both criteria enunciated by him, Ricardo asks, 'But as it is desirable that we should have one measure of value . . . , to which shall we give the preference[?]' (*Works* IV: 389). On the premiss that the criterion of technological invariability is met, what does invariability with respect to variations in income distribution mean? Since 'the value of all commodities resolves itself into wages and profits' (ibid.: 392), the proximate answer to be given is: that commodity is invariable in value, in which the fall in the profit component is equal to the rise in the wage component (consequent upon a rise in the real wage rate and a corresponding fall in the general rate of profits). This is in fact the answer implicit in Ricardo's argument (cf., e.g., ibid.: 372–3, 404, 407). The conclusion is close at hand that the commodity under consideration should 'require capital as well as labour to produce [it]' (ibid.: 371): 'To me it appears most clear that we should chuse a measure produced by labour employed for a certain period, and which always supposes an advance of capital' (ibid.: 405). Accordingly, the standard advocated by Ricardo is different from Malthus's:

It is not like Mr Malthus's measure one of the extremes it is not a commodity produced by labour alone which he proposes, nor a commodity whose value consists of profits alone, but one which may fairly be considered as the *medium between these two extremes*, and as agreeing more nearly with the circumstances under which the greater number of commodities are produced than any other which can be proposed.

(*Works* IV: 372; emphasis added)

In another place Ricardo is more explicit about what he thinks the 'medium' actually is:

> That a commodity produced by labour employed for a year is a mean between the extremes of commodities produced on one side by labour and advances for much more than a year, and on the other by labour employed for a day only without any advances, and the mean will in most cases give a much less deviation from truth than if either of the extremes were used as a measure.
>
> (ibid.: 405)

As can already be seen from the last few quotations, Ricardo was not content with the proximate answer referred to above. His concern was with rendering as precise as possible the causes which account for the dependence of relative prices on income distribution. Clearly, the major cause is 'the variety of circumstances under which commodities are actually produced' (*Works* IV: 368). This in conjunction with the fact that 'profits [are] increasing at a compound rate . . . makes a great part of the difficulty' (*Works* IX: 387; similarly IV: 388). Hence an important part of Ricardo's efforts was directed at describing more carefully the 'variety of circumstances' under which commodities are produced.

This Ricardo tried to effectuate in various terms. We have already seen that one way of differentiating between these circumstances was in terms 'of the different proportions in which the whole result of labour is distributed, between master and workers' (*Works* IV: 385). However, since these proportions are themselves but a reflection of differences in the underlying conditions of production, it is desirable to conceive of the differences more directly. As we have seen in the above, the most general distinction of the circumstances under discussion given by Ricardo is in terms of different proportions of fixed and circulating capital, where circulating capital includes the wages of labour, different durabilities of fixed capital and different durabilities of circulating capital (cf. also Sraffa 1951: xlii).

In addition, Ricardo used more compact formulas to express these differences. For example, he talks of the 'proportions in which immediate labour and accumulated labour enter into different commodities' (*Works* IV: 379), or the proportions in which 'labour and capital' are employed in their production. Apparently, Ricardo was aware that since the means of production are heterogeneous the concept of 'capital' is an intricate one.[8]

Therefore it comes as no surprise that Ricardo was in search of a description of the differences under consideration which is less assailable. In his letter to McCulloch of 13 June 1820 he had already hinted at what appeared to him to be the most abstract denomination of the circumstances which account for the deviation of relative prices from relative quantities of labour embodied in the various commodities: 'All the exceptions to the general rule come under this one of time', and 'there are such a variety of cases in which the time of completing a commodity may differ' (*Works* VIII: 193). This idea is taken up again in his essay 'Absolute Value and Exchangeable Value', in which he stresses: 'In this then consists the difficulty of the subject that the circumstances of time for which advances are made are so various' (*Works* IV: 370). Finally, it deserves mention that the reduction of all differences to one of time complies with Ricardo's preconception that the standard of value should ultimately be referred back to some 'object in nature'.

The 'medium between the extremes' standard

Let us now turn briefly to Ricardo's choice of a 'medium between the extremes'. According to Ricardo 'it is evident that by chusing a mean the variations in commodities on account of a rise or fall in wages would be much less than if we took either of the extremes' (*Works* IV: 373). The motivation for this choice comes out somewhat more clearly in the above-quoted letter to McCulloch of 13 June 1820:

> The medium . . . is perhaps the best adapted to the general mass of commodities; those commodities on one side of this medium, would rise in comparative value with it, with a rise in the price of labour, and a fall in the rate of profits; and those on the other side might fall from the same cause.
>
> (*Works* VIII: 193)

However Ricardo did not take the composite commodity 'social product', or, in his terms, the 'mass of commodities', as the standard of value. Ricardo considered this possibility, but rejected it on the grounds that '[i]f it be admitted that one commodity may alter in absolute value, it must be admitted that two, three, a hundred, a million may do so, and how shall I be able with certainty to say whether the one or the million had varied?' (*Works* IV: 401).[9] The same opinion is expressed in another place. Ricardo there declines the proposed measure, which was taken into consideration in the context of a discussion of the impact of distribution on relative value, given the technical conditions of production, with the argument that it does not meet the criterion of technological invariability: 'In our own times great improvements have been made in the mode of manufacturing cloth, linen and cotton goods, iron, steel, copper, stockings – great improvements have been made in husbandry all which tend to lower the value of these goods and of the produce of the soil and yet these are made a part of the measure by which you would measure the value of other things' (ibid.: 374).

The basic idea underlying the concept of the 'medium between the extremes' seems to be that the processes of production of the different commodities can somehow be expressed in terms of a single variable, that is, the time that elapses between an initial expenditure of labour and the completion of the product. In other words, Ricardo's approach appears to start from the supposition that commodities can somehow be distinguished in terms of the length of their production periods. With some circularity of production this idea necessarily breaks down, while with unidirectional processes of production it is applicable in very special cases only. There is ample evidence that Ricardo was aware of the fact that most commodities are produced by means of commodities. However, he did not succeed in grasping fully the implication of the inter-industry relationships for his specification of the standard of value.

A further remark concerns the fact that, even though Ricardo refrained from taking the aggregate of commodities as his measure of value, he nevertheless invoked 'the circumstances under which the greater number of commodities are produced' to rationalize his own choice. The measure is supposed to reflect to some extent the conditions of production of 'the generality of commodities which are the objects of the traffic of mankind', 'the greatest number of commodities which are the objects of exchange' (*Works* IV: 389, 405). Interestingly, whenever Ricardo gives examples of which particular commodities should by all means be taken into consideration in defining the properties of the standard, he always refers to necessaries (as opposed to luxuries). In one place he writes, 'The circumstance of this measure being produced in the same length of time as corn and most other vegetable food which forms by far the most valuable article of daily consumption would decide me in giving it a preference' (ibid.: 405–6).

SRAFFA'S INTERPRETATION OF RICARDO

In the above we frequently referred to Sraffa's Introduction to vol. I of Ricardo's *Works*, containing the *Principles*. Sraffa carefully delineates the development of Ricardo's approach to the theory of value and distribution. With regard to Ricardo's search for an invariable measure of value, Sraffa, as we have seen, arrives at the conclusion that the way in which the problem was formulated by Ricardo 'came close to identifying the problem of a measure with that of the law of value' (1951: xli). This remark might give rise to the impression that Ricardo's first and foremost concern was with the 'law of value'. However, this was not the case, as the previous section has demonstrated, nor is it implied in Sraffa's statement. What can be said about Sraffa's interpretation is that it emphasizes particularly those aspects of Ricardo's thought which point into the direction of the Standard commodity and its role as an analytic device to simplify the investigation of the mathematical properties of the system of production prices. This can best be seen by looking at Sraffa's treatment of Ricardo's successive attempts to simplify the problem of distribution, such that it can easily be solved (cf. Sraffa 1951: xxxi–xxxiii).

In Sraffa's interpretation, Ricardo's procedure may be divided into four steps. The *first* step consisted in eliminating the problem of rent: 'By getting rid of rent, which we may do on the corn produced with the capital last employed, and on all commodities produced by labour in manufactures, the distribution between capitalist and labourer becomes a much more simple consideration' (*Works* VIII: 194). The *second* step consisted in trying to get rid of the problem of value by assuming the 'corn model', in which the rate of profits can be ascertained directly as a ratio of quantities of corn without any need to have recourse to prices. Since Ricardo had to accept Malthus's criticism that there is no industry in which the product is exactly of the same kind as the capital advanced, in the *Principles* he presented (a *third* step) a fully fledged theory of value, according to which the relative value of commodities is governed by the quantities of total labour needed in their production. Hence, as Sraffa concludes, 'the rate of profits was no longer determined by the ratio of the corn produced to the corn used up in production, but, instead, by the ratio of the total labour of the country to the labour required to produce the necessaries of that labour' (1951: xxxii). However, Ricardo soon realized that the labour theory of value cannot generally be sustained. According to Sraffa the search for an 'invariable measure of value' may be considered the *final* step in Ricardo's efforts to simplify the theory of value and distribution. In particular, the measure was designed to corroborate Ricardo's dictum that the laws of distribution 'are not essentially connected with the doctrine of value' (*Works* VIII: 194). The parallel to Sraffa's ingenious concept of the Standard system is close at hand: in the latter '[t]he rate of profits . . . appears as a ratio between quantities of commodities irrespective of their prices' (Sraffa 1960: 22). In this interpretation the purpose of the invariable measure of value was basically to render a system with heterogeneous commodities in regard of some of its features as simple and transparent as the corn economy.

Summarizing the argument, it can be said that in his Introduction Sraffa focused his attention on those aspects of Ricardo's search for an invariable measure of value which concerned the theory of value and distribution with a given technological environment, whereas the intertemporal and interspatial aspect of Ricardo's problem is neglected. As a matter of fact there is no *general* theoretical solution to the problem of intertemporal and interspatial comparisons. A solution to the problem of intertemporal comparisons can be found only in special cases of technological change.

SRAFFA'S STANDARD COMMODITY[10]

We now turn to a detailed analysis of Sraffa's *Production of Commodities* and the role of the Standard commodity in it. The basic premiss Sraffa starts from is that commodities are produced by means of commodities. This then leads to the concept of surplus, to the distinction between basic and non-basic products, and to the assumption that there exists at least one basic commodity (chapters I and II, §§ 1–12). Chapter III (§§ 13–22) is highly relevant to the issue at hand and will be scrutinized here section by section, except for sections 17, 21, and 22, which will be put aside for the moment and analysed later. We want to stress that the main aim of chapter III is to provide a 'preliminary survey' (§ 20) of price movements consequent upon changes in distribution, on the assumption that the methods of production remain unchanged, the complete analysis of these movements being presented, as is well known, in chapter VI. Only sections 17, 21, and 22 serve a different aim.

A 'preliminary survey'

Section 13 states what will be done in the chapter, i.e. 'to give the wage (w) successive values' and 'to observe the effect of changes in the wage on the rate of profits and on the prices of individual commodities'. Section 14 is devoted to clarifying that, if 'the whole national income goes to wages', prices of commodities are proportional to 'the quantity of labour which directly and indirectly has gone to produce them', and, Sraffa adds, 'At no other wage-level do values follow a simple rule'.

When the wage rate w is decreased from its maximum level a rate of profits arises (§ 15). 'The key to the movement of relative prices consequent upon a change in the wage lies in the inequality of the proportions in which labour and means of production are employed in the various industries' (ibid.), whereas 'if the proportion were the same in all industries no price-changes could ensue' (ibid.). On the contrary, 'it is impossible for prices to remain unchanged when there is inequality of "proportions"' (§ 16). In order to clarify this Sraffa performs the intellectual experiment in which prices are unchanged and a profit rate arises: 'industries with a sufficiently low proportion of labour to means of production would have a deficit, while industries with a sufficiently high proportion would have a surplus, on their payments for wages and profits' (ibid.), and this would be so whatever the wage reduction and the corresponding rate of profits (ibid.). It is then clarified that 'with a wage reduction, price-changes would be called for to redress the balance in each of the "deficit" and each of the "surplus" industries' (§ 18).

But it is not possible to assert that 'the price of the product of an industry having a low proportion of labour to means of production . . . would necessarily rise, with a wage-reduction, relative to its own means of production', since 'the means of production of an industry are themselves the product of one or more industries which may in their turn employ a still lower proportion of labour to means of production' (§ 19). Finally, Sraffa can 'conclude this preliminary survey' (§ 20) by asserting that

> the relative price-movements of two products come to depend, not only on the 'proportions' of labour to means of production by which they are respectively produced, but also on the 'proportions' by which those means have themselves been produced, and also on the 'proportions' by which the means of production of those means of productions have been produced, and so on. The result is that the relative price of two products may move . . . in the opposite direction to what we might have expected on the basis of their respective 'proportions'; besides, the prices of their respective means of production may move in such a way as to reverse the order of the two products as to higher and lower proportions; *and further complications arise, which will be considered subsequently*.
>
> (ibid.; emphasis added)

We now turn to the complete analysis of price movements in chapter VI (§§ 45–9) and point out why the considerations contained in it were not to be found in the 'preliminary survey'.

The complete analysis

Section 45 states what will be done in the chapter, i.e. to consider prices 'from their cost-of-production aspect, and the way in which they "resolve themselves" into wages and profits'. Sraffa's doubts on when to present this analysis are also made explicit jointly with the reason for the choice which has been made and the reference to previous 'allusions' to the subject. Section 46 introduces the reduction to dated quantities of labour. The concept of the *Maximum rate of profits*, R, is assumed to be known. In section 47 the pattern of the movement of the value of each of the labour terms of the reduction to dated quantities of labour is analysed. This analysis is significantly simplified by the fact that the wage rate, w, is assumed to be a linear function of the profit rate, r:

$$w = \frac{R - r}{R} \qquad (1)$$

This allows Sraffa to prove that these patterns can be divided into two groups: those that correspond to labour performed $1/R$ or less years ago, 'which begin at once to fall in value and fall steadily throughout; and those representing labour more remote in time, which at first rise and then, as each of them reaches its maximum value, turn and begin the downward movement', where 'the rate of profits at which any term of date n is at its maximum is

$$r = R - \frac{1 + R}{n + 1}$$

(ibid.).

Section 48 enters into a discussion of the issue introduced in section 20 and presents the results announced there:

> The labour terms can be regarded as the constituent elements of the price of a commodity, the combination of which in various proportions may, with the variation of the rate of profits, give rise to complicated patterns of price-movement with several ups and downs.

As an example of these ups and downs Sraffa introduces the well known example of the 'old wine' and the 'oak chest'. Once again the analysis is dramatically simplified by the assumption that the wage rate as a function of the profit rate has the form (1). Section 48 concludes with the famous paragraph on the 'impossibility of aggregating the "periods" belonging to the several quantities of labour into a single magnitude which could be regarded as representing the quantity of capital'.

In the last section of chapter VI, section 49, it is clarified that there is 'a restriction to the movement of the price of any product: if as a result of a rise in the rate of profits the price falls, its rate of fall cannot exceed the rate of fall of the wage'. This is important, since if it is possible to prove that the wage rate is a decreasing function of the profit rate for some choice of the numeraire (as in equation (1)), then it is a decreasing function of the profit rate whichever is the numeraire.

To conclude, it should now be clear why the results presented in chapter VI could not have been contained in the 'preliminary survey'. This is so because it was first necessary to show that:

(i) The rate of profits, r, reaches a finite and unique maximum, R, when the wage rate, w, equals zero and the corresponding prices of basic commodities are positive (§§ 39–41).

(ii) R is the lowest positive real number such that the price equations are satisfied with $w = 0$ (§ 42).

(iii) For $0 \leq r \leq R$ the prices of basic commodities in general vary with r but remain positive and finite (§ 39).

(iv) In each system of production there exists a (composite) commodity such that, if it is chosen as numeraire, the wage rate w is a linear function of the profit rate with the form (1) (§ 43).

The Standard commodity: a tool of analysis

In order to demonstrate the above statements Sraffa introduces the *Standard commodity*, the *Standard system* and the *Standard national income* (§

26 and, in general terms, §§ 33–4). Then he shows that within the Standard system

$$r = R(1 - w) \tag{2}$$

where R is the *Standard ratio*, which coincides with the maximum rate of profits (§§ 27–30). This relation is then shown to be valid also in the 'actual economic system' if the Standard commodity is chosen as numeraire (§ 31).[11] Finally it is shown that non-basic products play no role in the construction of the Standard system (§ 35) and that there exists a Standard commodity on the assumption that there is at least one basic commodity (§ 37), and the former is unique (§ 41).

It deserves mention that these results can also be obtained by using the Perron–Frobenius theorem. In fact Sraffa's demonstration of the existence and uniqueness of the Standard commodity can be considered a (not fully complete) proof of this theorem. Yet Sraffa does even better, simultaneously providing an economic rationale of the analytical tools he uses. It should be clear now that for Sraffa the Standard commodity was first and foremost an analytical tool, useful in the study of price changes as income distribution changes (see Kurz and Salvadori 1987).

The Standard commodity: a physical analogue?

Until now we have left aside sections 17, 21–5, 32, 36 and 44. Section 36 states what is done in chapter V. Sections 17 and 21–5 will be scrutinized in the next sub-section; sections 32 and 44 will be analysed here. In section 44 the practice, common to the classical economists and Marx, of treating the wage rate rather than the rate of profits as the 'given' distribution variable is reversed. Sraffa remarks that since wages, besides the ever-present element of subsistence, may include a share of the surplus, the real wage rate can no longer be considered given. Hence, *if* the wage rate were still to be given from outside the system of production, it would have to be 'in terms of a more or less abstract standard, and [would] not acquire a definite meaning until the prices of commodities are determined'. On the contrary, '[t]he rate of profits, as a ratio, has a significance which is independent of any prices, and can well be "given" before the prices are fixed'. Section 32 applies the results of section 31 to the example of section 25 (mentioned also in section 27). But it contains also an interesting caveat which it is better to quote in full.

> [I]f in the actual system (. . . with $R = 20\%$) the wage is fixed in terms of the Standard net product, to $w = \frac{3}{4}$ there will correspond $r = 5\%$. But while the share of wages will be equal in value to $\frac{3}{4}$ of the Standard national income, it does not follow that the share of profits will be equivalent to the remaining $\frac{1}{4}$ of the Standard income. The share of

> profits will consist of whatever is left of the *actual* national income after deducting from it the equivalent of $\frac{3}{4}$ of the *Standard* national income for wages.
>
> (Sraffa's emphases)

Therefore, the fact that '[t]he rate of profits *in the Standard system* . . . appears as a ratio between quantities of commodities irrespective of their prices' (§ 29, emphasis added) cannot be generalized to the actual system even if the Standard commodity is the numeraire. These remarks contained in sections 32 and 44 constitute also an *ante litteram* criticism to the interpretation of the Standard commodity as a *physical or corn analogue.*[12] In the 'corn model' corn is also the only commodity consumed by workers and the only basic commodity.[13] Therefore, to give the real wage rate in terms of corn from outside the system is quite natural, whereas to give the real wage rate in terms of the Standard commodity requires one to know the value of the commodities which constitute the real wage rate, as an aggregate, in terms of the Standard commodity. Moreover, even if the real net national income is given, as in the thought experiment performed by Sraffa, its value in terms of the Standard commodity is variable; therefore to determine the point on the linear wage–profit relationship corresponding to a given share of wages requires knowledge of the function relating the value of net national income in terms of the Standard commodity to the rate of profits.[14]

A solution to Ricardo's search for an 'invariable measure of value'?

Sections 23–5 connect the Standard commodity with that part of Ricardo's problem of an 'invariable measure of value' which relates to the impact of (changes in) distribution on relative prices, taking the technical conditions of production as given and constant:

> The necessity of having to express the price of one commodity in terms of another which is arbitrarily chosen as standard, complicates the study of the price-movements which accompany a change in distribution. It is impossible to tell of any particular price-fluctuation whether it arises from the peculiarities of the commodity which is being measured or from those of the measuring standard.
>
> (§ 23)

Sections 17 and 21–2 prepare the field for this tribute to Ricardo. There does not exist a commonly accepted interpretation of these sections: for instance, Schefold (1986) criticized his own previous interpretation (Schefold 1976) in the course of criticizing an interpretation by Flaschel (1986). The one given here comes close to the later interpretation by Schefold (1986).

After having introduced 'deficit' and 'surplus' industries in section 16 (see above), Sraffa remarks:

> There would be a 'critical proportion' of labour to means of production which marked the watershed between 'deficit' and 'surplus' industries. An industry which employed that particular 'proportion' would show an even balance – the proceeds of the wage-reduction would provide exactly what was required for the payment of profits at the general rate. (§ 17)

It is obvious, and can easily be calculated, that for a given wage reduction this 'critical proportion' depends on the rate of profits, and, therefore, on the numeraire chosen.[15] But at the end of section 16 there is a parenthetical sentence stressing:

> Nothing is assumed at the moment as to what rate of profits corresponds to what wage reduction; all that is required at this stage is that there should be a uniform wage and a uniform rate of profits throughout the system.

Moreover, after the previously quoted sentences of section 17 there is another sentence, in the same paragraph, just asserting that, whatever is the value of that 'critical proportion', if there exist 'two or more basic industries, the industry with the lowest proportion of labour to means of production would be a "deficit" industry and the one with the highest proportion would be a "surplus" industry'. Thus it seems that such 'critical proportion' is not yet fixed and only its lower and upper bounds are determined: the way to fix it is postponed to a later section. The interpretation given here is also substantiated by section 2 of appendix D, where Sraffa refers explicitly to section 17 in asserting that '[t]he conception of a standard measure of value as a medium between two extremes (§ 17 ff.) . . . belongs to Ricardo'.

Section 17 is incidental with respect to the 'preliminary survey' of price movements consequent upon changes in distribution which constitute the main theme of chapter III. As soon as this survey is concluded, Sraffa reverts (§ 21) to the 'critical proportion' mentioned in section 17. He starts his reasoning by supposing not only that there is an industry employing labour and means of production in that proportion, but also that the means of production used by this industry, taken as an aggregate, are produced by labour and means of production in that proportion, and similarly for the aggregate means of production of those means of production, and so on. That is, the 'critical proportion' – still unknown – is supposed to recur in all the successive layers of the industry's aggregate means of production without limit. The commodity produced by such an industry would have two properties:

(i) It 'would be under no necessity, *arising from the conditions of production of the industry itself*, either to rise or to fall in value relative to any other commodity when wages rose or fell' (§ 21, emphasis added).

(ii) It 'would in any case be incapable of changing in value relative to the aggregate of its own means of production' (ibid.).

Therefore, when this commodity is compared with other commodities, the relative prices can go up and down, but these patterns will depend, not on the peculiarities of its production, but on the peculiarities of the production of the commodities it is compared with. However, when this commodity is compared with the aggregate of its own means of production the relative price is independent of distribution. Property (i) is the property required to solve that aspect of Ricardo's problem of an 'invariable measure of value' connected with the impact of changes in distribution within a given technical environment and in fact will be used for this purpose in section 23. Property (ii) is the property which is used to identify the 'critical proportion' (sometimes called also the 'balancing' proportion). When property (ii) holds, the ratio between the value of the product of the industry which exhibits the 'balancing' proportion to the value of its means of production is independent of distribution, but then such a ratio cannot differ from the Maximum rate of profits, since '[w]hen we make the wage equal to zero and the whole of the net product goes to profits, in each industry the value-ratio of net product to means of production necessarily comes to coincide with the general rate of profits' (§ 22).

Thus, the only candidate for being the 'balancing' proportion is the proportion of an industry whose ratio between the value of the net product to the value of its means of production equals *R*, the Maximum rate of profits. After having replaced 'the hybrid "proportion" of the quantity of labour to the value of the means of production' with 'the value-ratio of net product to means of production', which is one of the two 'corresponding "pure" ratios between homogeneous quantities' (§ 22), Sraffa can assert:

> the only 'value-ratio' which can be invariant to changes in the wage, and therefore is capable of being 'recurrent' in the sense defined in § 21, is the one that is equal to the rate of profits which corresponds to zero wage. And *that* is the 'balancing' ratio.
>
> (§ 22, Sraffa's emphasis)

Hence, if we could discover a commodity exhibiting a 'balanced' proportion between labour and means of production in all its 'layers', we would be 'in possession of a standard capable of isolating the price-movements of any other product so that they could be observed *as in a vacuum*' (§ 23; emphasis added).[16]

Such a commodity is not likely to be found among the individual commodities, yet it can be constructed from among them. In section 24 Sraffa argues that it can be obtained from the basic system by hypothetically reproportioning the industries in it in such a way that the product of the resulting artificial economy consists of the same commodities in the same proportions as does the aggregate of its own means of production. (Section 25 provides a three-industry example of the construction of such a composite commodity.) This is Sraffa's solution to Ricardo's search for a commodity produced under 'average' conditions of production, which, as we have seen, forms only a part of Ricardo's search for an 'invariable measure of value'.

Additional evidence

Next it is worthwhile to have a closer look at Sraffa's careful wording in his discussion of the problem of the measure of value. In the table of contents (cf. Sraffa 1960: ix) section 23 is announced under the heading '"An invariable measure of value"'.[17] Note that Sraffa put the term in inverted commas. Clearly, this is meant to refer back to the title of section VI of chapter I of Ricardo's *Principles*: 'On an invariable measure of value'. In the text of section 23 the term 'invariable measure of value' does not recur.

According to the index to Sraffa's book there are two other places in which the notion of an '[i]nvariable standard of value' makes an appearance. The first is in section 43; the second is in section 2 of appendix D. Sraffa's introductory remark to section 43, entitled 'Standard product replaced by equivalent quantity of labour', reads: 'The Standard system is a *purely auxiliary construction*. It should therefore be possible to present the essential elements of the mechanism under consideration without having recourse to it' (emphasis added). Sraffa then proceeds in two steps. First, he argues that if it is assumed that the wage rate is linearly related to the rate of profits, 'the wage and commodity-prices are then *ipso facto* expressed in Standard net product, without need of defining its composition' (ibid.). In other words, if we use formula (2) we actually *do* reckon in terms of the Standard commodity, and 'it is curious that we should thus be enabled to use a standard without knowing what it consists of' (ibid.). In the second step Sraffa then shows that there 'is available however a more tangible measure for prices of commodities which makes it possible to displace the Standard net product even from this attenuated function. This measure . . . is "the quantity of labour that can be purchased by the Standard net product"' (ibid.). Sraffa concludes, 'Thus all the properties of "an invariable standard of value", *as described in § 23*, are found in a variable quantity of labour, which, however, varies according to a simple rule which is independent of prices' (ibid.; emphasis added). With the annual labour of the system taken as unit, the quantity of 'labour commanded' referred to is given by

$$\frac{1}{w} = \frac{R}{R - r}$$

Any doubts the reader of Sraffa's book may still have, despite the unequivocal statements quoted in the above, as to whether Sraffa was, or was not, concerned with solving 'the' Ricardian enigma, are finally cleared away in the appendix D to the book, entitled 'References to the literature'. There Sraffa explicitly refers only to that aspect of Ricardo's search for an invariable measure which relates to the impact of distribution on relative value, and which prompted Ricardo to advocate '[t]he conception of a standard measure of value as a medium between two extremes' (ibid.: 94; see also pp. 131–2 above). The other aspect of Ricardo's search does not, and indeed cannot, play any role whatsoever in Sraffa's attempt to lay bare the connection of his work with the theories of the old classical economists.

CONCLUDING REMARKS

It has been shown that (i) the Standard commodity is a useful, although not a necessary, tool of analysis; (ii) Sraffa relates the Standard commodity to Ricardo's search for an 'invariable measure of value'; (iii) this is done only with regard to that aspect of Ricardo's search which is concerned with the impact of changes in distribution on relative prices within a given technique; (iv) whenever the notion of 'invariable measure of value' is utilized by Sraffa (1960) this is to refer to Ricardo's own wording (the sense in which the Standard commodity is an 'invariable measure of value' being that it is 'a standard capable of isolating the price-movements of any other product so that they [can] be observed as in a vacuum' (Sraffa 1960: § 23)).

Finally, can we say that Sraffa's Standard commodity has fulfilled Ricardo's dream of an 'invariable measure of value' at least with respect to the impact of changes in distribution? Even this would be an overstatement unless by 'a given technical environment' we mean 'a given technique'. What Sraffa has provided is a tool which allows us to say both when this part of the Ricardian problem is solvable (and when it is not), and to construct the solution whenever it exists.

In special cases of technological change the Standard commodity may even be used for intertemporal comparisons. A condition for the applicability of the Standard commodity to this problem would of course be that it is not affected by technological change. This holds good, for example, in the following cases: (i) technological change affects only non-basic commodities; (ii) and (iii) technological change is 'neutral' in the sense of Harrod or in the sense of Hicks as formulated in a linear multi-sectoral model by Steedman (1985); (iv) technological change transforms technique (**A**, **l**) in technique (λ**A**, μ**l**), with $0 < \lambda < 1$ and $0 < \mu < 1$). It would of course be possible to redefine as 'neutral' all forms of technological change which leave unaltered a given Standard commodity. However, even if this sort of neutrality would include Harrodian neutrality and Hicksian neutrality, next to nothing would be gained by it, since the class of cases captured by such a concept of neutrality would be rather insignificant.

Sraffa, for perfectly good reasons it seems, saw only a single analytical purpose of the Standard commodity, i.e. to simplify the analysis of the effects of changes in the division of the product between profits and wages on prices.

NOTES

1 There is a third aspect discussed in the literature which is highly controversial and which concerns the relationship between the Standard commodity and Marx's labour value-based approach to the theory of value and distribution. This aspect will be entirely set aside in the present chapter and will rather be dealt with in a separate study by us; for a discussion of some of the questions involved in this connection see Kurz and Salvadori (1987).

2 To a similar passage in chapter XX he added: 'still it [i.e. the correct standard of value] would not be a standard of riches, for riches do not depend on value' (*Works* I: 275).

3 Interestingly, even in the first and second editions Ricardo did not advocate a pure labour theory of value, according to which prices are proportional to quantities of labour embodied in the different commodities. In the first edition we read: 'Besides the alteration in the relative value of commodities, occasioned by more or less labour being required to produce them, they are also subject to fluctuations from a rise of wages, and consequent fall of profits, if the fixed capitals employed be either of unequal value, or of unequal duration' (*Works* I: 53). And in another passage Ricardo stressed that 'different proportions of fixed and circulating capital' in different trades and 'different degrees of durability' of fixed capital introduce 'a considerable modification to the rule, which is of universal application in the early stages of society' (*Works* I: 66). Hence relative prices are seen to depend on two circumstances instead of on only one: (i) the conditions of production of the various commodities and (ii) the division of the product between wages and profits, that is, the real wage rate. It deserves to be mentioned, however, that Ricardo did not think that this finding undermined his explanation of the rate of profits in terms of the quantities of labour embodied in the surplus product (net of rent) and capital advanced, respectively (see, for example, *Works* I: 49, 64).

4 Ong (1983) connects the first of these two aspects of Ricardo's search for an invariable measure of value to the measure of the 'difficulty of production'. He contends that the first aspect 'is central to Ricardo's argument regarding how income distribution is determined over the long-term course of capital accumulation by the deteriorating marginal conditions of production of a constant real-wage basket, while the second [aspect] is important chiefly in buttressing one side of his theory of short-run equilibrium movements in the labor market under constant conditions of production' (p. 208). This opinion cannot be sustained. There is ample evidence that Ricardo did not assume the real wage basket to be

constant in the long run. Changes in the real wage rate therefore cannot be limited to the short run. Hence long-run changes in (relative) prices are the combined results of changes in technical conditions of production and changes in the real wage rate. Ricardo was well aware of this. Indeed, his disenchantment with a measure of value which would be always produced under the same conditions of production resulted precisely from his clear understanding that such a measure would not at the same time be, and for ever remain, a measure which is also invariant with respect to changes in distribution.

5 It could be treated only in a theory of technical change; we will come back to this in the concluding remarks.

6 Similarly, in his letter to McCulloch of 21 August 1823 Ricardo stressed: 'When we measure the length of a piece of linen we measure length only, . . . but value is compounded of two elements wages and profit mixed up in all imaginable proportions' (*Works* IX: 361).

7 For example, in several places he assumes that 'an epidemic disorder carried off a vast number of the people', with a consequent rise in real wages (*Works* IV: 362); or that a 'vast number of people come into this country from Ireland and by their competition sink the price of labour' (ibid.: 408). (In this connection it is worth pointing out that the notion of 'substitution' between 'factors of production' and thus the explanation of distribution and employment in terms of opposing forces of supply and demand are absent in Ricardo. Hence there is no presumption that a fall in real wages will lead to full employment of labour. See on this Garegnani 1984.)

8 Commenting on a proposition by Torrens, he asks what the latter means by 'equal capitals': 'If he answer I mean what I have often mentioned equal quantities of loaves and suits of cloathing for the support of labourers I understand him, but I again ask him to compare the capital of the cloathier consisting of buildings steam engines, raw material & c[a]., with the capital of the sugar baker consisting of a very different set of commodities, and then to tell me what he means by equal capitals – he must answer that by *equal capitals* he means *capitals of equal value*' (ibid.: 393; emphasis added). In this argument it is implicitly acknowledged that to describe different technical conditions of production with reference to the 'capitals' applied is problematic, since it implies that the problem (of value) has already been solved, to the solution of which that very description was meant to provide a first step.

9 The reader will recall that the 'mass of commodities' as a standard had already been taken into consideration by Ricardo and then rejected in his contribution to monetary theory.

10 In what follows we shall concentrate on the simple case of single-product industries.

11 Clearly, the role of the Standard commodity is that of a special numeraire. The numeraire is chosen by the theorist; it neither depends on 'observed facts' nor can it alter their 'mathematical properties'. This simple fact does not seem to have been always understood properly. For example, Blaug in an entry in *The New Palgrave* contends: 'It is obvious . . . that an exogenous change in wages unconnected with a change in productive techniques alters the rate of profit but has no effect on relative prices measured in terms of the Standard commodity for the simple reason that the change alters the measuring rod in the same way as it alters the pattern of prices being measured' (Blaug 1987: 436; similarly Blaug 1985: 140). If this were true, by mere choice of numeraire prices could be made independent of distribution and therefore the choice of numeraire would affect relative prices! P. A. Samuelson in another entry showed full

awareness that the choice of the numeraire cannot affect relative prices, but insinuated that Sraffa was not so aware: 'Sraffa, for reasons not easy to understand, thought that [($w = 1 - (r/R)$)]'s truth somehow provided Ricardo with a defence for his labour theory of value' (Samuelson 1987: 456). There is no evidence whatsoever in support of this interpretation. On the contrary, Sraffa quite explicitly emphasized that the Standard commodity 'is a purely auxiliary construction' (p. 31) and 'cannot alter its [the system's] mathematical properties' (p. 23). For an opinion similar to Samuelson's see Burmeister (1980a, b, 1984). For a more detailed criticism of the view under consideration see Kurz and Salvadori (1987).

12 See, for instance, Medio (1972), Eatwell (1975), Broome (1977), Bacha *et al.* (1977). For a position which is similar to ours see Roncaglia (1978).

13 In appendix D to his book Sraffa points out: 'It should perhaps be stated that it was only when the Standard *system* and the distinction between basics and non-basics had emerged in the course of the present investigation that the [corn model] interpretation of Ricardo's theory suggested itself as a natural consequence' (Sraffa 1960: 93; emphasis added). This must certainly not be taken to support the physical analogue interpretation of the Standard *commodity*. In fact, in the paragraph preceding the one just quoted, Sraffa stresses that 'in the terms adopted [in Sraffa (1960)] . . . corn is the sole "basic product" in the economy' (ibid.) considered by Ricardo in the *Essay on Profits*.

14 Flaschel (1984) has made this clear in terms of a nice numerical example. However, he used this example to argue that the analysis of income distribution is 'obscured if the Standard [c]ommodity is used for *numeraire*' (p. 129). Clearly this 'obscurity' derives from the fact that the Standard commodity is used for a purpose it was not designed for. Flaschel (1984) is interested in determining the wage share in an economy with one technique and given produced quantities: in this case the most useful numeraire is perhaps the actual real net national income, so that its value is constant with respect to changes in distribution. It can be remarked, however, that if the thought experiment is different (for instance, to determine the wage share in an economy with one technique, constant returns to scale, a positive uniform growth rate and/or different consumption bundles for workers and capitalists), then 'actual real net national income' cannot be determined independently of distribution and a distribution numeraire is to be used.

15 This fact has been 'discovered' several times. Recently Woods (1987) has presented a simple proof to show that the Standard commodity satisfies the 'critical proportion' at any possible wage rate if and only if it itself it utilized as numeraire. Flaschel (1986) uses this fact to argue that there are flaws in the construction of the Standard commodity and that it cannot be an 'invariable measure of value' unless the actual system is a Standard system from the beginning. The whole criticism by Flaschel (1986) is based on the elementary misconception that an 'invariable measure of value' is a commodity whose price is constant in terms of the 'national income' (see, for instance, pp. 597 and 600). On the basis of this misunderstanding it comes as no surprise that the Standard commodity 'is devoid of economic content' (ibid.: 600).

16 This possibility of telling of any particular price fluctuation that it arises from the peculiarities of the commodity which is being measured and not from those of the measuring standard may perhaps be further clarified by the following argument. Let the pair ($\mathbf{A}$, $\mathbf{l}$) denote a technique, where $\mathbf{A}$ is the material inputs matrix and $\mathbf{l}$ is the labour input vector, the output matrix being set equal to the identity matrix $\mathbf{I}$ by appropriate choice of physical units. Let ($\mathbf{A}$, $\mathbf{y}$) be a

fictitious technique where the vector **l** has been replaced by vector **y** which is the eigenvector of matrix **A** corresponding to the eigenvalue of maximum modulus normalized in an appropriate way. Techniques (**A**, **l**) and (**A**, **y**) have the same maximum rate of profits, and at this rate of profits they have the same prices. In the fictitious technique (**A**, **y**) relative prices do not change as distribution changes: the conditions of production of each commodity do not necessitate a price change with respect to any other commodity. If any commodity produced under the conditions of the fictitious technique (**A**, **y**) should stay side by side with the commodities produced under the conditions of the actual technique (**A**, **l**) it would be a commodity whose conditions of production do not enforce a price change with respect to any other commodity and, therefore, any actual price change would be enforced by the conditions of production of the other commodities. *But* techniques (**A**, **l**) and (**A**, **y**) have the same Standard commodity. Hence the Standard commodity of technique (**A**, **l**) *is* produced under the conditions of the fictitious technique (**A**, **y**) and stays side by side with all the commodities produced under the conditions of the actual technique (**A**, **l**).

17 Notice that Sraffa uses the indefinite article. This can perhaps be considered as indirect evidence that he was aware of the fact that the Standard commodity does not need to be the only numeraire that yields a linear relationship between the wage rate and the rate of profits. (A complete analysis of this issue has been provided by Miyao 1977.) The following paragraph (§ 24) introduces the idea that both the input and the output of the standard may consist of quantities of the same commodity bundle and thus prepares the ground for the construction of the Standard system. Interestingly, now the definite article is used in the heading, which reads 'The perfect composite commodity'.

REFERENCES

Bacha, Edmar, Carneiro, Dionisio, and Taylor, Lance (1977) 'Sraffa and classical economics: fundamental equilibrium relationships', *Metroeconomica* 29: 39–53.

Blaug, Mark (1985) *Economic Theory in Retrospect*, fourth edition, Cambridge: Cambridge University Press.

—— (1987) 'Classical economics', in *The New Palgrave* 1, ed. John L. Eatwell, Murray Milgate and Peter K. Newman, London: Macmillan, pp. 434–45.

Broome, John (1977) 'Sraffa's Standard commodity', *Australian Economic Papers* 16: 231–6.

Burmeister, Edwin (1980a) *Capital Theory and Dynamics*, New York: Cambridge University Press.

—— (1980b) 'Critical observations on the labor theory of value and Sraffa's Standard commodity', in *Quantitative Economics and Development: Essays in Memory of Ta-Chung Lin*, ed. Lawrence R. Klein, Marc Nerlove and Sho Chieh Tsiang, New York: Academic Press, pp. 81–103.

—— (1984) 'Sraffa, labor theories of value, and the economics of real wage rate determination', *Journal of Political Economy* 92: 508–26.

Eatwell, John (1975) 'Mr Sraffa's Standard commodity and the rate of exploitation', *Quarterly Journal of Economics* 89: 543–55.

Flaschel, Peter (1984) 'The Standard commodity and the theory of income distribution – a critical note', *Australian Economic Papers* 23: 123–9.

—— (1986) 'Sraffa's Standard commodity: no fulfillment of Ricardo's dream of

an "invariable measure of value"', *Journal of Institutional and Theoretical Economics* 142: 588–602.
Garegnani, P. (1984) 'Value and distribution in the classical economists and Marx', *Oxford Economic Papers* 36: 291–325.
Kurz, H. D. and Salvadori, N. (1987) 'Burmeister on Sraffa and the labor theory of value: a comment', *Journal of Political Economy* 95: 870–81.
Lutz, F. A. and Hague, D. C. (eds) (1961) *The Theory of Capital*, London: Macmillan.
Marcuzzo, M. C. and Rosselli, A. (1986) *The Theory of the Gold Standard and Ricardo's Standard commodity*, Discussion Paper 13, Dipartimento di Economia Politica, Università degli Studi di Modena (Italy).
Medio, Alfredo (1972) 'Profits and surplus-value: appearance and reality in capitalist production' in E. K. Hunt and J. G. Schwartz (eds), *A Critique of Economic Theory: Selected Readings*, Harmondsworth: Penguin, pp. 312–46.
Miyao, T. (1977) 'A generalization of Sraffa's Standard commodity and its complete characterization', *International Economic Review* 18: 151–62.
Ong, Nai-Pew (1983) 'Ricardo's invariable measure of value and Sraffa's "Standard commodity"', *History of Political Economy* 15: 207–27.
Ricardo, D. (1951 *ssq.*) *The Works and Correspondence of David Ricardo*, 11 vols, ed. P. Sraffa with the collaboration of M. H. Dobb, Cambridge: Cambridge University Press.
Roncaglia, Alessandro (1978) *Sraffa and the Theory of Prices*, trans. J. A. Kregel, London: Wiley.
Samuelson, Paul Anthony (1987) 'Sraffian economics', in J. Eatwell, M. Milgate and P. Newman (eds), *The New Palgrave* 4, London: Macmillan, pp. 452–61.
Schefold, Bertram (1976) 'Nachworte', in Schefold, Bertram (ed.) *Warenproduktion mittels Waren*, German translation of Sraffa (1960), Frankfurt: Suhrkamp.
—— (1986) 'The Standard commodity as a tool of economic analysis: a comment on Flaschel', *Journal of Institutional and Theoretical Economics* 142: 603–22.
Sraffa, P. (1951) 'Introduction', in Ricardo (1951 *ssq.*) I, pp. xiii–lxii.
—— (1960) *Production of Commodities by Means of Commodities*, Cambridge: Cambridge University Press.
Steedman, Ian (1985) 'On the "impossibility" of Hicks-neutral technical change', *Economic Journal* 95: 746–58.
Woods, John E. (1987) 'Sraffa's critical proportion and the Standard commodity', *Economic Notes* 16: 60–6.

ACKNOWLEDGEMENTS

We thank without implicating Christian Bidard, Antonio D'Agata, Pierangelo Garegnani, Peter Flaschel, Geoff Harcourt, Bruno Jossa, Carlo Panico, Alessandro Roncaglia, Bertram Schefold and Ian Steedman for helpful comments and discussions. Neri Salvadori thanks the MPI (the Italian Ministry of Public Education) for financial support.

8

MORISHIMA ON RICARDO

Heinz D. Kurz and Neri Salvadori

[A review of Michio Morishima, *Ricardo's Economics: A General Equilibrium Theory of Distribution and Growth*, Cambridge: Cambridge University Press, 1989]

As Professor Morishima tells the reader in the preface, 'this volume is not primarily a book on history of economic analysis but a reappraisal of past great economists from the viewpoint of contemporary economic theory' (p. vii).[1] Together with *Marx's Economics* (1973) and *Walras' Economics* (1977) it forms a trilogy. Originally intending to conclude with a book on Keynes, Professor Morishima instead chose to write on Ricardo because the latter was 'Marx's and Walras' common guru' and thus occupies an important place in the history of the emergence of economic ideas. More particularly, Ricardo, who advocated 'Say's law of markets', seems to be the natural author to start with in order to study the 'transition' to Keynes, who rejected the law. It is indeed the investigation of this transition which forms the main concern of *Ricardo's Economics* (p. viii). Therefore, the book is almost as much about Marx, Walras and Keynes as it is about Ricardo.

Professor Morishima claims to concentrate on the main work: Ricardo's *On the Principles of Political Economy, and Taxation*. In the introduction he writes:

> I have never been a historian of economic thought but have been an economic theorist throughout my life. With such a speciality, I believe, I am allowed to concentrate solely on their main works; and by making this constraint I am able to read these works more deeply and more rigorously than specialists in the history of economic thought, so that present-day economists can learn from them.
>
> (p. 3)[2]

This is not the only limitation of Professor Morishima's book. Apart from setting aside most of Ricardo's correspondence, his other published and non-published works and his parliamentary speeches as they are available in the eleven volumes of *The Works and Correspondence of David Ricardo*, edited by Piero Sraffa with the collaboration of M. H. Dobb

(1951 *ssq.*, hereafter *Works*), Professor Morishima leaves out of consideration almost all the secondary literature on Ricardo. Indeed, there are few references to books or articles devoted to an investigation of Ricardo's analysis as a whole or specific parts of it. Yet there is an abundance of cross-references to Professor Morishima's own works. It should come as no surprise that the entire volume is largely Professor Morishima in the garb of Ricardo.

The main message of the book is that the analyses of Ricardo, Marx and Walras are much more similar than is generally held in contributions to the history of economic doctrines. Professor Morishima, in comparing the three approaches, sees essentially a *unité de doctrine*. Existing differences in the theory of value and distribution are 'of minor or secondary importance':

> We may thus conclude that Ricardo, Marx and Walras constitute a trio. The first developed a general-equilibrium model of economic growth verbally, logically, and the second extended it in a number of directions and examined interesting novel mathematical properties that were concealed within it, again with no explicit use of mathematical formulas, while the third put the model into a rigorous mathematical form and, by doing so, made it operationally more workable.
>
> (p. 4)

The book is divided into five parts, each of which is subdivided into two chapters, except the fifth part, which contains three chapters. Part I deals with Ricardo's theory of value and his explanation of extensive and intensive rent. Chapter 1 contains an attempt to establish the view that Ricardo's approach to the theory of prices is based on marginalism; chapter 2 is concerned with refuting Pasinetti's 1960 interpretation of Ricardo's theory of the rent of land. Part II is dedicated to a discussion of wages and profits. Chapter 3 focuses on the inverse relationship between the two distributive variables; in it Professor Morishima launches a frontal attack on Sraffa's concept of the Standard commodity and the distribution formula based on it. Chapter 4 is devoted to yet another exposition of what appears to be one of Professor Morishima's favourite subjects: the so-called 'Fundamental Marxian Theorem' and the generalized version of it. Professor Morishima takes the opportunity to reply to some of the critics of his earlier contributions on the matter. Part III turns to the theory of accumulation and growth. In chapter 5 the problem is discussed within the framework of a closed economy; the alternative interpretations suggested by Casarosa (1985) and Samuelson (1966) are rejected on the grounds that they 'distort Ricardo's theory immensely' (p. 121). Chapter 6 deals with the open economy and attempts to 'correct', 'revise' and 'modernize Ricardo's theory of foreign trade' (p. 134). In Part IV Say's law is discussed. In chapter 7 it is interpreted in such a way that it 'rules out unemployment of labour and capital' (p. 153). On the basis of this interpretation chapter 8 then argues that Ricardo, who advocated the law in the *Principles*, was wrong in maintaining that the introduction of machinery may cause unemployment. Finally, Part V compares what are called the 'three paradigms', which are now identified as the economics of Ricardo, Walras and Keynes, respectively. Chapter 9 deals with several authors, ranging from Marx and J. S. Mill to Walras, Wicksell and Schumpeter, certain elements of whose analyses point in the direction of an abandonment of Say's law. It is in fact Professor Morishima's contention that the various contributions to economic theory should be divided into two groups only: those which are based on Say's law, and those which are not. Chapter 10 highlights what Professor Morishima considers to be the main difference between the economics of Ricardo and Walras and that of Keynes in terms of a two-sectoral model. The concluding chapter is concerned with the problem of the periodization of economic theory and attempts to locate what is called 'the epoch of Ricardo's economics'. To this effect an 'anti-Say's law index' is constructed, which relates that part of investment which 'is decided entirely independently of savings' (p. 237) to total investment undertaken in the economy.

In what follows, attention will focus on those parts and passages of the book which, in our view, are either based on a misreading of Ricardo or major interpreters of Ricardo, such as P. Sraffa and L. Pasinetti, or are difficult to sustain from a theoretical point of view. We shall not enter into a discussion of Professor Morishima's extensive digressions into Marx's and Walras's economics. Taking the title of the book seriously, emphasis is placed on what *Ricardo's Economics* has to offer on the economics of Ricardo.

While the present chapter is mostly critical of Professor Morishima's book on Ricardo, the authors wish to emphasize that in their view his book deserves the credit for having enriched the debate about the interpretation of the classical economists, and in particular Ricardo, with new and original ideas. Moreover, Professor Morishima has contributed in important ways to the time-honoured question of how different schools of economic thought relate to one another. Last but not least, the authors wish to express how much they owe to the works of Professor Morishima for their own training as economists. Therefore, the critical remarks that follow should be seen in the light of Ricardo's last letter to T. R. Malthus, dated 31 August 1823 (see *Works* IX: 382).

The structure of the chapter is as follows. In the next section we shall briefly deal with the length of the period of production in agriculture and manufacturing, respectively. The subsequent section (pp. 152–8) turns to the theory of rent and Professor Morishima's criticism of the interpretation put forward by L. Pasinetti some thirty years ago. Pages 158–9 deal with the treatment of fixed capital in Ricardo's theory of value. Professor

Morishima's discussion of the problem of the standard of value is scrutinised in the fifth section (pp. 159–63). Next, in the sixth (pp. 163–4), we shall briefly comment on his view of Ricardo's dynamical analysis. The seventh section (pp. 164–6) turns to Ricardo's approach to trade theory. Say's law and Ricardo's opinion on machinery are dealt with in section eight (pp. 166–71). The final section contains some conclusions.

THE PRODUCTION PERIOD

Professor Morishima contends that Ricardo 'actually assumed the production period to be 1 [year] for agriculture and 0 for manufacturing industries' (p. 20). However, he provides no textual evidence in support of his view that in Ricardo production is instantaneous in manufacturing. Indeed, no evidence to this effect exists in Ricardo's writings.

Ricardo's views on the production process are most clearly expressed in his disquisitions on the 'invariable measure of value'. As is well known, Ricardo was of the opinion that relative natural prices are generally not fully explained in terms of the quantities of labour needed directly and indirectly in their production. The deviation of relative prices from relative quantities of labour 'embodied' derives from the differences in the technological characteristics of the various production processes. These differences Ricardo attempted to capture in various ways (see Kurz and Salvadori 1993). In his letter to McCulloch of 13 June 1820 Ricardo hinted at what appeared to him to be the most abstract formulation of the circumstances which account for the deviation under consideration: 'All the exceptions to the general rule [i.e. the labour embodiment rule] come under this one of time'; and 'there are such a variety of cases in which the time of completing a commodity may differ' (*Works* VIII: 193). This idea was taken up again in his essay 'Absolute Value and Exchangeable Value', in which he emphasized: 'In this, then, consists the difficulty of the subject, that the circumstances of time for which advances are made are so various' (*Works* IV: 370).

The commodity Ricardo was in search of as a 'perfect' standard of value was supposed to somehow reflect the 'medium between the extremes' (cf. *Works* IV: 372):

> That commodity produced by labour employed for a year is a mean between the extremes of commodities produced on one side by labour and advances for much more than a year, and on the other by labour employed for a day only without any advances, and the mean will in most cases give much less deviation from truth than if either of the extremes were used as a measure.
>
> (*Works* IV: 405)

The basic idea underlying this concept seems to be that 'the variety of circumstances under which commodities are actually produced' (*Works* IV: 368) can be expressed in terms of a single variable, that is, the time that elapses between an initial expenditure of labour and the completion of the product. In other words, Ricardo appears to start from the supposition that commodities can be distinguished in terms of the length of their production periods. He explicitly rejected the standard suggested by Malthus, i.e. a commodity produced by labour employed for a day only without any advances. A particular case of such instantaneous production introduced by Malthus for illustrative purposes consists of silver picked up at the seashore. Malthus's measure, Ricardo objected, is of such an extreme and exceptional nature that it cannot be considered to represent 'the circumstances under which the greater number of commodities are produced' (*Works* IV: 372). Hence to maintain, as Professor Morishima does, that Ricardo envisaged the entire manufacturing sector as characterized by instantaneous production appears to be in stark contrast to Ricardo's own writings.[3]

To conclude, it deserves to be mentioned that with some circularity of production Ricardo's idea of a (finite) production period necessarily breaks down, while with unidirectional processes of production it is applicable in very special cases only. There is ample evidence that Ricardo was aware of the fact that most commodities are produced by means of commodities. However, he did not succeed in grasping fully the implication of the inter-industry relationships for his theory of value and distribution and his specification of the standard of value. (On the latter, see pp. 159–63 below.)

RENT THEORY

While Professor Morishima assumes all land to be homogeneous in quality in chapter 1, he extends the analysis to cover the case where land 'is differentiated in quality into several or infinitely many classes' (p. 36) in chapter 2. The assumptions underlying Professor Morishima's simplified analysis are essentially the same as those adopted by Pasinetti in his article 'A mathematical formulation of the Ricardian system', published in 1960.[4] The assumptions are (cf. Pasinetti 1974: 7):

(i) There is only one type of agricultural product, called 'corn'.
(ii) Corn is the only wage-good and capital consists entirely of the wage-bill, i.e. corn is produced by labour and land only.

According to Professor Morishima, Pasinetti's formalization of Ricardo's approach to the theory of rent is fundamentally flawed. His main objection reads:

> Pasinetti does not classify various sorts of land according to their quality. He instead has only one aggregate production function for

agriculture as a whole, with the logical consequence that he is unable to explain the rent of a land as the surplus which it yields . . . His theory of rent, accordingly, can hardly be a theory of differential rent, though it may be called a marginal productivity theory of rent.

(pp. 50–1; similarly p. 38)

Professor Morishima maintains that, given these assumptions, 'there is no simple aggregate production function for agriculture' (p. 103) if land is diversified in quality. The solution he suggests is a separate production function for each quality of land.

This claim, however, cannot be sustained. In what follows, Pasinetti's approach to Ricardo's theory of rent will be reconstructed starting from Sraffa's chapter on 'Land' (Sraffa 1960: chapter XI). For this purpose Sraffa's analysis of extensive and intensive rent will be summarized briefly and, given the simplifying assumptions (i) and (ii), a production function for agriculture as a whole will be constructed.

Sraffa's analysis

In his chapter 'Land', Sraffa extends his analysis to cover the case of natural resources which are used in production and, if they are in short supply, enable their owners to obtain a rent. In accordance with previous chapters, Sraffa starts from a given *system of production*, i.e. given quantities of the commodities produced and given methods of production in use, and a given distribution of income between wages and profits. He then indicates how such a situation can be conceived 'as the outcome of a process of "extensive" . . . [or] "intensive" diminishing returns' (Sraffa 1960: 76). Elaborating on Sraffa's approach, several contributions were concerned with the study of changes in the relations between the distributive variables (including rents) and prices, corresponding to autonomous changes in one of the distributive variables (the rate of profits r or the wage rate w) or in outputs.[5]

In general, the scarcity of natural resources is reflected in the coexistence of two or more processes producing the same commodity.[6] In the pure case of *extensive* diminishing returns, in which there exists only one process for the production of corn for each quality of land, different qualities of land will be used side by side in order to produce the amount of corn required. If there were no scarcity, cost minimization would imply that only one quality of land (and only one method of production), i.e. the one that allows production of the commodity at lowest cost per unit, would be used, and there could be no rent. However, if the best-quality land is in short supply, one or several additional qualities of land have to be cultivated and hence one or several additional methods of production are used to produce the required amount. That quality of land which, among all those cultivated, exhibits the highest cost per unit of production (but no higher unit cost than any of the lands lying fallow) yields no rent, whereas the scarcity of the other lands in use is reflected in positive differential rents, and rents are such that corn is produced at the same unit cost by all the processes operated.

In the pure case of *intensive* diminishing returns, in which there exists only one quality of land but a variety of methods of production to cultivate it, 'the only evidence of [the] scarcity [of land] to be found in the process of production is the duality of methods' (Sraffa 1960: 76). If land were available in abundant supply, only the cheapest method of production would be operated and there could be no rent. However, as soon as the required amount of the product can no longer be produced by this method, even if it occupies all the land, the price of corn has to rise to the point where an additional method becomes eligible which, although characterized by a higher cost per unit of output, yields more corn per acre. Thus, with scarce homogeneous land, two methods of production will be employed concurrently in general and will allow the determination of the (uniform) rent of land and the price of corn. With an increase in demand for corn, output will increase 'through the gradual extension of the method that produces more corn at a higher unit cost, at the expense of the method that produces less' (ibid.). When the second method has completely replaced the first one, further increases in output presuppose that a third method will be introduced which produces still more corn per acre at still higher unit cost, etc.

As should be clear from the foregoing, in answering questions like 'Which kinds of land (or methods of production) will be used in order to produce given outputs?' a problem of the choice of technique has to be solved. This problem consists of finding, for a given wage rate (or, alternatively, a given rate of profits), a cost-minimizing system of production, in which commodity prices, rents and the rate of profits (wage rate) are non-negative and no process yields extra profits. Since the prices of commodities and hence the cost of production cannot generally be determined independently of distribution, i.e. the level of wages (the rate of profits), the implication is close at hand that in order to produce the same vector of outputs, at different levels of w (r) the criterion of cost minimization may lead to the cultivation of different kinds of land and/or the activation of a different pair of methods on a given kind of land. Furthermore, if produced means of production are used there is no reason to exclude the possibility that the same system of production can return at different levels of w (r); i.e. the reswitching of techniques that use non-produced means of production can occur. The view frequently to be found in the economic literature that there exists a 'natural' ranking of the various plots of land in decreasing order of profitability (or 'fertility'), and the related view that this ranking coincides with a parallel one according to rent per acre, are generally unwarranted. Both orders 'may vary with the variation of r and w' (Sraffa 1960: 75) and may deviate from one another. It should also be clear that with heterogeneous capital goods no production function can be constructed. Yet this is *not* the case dealt with by Pasinetti and Morishima in their simplified analyses of rent.

A production function for agriculture as a whole

A production function for agriculture as a whole expresses the following 'course of events' in an economy satisfying assumptions (i) and (ii) (stated on p. 152), in which capital is accumulated and a growing labour force has to be provided with corn. At first only one method of production will be employed, that which maximizes the output per worker (since there are no produced means of production). Total output can be increased by gradually extending the cost-minimizing method to the entire available amount of the quality of land (call it quality A) utilized by this method. In Figure 8.1 the maximum output to be produced with this method is given by X_1^1; the corresponding employment on land of quality A is N_1^1; $tg\ \alpha$ is the output–labour ratio.

A further increase of output can take place either by taking into cultivation another quality of land (call it quality B) or by gradually replacing the first method of production by another one which utilizes the same quality of land but produces more corn per acre at a higher unit cost, i.e. a higher quantity of labour per unit of output. Farmers will choose the cheapest method available. If the cheapest method available happens to be the one utilizing land of quality B, then in Figure 8.1 the maximum output to be produced with this method is given by $(X_1^2 - X_1^1)$; the corresponding

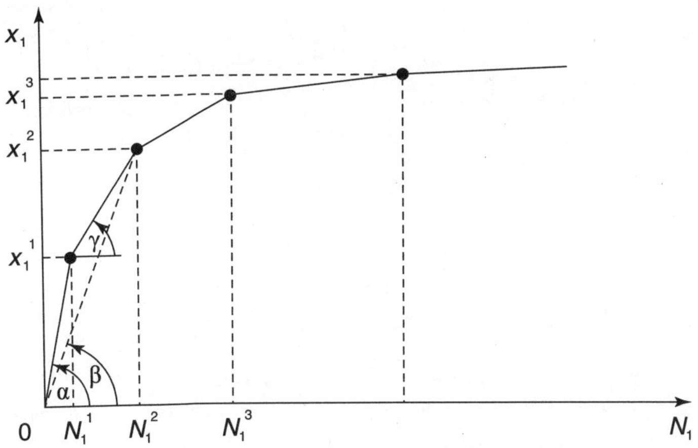

Figure 8.1 The production function.

employment on land of quality B is $(N_1^2 - N_1^1)$; $tg\ \gamma$ is the output–labour ratio. On the other hand, if the cheapest method available is another method utilizing land of quality A, then in Figure 8.1 the maximum output to be produced with this method is given by X_1^2; the corresponding employment is N_1^2; $tg\ \beta$ is the output–labour ratio.

Similarly, a further increase in output can take place either by taking into cultivation yet another quality of land or by gradually replacing (one of) the operated method(s) of production by another one which utilizes the same quality of land but produces more corn per acre at a still higher labour input per unit of output. Once again farmers will choose the cheapest method available.

With a continuum of methods of production available to cultivate each quality of land, the production function for agriculture as a whole need not, as in Figure 8.1, consist of a series of straight lines.

Let us now construct this function.[7] Because of assumptions (i) and (ii), the technology of the agricultural sector can be described in terms of the labour input vector **l**, the land input matrix **C** and the output vector **b**. The number of rows of **l**, **C** and **b** equals the number of the available methods (or processes) of production; the number of columns of **C** equals the number of existing qualities of land. It is assumed that **l** and **b** are positive vectors and that each row and column of matrix **C** is semipositive. This means that each process produces a positive amount of corn by employing a positive amount of labour (and, as a consequence, capital) and at least one quality of land. All qualities of land may be used in the production of corn.[8]

For each amount of labour employed in corn production, N_1, the following set of inequalities and equations must hold,

$$\mathbf{x}^T\mathbf{C} \leqq \mathbf{h}^T \tag{1}$$

$$\mathbf{x}^T\mathbf{C}\mathbf{q} = \mathbf{h}^T\mathbf{q} \tag{2}$$

$$\mathbf{b} \leqq w(1 + r)\mathbf{l} + \mathbf{C}\mathbf{q} \tag{3}$$

$$\mathbf{x}^T\mathbf{b} = w(1 + r)\mathbf{x}^T\mathbf{l} + \mathbf{x}^T\mathbf{C}\mathbf{q} \tag{4}$$

$$\mathbf{x}^T\mathbf{l} = N_1 \tag{5}$$

$$\mathbf{x} \geqq \mathbf{0} \tag{6}$$

$$\mathbf{q} \geqq \mathbf{0} \tag{7}$$

$$w(1 + r) \geq \mathbf{0} \tag{8}$$

where **x** is the process intensity vector, **h** is the vector of the available amounts of the different qualities of land, **q** is the vector of rent rates, w is the wage rate in terms of corn and r is the profit rate.

Because of the Equilibrium Theorem of Linear Programming (see, e.g.,

Franklin 1980: 66), system (1)–(7) is satisfied if and only if the following two dual linear programmes have optimal solutions:

Maximize $\mathbf{x}^T\mathbf{b}$ subject to

$$\mathbf{x}^T\mathbf{C} \leqq \mathbf{h}^T \tag{9}$$
$$\mathbf{x}^T\mathbf{l} = N_1$$
$$\mathbf{x} \geqq \mathbf{0}$$

Minimize $\mathbf{h}^T\mathbf{q} + w(1 + r)N_1$ subject to

$$\mathbf{b} \leqq w(1 + r)\mathbf{l} + \mathbf{C}\mathbf{q} \tag{10}$$
$$\mathbf{q} \geqq \mathbf{0}$$

Let

$$N_1^* = \text{Max } \mathbf{z}^T\mathbf{l} \text{ subject to}$$
$$\mathbf{z}^T\mathbf{C} \leqq \mathbf{h}^T$$
$$\mathbf{z} \geqq \mathbf{0}$$

Then programme (9) has a feasible solution for each N_1, such that $0 \leqslant N_1 \leqslant N_1^*$, whereas programme (10) always has a feasible solution. Hence both programmes have optimal solutions for $0 \leqslant N_1 \leqslant N_1^*$. Moreover, the theory of parametric programming (see, for example, Franklin 1980: 70) ensures that the function

$$X_1 = f(N_1) \tag{11}$$

where X_1 is the value of the maximum of programme (9), is continuous, concave and piecewise linear for $0 \leqslant N_1 \leqslant N_1^*$. Moreover, since

$$X_1 = \mathbf{h}^T\mathbf{q} + w(1 + r)N_1$$

$f'(N_1) = w(1 + r)$ for each point in which the function $f(N_1)$ is differentiable. Finally, let

$$X_1^{**} = \text{Max } \mathbf{z}^T\mathbf{b} \text{ subject to}$$
$$\mathbf{z}^T\mathbf{C} \leqq \mathbf{h}^T$$
$$\mathbf{z} \geqq \mathbf{0}$$

and let

$$N_1^{**} = \text{Max } \mathbf{z}^T\mathbf{l} \text{ subject to}$$
$$\mathbf{z}^T\mathbf{C} \leqq \mathbf{h}^T$$
$$\mathbf{z}^T\mathbf{b} \geq X_1^{**}$$
$$\mathbf{z} \geqq \mathbf{0}$$

Obviously, $N_1^{**} \leqslant N_1^*$ and $X_1^{**} > 0$, where X_1^{**} is the maximum output producible with the given technology and the given amounts of the different qualities of land available. Therefore, for $0 \leqslant N_1 \leqslant N_1^{**}$ the function is non-decreasing. Thus for $0 \leqslant N_1 \leqslant N_1^{**}$ the system (1)–(8) has a solution and function (11) is the production function used by Pasinetti to represent the production of the corn sector as a whole.

Whereas the production function just derived is not continuously differentiable, Pasinetti in his original formulation assumed the function to be so. However, this assumption is introduced for the sake of simplicity only (Pasinetti 1974: 4). This becomes crystal-clear in a note on his model published two decades later. In this note Pasinetti points out:

> For didactical purposes, continuous functions are very useful. I have myself, most of the time, used the device of considering the derivative $f'(N_1)$ as a continuous function of N_1, . . . However, there is no reason why the derivative of function $f(N_1)$ should be a continuous one. Let us remember that the first derivative of $f(N_1)$ represents the productivity of the worker who is put to work on the least fertile piece of cultivated land. Ricardo always considered the various pieces of land, ranked in order of fertility, in *finite* terms (not in infinitesimal terms).
>
> (Pasinetti 1981: 673–4; Pasinetti's emphasis)

Professor Morishima's proposition that 'there is no simple aggregate production function for agriculture' (p. 103) if land is diversified in quality is therefore untenable, and his criticism of Pasinetti's formulation has to be rejected.

FIXED CAPITAL

Professor Morishima's formalization of Ricardo's theory of relative prices contains an inadequate treatment of fixed capital. Using our notation, the price system suggested can be written as

$$\mathbf{p} = w\mathbf{l} + \mathbf{K}\delta\mathbf{p} + r(w\mathbf{l} + \mathbf{K}\mathbf{p})$$

where $\mathbf{p}$ is the vector of prices, $\mathbf{K}$ is the matrix of capital coefficients and δ is the diagonal matrix 'with the ith diagonal element δ_i being the rate of depreciation of capital good i' (p. 20; similarly p. 62). The latter assumption is known as 'depreciation by radioactive decay' or 'depreciation by evaporation' (Hicks), an assumption which has been criticized by Professor Morishima himself (see Morishima 1969: 89).

A proper treatment of durable capital goods has been suggested by von Neumann (1945–6: 2) and was dealt with in some detail by Sraffa (1960: chapter X) and the literature following the publication of these two seminal contributions.[9] As is well known, the method of treating what remains of fixed capital goods at the end of the production period as part of the gross output allows the correct calculation of the annual charge on the fixed capital. This charge consists of the payment of profit at the uniform rate and the depreciation that makes possible the replacement of the durable instrument of production when it is worn out. It is shown that the depreciation quotas and thus the prices of ageing fixed capital items cannot be ascertained independently of distribution. Hence *ad hoc* rules of depreciation such as 'depreciation by evaporation' cannot generally be sustained.

As Sraffa pointed out, the method of treating fixed capital as a joint product 'fits easily into the classical picture'. He added:

> It was only after Ricardo had brought to light the complications which the use of fixed capital in various proportions brings to the determination of values that the plan in question was resorted to. It was first introduced by Torrens in the course of a criticism of Ricardo's doctrine . . . Thereafter the method was generally adopted, even by the opponents of Torrens's theory: first by Ricardo in the next [i.e. third] edition of his *Principles*.
>
> (Sraffa 1960: 94–5)

The reference is to a passage in Ricardo in which the value of corn, which is taken to be produced by unassisted labour, is compared with the value of 'the machine and cloth of the clothier together . . . and the machine and cotton goods of the cotton manufacturer' (*Works* I: 33).

While Ricardo recognized the possibility of treating fixed capital in terms of the joint production method, he did not develop it. However, as numerical examples in the *Principles* indicate, Ricardo knew the annuity formula

$$y = p_{m0} \frac{r(1 + r)^n}{(1 + r)^n - 1}$$

where y is the annual charge, p_{m0} is the price of the new machine, r is the general rate of profits and n is the life of the machine (cf. *Works* I: 54–62). It would, of course, have been most surprising had a highly successful stockbroker like Ricardo not known this result. As is well known, this formula gives the correct annual charge to be paid for interest and depreciation in the special case of a machine operating with constant efficiency throughout its lifetime of n years. Ricardo was thus also well aware of the fact that the pattern of depreciation cannot be ascertained independently of income distribution, i.e. the level of the rate of profits.

THE STANDARD OF VALUE

Professor Morishima stresses that 'the wage–profit frontier . . . plays a most crucial role in the Ricardian economics'; he therefore considers it appropriate to 'carefully examine the various methods of deriving the frontier and discuss their merits and demerits' (p. 28). This is done in the third chapter. There he writes:

> In this sort of analysis, we must clearly define, as Ricardo did, what is taken as the standard of measure of prices and wages. This is Sraffa's problem of standard commodity or the problem of numeraire, which is dealt with significantly differently by Ricardo, Sraffa and myself.
>
> (p. 61)

As regards the 'significant differences' alluded to, Professor Morishima points out that his position is similar to the one entertained by Walras, i.e. that any commodity, or any bundle of commodities, could serve as numeraire. He rejects Ricardo's concept of an 'invariable measure of value' on the grounds that 'I do not assume existence of such a commodity because I do not take the labour-value theoretic approach' (p. 61).

Against Sraffa's Standard commodity, which he dubs a 'metaphysical concept' (p. 76), he objects:

> Whatever terminology and rhetoric are used, the hypothetical character of the standard system is clear. It is doubly hypothetical. First, it neglects the workers' demand for commodities as well as the wage payment [*sic*!]. Secondly, it assumes that commodities are produced in the fixed proportions necessary for the standard economy to grow at a uniform rate. Such an imaginary state is extremely remote from the actual observed economy, and Sraffa's share *W* [the share of wages], as a proportion of 'the standard net product', has nothing to do with the workers' share in the actual economy. In addition to this, Sraffa's formula [$r = r^*(1 - w)$] has a defect in that this real wage rate in terms of the standard commodity . . . does not accurately reflect the consumers' true 'real wage rate' in terms of their consumption bundle . . . although there is some parallelism between them.
>
> (p. 65)

On the construction of the Standard system he comments: 'Of course in this system too, labour is needed for producing commodities, even though no wage payment is made.' And in parentheses he adds, 'I ignore . . . this paradoxical character of the standard system and do not ask whether workers will work without reward. Even slaves would not really work if they were not rewarded, in the form of food at least' (p. 64).

There are various misconceptions here, some of which are also to be found elsewhere in the literature on Ricardo and Sraffa (cf. Kurz and Salvadori 1986, 1987, 1989).

A standard of value or numeraire is chosen by the theorist and does not depend on 'observed facts'. However, some standards have useful properties that can be utilized by the theorist. As is well known, Ricardo's search for an 'invariable measure of value' aimed at rendering precise the properties a standard would have to exhibit[10] in order to answer his concern with (i) intertemporal and interspatial comparisons and (ii) the impact of changes in distribution on relative prices (see also Pasinetti 1974: 3–4). While the first refers to measurement with respect to *different* technical environments, the second refers to measurement with respect to the *same* technical environment but a changing distribution of income. Ricardo considered the first property to be fulfilled by a commodity (or a bundle of commodities) used as a standard which 'now and at all times required precisely the same quantity of labour to produce it' (*Works* I: 17 n. 3). As to the second property, he was of the opinion that the commodity (or the bundle of commodities) used as a standard had to be produced with a proportion of labour to means of production 'which may fairly be considered as the medium between [the] extremes, and as agreeing more nearly with the circumstances under which the greater number of commodities are produced than any other which can be proposed' (*Works* IV: 372). There is, however, no reason to presume that there exists a commodity (or a bundle of commodities) which will be produced at all times with a constant amount of (direct and indirect) labour. And even if such a commodity (or bundle of commodities) existed, there would be no reason to presume that it would at all times be the medium between the extremes. Hence Ricardo's search for an 'invariable measure of value' which fulfilled both requirements resembled, as Ricardo became increasingly aware, the search for a will-o'-the-wisp.

Scrutiny shows that Sraffa in *Production of Commodities by Means of Commodities* (1960) saw only a single analytical purpose for the concept of the Standard commodity elaborated by him: it is conceived as a tool capable of simplifying the study of the effects of changes in the distribution of income on relative prices, given the technical conditions of production. When Sraffa in his book relates the Standard commodity to an 'invariable measure of value', his intention seems to be to pay a tribute to Ricardo by using the latter's own expression. However, Sraffa's concern is explicitly with the second aspect of Ricardo's problem only, whereas the first aspect plays no role whatsoever.[11]

In the literature on Sraffa there is an unfortunate tendency to assign meanings to the Standard commodity other than the one just mentioned. A case in point is Professor Morishima's interpretation quoted above. The Standard commodity was explicitly designed by Sraffa as a numeraire (with useful properties) and only that. If Professor Morishima's objections – that the Standard commodity 'neglects the workers' demand for commodities as well as the wage payment' and that it 'does not accurately reflect the consumers' true "real wage rate" in terms of their consumption bundle' – were to be taken seriously, then they would also have to be applied, for example, to the Walrasian normalization favoured by Professor Morishima (that is, setting the price of any commodity, or any bundle of commodities, equal to 1). As will become clear below, the Standard commodity was most certainly *not* designed as a method of measuring 'real wages'. Hence Professor Morishima is worried about an issue that cannot even arise with respect to the standard of value used by Sraffa.

It has been stated in the above that the numeraire chosen by the theorist does not depend on 'observed facts'. It goes without saying that the reverse is also true, i.e. the observed facts do not depend on the numeraire chosen. As Sraffa emphasized, the Standard system is 'a purely auxiliary construction' which 'may give transparency to a system and render visible what was hidden, but . . . cannot alter its mathematical properties' (1960: 31, 23).[12] Hence speculations like that entertained by Professor Morishima – that the construction of the Standard system implies that 'workers will work without reward' – are unwarranted.

Since Professor Morishima rejects both Ricardo's measure of value and Sraffa's Standard commodity, it is interesting to see which numeraire he proposes. He favours a bundle of commodities as a standard of value which in chapter 1 of his book has been identified as 'the consumption vector at some basic level' (p. 22). He calls the wage rate in terms of units of this bundle 'the real wage rate ω' and the relationship between ω and the rate of profits r the 'wage–profit frontier'. Professor Morishima appears to be of the opinion that the latter is in general the only meaningful expression of the constraint binding changes in the distribution of income.

This becomes clear when he confronts the wage–profit frontier with Sraffa's distribution formula. He points out that the two coincide with each other in the case in which the proportion between labour and the means of production is the same in all industries, i.e. the case in which the simple labour theory of value holds. He adds:

> We may now conclude that this is the only case in which Sraffa's formula . . . is meaningful; otherwise it deviates from the wage–profit frontier, because of the relative price effects, and is nothing else but a law concerning the *imaginary* 'standard' system.
>
> (p. 67; Morishima's emphasis)

This contention is best answered in terms of Sraffa's own argument. Sraffa begins his analysis by assuming that wages consist of the necessary subsistence of workers. Accordingly, *real* wages are given. He then observes that wages, besides the ever-present element of subsistence, may include a share of the surplus. Consequently, the real wage rate can no longer be considered given.[13] Hence, *if* the wage rate were still to be given from outside the system of production, it would have to be 'in terms of a more or less abstract standard, and [would] not acquire a definite meaning until the prices of commodities are determined' (Sraffa 1960: 33). To start, as Professor Morishima does, from a given and constant composition of the goods bundle consumed by workers evades the issue mentioned by Sraffa:

of two measures of value neither of which can be said to 'accurately reflect the consumers' "real wage rate"' (p. 65), Professor Morishima criticizes the one which has expressly been designed for a different purpose and adopts the one which was indeed meant to accomplish this task but fails to do so.

Professor Morishima also attempts to restrict the meaningfulness of the Standard system to the case of equal proportions of labour to means of production in all industries. While the Standard system is a *construction* related to a given actual system, equal proportions are an extremely special *assumption* about the actual system. With equal proportions no question would arise whether any particular change in the relative price of a commodity is due to the peculiarities of the commodity which is being measured or those of the measuring standard, since no change in relative prices could occur. Therefore, with equal proportions, no problem of a standard of value which is invariable with respect to changes in distribution could arise. Hence, rather than being the only case in which the Standard system is 'meaningful', equal proportions are the only case in which it is meaningless.

We may conclude that Professor Morishima's treatment of the problem of the standard of value is not convincing. His objections against Sraffa's Standard commodity are either wrong or not pertinent because they concern problems to the solution of which the Standard commodity has not been designed by Sraffa. The numeraire adopted by Professor Morishima, on the other hand, fails to accomplish the task ascribed to it by him, i.e. to reflect accurately the 'true "real wage rate"'.

ON THE NATURAL WAGE RATE

A brief comment should be made on Professor Morishima's discussion of which variables should be regarded as exogenous. In his analysis Professor Morishima considers as given the existing amounts of wage goods and capital goods and the number of workers in the economy. He contends that Pasinetti (1960) takes as given the existing amount of capital and the natural wage rate, defined as the wage rate which keeps population constant, and comments:

> This means that [Pasinetti's] model . . . is concerned with an 'open' economy where workers freely emigrate or immigrate so as to keep the real wage rate at a given level.
>
> (pp. 51–2)

From this Professor Morishima derives a further criticism:

> In the long-run analysis Pasinetti defines the long-run equilibrium as a state where the real wage rate is set at the natural rate and the profits

> are zero. There is no doubt that Ricardo also has the same definition. But there is a big difference between the models of the two authors. Ricardo's economy is a closed economy, whilst Pasinetti's is open. If Pasinetti had correctly taken the openness of his economy into consideration, that is, if he had not forgotten that workers can freely immigrate or emigrate, he would have seen that the long-run equilibrium real wages need not be at the natural level, because the wage rate at which the population remains stationary has no relevance in such an 'open' economy. The wage rate can be kept at an arbitrary level even in the long run.
>
> (p. 52)

As against this the following may be said. In Pasinetti's analysis two dynamic processes are considered: first, a sequence of market equilibria which leads to a 'natural' equilibrium and, second, a sequence of 'natural' equilibria which leads to the stationary state equilibrium. It is only in investigating the latter dynamic process that Pasinetti takes as given the natural wage rate. In contradistinction, in investigating the former dynamic process he takes as given the existing amount of capital and the number of workers in the economy.[14] Thus the forces which are envisaged to push the wage rate to a specific level are not immigration or emigration of workers, but those of Malthus's 'law of population'. Therefore, this specific level cannot be different from the natural real wage rate.

FOREIGN TRADE

In chapter 6 Professor Morishima deals with Ricardo's theory of foreign trade as it is expounded in chapter VII of the *Principles*. According to Professor Morishima the chapter 'begins on the wrong foot and results in confusion and incomprehensibility' (p. 128). Its main flaw, as seen by Professor Morishima, consists in Ricardo's rejection of the view advocated by Adam Smith that the opening or extension of trade leads to an increase in the general rate of profits: Ricardo's 'mistake' is already to be found 'at the very beginning of the chapter on foreign trade and therefore it affects the whole chapter' (p. 127). Professor Morishima thus attempts to demonstrate, in terms of some formal argument, that Ricardo was wrong, i.e. 'there is no reason to suppose that the wage–profit frontier will stay at the same place' (p. 127). However, as we shall see, there is no need for this 'revision' of Ricardo's trade theory, since Ricardo did not hold the opinion ascribed to him by Professor Morishima.

Professor Morishima begins by quoting the following passage from Ricardo's chapter:

> It has been my endeavour to shew, throughout this work, that the rate of profits can never be increased but by a fall in wages, and that there

> can be no permanent fall of wages but in consequence of a fall of the necessaries on which wages are expended. If, therefore, by the extension of foreign trade, or by improvements in machinery, the food and necessaries of the labourer can be brought to market at a reduced price, profits will rise.
>
> (*Works* I: 132)

Professor Morishima objects that 'this argument is incorrect . . . [W]hen the wage–profit frontier shifts upwards the rate of profits can be increased without a fall in wages, and, in fact, this is what happens when a country embarks on international trade' (pp. 126–7).

Apparently, Professor Morishima takes Ricardo to mean *real* rather than nominal wages when the latter talks of 'a fall in wages' in the above statement, in the same way as he requires the reader of his objection to Ricardo to interpret the reference to 'a fall in wages' in it in real terms. Yet there cannot be the least doubt that Ricardo, in this context, meant *nominal* wages and assumed real wages, i.e. 'the food and necessaries of the labourer', to be given. In order to see this, it is useful to recall how Ricardo defined 'the natural price of labour', or 'natural wage', at the beginning of his chapter 'On wages'. It is:

> that price which is necessary to enable the labourers, one with another, to subsist and to perpetuate their race, without either increase or diminution . . . The natural price of labour, therefore, depends on the price of food, necessaries, and conveniences required for the support of the labourer and his family. With a rise in the price of food and necessaries, the natural price of labour will rise; *with the fall in their price, the natural price of labour will fall.*
>
> (*Works* I: p. 93; emphasis added)[15]

It is precisely the latter constellation which is contemplated by Ricardo in the passage criticized by Professor Morishima. This becomes clear when we turn to the continuation of the passage: 'If, instead of growing our own corn, or manufacturing the clothing and other necessaries of the labourer, we discover a new market from which we can supply ourselves with these commodities at a cheaper price, wages will fall and profits rise' (*Works* I: 132). Hence in Ricardo's opinion the fall in (nominal) wages is due to a fall in (nominal) prices of wage goods, leaving real wages unaffected. This interpretation is further confirmed by Ricardo's subsequent remark, which refers to luxuries:

> [B]ut if the commodities obtained at a cheaper rate, by the extension of foreign commerce, or by the improvement of machinery, be exclusively the commodities consumed by the rich, no alteration will take

place in the rate of profits. *The rate of wages would not be affected . . . , and consequently profits would continue unaltered.*

(*Works* I: 132; emphasis added)

Clearly, Ricardo did not deny that the extension of foreign trade may entail a rise in the general rate of profits. He rather attempted to render precise the circumstances under which this will indeed be the case. He arrived at the conclusion that profitability increases if the extension of trade entails a lowering of the price of wage goods, whereas a lowering of the price of luxuries would have no such effect. Ricardo stressed that this finding is in harmony with the rest of his doctrine: 'The remarks which have been made respecting foreign trade, apply equally to home trade' (*Works* I: 133). We may conclude, therefore, that Professor Morishima's main criticism of Ricardo's theory of foreign trade is ill-conceived.

ON MACHINERY AND 'SAY'S LAW'

In chapter 8 Professor Morishima deals with Ricardo's chapter 'On machinery'.[16] In the chapter, added to the third edition of the *Principles*, Ricardo informed the reader about an important change of opinion concerning the effects of the introduction of improved machinery on employment. While in earlier times Ricardo had advocated the view that the introduction of machinery is beneficial to all classes of society, i.e. a 'general good' (*Works* I: 386), he now attempted to establish, in terms of an argument making use of two numerical examples, the doctrine 'that the substitution of machinery for human labour, is often very injurious to the interests of the class of labourers' (*Works* I: 388). For, Ricardo maintained, if the mechanization of production involves a decrease in the circulating part of capital, which he tended to identify with wages, 'there will necessarily be a diminution in the demand for labour, population will become redundant, and the situation of the labouring classes will be that of distress and poverty' (*Works* I: 390).

Professor Morishima questions the logic of Ricardo's argument and arrives at the conclusion that it is fundamentally flawed. Since Ricardo assumed 'Say's law' in the machinery chapter as well as in the rest of the *Principles*, he 'should have stuck to his original view, because unemployment is impossible under Say's law' (p. 11). It follows that all those who have praised Ricardo because of his change of opinion on the matter must be wrong, too. This includes, among others, Marx ([1867] 1954: 412), Hicks (1969, 1973) and most recently Samuelson (1988, 1989).

In his discussion of Say's law Professor Morishima stresses that the law 'is open to interpretation and has been given diverse meanings throughout its history. It is clear that Ricardo welcomed and accepted it.' Yet, surprisingly, the focus is not on Ricardo's version of Say's law: 'In what follows, we define the law in the same way that Keynes did' (p. 54; similarly p. 164), implying that investment tends to equality with full employment savings. While it is true that Ricardo assumed every act of saving to imply an act of investment of the same magnitude, and therefore ruled out the possibility of a 'general glut' of commodities, there is no indication that this implied of necessity the full employment of labour. Indeed, it should be noticed that in Ricardo's discussion of Say's law reference is exclusively to the employment of *capital*: 'M. Say has . . . most satisfactorily shewn, that there is no amount of capital which may not be employed in a country, because demand is only limited by production.' And 'there is no limit to demand – no limit to the employment of capital while it yields any profit' (*Works* I: 290, 296). Whether the amount of capital actually in existence at a given moment of time is able to give work to all those seeking employment at the given wage rate is not answered by the version of Say's law adopted by Ricardo, which refers to capitalistically produced commodities only. As Ricardo clarified, 'It is . . . always a matter of choice in what way a capital shall be employed, and therefore there can never, for any length of time, be a surplus of any commodity; for if there were, it would fall below its natural price, and capital would be removed to some more profitable employment' (*Works* I: 291n.). Hence Ricardo's finding that the introduction of improved machinery may displace workers does not, in itself, contradict his version of the 'law of markets'.

Ricardo's argument in the chapter on machinery is centred on the following numerical example:

> A capitalist we will suppose employs a capital of the value of 20,000 *l.* and that he carries on the joint business of a farmer, and a manufacturer of necessaries. We will further suppose, that 7000 *l.* of his capital is invested in fixed capital, viz. in buildings, implements, &c. &c. and that the remaining 13,000 *l.* is employed as circulating capital in the support of labour. Let us suppose, too, that profits are 10 per cent., and consequently that the capitalist's capital is every year put into its original state of efficiency, and yields a profit of 2000 *l.*
>
> (*Works* I: 388)

All profits are assumed to be spent for consumption purposes, so that the business is in a stationary state. The miniature system under consideration is perhaps best seen as a vertically integrated firm which manages to make good any wear and tear of the durable capital goods utilized and to reproduce all circulating capital goods (i.e. means of production used up and means of subsistence) needed annually to carry on the business. However, since Ricardo is not explicit about the depreciation pattern of the fixed capital items employed, we may for simplicity assume that they are ultra-long lived, i.e. represent perennial capital. In addition to the reproduction of the inputs used up the miniature system generates a surplus product which consists of food and necessaries, of which the capitalist 'consumes himself, or disposes of as may best suit his pleasure and gratification' (*Works* I: 388–9). Therefore the 'gross produce' consisting of the wages bill and profits amounts to £15,000, and the 'net produce' consisting of profits of £2,000. (The rent from land, which like profits has its origin in the surplus and thus is a component of the net produce, is for simplicity set aside by Ricardo.) Hence Ricardo's accounting reads as follows:

gross produce		circulating capital		total capital		rate of profits	
15,000	=	13,000	+	20,000	×	0.1	(R)

On this Professor Morishima comments: '[S]ince his [i.e. Ricardo's] formulas of accounting are a bit confusing, I shall begin with correcting his numerical example' (p. 171). The 'correction' suggested by Professor Morishima consists in reckoning what in Ricardo's example is the value of the *fixed capital* employed in the business, i.e. £7,000, as the *fixed capital cost*. Therefore, in terms of Professor Morishima's accounting, the value of the gross produce amounts to £22,000, and not, as Ricardo assumed, to £15,000: 'The difference between the two gross products, i.e. £22,000 versus £15,000, is not a matter of definition, but arises from incorrect methods of accounting' (p. 171). Professor Morishima thus replaces (R) by

gross produce		fixed capital cost		circulating capital cost		profits	
22,000	=	7,000	+	13,000	+	2,000	(M)

While it is true that Ricardo is not as explicit as he could or should have been with regard to the wear and tear of the durable capital items utilized by the joint business, i.e. 'buildings, implements, &c. &c.', there is no evidence in support of Professor Morishima's contention that the £7,000 was meant to represent the costs due to wear and tear, i.e. depreciation. What Professor Morishima's procedure amounts to is assuming away the existence of *any* kind of fixed capital, and the fact that he keeps using this term should not give rise to the impression that this is not so. Indeed, as in Ricardo's example, Professor Morishima takes the total capital advanced at the beginning of the production period to be worth £20,000, which in his case implies that the *entire* capital is taken to be used up in the course of the production cycle and has to be annually reproduced.

Ricardo supposes 'that the following year the capitalist employs half his men in constructing a machine, and the other half in producing food and necessaries as usual' (*Works* I: 389). On the assumptions (i) that also the existing fixed capital is divided equally between the two different kinds of productive activities, and (ii) that the value of the newly constructed machine is determined by its current cost of production plus profits at the going rate of 10 per cent on the capital advanced, Ricardo arrives at the following accounting scheme for the two intra-firm production lines:

	gross produce		circulating capital		total capital		rate of profits	
food and necessaries	7,500	=	6,500	+	10,000	×	0.1	(R.I)
machine	7,500	=	6,500	+	10,000	×	0.1	(R.II)

The implication of the reallocation of productive resources is close at hand: 'While the machine was being made, only one-half of the usual quantity of food and necessaries would be obtained, and they would be only one-half the value of the quantity which was produced before' (*Works* I: 389). On the premiss that the capitalist still consumes his entire profits, which amount to £2,000, 'he would have no greater circulating capital than 5500 *l.* with which to carry on his subsequent operations; and, therefore, his means of employing labour, would be reduced in the proportion of 13,000 *l.* to 5500 *l.*, and, consequently, all the labour which was before employed by 7500 *l.*, would become redundant' (*Works* I: 389).

Given the real wage rate, the reduction in employment in the subsequent period is due to the decreased amount of food and necessaries available in the support of labour, i.e. the decreased circulating capital. The value of the total capital at the firm's disposal is still the same as before, i.e. £20,000, yet its composition has drastically changed. While originally the ratio of fixed to circulating capital was 7,000/13,000 = 77/143, it has now risen to (7,000 + 7,500)/5,500 = 377/143, i.e. it has almost quintupled. This increase in the fixed capital intensity, given total capital, is the very cause of the displacement of workers analysed by Ricardo. For, as Ricardo stresses in the entry 'Capital' in the index to the *Principles* with reference to the machinery chapter, 'The increase of circulating not of fixed capital, regulates the demand for labour' (*Works* I: 432). Here Ricardo deliberately echoes an opinion entertained by John Barton, who in his *Observations on the Circumstances which Influence the Condition of the Labouring Classes of Society*, published in 1817, had stated, 'The demand for labour depends on the increasing of circulating, and not of fixed capital.' Ricardo quotes the passage starting with this line and makes it clear that he approves of this part of Barton's doctrine. He does not, however, follow Barton in the latter's more radical claim that '[i]t is easy to conceive that, under certain circumstances, the whole of the annual savings of an industrious people might be added to fixed capital, in which case they would have no effect in increasing the demand for labour' (cf. *Works* I: 395–6 n.). As Ricardo emphasizes in the chapter on machinery, capital accumulation is the key to a compensation of any labour displacement, notwithstanding the fact that in the course of the accumulation of capital the proportion between fixed and circulating capital tends to rise: 'The demand for labour will continue to increase with an increase of capital, but not in proportion to its increase; the ratio will necessarily be a diminishing ratio' (*Works* I: 395; similarly, p. 390).

Professor Morishima on the other hand replaces equations (R.I) and (R.II) by

	gross produce		fixed capital		circulating capital		profits	
food and necessaries	11,000	=	3,500	+	6,500	+	1,000	(M.I)
machine	11,000	=	3,500	+	6,500	+	1,000	(M.II)

and asks, '[W]here did Ricardo stray from the straight and narrow? Where did he admit an obstacle which would make Say's law unworkable, in spite of his superficial support of it, and resulted in a creation of unemployment?' (pp. 172–3).

The answer given by him reads: the system described by equations (M.I) and (M.II) 'is not an equilibrium' (p. 173). While there is a supply of food and necessaries worth £11,000, the demand for these items stemming from workers and the capitalist is worth £15,000(= 2 × £6,500 + 2 × £1,000). Hence there is £4,000 'of excess demand for food and necessaries' (p. 173). On the other hand, with the total 'demand for fixed capital for replacement' worth £7,000(= 2 × £3,500) and the supply worth £11,000, 'there is an excess supply of machines amounting to £4,000'. Professor Morishima comments on this, 'We have obtained this state of disequilibrium because Ricardo arbitrarily assumed that half the workers were employed in the production of machines.' The wage fund would thus be reduced from its previous level of £13,000 to £9,000 (rather than Ricardo's £5,500), and, with a given real wage rate, employment would fall to nine-thirteenths of its former size.

Seen from this perspective, the question arises, which allocation of the work force among the two production lines Ricardo, or rather the capitalist contemplated in his example, *should* have assumed in order not to end up with a 'disequilibrium'? The constellation satisfying the condition that both 'markets' internal to the firm clear, is easily calculated (p. 174):

	gross produce		fixed capital		circulating capital		profits	
food and necessaries	15,000	=	4,773	+	8,864	+	1,364	(M.I*)
machine	7,000	=	2,227	+	4,136	+	637	(M.II*)

Here the total supply of food and necessaries at current prices (£15,000) matches with the total consumption demand (£8,864 + £4,136 + £1,364 +

£637), and the total supply of machines (£7,000) matches with replacement requirements (£4,773 + £2,227). Professor Morishima concludes:

> Thus, where the labourforce is distributed between the two sectors in the equilibrium proportions, 68.2 per cent: 31.8 per cent, the demand for labour after the production of machines will be the same as before such an operation was commenced; thus, it does not cause unemployment. In Ricardo's example unemployment is generated because the labourforce is distributed between the two sectors in the wrong proportions, 50 per cent: 50 per cent. There is, however, no reason why it should be so. Where there is an excess supply of one commodity, an excess demand arises from some other commodity. Outputs are then adjusted in order to remove excess demand and supply. When the state of equilibrium is finally brought about, the employment of labour will be as high as it was before, because Say's law is assumed.
>
> (p. 174)

And a few pages later he writes, 'Thus, contrary to Ricardo, we conclude that, *under Say's law*, the substitution of machinery for human labour is not injurious to the interests of the class of labourers, provided that machines are introduced appropriately' (p. 177; Professor Morishima's emphasis).

Professor Morishima's argument cannot be accepted as a demonstration that Ricardo was wrong. In fact the interpretation suggested has emptied Ricardo's reasoning of its very content, i.e. the analysis of the employment consequences of a physical restructuring of the joint business's capital in favour of the fixed parts via the introduction of a machine. Since, according to Ricardo, the employment capacity of the miniature system is proportional to the circulating part of capital, a shift in favour of the fixed parts entails, of necessity, a reduction in employment. In Professor Morishima's interpretation there is no such shift, indeed there is no fixed capital at all. Comparing accounting systems (M) and [(M.I.*), (M.II*)], what is dubbed 'fixed capital cost' in the former and 'fixed capital' in the latter amounts to £7,000 in both cases. Similarly, the value of what is called 'circulating capital cost' in the former and 'circulating capital' in the latter is the same, i.e. £13,000. Hence, contrary to Professor Morishima's claim, his entire argument contains no discussion of 'the substitution of machinery for human labour', let alone whether this substitution is carried out 'appropriately' or not. Therefore, as a matter of logic, it cannot disprove Ricardo's opinion on the matter.

CONCLUSION

The present chapter provides a critical account of Professor Morishima's recent book *Ricardo's Economics*. Emphasis is on those parts of the book which, in our view, are either based on a misreading of Ricardo or major interpreters of Ricardo, or appear to be misconceived from a theoretical point of view. In particular, we deal with the following issues: Professor Morishima's opinion that in Ricardo production in manufacturing is taken to be instantaneous; his claim that, despite the simplifying assumptions underlying his analysis of extensive and intensive rent, a production function for agriculture as a whole does not exist; his interpretation of Ricardo's approach to fixed capital and depreciation; his discussion of the problem of the standard of value in Ricardo and Sraffa; his criticism of Pasinetti's treatment of the natural wage rate; his objections to Ricardo's analysis of foreign trade; and his opinion on the (in)compatibility of Ricardo's new view on machinery and Say's law. It is shown that with respect to the issues under consideration Professor Morishima's views are difficult to sustain.

NOTES

1 References to *Ricardo's Economics* are indicated by page numbers alone. Ricardo's writings are referred to as *Works*, volume number and page number (Sraffa edition).

2 On p. 4 of his book Professor Morishima points out 'that, for all editions [of the *Principles*] published while Ricardo was alive, there was a comma between "political economy" and "and taxation" in the title'. While this is correct, it seems to have escaped Professor Morishima's attention that the title reads '*On* the Principles . . .' rather than 'The Principles . . .'(p. 2 n. 5).

3 In private correspondence Professor Pasinetti pointed out to us that since Ricardo took both the production period in agriculture and the average production period of all commodities to be one year (the first fact being acknowledged by Professor Morishima), it would have been impossible for Ricardo to assume the average production period in manufacturing to be zero.

4 See Pasinetti (1960), reprinted in Pasinetti (1974); in what follows all references will be to the 1974 collection of essays.

5 See, for example, the papers on rent theory by Montani (1975) and Kurz (1978) reprinted in Steedman (1988 II, part II), the article by Quadrio-Curzio in Pasinetti (1980) and Salvadori (1986).

6 For the sake of the argument, we shall, in what follows, assume that there is only one product, say 'corn', in the production of which land is used. The complications which arise when there is more than one agricultural product have been investigated by D'Agata (1984).

7 Professor Samuelson in private correspondence has drawn our attention to his 1959 paper on Ricardo, which contains an early discussion of the existence of a production function in the case considered above; see Samuelson (1959: 28–32). The following argument draws on some of the material contained in the *Laurea* thesis submitted by Giuseppe Freni to the University of Catania (1987); we are grateful to Giuseppe Freni for allowing us to do so. It is hoped that he will publish his dissertation soon.

8 With Professor Morishima's description of agricultural technology (cf. p. 37) each row of matrix **C** would have one and only one positive element, all other elements being zero. We do not need this assumption, so we can allow, for example, that corn is produced by using a particular quality of land and water,

both in short supply, the water coming from a source located on another quality of land whose proprietor obtains a rent for the use of the source.

9 A major author in the tradition of von Neumann is of course Professor Morishima himself; with regard to the treatment of fixed capital see Morishima (1969: 89–91, 1973: 164–70). Important contributions to the analysis of fixed capital in the Sraffian tradition are collected in Pasinetti (1980), Steedman (1988, II, part I) and Salvadori and Steedman (1990).

10 In the *Principles* Ricardo stresses, 'It is . . . of considerable use towards attaining a correct theory, to ascertain what the essential qualities of a standard are, that we may know the causes of the variation in the relative value of commodities, and that we may be enabled to calculate the degree in which they are likely to operate' (*Works* I: 17 n. 3).

11 For a detailed discussion of the role of the Standard commodity in Sraffa's analysis and its relationship to Ricardo's search for an 'invariable measure of value' see Kurz and Salvadori (1989).

12 This has not always been properly understood. See, for example, the opinion expressed by Blaug that a change in distribution 'has no effect on relative prices measured in terms of the Standard commodity for the simple reason that the change alters the measuring rod in the same way as it alters the pattern of prices being measured' (1987: 436). If this were true, by mere choice of numeraire prices could be made independent of distribution and therefore the choice of numeraire would affect relative prices.

13 As Joan Robinson succinctly remarked, 'we could hardly imagine that, when the workers had a surplus to spend on beef, their physical need for wheat was unchanged' (1961: 54).

14 The literature following the publication of Pasinetti's formulation has criticized the fact that the second process begins when the first is concluded. Yet Pasinetti was aware of the incompleteness of his analysis: in the third section of the appendix to his paper he studies the local stability of the stationary state equilibrium when both dynamic processes are considered.

15 It is worth mentioning that Professor Morishima earlier in his book seems to have been well aware of the mechanism contemplated by Ricardo, at least with regard to the case of a *rise* in the price of a wage good: 'Where the price of corn rises, the workers' cost of living will also rise, and therefore [*sic*!] wages should rise' (p. 60; see also the discussion on pp. 72–3).

16 After this section had been written we had the opportunity to read a paper by T. Negishi (1990) which is devoted to a critical discussion of Professor Morishima's treatment of Ricardo on machinery and which raises some similar points.

REFERENCES

Blaug, M. (1987) 'Classical economics', in Eatwell, J., Milgate, M. and Newman, P. (eds), *The New Palgrave: a Dictionary of Economics* I, London: Macmillan.

Casarosa, C. (1985) 'The "new view" of the Ricardian theory of distribution and economic growth', in Caravale, G. A. (ed.), *The Legacy of Ricardo*, Oxford: Blackwell.

D'Agata, A. (1984) 'Molteplicità di merci agricole e rendita differenziale estensiva', *Ricerche Economiche* 38 (1).

Franklin, J. (1980) *Methods of Mathematical Economics*, New York: Springer.

Freni, G. (1987) *Modelli dinamici dell'analisi ricardiana*, Laurea thesis, Facoltà di Economia e Commercio, University of Catania.

Hicks, J. R. (1969) *A Theory of Economic History*, London: Oxford University Press.

—— (1973) *Capital and Time*, London: Oxford University Press.

Kurz, H. D. (1978) 'Rent theory in a multisectoral model', *Oxford Economic Papers* 30, reprinted in Steedman (1988).

Kurz, H. D. and Salvadori, N. (1986) 'A comment on Levine', *Journal of Post-Keynesian Economics* 9 (1).

—— (1987) 'Burmeister on Sraffa and the labor theory of value: a comment', *Journal of Political Economy* 95 (4).

—— (1993) 'The "Standard commodity" and Ricardo's search for an "invariable measure of value"', in M. Baranzini and G. C. Harcourt (eds), *The Dynamics of the Wealth of Nations. Growth, Distribution and Structural Change: Essays in Honour of Luigi Pasinetti*, New York: St. Martin's Press, pp. 135–63.

Marx, K. (1954) *Capital* I, Moscow: Progress Publishers (first German edition 1867).

Montani, G. (1975) 'Scarce natural resources and income distribution', *Metroeconomica* 27, reprinted in Steedman (1988).

Morishima, M. (1969) *Theory of Economic Growth*, Oxford: Clarendon Press.

—— (1973) *Marx's Economics*, Cambridge: Cambridge University Press.

—— (1977) *Walras' Economics*, Cambridge: Cambridge University Press.

—— (1989) *Ricardo's Economics: a General Equilibrium Theory of Distribution and Growth*, Cambridge: Cambridge University Press.

Negishi, T. (1990) 'Ricardo and Morishima on machinery', *Journal of the History of Economic Thought* 12 (2).

Neumann, J. von (1945–6) 'A model of general economic equilibrium', *Review of Economic Studies* 13 (33).

Pasinetti, L. L. (1960) 'A mathematical formulation of the Ricardian system', *Review of Economic Studies* 27, reprinted in Pasinetti (1974).

—— (1973) 'The notion of vertical integration in economic analysis', *Metroeconomica* 25, reprinted in Pasinetti (1980).

—— (1974) *Growth and Income Distribution: Essays in Economic Theory*, Cambridge: Cambridge University Press.

—— (ed.) (1980) *Essays on the Theory of Joint Production*, London: Macmillan.

—— (1981) 'On the Ricardian theory of value: a note', *Review of Economic Studies* 48 (4).

Quadrio-Curzio, A. (1980) 'Rent, income distribution, and orders of efficiency and rentability', in Pasinetti (1980).

Ricardo, D. (1951 *ssq.*) *The Works and Correspondence of David Ricardo*, ed. Piero Sraffa with the collaboration of M. H. Dobb, referred to as *Works*, Cambridge: Cambridge University Press.

Robinson, J. (1961) 'Prelude to a critique of economic theory', *Oxford Economic Papers* 13 (1).

Salvadori, N. (1986) 'Land and choice of techniques within the Sraffa framework', *Australian Economic Papers* 25 (46).

Salvadori, N. and Steedman, I. (eds) (1990) *Joint Production of Commodities*, Aldershot: Edward Elgar.

Samuelson, P. A. (1959) 'A modern treatment of the Ricardian economy' I, 'The pricing of goods and of labor and land services', *Quarterly Journal of Economics* 73 (1).

—— (1966) 'Wages and interest: a modern dissection of Marxian economic models', in *The Collected Scientific Papers of Paul A. Samuelson* I, Cambridge, Mass.: MIT Press.

—— (1988) 'Mathematical vindication of Ricardo on machinery', *Journal of Political Economy* 96 (2).
—— (1989) 'Ricardo was right!' *Scandinavian Journal of Economics* 91 (1).
Sraffa, P. (1960) *Production of Commodities by Means of Commodities*, Cambridge: Cambridge University Press.
Steedman, I. (ed.) (1988) *Sraffian Economics* I and II, Aldershot: Edward Elgar.

ACKNOWLEDGEMENTS

We should like to thank without implicating Mauro Baranzini, Piero Garegnani, Harvey Gram, Geoff Harcourt, Mark Knell, Perry Mehrling, Luigi L. Pasinetti, Paul A. Samuelson, Ian Steedman – and the participants at a session at the ASSA meeting in Washington, D.C., in December 1990 and at a seminar in the University of Stuttgart–Hohenheim in January 1991 – for helpful comments on previous versions of this chapter. We should also like to thank an anonymous referee and the editors of the *Cambridge Journal of Economics* for useful remarks and suggestions.

9

PEACH ON RICARDO

Heinz D. Kurz

[A review of Terry Peach, *Interpreting Ricardo*, Cambridge: Cambridge University Press, 1993]

The declared objectives of the book are: (i) to reconstruct the development of Ricardo's theory of value, distribution and accumulation; and (ii) to comment on the interpretative literature, focusing attention on the contributions subsequent to the publication of *The Works and Correspondence of David Ricardo* (eleven volumes), edited by Piero Sraffa (with the collaboration of Maurice H. Dobb) (cf. p. xi). The author indicates that the book had a gestation period of over ten years (cf. p. xiv). During that period Peach contributed some papers to the debate amongst advocates of alternative interpretations of Ricardo in which he anticipated some of the material contained in the book. This concerns his questioning of Sraffa's 'corn ratio' interpretation of Ricardo's early theory of profits and his rejection of Samuel Hollander's 'revisionist' view of Ricardo.

The book consists of seven chapters. Chapter 1, 'Interpretations of Ricardo' (pp. 1–38), introduces the interpretative literature and summarizes the author's own views on the matter and his criticisms of others; in addition, it gives an overview of the structure and content of the following chapters. Chapter 2, 'From bullion to corn: the early writings' (pp. 39–86), attempts to reconstruct the evolution of Ricardo's theory of profits up to the period following the publication of his *Essay on Profits* in 1815. Chapter 3, 'The falling rate of profit, wages and the law of markets' (pp. 87–144), is concerned with the dynamic setting of the process of accumulation within which Ricardo studied the problem of income distribution. Then follow two chapters on 'The labour theory of value', part I and part II. Chapter 4 (pp. 145–88) focuses on the development of Ricardo's theory of value prior to the third edition of the *Principles* (1821), while chapter 5 (pp. 189–240) covers the period thereafter. Chapter 6 deals with attempts aiming at 'The appropriation of Ricardo' (pp. 241–93); emphasis is on the interpretations of Ricardo by Marshall, Samuel Hollander, Morishima, Sraffa and a group of authors Peach calls the 'Sraffians'. The final chapter contains 'Concluding remarks' (pp. 294–303). There is a name and a subject index. Setting aside several misprints, the book has been produced with the usual care the publisher is known for. It comes as a surprise that with regard to several quotations only the author and the year of publication but not the page number of the work are given; the name of Böhm-Bawerk is consistently misspelled.

Seeking 'the (truly) "historical Ricardo"' (cf. p. 292) is an intrinsically difficult and troublesome task. The micro-surgery of the available bits and pieces of literature stemming from Ricardo's pen and the author's seemingly untiring endeavour to relate the development of Ricardo's ideas to the inspiration Ricardo may have got from reading the works of others and discussing with friends and adversaries, in particular Malthus, do not exactly provide the stuff of exciting prose. In places the less patient reader might be close to despair at missing the forest for the trees. These difficulties are not lessened by the pronounced desire of the author to earn himself the reputation of an independent and original scholar in the field. It forces Peach to enter into competition with several eminent interpreters of Ricardo, most notably Piero Sraffa. While there is no doubt that Peach deserves credit for enriching our understanding of some aspects of Ricardo's analysis, there is a tendency in the book to play down the similarities and magnify the differences between his and alternative interpretations. In places I also had the impression that the author finds enjoyment in discounting the achievements of the sung heroes of our subject.

Given the objectives of the book, certain important themes in Ricardo's writings are either completely neglected or dealt with only to the extent to which Peach sees them as contributing to these objectives. While the origins and substance of Ricardo's version of the 'law of markets' are given detailed consideration (pp. 131–42), there is, somewhat surprisingly, no discussion of his new view on machinery, published in the third edition of the *Principles*, and its compatibility, or otherwise, with the 'law of markets'.

A major concern of Peach in chapter 2 is Sraffa's interpretation of Ricardo's agricultural theory of the general rate of profit (cf. Ricardo's statement that 'it is the profits of the farmer which regulate the profits of all other trades' in *The Works* VI: 104), referred to as the 'corn model' interpretation. He points out that there is no *direct* textual support of that interpretation in Ricardo's writings, a point stressed also by Sraffa in his introduction to vol. I of *The Works* (pp. xxxi–ii) and then again in Sraffa (1960: 93–4). Since Ricardo's correspondence between late summer 1813 and spring 1814 and also his 'papers on the profits of Capital' which had been drafted during that period are missing, in Peach's view any attempt to reconstruct Ricardo's intellectual development in that period 'must be highly speculative' (p. 50). He does not, however, really mean it, as becomes clear when he turns to the examination of three different interpretations of Ricardo's pre-*Essay* theory of profits: the versions proposed by Sraffa, Samuel Hollander and the 'new' one by Peach himself. A minimum criterion to be fulfilled by any version is that it must not contradict 'core' elements of Ricardo's economic analysis in the period under consideration, especially his doctrine of the tendency of the rate of profit to fall. While, as Peach concedes, Sraffa's interpretation does not fail on this count, it is otherwise in the case of Professor Hollander's version (cf. Hollander 1979). Peach's own reconstruction rests on two pillars (cf. pp. 5–6 and pp. 54ff.). He argues that the 'Smithian' view that all prices rise with the corn price was the basis of Ricardo's early theory of profits. This together with diminishing returns in agriculture suffices to explain, *ceteris paribus*, i.e. setting aside agricultural 'improvements', the tendency of profitability to decline when, with the expansion of corn production, more and more (agricultural and manufactured) inputs are needed per unit of corn output.

Peach stresses, 'All the evidence cited in favour of this reconstruction . . . is avowedly indirect but, then again, so too was the evidence cited by Sraffa in support of his "corn model" interpretation (which I reject)' (p. 39). While this appears to be a fair statement, one page earlier we are told that 'the basic problem with Sraffa's interpretation would seem to stem from a tendency to read more of himself into Ricardo than was warranted. Thus, the "corn model" interpretation . . . [is an instance] of Sraffa having reconstituted Ricardo in his own image.' Since no conclusive evidence is put forward in support of this, one can only wonder what is the foundation, and status, of Peach's accusation. Later in the book Peach even talks of 'Sraffa's interpretative error' (p. 289), yet, again, nothing resembling proof of the 'error' is provided. Given the uncertainty surrounding Ricardo's early theory of profits, stressed by Peach, one ought to refrain from judgements the correctness of which cannot be established.

Peach is correct in stressing 'that, in any case, the "corn model" is not required in order to understand Ricardo's confidence that agricultural profitability falls as conditions of production deteriorate'. He continues: 'My interpretation is not one which has Ricardo constructing, or relying upon, a logically consistent model, but I do not regard this as a weakness' (p. 68). While it may not be a weakness, neither can it be regarded as a strength. Here it is not the place to discuss in detail Peach's version and his criticism of Sraffa's. It is up to the specialists in the field to carry out this task. I confine myself to two observations. First, I am not clear whether Peach is fully aware of the negative implication of his claim that there is no reason 'to *presume* consistency on Ricardo's part' (p. 83; emphasis in the original) for the project of providing a 'rational' reconstruction of Ricardo's early theory of profits. Second, I had difficulties with his explanation of why Ricardo in the *Essay* conducted his analysis on the premiss of given and constant *corn* value inputs to agriculture even though conditions of production deteriorate as less fertile plots of land are cultivated. As is well known, Sraffa saw the analysis in the *Essay* to 'reflect' the 'corn model', i.e. he took the numerical example in it to refer to corn quantities. In contradistinction, Peach claims that the analysis in the *Essay* 'was in fact based on the corn valuation of *heterogeneous* inputs on the assumption that all prices remain constant: any "reflection" of a "corn model" analysis is wholly superficial' (p. 85; emphasis in the original). The 'tacit assumption of *constant* prices' (p. 75) attributed to Ricardo by Peach is, however, squarely contradicting the fact that Ricardo by the time of the *Essay* saw clearly that due to diminishing returns in agriculture the price of manufactures will *fall* relative to corn. Peach is of course aware of this. To him there is no doubt that the blame is to be put on Ricardo: 'That this [i.e. the fall in the price of manufactures relative to corn] should have been overlooked may reflect the *Essay*'s hasty composition' (p. 74). It may also reflect a misinterpretation on Peach's part. Finally, I am not convinced by Peach's attempt to deny any connection between the 'corn model' formulations, or reflections, in the writings of several other contemporary authors, especially Malthus, and Ricardo's early theory of profits. Whether Ricardo was the 'inventor' of the 'corn model' or was introduced to it by someone else is one thing. If it *could* be established that he was not the inventor, this does not imply that the model played no role in the evolution of his theory of profits.

In chapter 3 Peach attempts to establish the following three propositions. First, Ricardo in his later writings continued to be concerned with demonstrating a downward trend in the rate of profit in consequence of diminishing agricultural returns. Second, the 'new view' passages in Ricardo's treatment of wages first pointed out by Edwin Cannan and more recently taken by Samuel Hollander, John Hicks, Carlo Casarosa and Giovanni Caravale to reflect Ricardo's mature or 'true view' cannot be reconciled with Ricardo's 'natural wage' doctrine and are incompatible with his view of the long-term movements of profitability. Third, Ricardo was a staunch advocate of the 'law of markets', which he believed to reflect real-world tendencies. In arguing the first proposition Peach takes the opportunity to refute Hollander's claim that Ricardo's case against the Corn Laws was not based upon the secular tendency of the profit rate to fall (cf. Hollander 1979: 604). As to the second proposition, it is conceded that there are in fact two conflicting treatments of wages in the *Principles*: first, Ricardo's 'natural wage' doctrine, which conceives the natural wage an effective attractor, or 'centre of gravitation', of market wages at any point in time; and, second, the 'new view' which suggests that the natural wage is a centre of gravitation in the diluted sense that market wages only tend towards it as the economy approaches the 'stationary state'. Peach confronts the reader with a large amount of evidence indicating that Ricardo was 'at no discernible time a fully committed new view theorist' and that even in his later writings, responding to Malthus's claim that a deceleration of the process of accumulation would exert a downward pressure on real wages, he states that 'his clear preference was for the treatment of real (commodity) wages as an analytical *datum* and not, contrary to the spirit of the new view analysis, as an endogenous variable' (p. 131; emphasis in the original).

It has been noted above that Peach's treatment of the 'law of markets' in Ricardo may be considered incomplete, since the machinery question is not dealt with. It is also not made sufficiently clear that Ricardo's attachment to this 'law' is *implied* by the view he had adopted from Adam Smith that any reduction in effective demand due to acts of saving can always be expected to be offset by an increase in effective demand due to corresponding acts of investment. (It can even be doubted that in the earlier authors there is a clear distinction between saving and investment.) I would not therefore talk of a 'creed' of Ricardo's (cf. p. 298). Since Malthus, too, shared this view, Ricardo was at a loss to understand the rational foundation of Malthus's doctrine of general 'gluts' of commodities and what the latter called the 'regulating principle' of profits. (I found the author's use of the term 'net saving' unfortunate: when he talks of 'aggregate net savings [being] zero' or of a 'no-saving "equilibrium"' (pp. 135–6), he apparently means a situation in which total savings, which need not be zero, equal total investment.)

The chapters on the labour theory of value expound in great detail the evolution of Ricardo's theorizing on value. Emphasis is on the role of the labour theory as a device to express the 'difficulty or facility of production' independently of general exchange relationships, an aspect already stressed by Sraffa. There are several issues with regard to which I believe the opinions or at least formulations entertained by Peach are difficult to sustain. The first concerns the problem of heterogeneous labour. Ricardo was perfectly aware of it and, as Peach points out, treated it essentially in the same way as Adam Smith, whose detailed analysis in chapter 10 of Book I of *The Wealth of Nations* Ricardo mentioned approvingly. Both in Smith and Ricardo quantities of different qualities of labour are aggregated via the relative wage rates of those different labours. However, in order to be consistent with the long-period method adopted by these authors, relative wages ought not to change too much with changes in the methods of production used (and changes in the overall level of the rate of profit). Ricardo endorsed explicitly Smith's analysis of wage differentials and the latter's attempt to show that the factors affecting these differentials can be assumed to change very little over time. Hence, whereas Ricardo's treatment of the problem may be called terse, this is no reason to contend, as Peach does, that 'neither here [i.e. in chapter 1 of the *Principles*], nor anywhere else in his writings, did Ricardo take the problem seriously' (p. 157). On the following page Peach, commenting on Ricardo's doctrine that changes in relative prices are governed by changes in relative labour costs, goes even a step further and maintains that 'Ricardo did not confine himself to such a limited interpretation of the labour theory. Having mentioned the "heterogeneous labour" problem, he proceeded as if it did not exist. He may therefore be read "as if" the assumption of homogeneous labour had been made.' I conjecture that if Peach were to apply the standards used by him to assess, for example, Sraffa's 'corn model' interpretation to this statement, he would have to recant it.

The second issue concerns the question of whether Ricardo 'determined the general rate of profit with reference to *social* aggregates . . . [or whether] the general rate of profits is calculated with reference to the distribution of produce obtained by a given amount of labour on the last (portion of) land cultivated: a "micro" determination' (p. 164 n.). It seems to be evident that a theory of value and distribution, concerned with the 'natural' levels of the respective variables obtaining in conditions of free competition, presupposes a *general* framework of the analysis. Indeed, without such a general framework, which has amongst its data the total amounts of the different commodities to be produced, it would be impossible to ascertain which of the different qualities of land will be cultivated and which quality will be 'marginal'. It would *a fortiori* also be impossible to know the labour values (or 'natural' prices) of the means of production entering the production of agricultural and manufactured products needed to 'calculate' the profit rate on the marginal land. Hence there is no 'micro', or rather partial, determination of distribution.

Finally there is Ricardo's problem of the 'invariable measure of value'. While Peach for perfectly good reasons refutes the idea put forward by some interpreters that Sraffa's 'Standard commodity' is 'the' solution to that problem, I found his discussion of this problem in Ricardo, Sraffa's interpretation of it and the latter's assessment of how the 'Standard commodity' relates to it unsatisfactory. As expounded in some detail in Kurz and Salvadori (1993), the main problem with Ricardo's search for an 'invariable measure of value' is that he tried to kill two birds with one stone. In his earlier writings he was exclusively concerned with a standard which would measure the value of commodities at different times and places, that is, he was interested in intertemporal and interspatial comparisons, or measurement with respect to *different* technical environments. To this was added later a concern with the altogether different problem of measurement with respect to the *same* technical environment, but changing distributions of income. As regards the 'Standard commodity', it can be shown that Sraffa saw only a single analytical purpose for it, i.e. to simplify the analysis of the effects of changes in the division of the product between wages and profits on prices. While he *relates* the 'Standard commodity' to the second part of Ricardo's search for an 'invariable measure', and only to it, there is no claim that his device provides a *solution* at least to this part.

Such a claim would indeed be unwarranted, unless by 'a given technical environment' we mean 'a given technique (or system of production)'. The cases in which the 'Standard commodity' may be used for interspatial or intertemporal comparisons are far too special to command greater attention.

Chapter 6 is devoted to an assessment of major attempts to locate Ricardo's work within an intellectual tradition. Peach refutes the opinion, entertained by Alfred Marshall and Samuel Hollander, that Ricardo can be absorbed within a 'utility' tradition of analysis, and Hollander's contention that in Ricardo we encounter a 'particularly sophisticated' treatment of demand. He is also highly critical of interpretations which depict Ricardo as a kind of 'early and rude' supply and demand theorist. On the 'Ricardo–Say–Walras tradition' invoked by Hollander he passes the verdict: 'purely fictitious' (p. 277). He considers the attempts by Hollander (1979) and Morishima (1989) to present Ricardo as a 'general equilibrium' theorist of sorts to be fundamentally mistaken. On Hollander's version he comments that it is nothing but 'wishful thinking, with the unreality of his vision further evidenced by "the entire set of final demand curves" which he thinks he can find in "Ricardian logic"' (p. 282). Morishima gets only slightly better marks: it is noted to his credit that 'at least he is clear what he means by general equilibrium' (p. 283). Both authors are chastised for relying, 'primarily, on what Ricardo *might* have done had he followed a line of reasoning supplied by them' (p. 286; emphasis in the original).

The final section in chapter 6 is devoted to 'Ricardo and Sraffa'. Initially Peach reports what he considers to be 'various salient features of Sraffa's own work' (p. 286). One of these is that, given the system of production in use and one of the distributive variables (the wage rate and the profit rate), 'prices are determined at a *secondary* stage in the analysis (*after* the determination of the unknown distributive variable)' (pp. 286–7; emphases in the original). This is a misconception. A central finding of Sraffa's analysis was precisely that the remaining distributive variable and relative prices can be determined only *simultaneously* and not successively. 'The result is', Sraffa stresses with regard to the case in which the real wage rate is given, 'that the distribution of the surplus [profits] must be determined through the same mechanism and at the same time as are the prices of commodities' (Sraffa 1960: 6). It is also not generally true that it is only the conditions of production of 'basic' commodities 'which are relevant to the determination of the general rate of profit' (p. 287); think of the case in which 'non-basics' enter the wage basket.

Next Peach turns to similarities and differences between the analyses of Sraffa and Ricardo. After further remarks on the 'corn model' and the 'Standard commodity' he deals with two additional issues. The first concerns the question whether, in approaching the problem of income distribution, Ricardo held constant, as is claimed by Sraffa and the 'Sraffians', all outputs and methods of production. Peach admits that there are passages in Ricardo's writings 'where Ricardo at least came close to exhibiting the approach adopted by Sraffa. But again,' he continues, 'the similarities with Sraffa's work evaporate when we turn to "the principal problem in Political Economy" [the long-term development of income distribution] . . . , in which the output and conditions of producing corn, in particular, were certainly *not* treated as given constants' (p. 291; emphasis in the original). Hence any attempt 'to saddle Ricardo with a *static* analysis of distribution' (p. 295; emphasis in the original) is ill-conceived. These observations are superficial and indeed incorrect. First, to determine the rate of profit and the rent(s) of land(s), given the real wage rate, presupposes *given* levels of output and given technical alternatives from which cost-minimizing producers can choose. In Ricardo these technical alternatives were defined with regard to the amounts of the different qualities of land available in the economy. Ricardo was also interested in investigating *changes* in distribution implied by *changes* in the levels of output, keeping the set of technical alternatives constant, that is, setting aside 'improvements' in the economy. So was Sraffa. It seems to have escaped Peach's attention that in his chapter XI, 'Land', Sraffa extends his analysis to cover the case of natural resources which are used in production and, if they are in short supply, enable their owners to obtain a rent. He indicates how a given system of production can be conceived 'as the outcome of a process of "extensive" . . . [or] "intensive" diminishing returns' (Sraffa 1960: 76). Sraffa points out that it is a characteristic feature of systems of production with scarce natural resources that 'the output may increase continuously, although the methods of production are changed spasmodically' (ibid.). This underscores the above statement that, in order to determine the shares of income other than wages and relative prices, the levels of output have to be taken as given.

The second issue concerns the role of supply and demand analysis in Ricardo and Sraffa, respectively. Peach sees reason to point out 'dissimilarities' between the two in that 'Ricardo, unlike Sraffa, did provide a supply and demand rationalisation for the convergence of market prices to natural prices (but not for the *level* of natural prices)' (p. 292; emphasis in the original). Sraffa, it will be remembered, in the preface of his book stressed that he had adopted the 'standpoint . . . of the old classical economists from Adam Smith to Ricardo' (Sraffa 1960: v). And later he pointed out with regard to the concept of price adopted in his analysis, 'Such classical terms as "necessary price", "natural price" or "price of production" would meet the case, but value and price have been preferred as being shorter and in the present context (which contains no reference to market prices) no more ambiguous' (ibid., p. 9). This should be enough to excuse him from the task of repeating everything he broadly agreed to in the writings of Smith and Ricardo.

Towards the end of the section Peach mentions, almost as an aside, that 'a more pronounced similarity [between the analyses of Sraffa and Ricardo] exists over the general treatment of distribution' (p. 292). It is indeed the *asymmetrical* treatment of the distributive variables – one given from outside, the other determined as a residual – which distinguishes the analyses of Ricardo and Sraffa sharply from neoclassical theory with its *symmetrical* treatment in terms of supply and demand. Compared with this similarity all other differences and dissimilarities, real and imagined, seem to count for little.

To conclude, Peach's book is instructive, interesting, provocative and often correct. It is strong on certain aspects of the intellectual evolution of Ricardo, pungent on the interpretations of Ricardo put forward by Hollander and Morishima, and weak on Sraffa, especially as regards the latter's book. I found Peach's attempt to refute elements of Sraffa's 'classic' interpretation of Ricardo on the whole unconvincing. It goes without saying that Peach's study is a must for all interested in Ricardo's and Ricardian economics.

REFERENCES

Hollander, S. (1979) *The Economics of David Ricardo*, London: Heinemann.

Kurz, H. D. and Salvadori, N. (1993) 'The "Standard commodity" and Ricardo's search for an "invariable measure of value"', in M. Baranzini and G. C. Harcourt (eds), *The Dynamics of the Wealth of Nations: Growth, Distribution and Structural Change, Essays in Honour of Luigi Pasinetti*. New York: St. Martin's Press, pp. 95–123.

Morishima, M. (1989) *Ricardo's Economics: a General Equilibrium Theory of Distribution and Growth*, Cambridge: Cambridge University Press.

Ricardo, D. (1951 *ssq.*) *The Works and Correspondence of David Ricardo*, 11 vols, ed. Piero Sraffa with the collaboration of M. H. Dobb, Cambridge: Cambridge University Press.

Sraffa, P. (1960) *Production of Commodities by Means of Commodities: Prelude to a Critique of Economic Theory*, Cambridge: Cambridge University Press.

Part III

ON THE LABOUR THEORY OF VALUE

10

KARL MARX ON PHYSIOCRACY

Christian Gehrke and Heinz D. Kurz

> How long is it since economy discarded the Physiocratic illusion, that rents grow out of the soil and not out of society?
>
> (Karl Marx, *Capital* I: 86)

François Quesnay was born in 1694. Two centuries later, in 1894, Friedrich Engels edited the third volume of Karl Marx's *Das Kapital*. This chapter commemorates the two events in terms of an investigation of Marx's reading of the physiocrats, in particular Quesnay, and the way he absorbed physiocratic concepts in his own analysis. The chapter is on Marx *on* physiocracy rather than on Marx *and* physiocracy. That is, our concern is first and foremost with what *Marx thought* the physiocrats had done or had aimed at doing and to what extent he benefited from what *he saw* in their works. With such a perspective it is of secondary importance whether his views on the physiocrats are faithful to their writings. (We shall, however, take the opportunity to comment on some problems of Marx's interpretation of the physiocrats). What matters is the productive use Marx made of the physiocratic doctrines *as he understood them*. It should be kept in mind that Marx, a foremost historian of economic thought, was not so much interested in the history of economic thought for its own sake. He rather conceived of a careful and critical study of earlier political economists as an indispensable task in the development of a coherent analysis of modern society. He entertained the view that he or she who wanted to promote economic analysis had to study the history of the subject as well as the history of the subject matter, that is, economic and social history.

The existence of a number of remarkable parallels and striking similarities between Marx's system of political economy and that of the physiocrats has often been noticed.[1] It has also been widely acknowledged that Marx was the first to point out the importance of the physiocrats' achievements in analysing the capitalist process of reproduction as a whole and that we owe to him the resurrection (and further development) of Quesnay's *Tableau économique* (see Samuelson 1982: 46). Marx's assessment of the physiocrats' approach to the explanation of value and distribution, on the other hand, has met with much less approval and was indeed criticized by several authors.[2]

The purpose of this chapter is to discuss what we consider to be the central elements of Marx's interpretation of the political economy of *les économistes* and to point out the analytical importance of certain physiocratic doctrines for the evolution of his own conceptualization of the process of production of capital. It will be argued that physiocratic ideas stood godfather to crucial elements of Marx's own system of economic thought. This is also the deeper reason why Marx showed so much admiration for the achievements of the physiocrats. In the course of tracing back major concepts used by Marx to the contributions of the French *secte* we shall also take the opportunity to question some received views on the relationship between the two.

Since we are predominantly interested in Marx's reception, transformation and eventual absorption of the ideas of the physiocrats in his own analysis, it is important to be clear about the sources he actually used. In order not to disrupt the main argument of the chapter this is done in the appendices. While appendix A provides a brief chronological account of Marx's studies of the physiocratic writings available to him, appendix B focuses attention on his attempts to come to grips with Quesnay's *Tableau économique*. The chronological account also throws some light on the question of lacunas and omissions in Marx's interpretation. Although there is reason to presume that the material available to us does not fully document Marx's discussion of physiocracy and the sources he used, the following can be said. From the very beginning of his studies in political economy he considered the physiocrats the 'true fathers' of that new scientific subject. Given the openly displayed admiration for their work, it comes as no surprise that he made several efforts to come to grips with their doctrines. In his view there was a direct lineage from their conception of the capitalist process of production via Adam Smith and David Ricardo to his: what they had begun and Smith and Ricardo had continued, Marx sought to complete.

The structure of the chapter is as follows. The next section deals with what Marx appears to have considered the essence of the physiocratic theory of income distribution, centred around the concept of the *produit net*, or surplus product. In addition, we shall discuss Marx's view that in the writings of the physiocrats we encounter elements of both a material-based and a labour-based approach to the theory of value. The following section (pp. 196–203) points out the importance of the *Tableau* in the development of Marx's schemes of simple and extended reproduction; the reader may want to read this section together with the summary statement of Marx's interpretation of the *Tableau* in appendix B. It is then shown in the subsequent section (pp. 203–6) that the *Tableau*'s conceptualization of the process of production and distribution in the economy as a whole played also a significant role in Marx's approach to the determination of the general rate of profit and prices of production. The final section contains some concluding observations.

THE CONCEPT OF SURPLUS AND THE PROBLEM OF VALUE AND DISTRIBUTION

As is well known, Marx was critical of most economists: few were in moderate and only a handful in high esteem with him. David Ricardo is perhaps the one author whom Marx respected most, notwithstanding Marx's many objections to Ricardo's analysis. Adam Smith, too, is variously credited for what he wrote, yet more often he is discredited for the same reason and also for what he did not write. The deeper reason why Marx was so critical of Smith was that in his view the Scotsman bore a large responsibility for the decline of classical political economy in the first half of the nineteenth century. The 'exoteric' parts of his analysis submerged the classical core of his theory of value and distribution. Unconsciously Smith thus lent authority to approaches to that theory which Marx dubbed 'vulgar'. The questions Marx put to himself were: Why and when did the story go wrong? Why did classical political economy gradually decay and finally fall into oblivion? What had to be done to resurrect that theory and develop its full potential? An answer to these questions necessitated, among other things, a careful investigation of Smith's doctrine and the doctrines of his precursors. In the course of his 'excavation' of the roots of classical political economy Marx arrived at the conclusion that 'The analysis of capital, within the bourgeois horizon, is essentially the work of the physiocrats. It is this service that makes them the true fathers of modern political economy' (*Theories of Surplus Value* (*TSV*) 1: 44). Hence a proper understanding of the contribution of the physiocrats was a major requirement in the task of reconstructing classical political economy. A clear perception of the merits and demerits of their analysis and the way it was received and absorbed in later contributions was at the same time seen to hold the key to an explanation of the decline of classical political economy.

Laws of production, real wages and surplus

According to Marx the linchpin of the classical approach to the theory of value and distribution is the concept of 'surplus product', that is, all shares of income other than wages, and its relationship to the real wage rate. Taking the methods of production employed and thus the productivity of labour and the length and intensity of the working day as given, the higher the real wage rate, the smaller is the surplus product, and vice versa. This idea constituted also the nucleus of the elaborate form of the classical argument in Ricardo, with its emphasis on the inverse relationship between the *rate of profit* on the one hand and the real wage rate or rather the total amount of labour needed to produce the wage commodities on the other.

In Marx's view the physiocrats, and especially Turgot, are to be credited with having anticipated the concept of surplus. They started from the assumption of 'a given productivity of labour' and took the day's labour 'to be a fixed quantity' (*TSV* 1: 49, 51). Most important, they recognized that the basis for the development of capitalist production was the emergence of a separate commodity, 'labour power', the *value* of which was ascertained in physical terms as the minimum amount of use-values or means of subsistence needed 'for the existence of the worker as a worker'. Marx expounded:

> The foundation of modern political economy, whose business is the analysis of capitalist production, is the conception of the *value of labour-power* as something fixed, as a given magnitude – as indeed it is in practice in each particular case. The *minimum of wages* therefore correctly forms the pivotal point of Physiocratic theory. They were able to establish this although they had not yet recognised the nature of value itself, because this *value of labour-power* is manifested in the price of the necessary means of subsistence, hence in a sum of definite use-values.
>
> (ibid.: 45; similarly, 50–1)

The fact that, in Marx's opinion, the physiocrats considered this minimum of wages – the 'pivotal point' of their theory – an unchangeable magnitude, 'determined by nature and not by the stage of historical development' (as, for example, in Smith, Ricardo and Marx himself), counts for little: 'this in no way affects the abstract correctness of their conclusions, since the difference between the value of labour-power and the value it creates does not at all depend on whether the value is assumed to be great or small' (ibid.). In other words, whether the real wage rate is high or low is relevant for the question of whether shares of income other than wages are low or high, but does not affect the truth of the statement that these shares exist if and only if there is a surplus product.

In order to develop the notion of surplus the physiocrats had to solve several problems. First, they had to come to grips with 'the various *material components* in which capital exists and into which it resolves itself in the course of the labour-process'. We owe to the physiocrats a clear distinction between the different forms which capital assumes, including the distinction between circulating and fixed capital, and a study of 'the connection between the process of circulation and the reproduction process of capital' (ibid.: 44). Secondly, we owe to the physiocrats the distinction between 'productive' and 'unproductive' labour: 'Quite correctly they lay down the fundamental principle that only that labour is *productive* which creates a *surplus-value*, in whose product therefore a higher value is contained than the sum of the values consumed during the production of this product' (ibid.: 46).[3] That is, the value of the product, p, must be larger than the value of raw materials, machinery, etc., used up, c (constant capital), plus the value of labour power, v (variable capital), which is taken to be equal to the minimum of wages, that is,

$$p > c + v$$

As regards the determination of value, Marx saw elements of two different, but not necessarily contradictory, theories in the physiocratic writings: a material-based and a labour-based determination of value. While the former is said to be characteristic of the earlier authors, the latter is particularly attributed to Turgot. We shall come back to this question in the following sub-section. Here it is to be pointed out that Marx was aware of the fact that in the physiocrats an explanation of income distribution in terms of the surplus product did *not* require a labour-based concept of value, indeed, it seemed, any concept of value at all. The physiocrats, Marx argued, could do without such a concept because of their 'general view of the nature of value, which to them is not a definite social mode of existence of human activity (labour), but consists of material things – land, nature, and the various modifications of these material things' (ibid.: 46). In their system, the generation of surplus can be *directly* seen. It

> appears most palpably, most incontrovertibly, of all *branches of production*, in *agriculture*, the primary branch of production . . . . In agriculture it shows itself directly in the surplus of use-values produced over use-values consumed by the labourer, and can therefore be grasped without an analysis of value in general, without a clear understanding of the nature of value.
>
> (ibid.: 46; similarly, 51 and *TSV* 3: 115–16)

In contradistinction, in manufacture, where 'the workman is not generally seen directly producing either his means of subsistence or the surplus in excess of his means of subsistence', the analysis of value is indispensable for an understanding of the generation of surplus (*TSV* 1: 46; similarly, 51 and *TSV* 3: 115–16).

This reasoning would only be correct if agriculture produced (and *re*produced) all products that are needed in agriculture as means of production or as means of subsistence in support of the agricultural labourers, that is, if agriculture were totally independent of the manufacturing sector as a supplier of capital goods or necessaries. This is, of course, not generally true and it is not even true with regard to the physiocratic system as represented by the *Tableau économique* (see Appendix B).[4] Marx was perfectly aware of this. However, he thought that such an abstraction was or at any rate should have been at the back of their minds: in accordance with their attempt to locate the genesis of the surplus in the sphere of production rather than in the sphere of circulation the physiocrats 'necessarily begin . . . with that branch of production which *can be thought of in complete separation from and independently of circulation, of exchange*; and which presupposes exchange not between man and man but only between man and nature' (ibid.: 49, emphasis added; similarly, 50).[5] It was 'the great and specific contribution of the Physiocrats' that they engaged in these kinds of abstraction, that they *thought* of agriculture as a branch in which the self-same commodity and only it figures both as input and output. The importance of this abstraction can hardly be exaggerated since, in Marx's view, it formed the starting point of classical political economy.[6]

There is a second reason why the need to develop a theory of value was felt less strongly, and consequently was given less prominence in their analytical edifice, by the physiocrats relative to their classical successors. With some notable exceptions, especially Turgot, the physiocrats knew essentially only one type of non-wage income. For them

> agricultural labour is the only *productive labour*, because it is the only labour that *produces a surplus-value*, and *rent* is the *only form of surplus-value* which they know . . . . *Profit* on capital in the true sense, of which rent itself is only an offshoot, therefore does not exist for the Physiocrats. Profit is seen by them as only a kind of higher wages paid by the landowners, which the capitalists consume as revenue.
>
> (ibid.: 46–7)

Since they had no concept of profit they also had no concept of the general *rate of profit*, that is, the relationship, in physical terms, between two bundles of heterogeneous goods: the social surplus exclusive of the rent of land and the capital employed in production. Had the physiocrats developed the concept of the *rate* of profit, they of necessity would have had to face 'the question of valuation' in order to render commensurable the two bundles. By identifying the social surplus with the rent of land they evaded a major problem the classical economists were concerned with.

Material-based and labour-based concepts of value

While the need to develop a theory of value was not felt with the same urgency as in later authors, the physiocrats saw, of course, that in a system characterized by a division of labour, private property, etc., agricultural and manufactured products had to circulate as *commodities*. And Marx was aware of at least some of their attempts to tackle the problem of value.[7] He was clear about the fact that his depiction of 'agriculture' as a sphere of production which is independent of exchange involved some bold abstraction. He justified it in the interest of bringing out what he thought was the essence of the physiocratic doctrine. However, useful as it may have been in order to illustrate the principle of surplus generation in pure and simple terms, the abstraction contradicted an indisputable fact of life: the heterogeneity of commodities. How did the physiocrats cope with this problem and did it affect the basic structure of their approach? Broadly speaking, Marx discerned elements of two explanations of value in physiocratic authors: a *material*-based one and a *labour*-based one.[8] According to Marx both explanations are, in principle, in perfect harmony with the explanation of non-wage incomes in terms of a surplus product. However, the former is said to meet with serious difficulties and therefore cannot be sustained. The labour-based theory of value is taken to belong predominantly to Turgot, who is credited with having provided 'a deeper analysis of capitalist relations' (*TSV* 1: 54).

It is a characteristic feature of the *material-based* explanations that the exchange values of primary products, on which attention focused, were somehow taken to be given, springing *directly* from the conditions of production. Indeed, Marx attributed to the physiocrats the idea that the different products, containing different *concrete* materials such as specified qualities of corn, iron, coal and wood, can be reduced to some common denomination: material *in genere*, or, to apply an adjective that played an important role in Marx's own theory of value, *abstract* material. He wrote:

> Their error was that they confused the *increase of material substance*, which because of the natural processes of vegetation and generation distinguishes agriculture and stock-raising from manufacture, with the *increase of exchange-value*. Use-value was their starting point. *And the use-value of all commodities, reduced, as the scholastics say, to a universal, was the material substance of nature as such, whose increase in the same form occurs only in agriculture.*
>
> (ibid.: 62–3; the last emphasis is ours)

While Marx was critical of this approach to the problem of value, interestingly his criticism was moderate. The underlying idea of *tertium comparationes* was not dismissed by him as an old-fashioned and wrong idea of Aristotelian descent which ought to be exorcized from economic reasoning. On the contrary, in chapter I, 'Commodities', of volume I of *Capital*, Marx himself was to rely on this idea. His investigation there can be interpreted, *inter alia*, as echoing his discussion of the material-based view of value of the physiocrats. As is well known, his search for a 'common factor' of commodities led him to conclude:

> This common 'something' cannot be either a geometrical, a chemical, *or any other natural property of commodities*. Such properties claim our attention only in so far as they affect the utility of those commodities,

> make them *use-values*. But the exchange of commodities is evidently an act characterised by a total abstraction from use-value.
>
> (*Capital* I: 45; emphases added)

The *tertium comparationes*, we are told, is *abstract* human labour.[9]

Marx's discussion of elements of a *labour-based* reasoning in the physiocrats is concentrated in sections 2 and 3 of chapter II of *TSV* 1. His main message is well captured in the title of section 2: 'Contradictions in the system of the physiocrats: the feudal shell of the system and its bourgeois essence: the twofold treatment of surplus-value'. Marx's argument proceeds in two steps. He first tries to establish that the physiocratic attempt to explain the rent of land in terms of a 'free gift of nature' is inherently contradictory. Scrutinizing carefully the texts of Quesnay, Mirabeau and especially Turgot shows that any surplus product is finally to be traced back to agricultural surplus labour, that is, it has its origin not in the productivity of land, or nature, but in the 'productivity' of the agricultural labourer who produces more than he gets in the form of wages. In a second step Marx attempts to show that it is not only labour employed in agriculture which is productive in the sense specified, but also labour employed in the manufacturing sector.

Marx stresses that

> The first condition for the development of capital is the separation of landed property from labour – the emergence of land, the primary conditions of labour, as an independent force, a force in the hands of a separate class, confronting the free labourer. Feudalism is thus portrayed and explained from the viewpoint of bourgeois production.
>
> (*TSV* 1: 50)

The crucial historical precondition of the development of the physiocratic doctrine is thus seen to be the emergence of wage labour, with the labourer owning nothing but his labour power and with the wage rate fixed on some minimum level, 'the *strict nécessaire*' (ibid.: 51).

The contradictions in the economic doctrine of the physiocrats are said to be clearly seen in their advocacy of *La Grande Culture*, in Marx's terms: 'large-scale capitalist agriculture'. Commenting on some passage in Quesnay's *Maximes générales du gouvernement économique d'un royaume agricole*, Marx expounds that there

> Quesnay admits that the increased productivity of agricultural labour accrues to the 'net revenue', and therefore in the first place to the landowner, i.e. the owner of surplus-value, and that the relative increase of the latter arises not from the land but from the social and other arrangements for raising the productivity of labour.
>
> (ibid.: 65)

However, Marx claims, it is only with Anne Robert Jacques Turgot that 'the Physiocratic system is presented as the new capitalist society prevailing within the framework of feudal society. This therefore corresponds to bourgeois society in the epoch when the latter breaks its way out of feudal society.' With Turgot the 'illusion disappears completely' that agriculture is the branch in which 'capitalist production – that is, the production of surplus-value – exlusively appears' (ibid.: 50). Hence it is to Turgot's writings, in particular his *Réflexions sur la formation et la distribution des richesses*, written in 1766 but not published till 1769–70 in serial form in the *Ephémérides*, that one has to turn in order to see the good harvest which grew by necessity out of the good seed sown by Dr Quesnay and his followers. This is what Marx does in section 3 of the chapter on 'The Physiocrats'.

The good harvest referred to was of course, in Marx's perspective, the gradual emergence of a labour-based theory of value which complemented the older material-based conception. This development is insolubly intertwined with – and is indeed only another expression of – the shift from the notion of social surplus as a *pur don de la nature* to the notion of surplus as the product of surplus labour, *unpaid labour*:

> [With] Turgot [the physiocratic system is] most fully developed. In some passages in his writings the pure gift of nature is presented as surplus-labour, and on the other hand the necessity for the labourer to yield up what there is in excess of his necessary wage [is explained] by the separation of the labourer from the conditions of labour, and their confronting him as the property of a class which uses them to trade with.
>
> (ibid.: 54)

Marx puts forward some evidence from the *Réflexions* that 'this pure gift of nature becomes imperceptibly transformed into the surplus-labour of the labourer which the landowner has not bought, but which he sells in the products of agriculture' (ibid.: 55). Marx quotes approvingly, and italicizes, Turgot's observation that '*The proprietor has nothing except through the labour of the cultivator*' and adds, in brackets: 'therefore not through a pure gift of nature' (ibid.: 57). Hence in Turgot the surplus approach to the theory of value and distribution is at the crossroads. There is a clear perception that the surplus product is due to surplus labour and yet the 'productivity' of agricultural labour is explained in terms of a material-based reasoning: nature is taken to 'give back' to the agricultural labourer more 'material' than is 'used up' by him (as food, seed, etc.)

We may conclude that in Marx's view the theory of value is *instrumental* to an explanation of the sharing out of the product amongst the different classes of society. If the physiocrats had succeeded in elaborating a satisfactory explanation of the exchange ratios of commodities based on real physical costs of production in terms of some use-value *in genere*, it may be conjectured that Marx would have accepted it. He rejected the physiocratic material-based view because of its failure to perform that instrumental role. To Marx the labour theory of value was not fundamental in the sense that it was considered 'true' *independently* of whether it served the purpose of providing a logically coherent foundation of the theory of income distribution. Marx endorsed the labour theory of value precisely because he was convinced that it would offer that foundation, that is, allow one to elaborate a logically unassailable theory of the general rate of profit. He held the physiocrats in high esteem also because it was another achievement of theirs which he thought had paved the way to the development of such a theory. The achievement under consideration is the *Tableau économique*.

MARX'S SCHEMES OF REPRODUCTION AND THE *TABLEAU ÉCONOMIQUE*

Marx on the significance of the *Tableau*

Marx was full of praise for the *Tableau* ever after he had carefully studied it in 1862–3 (see also Appendix B). In the section 'Significance of the Tableau Économique in the history of political economy' in volume 1 of *Theories of Surplus Value* he calls it 'an extremely brilliant conception, incontestably the most brilliant for which political economy has up to then been responsible' (*TSV* 1: 344; similarly in *MEGA* I.27 (Text): 214). Marx explains:

> In fact it was an attempt to portray the whole production process of capital as a *process of reproduction*, with circulation merely as the form of this reproductive process; and the circulation of money only as a phase in the circulation of capital; at the same time to include in this reproductive process the origin of revenue, the exchange between capital and revenue, the relation between reproductive consumption and final consumption; and to include in the circulation of capital the circulation between consumers and producers (in fact between capital and revenue); and finally to present the circulation between the two great divisions of productive labour – raw material production and manufacture – as phases of this reproductive process; and all this depicted in a *Tableau* which in fact consists of no more than five lines which link together six points of departure or return.
>
> (*TSV* 1: 344)

In Marx's view the *Tableau* had been unduly neglected by the British political economists, so that an important achievement of economic analysis had been lost sight of for almost an entire century. Adam Smith, Marx claims,

> in fact only took over the inheritance of the Physiocrats and classified and specified more precisely the separate items in the inventory. But his exposition and interpretation of the movement as a whole was hardly as correct as its presentation in outline in the Tableau économique, in spite of Quesnay's false assumptions.
>
> (ibid.)

Marx's appreciation of the physiocrats permeates also his later works. The importance of the *Tableau* is emphasized, for example, in chapter XIX of volume II of *Capital*: 'Quesnay's *Tableau Économique* shows in a few broad outlines how the annual result of the nation production, representing a definite value, is distributed by means of circulation in such a way that, other things being equal, simple reproduction, i.e., reproduction on the same scale, can take place' (*C* II: 363). Marx credits Quesnay with developing the *Tableau* in terms of 'great functionally determined economic classes of society' and with striking upon 'the main thing, thanks to the limitation of his horizon, within which agriculture is the only sphere of investment of human labour producing surplus-value, hence the only really productive one from the capitalist point of view.' It is a characteristic feature of agriculture that in it the economic process of reproduction, 'whatever may be its special social character, always becomes intertwined . . . with a natural process of reproduction. The obvious conditions of the latter throw light on those of the former, and keep off a confusion of thought which is called forth by the mirage of circulation' (ibid.).

Marx calls the system of the physiocrats 'the first systematic conception of capitalistic production' (ibid.: 363; similarly, *C* I: 554). This judgement is justified as follows: 'The representative of industrial capital – the class of tenants – directs the entire economic movement. Agriculture is carried on capitalistically, that is to say, it is the enterprise of a capitalist farmer on a large scale; the direct cultivator of the soil is the wage-labourer.' Marx then turns to the problem of the generation and appropriation of a social surplus: 'Production creates not only articles of use but also their value; its compelling motive is to the procurement of surplus-value, whose birth-place is the sphere of production, not of circulation' (*C* II: 364). As to the roles performed by the classes other than the class of workers in this 'social process of reproduction' he writes: 'the immediate exploiter of productive labour, the producer of surplus-value, the capitalist farmer, is distinguished from those who merely appropriate the surplus value' (ibid.).

The schemes of reproduction

Quesnay's *Tableau* was the foil against which Marx developed his own schemes of reproduction (see, in particular, *C* II: Part III). The schemes are concerned with the distribution of labour amongst the different sectors of the economy. That distribution was envisaged by Marx to depend on the socially dominant techniques of production, the distribution of income between wages and profits, and the expenditures out of these incomes, especially whether or not parts of profits are saved and invested, that is, accumulated. Hence the schemes were essentially an attempt to come to grips with the *quantity* system of the economy under consideration. In principle the quantity system could be studied without any recourse to the problem of valuation. However, Marx chose to provide both a description of the requirements of (simple or extended) reproduction in physical terms, that is, with reference to use values, and in value terms, that is, with reference to labour values. (In addition he was concerned with the problem of money circulation.) Thus he intended to show that the physical reproduction of capital and its value reproduction are two aspects of the same thing, two sides of a single coin. However, Marx was aware of the fact that what matters as regards the value aspect of capital reproduction was that the single items constituting social capital fetched 'prices of production' and not labour values, that is, prices including the normal rate of profit on the capital advanced in each line of production. His explicit assumption that commodities are exchanged according to labour values was considered a legitimate device to simplify a piece of analysis in which the problem of value and distribution played at best a side role.[10] Yet once Marx turned to a proper discussion of that problem the device had to be abandoned because it contradicted the idea that in conditions of free competition a tendency towards the establishment of a uniform rate of profit would make itself felt. Interestingly, Marx entertained the view that the scheme of reproduction, or quantity system of the economy, provided also the framework within which a theory of 'prices of production' could be developed (see, in particular, *C* III: Part II). In this section we shall deal with the quantity aspect and in the next one with the price aspect.

An early version of the scheme of simple reproduction was elaborated in Marx's letter to Engels of 6 July 1863.[11] He wrote to Engels, 'If it is possible in this heat, please look carefully at the enclosed "*Tableau Économique*" which I have put in the place of Quesnay's Tab[leau] and let me know any deliberations [*Bedenken*] you may have. It encompasses the entire process of reproduction' (*MEW* 30: 362). The scheme (including the handwritten version of it by Marx) is given in Figure 10.1. The importance Marx attributed to, and the inspiration he derived from, Quesnay's *Tableau* is also reflected in the fact that he reproduced the latter underneath his alternative construction.

Marx divides the economy into two 'classes' or 'categories': class I represents the production of the means of subsistence, class II that of the means of production, that is, commodities 'which enter as raw materials, machinery etc. in the process of production'; the latter commodities 'form the *constant capital*' (*MEW* 30: 363). (In volume II of *Capital* the number-

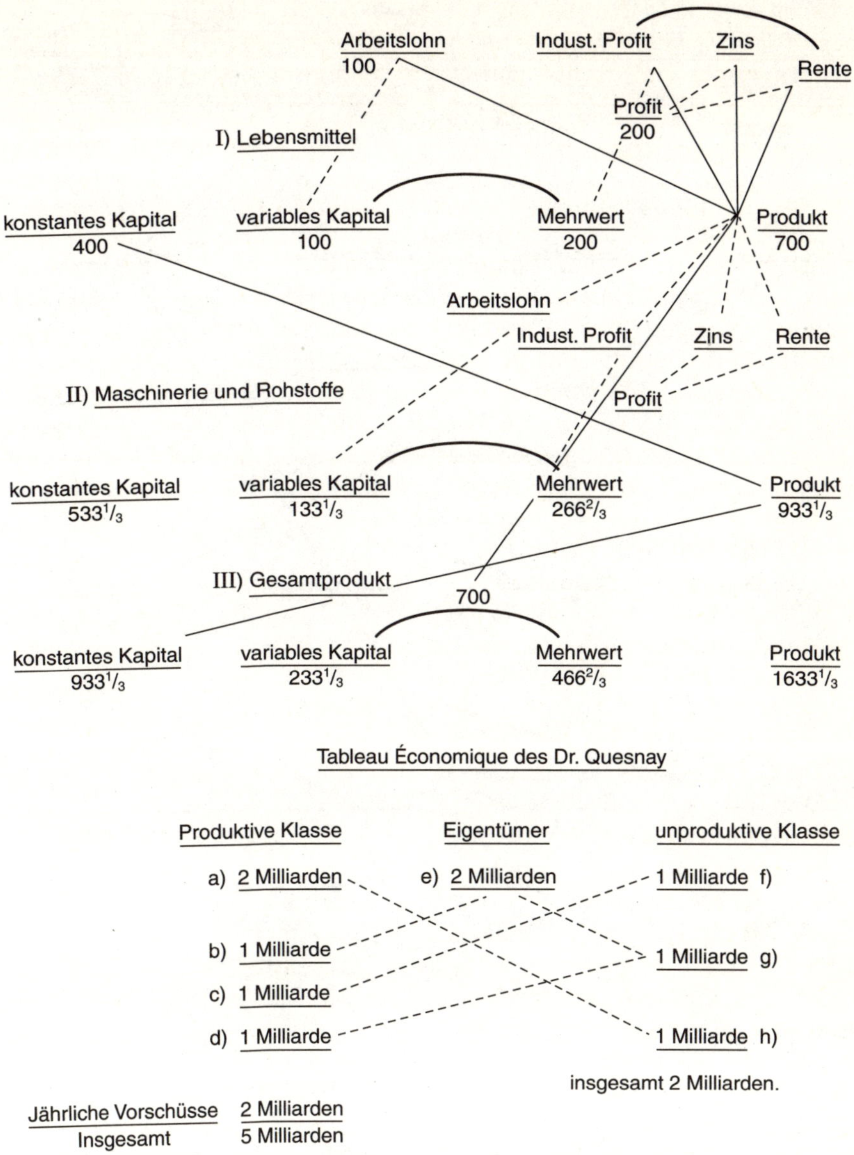

Figure 10.1(a) The scheme of simple reproduction.

ing of departments is reversed.) Marx emphasizes that the two classes or departments represent productive *aggregates* in a special sense.[12] This becomes clear with regard to agriculture, in which 'a part of the same products (e.g. corn) forms means of subsistence, whereas another part (e.g. corn) enters again as a raw material in its natural form (e.g. as *seeds*) into

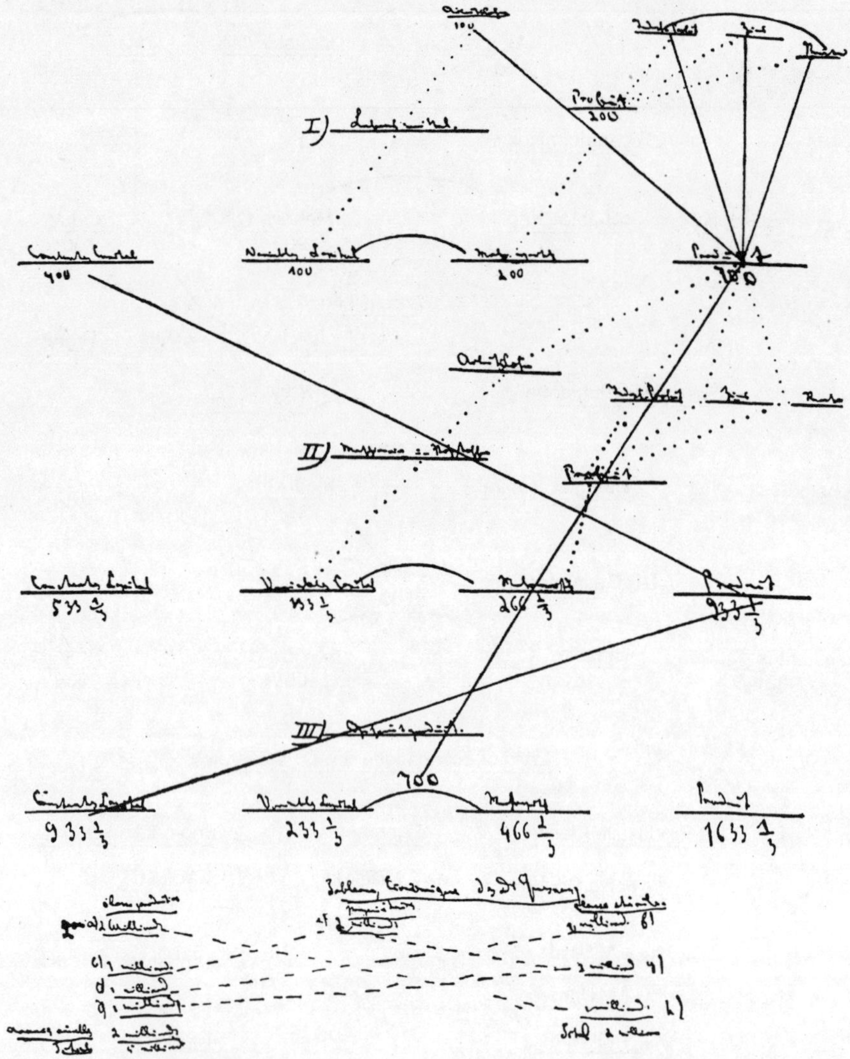

Figure 10.1(b) Marx's handwritten version.

the reproduction. This does not change things, since according to one characteristic these branches of production belong in class II and according to the other in class I' (ibid.). The broken lines indicate payments by industrial capitalists to workers (wages), monied men (interest) and landlords (rent), the solid lines expenditures by the different income recipients on means of consumption and means of production.

The numerical example of Figure 1 can be rewritten in a form which became prominent with volume II of *Capital* (*C* II: chapter XX), i.e.

class I: $700 = 400_c + 100_v + 200_s$
class II: $933\frac{1}{3} = 533\frac{1}{3}{}_c + 133\frac{1}{3}{}_v + 266\frac{2}{3}{}_s$

where the subscripts *c*, *v*, and *s* stand for 'constant capital', 'variable capital' and 'surplus value', respectively. Simple reproduction requires that the constant capitals used up in both sectors ($400_c + 533\frac{1}{3}{}_c$) are equal to the total product of class II ($933\frac{1}{3}$); and that the variable capitals, or wage bills ($100_v + 133\frac{1}{3}{}_v$),[13] plus the surplus values, or profits ($200_s + 266\frac{2}{3}{}_s$), of the whole system are equal to the total product of class I (700). Accordingly, simple reproduction involves (using again the notation employed in volume II of *Capital*)

$$\text{I}\ (400_c) = \text{II}\ (133\tfrac{1}{3}{}_v + 266\tfrac{2}{3}{}_s)$$

Marx stresses that the constant capitals include only '*that* part of working material which enters the yearly product as *dechet* [wear and tear]; the non-consumed part of machinery etc. does *not* figure in the table'. He also points out that as regards the ratio of variable capital to surplus value 'it is assumed that the worker works $\frac{1}{3}$ of the working day for himself and $\frac{2}{3}$ for his natural superiors'. Hence, the rate of surplus value in both classes is taken to be 200 per cent. In addition it is assumed that the entire surplus value is realized as profit, which in turn is taken to split up 'in *industrial profit* (including the *commercial* one), then *interest*, which the industrial capitalist pays in money, and rent, which he also pays in money' (ibid.: 363–4). With simple reproduction all the money paid for industrial profit, interest and rent is 'unproductively used' (*C* II: 401), that is, spent on consumption goods, and thus flows back to the capitalists in class I.

While the capitalists in class I can realize their revenue in terms of the products produced in that class, this is not so with regard to the capitalists in class II: they have to buy consumption goods from class I. Conversely, while the capitalists in class II can replace the used-up parts of their constant capital in terms of the products produced in that class, this is not so with regard to the capitalists in class I: they have to buy investment or capital goods from class II. The total effective demand for products of class I coming from agents (capitalists and workers) in class II amounts to ($133\frac{1}{3}{}_v + 266\frac{2}{3}{}_s$), whereas the total effective demand for products of class II coming from agents (capitalists) of class I amounts to (400_c): the *inter-sectoral* exchange is *balanced*. 'The movement partly within category I, partly between categories I and II, shows at the same time how the money with which they pay anew the wages of labour, interest and ground rent flows to the respective industrial capitalists in both categories' (ibid.: 364). In 'category III' Marx also gives the aggregate figures for the economy as a whole.

In contrast to Quesnay's *Tableau*, here the labour performed in both sectors is taken to be productive, that is, generating a surplus value which is appropriated by the industrial capitalists and then shared out between themselves, the financial capitalists and the landowners.[14] The criteria according to which total surplus value is split up into industrial (and commercial) profit, interest and rent are not expounded in Marx's letter. Emphasis is on what Marx considered to be the crucial point: *all* kinds of non-wage incomes, whether profit, interest or rent, have a common source – '*unpaid surplus labour*'. It is labour applied capitalistically, not nature, which generates a surplus. It is also assumed that commodities exchange according to the quantities of labour needed (directly and indirectly) in their production, that is, the labour theory of value holds as a theory of relative prices. Since the 'organic composition of capital' differs between the two sectors, with a uniform rate of surplus value the sectoral rates of profit are necessarily unequal. (As Samuelson (1974: 271) has emphasized, Marx assumed equal organic composition of capital in his analysis of 'simple reproduction' in volume II of *Capital*.)

Both Quesnay's *Tableau*, as seen by Marx, and Marx's own scheme of reproduction share the following features. First, they start from the same set of data: the system of production in use, defined in terms of (i) the (average) methods of production employed to produce (ii) given levels of (aggregate) output; and (iii) a given real wage rate. Second, all shares of income other than wages are explained in terms of the surplus product (representing a certain surplus value), or residual, left after the means of subsistence in the support of labourers, and what is necessary for the replacement of the used-up means of production have been deducted from the annual output. Hence the distributive variables are treated *asymmetrically*: the wage rate is taken to be an *exogenous* variable, whereas the (rate of) rent in the case of Quesnay and the rate of profit (and also the interest and rent rates) in the case of Marx are *endogenous* variables.[15] Third, and closely related to what has just been said, both the physiocrats and Marx conceive of any surplus product that may exist as *generated* in the sphere of production and *realized* only in the sphere of circulation (cf. also *TSV* 1: 45). Fourth, it is assumed in both representations that the process of circulation works out smoothly. This involves, *inter alia*, the existence of a system of *relative* prices which support the process of reproduction (see also the following section), and a system of *absolute* prices compatible with the stock of money available in the system and the going habits of payment. Fifth, both schemes distinguish between fixed and circulating capital, where both kinds of capital relate to productive capital only. Exclusively those parts of capital which are used up during the process of production and have to be replaced periodically are taken into account in the tables. This presupposes that the stocks of durable means of production employed in the different sectors, their modes of utilization and thus their patterns of wear and tear (and therefore depreciation) are known. Sixth, in both versions reference is to some 'normal' levels of output, defined in terms of some average of the conditions of production over a sequence of years.

While in the *Tableau* the problem of accumulation of capital is set aside, it is well known that Quesnay was concerned with the sources of economic growth and stressed the role of accumulation.[16] In Marx the problem of balanced growth of the two departments in the absence of technological change is dealt with in his schemes of extended reproduction (cf. *C* II: Chapter XXI) which provide a theory of the relationship between quantities, or sectoral proportions, and the rate of growth of the economic system as a whole.

PRICES OF PRODUCTION

After having studied Ricardo's labour-based approach to the theory of value and profits Marx felt the need to go back once more to the physiocrats and particularly the *Tableau* and investigate the implications of that approach within a *general* framework of the analysis.[17] He hoped within that framework to be able to consistently determine the general rate of profit. While Ricardo deserved the credit for having had a clear view of the inverse relationship between the rate of profit and the real wage rate, he had failed to show how the level of the rate of profit was actually ascertained, given the real wage rate.[18] Marx saw that the data on which Ricardo's argument was based were essentially the same as the data (i)–(iii) underlying the *Tableau*. There was a single important difference between the physiocratic and the classical scheme: the rule according to which the social surplus is distributed – as rent in the case of the physiocrats, and as rent and profits in the case of the classical economists from Smith to Ricardo. It was indeed the determination of the general rate of profit which became a major focus of classical analysis.[19] The question was close at hand whether Ricardo's labour-based approach could be integrated with an appropriately modified *Tableau*. This reformulation had to leave the basic structure of the approach defined in terms of the *exogenous variables*, or givens, untouched. Marx's theory of the general rate of profit and prices of production in Part II of volume III of *Capital* can indeed be interpreted as an amalgamation and elaboration of insights Marx owed first and foremost to the physiocrats, Smith and Ricardo. There the problem of the rent of land is set aside altogether. The entire surplus is assumed to accrue in the form of profits, which, in conditions of free competition, are distributed at a uniform rate on the capitals invested in the different sectors of the economy. In chapter X of that part, 'Equalisation of the general rate of profit through competition', Marx informs the reader about his sources and also about what he intends to achieve beyond the contributions of his precursors:

> The price of production includes the average profit. We call it price of production. It is really what Adam Smith calls *natural price*, Ricardo calls *price of production*, or *cost of production*, and the physiocrats call *prix nécessaire*, because in the long run it is a prerequisite of supply, of the production of commodities in every individual sphere.

He adds, 'But none of them has revealed the difference between price of production and value' (*C* III: 198). It was precisely this problem Marx took pride in having solved: 'this intrinsic connection is here revealed for the first time' (ibid.: 168). The solution consisted of a combination of Ricardo's labour-based valuation of commodities and a modified version of the physiocratic description of the system of production of the economy as a whole.

A brief summary statement of Marx's analysis must suffice. He makes it clear that a determination of the general rate of profit and relative prices presupposes a *general* framework of the analysis, taking into account the 'total social capital' and its distribution in the different 'spheres of production' (ibid.: 158, 163). Marx's two-step procedure was aptly dubbed 'successivist' (as opposed to 'simultaneous') by Ladislaus von Bortkiewicz (1906–7: 38). In a first step he specifies the general rate of profit as the ratio between the (labour) value of the economy's surplus product, or 'surplus value', and the (labour) value of social capital, consisting of a 'constant capital' (means of production) and a 'variable capital' (wages). In a second step the (value) rate of profit is then used to calculate prices. We may illustrate his procedure as follows. Marx starts from a description of the economic system divided into several sectors or spheres of production, each of which is represented by an equation giving the value of the sectoral output (λ_i) as the sum of the sectoral constant capital (c_i), its variable capital (v_i) and the surplus value (s_i) generated in the sector (cf. *C* III: chapter IX). This description involves, of course, given methods of production in the sectors and a given real wage rate. Otherwise it would be impossible to derive the labour-value magnitudes. With a given and uniform real wage rate and a given and uniform length of the working day (reflecting, *inter alia*, free competition in the labour market), the rate of surplus value is uniform across sectors. The larger the real wage rate, the larger is the variable capital and the smaller is the sectoral surplus value. Assuming only two sectors in order to facilitate a comparison with the *Tableau*, and setting aside the problem of fixed capital, we have

$$\lambda_I = c_I + v_I + s_I \tag{1.1}$$

$$\lambda_{II} = c_{II} + v_{II} + s_{II} \tag{1.2}$$

where sector I produces means of production and sector II means of subsistence. It is Marx's contention that from this system *alone*, reflecting the set of data specified above, both the general rate of profit and prices of production can be determined.[20] Setting aside the problem of fixed capital, the rate of profit, ρ, is taken to be determined by the following equation:

$$\rho = \frac{s_I + s_{II}}{c_I + v_I + c_{II} + v_{II}} = \frac{\Sigma_i s_i}{\Sigma_i (c_i + v_i)} \qquad (2)$$

In Marx's view it is here that the labour theory of value is indispensable, because it allegedly allows the determination of the rate of profit *independently of, and prior to*, the determination of relative prices.

In a second step this 'value' rate of profit, ρ, is then used to discount forward sectoral costs of production, or 'cost prices', measured in terms of labour values (cf. ibid.: 164). This is the (in)famous problem of the 'Transformation of values of commodities into prices of production' (*C* III: Part II). With p_i as the value-price transformation coefficient applied to the product of department i, i = I, II, we have, following Marx's procedure,

$$\lambda_I p_I = (1 + \rho)(c_I + v_I) \qquad (3.1)$$

$$\lambda_{II} p_{II} = (1 + \rho)(c_{II} + v_{II}) \qquad (3.2)$$

Counting the number of equations and that of the unknowns, there are two equations with two unknowns: the value-price transformation coefficients p_I and p_{II}. Hence the 'prices of production' seem to be fully determined.[21]

Here there is no need to enter into a detailed discussion of why Marx's 'successivist' procedure to determine the general rate of profit and relative prices cannot be sustained. A few critical remarks must suffice (see also Garegnani 1987). A first and obvious error concerns the fact that in the above price equations (3.1–2) the constant and variable capitals ought to be expressed in price terms rather than in value terms. Marx was aware of this slip in his argument (cf. *C* III: 164–5, 206–7), but apparently he was convinced that it could easily be remedied. Reckoning the two kinds of capital advances in price terms would not, he thought, contradict the labour-based determination of the general rate of profit in equation (2). It is basically this conviction that made him rely on the labour theory of value. The latter was taken to provide a coherent foundation of the theory of distribution, that is, was seen to allow a logically consistent determination of the key variable of the capitalist economy: the general rate of profit. Had Marx seen that the labour-based theory of value failed to perform the instrumental role it was devised for, he would have had to reject it as he rejected the physiocrats' material-based view of value.

Wherein consists the flaw of Marx's argument? Once the necessary corrections suggested by Marx himself are carried out, that is, the two types of capital advances are expressed in price terms, it becomes clear that it cannot generally be presumed that the 'transformation' of values into prices of production is relevant with regard to single commodities only, while it is irrelevant with regard to commodity aggregates, such as the surplus product or the social capital, the ratio of which gives the rate of profit. In other words, it cannot generally be excluded that the assumed '*re*distribution' of the surplus value involves a deviation of the price expressions of the surplus product and the social capital from their value expressions in the same way as it involves a deviation of the prices of single commodities from their values. Hence there is no presumption that the 'price' rate of profit equals the 'value' rate of profit, ρ. Marx's equation (2) cannot, therefore, be correct in general. Since the rate of profit cannot be determined before knowing the prices of commodities, and since the prices cannot be determined before knowing the rate of profit, the rate of profit and prices have to be determined *simultaneously* rather than successively.

Does Marx's blunder also falsify his intuition that starting from the set of data (i)–(iii), which he had discerned in the *Tableau* and Ricardo, relative prices and the rate of profit can be determined in a logically coherent way, assuming a capitalist economy in which the problem of the rent of land is set aside? The answer is no. This has been shown, explicitly or implicitly, within various analytical frameworks which differ in terms of generality by authors such as Vladimir K. Dmitriev, Ladislaus von Bortkiewicz, Georg von Charasoff, Wassily Leontief, John von Neumann and Piero Sraffa (cf. Kurz and Salvadori 1995: chapter 13).

We may summarize our findings as follows. Marx was convinced that the determination of the rate of profit and relative prices could be approached only in a *general* framework of the analysis, allowing for the interdependences of the different spheres of production in the economy. He thought he could accomplish this task in terms of a *set of data* which he had encountered, or so he thought, at least *in nuce*, in the *Tableau économique*. These data would be sufficient to determine the labour values of the different commodities and, given the real wage rate, also the aggregate magnitudes of 'surplus value', 'variable capital' and 'constant capital', and thus the general rate of profit. With the latter as a known magnitude, prices of production could be calculated.

CONCLUSION

We have seen how much Marx owed to the physiocrats for the development of his own views on the laws of production, distribution and circulation governing a capitalist economy. This is the deeper reason why Marx spoke so respectfully of Dr Quesnay and the physiocrats. After all, *les économistes* were amongst the true forerunners of his own analysis, which was in important respects but a metamorphosis and development of theirs. He appears to have been particularly fascinated by the fact that in the physiocratic system, as he saw it, the theory of quantities and growth and the theory of prices and distribution do have a common origin in the concepts of social surplus and production as a circular flow. Marx can indeed be said to have seen through the lens of the physiocratic writings the essence of the *duality* relationship between the two sets of variables emphasized by later theorists and particularly by John von Neumann.[22] Hence it may be argued that there exists a direct lineage from physiocracy to modern formulations of the classical theory.

APPENDIX A

On Marx's studies of physiocracy and his sources

Since Marx studied, and commented on, physiocratic authors in different phases of his life, extending over a period of more than thirty years, it may be useful to provide the reader with a brief overview of major stages in the development of Marx's studies of physiocracy. To begin with, some general remarks about the character of Marx's own writings seem appropriate.

One of the princical sources for Marx's views on physiocracy is the first part of the *Theories of Surplus Value* (*TSV* 1) – a manuscript written in 1862–3 which contains Marx's 'working notes', and which was not meant to be published in its present form. The same applies also to Marx's *Economic & Philosophic Manuscripts of 1844* (*EPM* 1844), to his *Grundrisse* manuscript of 1857–8 (*Grundrisse*), and to the *Marx–Engels Correspondence* (*MEW* 30).[23] The reader is therefore asked to keep in mind that any exposition of Marx's views on physiocracy relies to a large extent on material that Marx had not prepared for publication. It should also be emphasized that Marx's first and foremost objective in all these manuscripts, including those of the *TSV*, was *self-clarification*. With regard to the sources used by Marx in his assessment of physiocracy, it must first be noted that Marx did not have access to all the writings of the physiocrats that are available to us. Moreover, in some cases some of the material, though available in principle, was not at his disposal when he was writing (cf. *TSV* 1: 484 n. 88).

The first time Marx came into contact with physiocratic ideas appears to have been during his stay in Paris, where – most probably in 'early 1844' (cf. Oakley 1983: 23; see also *MEGA* IV.2 (Apparat): 714) – he started to study systematically the works of political economists. Marx recorded his work in a series of notebooks (now known as the *Paris Notebooks*), containing his excerpts, summaries and commentaries. Among the sixteen authors from whose works Marx took excerpts, there is none that would be considered a physiocrat (cf. *MEGA* IV.2 (Apparat): 710–24). However, in the so-called *Economic & Philosophic Manuscripts of 1844* – frequently also referred to as the *Paris Manuscripts* (1844) – which emerged from Marx's attempt to collate the material collected in the notebooks and to clarify his views on political economy, he included a discussion relating to physiocracy of roughly one page in length. Marx provides no hints as to the sources on which he based the following characterization of the 'physiocratic doctrine':

> The physiocratic doctrine of Dr *Quesnay* forms the transition from the mercantile system to Adam Smith. *Physiocracy* represents in political economy directly the decomposition of feudal property, but it therefore just as directly represents its *metamorphosis* and restoration . . . All wealth is resolved into *land* [*Erde*] and *cultivation* (agriculture). Land is not yet *capital*: it is still a special mode of its existence . . . Yet land is a general natural *element*, whilst the mercantile system admits the existence of wealth only in the form of *precious metal*. Thus the *object* of wealth – its matter – has [straight away] obtained the highest degree of generality within the *bounds of nature*, in so far as nature is its immediate objective wealth. And land only exists for *man* through labour, through agriculture. Hence the subjective essence of wealth has already been transferred to labour. But at the same time agriculture is the *only productive* labour. Hence, labour is not yet grasped in its generality and abstraction . . . Physiocracy denies *particular*, external, merely objective wealth by declaring labour to be the *essence* of wealth.
>
> (*EPM* 1844: 130–1)

Marx was thus already familiar with physiocratic ideas when he first set out the basic conceptions of 'historical materialism' in *Die deutsche Ideologie* (*The German Ideology*), written in collaboration with Friedrich Engels in 1845–6. But apart from a side remark, in which *les économistes* are credited with having originated the science of political economy,[24] there are no other references to physiocratic writers.

According to Marguerite Kuczynski (1976: 18–20; cf. also Oakley 1983: 31), Marx first took excerpts from Quesnay's writings in the autumn of 1846, when he planned to rewrite the manuscript for his contracted book entitled *Kritik der Politik und Nationalökonomie* (*Critique of Politics and Political Economy*). Kuczynski also reports that Marx had emphasized, in the draft of a letter to the publisher K. W. Leske, the necessity of 'now' having to include 'a thorough examination of Daire's edition of the *Physiocrates* (1846)', which have just been published (but which Marx had not yet received). Marx's study of Daire's volume resulted in extensive excerpts from two articles of Quesnay that he collected under the heading 'Quesnay, François: a) Le droit naturel; b) Analyse du tableau économique. In: Physiokrates [*sic*]. Quesnay, Du Pont de Nemours . . .', in the (unpublished) 'Exzerptheft XII, 1846'.[25]

The revision of the manuscript for *Critique of Politics and Political Economy* was, however, not carried out.[26] Some traces of Marx's examination of Daire's volume can be detected in *Misère de la philosophie*

(1847), which he wrote from December 1846 to April 1847. Section '1. The method' of 'Chapter II. The metaphysics of political economy' was divided by Marx into seven 'Observations', in analogy with the structure used by Quesnay in summarizing the main ideas of his *Analyse* in seven 'Observations importantes'. And in the paragraph preceding this section Marx refers to Quesnay as the leading economist of France, who had 'turned political economy into a science' (*MEW* 4: 125).

A decade later, in the *Grundrisse der Kritik der Politischen Ökonomie, Rohentwurf 1857–8* (*Foundations of the Critique of Political Economy* (*Rough Draft 1857–58*)), Marx again characterizes the physiocrats as 'the fathers of modern political economy' (*Grundrisse*: 234). Almost all of Marx's comments on physiocracy in the *Grundrisse* are contained in the section 'The chapter on capital. – Production process. Theories of surplus value' (*Grundrisse*: 232–5) and most of them reappear (in very similar formulations) in chapter 2 of *TSV* 1. The first text that was to emerge from Marx's subsequent revision and further elaboration of the *Grundrisse* manuscript, *Zur Kritik der Politischen Ökonomie* (*A Contribution to the Critique of Political Economy*), first published (in German) in 1859, contains only a brief passage on physiocracy (cf. *Critique*: 57–8).[27]

We may thus conclude that from his first contact with physiocratic ideas onwards Marx spoke very respectfully of the physiocrats, and in particular of Quesnay, although there is no evidence that he had thoroughly examined Daire's *Physiocrates*, or the writings of other physiocrats, other than that from 1846.

From August 1861 to July 1863 Marx then wrote a set of economic manuscripts, the greater part of which was later to become the *TSV*; another part was redrafted in 1863–5 for *Capital*. Marx collected these manuscripts in altogether twenty-three notebooks. The chapter on 'The Physiocrats' in *TSV* 1, originally contained in notebook VI, was written in March 1862 (cf. *MEGA* II.3.1 (Apparat): 12). It is remarkable that in this chapter almost all the quotations provided by Marx in order to substantiate his characterization of physiocracy are from Turgot's *Réflexions* ([1766] 1844).[28] Other physiocratic or secondary sources used by Marx include Mercier de la Rivière's *L'ordre naturel* (1767), Schmalz's *Économie politique* (1826) and Blanqui's *Histoire de l'économie politique* (1839). There is no indication that Marx consulted the texts in Daire's *Physiocrates* while he was writing the chapter on 'The Physiocrats'.

Chapter 6 of *TSV* 1, the original German title of which is 'Abschweifung [Digression] *Tableau économique* suivant Quesnay', is based on a manuscript that Marx had first put in a 'separate notebook' (which he then, however, relabelled 'notebook X').[29] It was written in April or in May 1862,[30] and it is based on the exposition of Quesnay's *Tableau* in Schmalz's *Économie politique*, the French translation of the German original (cf. Schmalz 1826: 329). The fact that there are hardly any quotations from the physiocrats 'leads to the conclusion that when he was writing his "Digression" Marx did not have by him the works of Quesnay and of the other authors mentioned' (*TSV* 1: 484 n. 88).

A first formulation of the transformation of values into prices of production is to be found in a 'Digression' on Rodbertus's theory of rent in notebook X of the economic manuscripts of 1861–3. This 'Digression', which was later to appear in volume 2 of the *TSV* (cf. *TSV* 2: 64–71), was written in mid June 1862 (cf. *MEGA* II.3.1. (Apparat): 13), that is, shortly after the 'Digression' on the *Tableau économique*. In this analysis Marx calculates an average rate of profit by aggregating the sectoral value rates of profit and then averaging them out, or alternatively, by forming the ratio of the aggregated sectoral surplus values to the aggregated capital advances (in value terms). As Oakley (1985: 85–8) has noted, this analysis anticipates the presentation in chapter 9 of volume III of *Capital*, except that Marx here 'made no comment on the fact that the total surplus value equals the total profit and the total immediate exchange value equals the total average price' (Oakley 1985: 87).

In December 1862, after he had finished notebook XV (that is, almost all of the manuscripts that were later to appear in volumes 1–3 of the *TSV*), Marx began to work on a manuscript that includes a section entitled 'Capital und Profit', which contains the original form of the argument of the first parts of volume III of *Capital*. A central piece of analysis of Part II of the third volume of *Capital*, i.e. the 'Transformation of values of commodities into prices of production', is, however, not developed in this manuscript (cf. *MEGA* II.3.5. (Text): 1,598–1,674).[31]

In the period from May to July 1863[32] Marx took extensive excerpts from Quesnay's *Le Droit naturel* from the *Analyse du Tableau économique*,[33] from Quesnay's two *Encyclopédie* articles, 'Fermiers' and 'Grains', from the two *Dialogues*, from the (*Premier*) *Problème économique* and from the *Maximes générales* as found in Daire (1846). During this period Marx was working on manuscripts he collected in notebooks XXII and XXIII. Notebook XXIII contained a discussion of Quesnay's *Tableau économique*, entitled 'Addendum to the chapters on the Physiocrats' which was later to appear in volume 1 of the *TSV* (cf. *TSV* 1: 378–80).[34] In the same notebook Marx also collected comments on some passages from John Gray's *The Essential Principles of the Wealth of Nations* (1797), which were later also included in *TSV* 1 (cf. *TSV* 1: 382–6).[35] We may therefore conclude that Marx had intensively studied physiocratic authors, and in particular Quesnay's *Tableau économique*, in the period from May to July 1863.

Marx again studied the articles in Daire's *Physiocrates* edition, and particularly Quesnay's *Analyse*, in 1877, when he was engaged in preliminary work for his contribution to Engels's *Anti-Dühring*. As is well known, Marx drafted the whole of chapter X of Part II of Friedrich

Engels's *Herrn Eugen Dühring's Umwälzung der Wissenschaft* (*MEW* 20: 210–38). The work on this manuscript was largely done in the period from January to March 1877 (*MEGA* I.27 (Apparat): 856–8), and in March 1877 Marx sent his draft of the chapter to Engels. However, Marx had encountered difficulties in his exposition of Quesnay's *Tableau économique*, and in August 1877 he sent Engels a supplementary note entitled 'Das Tableau économique mit einigen Randglossen [The *Tableau économique* with some marginal comments]' (*MEGA* I.27 (Text): 210–14). The final version of chapter X was then written by Engels in November 1877.

APPENDIX B

Marx's discussion of the *Tableau économique*

Since Marx's examination of and elaboration on Quesnay's *Tableau économique* is of particular interest in this chapter, it seems appropriate to provide also a short chronological outline specifically referring to Marx's intensive and repeated studies of it.[36] It has already been mentioned in Appendix A that Marx first took excerpts from the *Analyse* in 1846 (cf. Kuczynski 1976: 74–5). Quesnay's *Tableau* seems immediately to have fascinated Marx, although he was apparently still rather unclear about its meaning, as can be inferred from a side-remark in *Misère de la philosophie* (1847): 'We must therefore seek to clarify the method of Mr Proudhon which is at least as dark as the "*Tableau économique*"' (*MEW* 4: 125–6). The *Tableau* was then taken up neither in the *Grundrisse* manuscript nor in the *Critique*, and there is no indication that Marx had attempted an 'illumination' of it before he wrote the 'Abschweifung [Digression] *Tableau économique* suivant Quesnay', which was later to become chapter 6 of *TSV* 1, in 1862.

Within this 'Digression' of some forty pages there are several other digressions, so that only the smaller part of the chapter is actually devoted to the *Tableau* and its *problématique*. It is obvious that Marx's foremost interest in this manuscript was to clarify his own, incompletely worked-out ideas on 'the capitalist process of reproduction as a whole'. Reading through the chapter gives one the impression that Quesnay's 'brilliant conception' (*TSV* 1: 344) has caused Marx considerable headaches.[37]

Marx first reproduces the *Tableau* from Schmalz's *Économie politique* (cf. Schmalz 1826: 329), adding small letters (a, b, c and d) and signs (′ and ″) to indicate the starting points of economic transactions. (See Figure 10.2a; Figure 10.2b gives Marx's handwritten version of it.) He then subdivides his discussion into four parts, contained in subsections 2 to 5, respectively.

The *first* part refers to 'Circulation between farmers and landowners. The return circuit of money to the farmers, which does not express

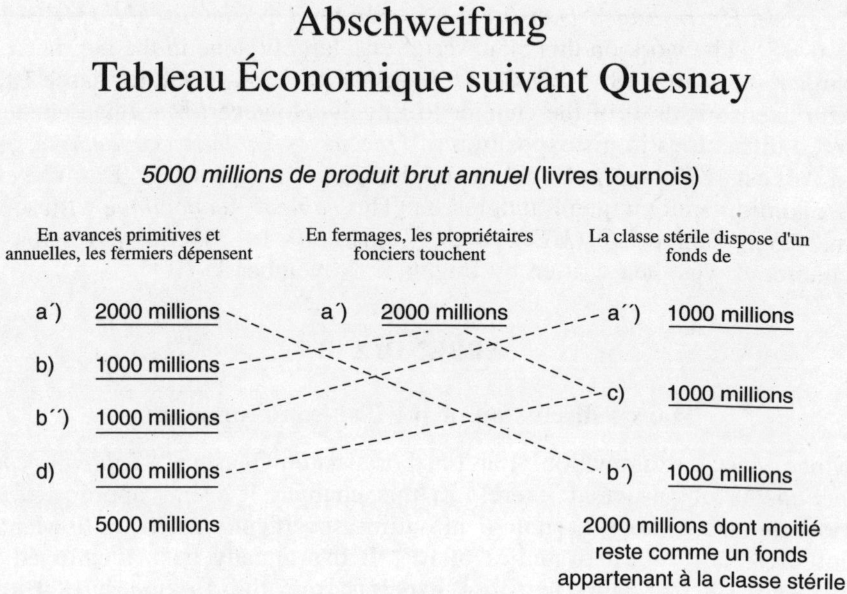

Figure 10.2(a) The *Tableau* from Schmalz's *Économie politique*.

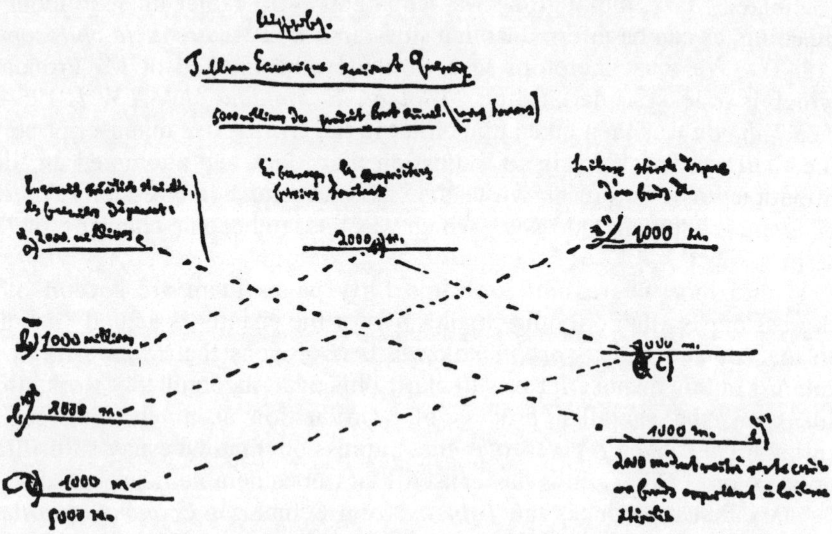

Figure 10.2(b) Marx's handwritten version.

reproduction'. According to Marx, the farmer[38] first pays 2 milliards [billion] in money as rent to the landlord, the *propriétaire*, which the latter then spends entirely and in equal proportion to buy from the farmer by means of subsistence and from the 'sterile class' manufactured commodities. By selling his commodities to the landlord the farmer, Marx observes, '*in fact . . . only pays back the money with which he paid the landlord the rent . . . He* [the landlord] *pays the farmer* with the money which he has received *from the farmer without any equivalent*' (ibid.: 310). Marx then counterposes the circulation between farmer and landowner to the *M–C–M* circuit of simple commodity production in which the flowing back of the money to its starting point expresses continuous reproduction, and notes, 'In contrast with this, in the case given above no reproduction process takes place when the money flows back from the landlord to the farmer' (ibid.: 311).

The *second* part, largely a digression within the 'Digression', is 'On the circulation of money between capitalist and labourer', and consists of two subsections. There is no *direct* reference to Quesnay or any other physiocrat. In the first subsection Marx indeed expounds his own theory of surplus value (in the literary form of a dialogue between a capitalist and his workers), and attempts to reject the idea, also present in the physiocratic concept of *avances annuelles*, that the capitalist 'advances' money or rather that part of the product which is the labourers' share as wages, and that the profits he pockets are a reward for the risk that he takes on (ibid.: 315). The second subsection is concerned with 'Commodities which the labourer buys from the capitalist'. The main point Marx wants to establish is that a retransformation of money wages into commodities signifies an *M–C–M* circuit from the capitalist's, and a *C–M–C* circuit from the labourer's, point of view: the former buys with money labour power, and with the product of labour power 'he buys money' (ibid.: 321); the latter sells labour power, and with the money he buys commodities that allow him to reproduce his labour power.

After several further digressions Marx finally turns to the *third* part, that is, to the 'Circulation between farmer and manufacturer according to the Tableau Économique'. The landlord, or, for short, *L*, spends half his rent, i.e. 1 milliard, on manufactures sold by the sterile class, *S*. With this amount of money *S* buys means of subsistence from the farmer, *F*. Comparing this transaction with the first one, in which L is buying commodities from *F*, Marx observes, 'This retransformation of the 1 milliard into means of subsistence expresses, in the case of *L*, mere consumption, but in the case of *S* it expresses industrial consumption, reproduction; for he transforms a part of his commodity into one of the elements in its production – means of subsistence' (ibid.: 329). *F* has now received back the 2 millards in money initially paid out as rent to *L*, and buys commodities for 1 milliard from *S* 'to replace his annual and original advances, in so far as these consist partly of tools, etc., and partly of manufactured goods which he consumes during the process of production' (ibid.: 331). This is a 'simple process of circulation', Marx stresses, and 'On both sides there is metamorphosis of capital' (ibid.): *F* reconverts 1 milliard in money into elements of production needed in reproduction, and *S* is thereby enabled to obtain the elements of production needed for reproduction in his sphere. The reconversion of the money into raw materials channels the 1 milliard in money back to *F*.

Marx then summarizes what has happened with total agricultural production: 'one-fifth goes into reproduction for the farmer, and does not come into circulation; the landlord consumes one-fifth (that makes two-fifths); *S* gets two-fifths; in all, four-fifths' (ibid.). At this point Marx thinks he has detected 'an obvious gap in the explanation' (ibid.). He explains:

> Quesnay seems to reckon like this: *F* gives *L* (line a–b) 1 milliard (one-fifth) in means of subsistence. With 1 milliard of his raw materials he replaces S's fund (a″–b″). And 1 milliard in means of subsistence form wages for S, which he adds as value to the commodities and consumes in food while he is doing it (c–d). And 1 milliard remains in reproduction (a′), not entering into circulation. Finally, 1 milliard of the product replaces advances (a′–b′).
>
> (*TSV* 1: 332)

Then follows his criticism: 'Only he overlooks the fact that S buys for the 1 milliard in manufactured goods, neither means of subsistence nor raw materials from the farmer, but pays back to him his own money' (ibid.: 332).[39] Next Marx maintains that Quesnay has wrongly excluded the products of the manufacturing sector from the gross annual production, which correctly amounts to 7 milliards (i.e. 5 milliards in agricultural and 2 milliard in industrial product), rather than 5 milliards, as in Quesnay (ibid.: 332).[40]

The *fourth* part of Marx's 'Digression' contains a (tedious) discussion of 'Different cases in which the money flows back to its starting point'. The cases dealt with differ with respect to the starting points of the money flows, the number of transactions carried out between the three parties and the question of whether or not all the transactions can be carried out with the existing 2 milliards in money. In some of the cases a 'development of credit, and consequently economy in payments', must be assumed (ibid.: 337). Marx then uses the *Tableau* to check some of his own ideas developed elsewhere, and arrives at the conclusion: 'the cases set out above do not contradict the law explained earlier: "that with a given rapidity of circulation of money and a given total sum of prices of commodities the quantity of the circulation medium is determined"' (ibid.: 341).[41] Marx concludes this part with a remark which shows that he had not yet fully understood the money and commodity circuit implied in a process of 'simple reproduction': what is not explained in Quesnay's *Tableau*, Marx notes, is the fact that 'the capitalist draws more money out of circulation than he threw into it' (ibid.: 343), reflected in the famous formula *M–C–M′*.

It is interesting to note that shortly after Marx had written the 'Digression' in April or May 1862, he made the following request in a letter to Engels (from 18 June 1862):

> Apropos! If it can be done in all brevity, without making heavy demands on you, I would wish a paradigm (plus an explanation) of Italian book-keeping. It would be useful in the illumination of the 'Tableau Economique' of Dr. Quesnay.
>
> (*MEW* 30: 249)

However, Marx was only to examine the *Tableau* again in the period from May to July 1863, when he worked on the notebooks XXII and XXIII of the 'Economic manuscripts of 1861–3'. The 'Addendum to the chapters on the Physiocrats' (*TSV* 1: 378–80), written in June 1863,[42] gives a short but much clearer exposition of the *Tableau*. Its content and its composition suggest that it was mainly a record of what Marx had, and had not yet, been able to clarify with regard to Quesnay's *Tableau économique*. Marx first reproduces the *Tableau* as found in Quesnay's *Analyse* (in Daire 1846), and adds, 'This is the simplest form of the *Tableau Économique*.' Marx's exposition begins with: '1. *Money circulation* . . . The money circulation starts out from the spending class, the landlords' (ibid.: 378), and after a brief account of the succession of the various transactions depicted in the *Tableau* Marx arrives at the result: 'In this way the [2] milliards in money have flowed back to the productive class' (ibid.: 379). Next Marx again notes, and again leaves out for later investigation, the problem of what happens to the last *one-fifth* of the agricultural gross produce. Then follows a new aspect that is first (and last) mentioned in the 'Addendum'. It is Quesnay's alleged omission of the existence of fixed capital items in the manufacturing sector, an aspect which Marx at this time apparently considered an important criticism of the physiocrat's construction: [43]

> Even from Quesnay's point of view, according to which the whole sterile class in fact consist[s] only of wage-labourers, the falsity of the assumptions made is evident from the Tableau itself. The original advances (fixed capital) made by the productive class are assumed to be five times the size of the annual advances. In the case of the sterile class this item is not mentioned at all – which naturally does not prevent it from existing.
>
> (*TSV* 1: 379)

Another problem that Marx first notes in the 'Addendum' (and that he again mentions in his later account of the *Tableau*),[44] is the question of how the sterile class can provide itself with manufactures when it buys foodstuff and raw materials for 2 milliards, adds no additional value in the production process, and then sells the whole of its annual production, amounting to a value of 2 milliards, to the other two classes. In the 'Addendum' Marx follows the Abbé Baudeau's 'Explication', according to which the sterile class holds back an appropriate portion of its total production while it sells the larger part of it to the other classes for 2 milliards, that is, '*above* its *value*' (ibid.: 379). This explanation clearly amounts to a return to mercantilistic habits of thought, as Marx immediately points out, and reintroduces the notion of 'profit upon alienation'. In the following section of the 'Addendum' Marx then records, without any comment, four statements from Quesnay's writings about the exchange of equivalents in the market, that is, about the impossibility of a creation of value in exchange (ibid.: 380).

The available material suggests that Marx, after a first attempt in 1862, worked intensively on and with the *Tableau économique* during the (hot) summer of 1863 – *after* he had written the main contents of notebooks VI to XV, that is, almost all of the material that was later to appear in volumes 1–3 of the *TSV*, and *before* he drafted the manuscript version of Part II of volume III of *Capital* in 1864–5.

Finally, two further remarks are in order. First, it should be noted that Marx presumably only knew Quesnay's *Tableau* in the version of the *Analyse* (as contained in Daire 1846), and not in the earlier *zigzag* version. His remark in the 'Addendum' – 'This is the *simplest* form of the *Tableau Économique*' (*TSV* 1: 378; emphasis added) – was in all probability not meant to refer to Quesnay's earlier *zigzag* version but to another exposition of the *Tableau* that was known to him: the one contained in Schmalz's volume (cf. also Gilibert 1977: 53). Second, it must be noted that of the different versions of Marx's interpretation of the *Tableau* the only one published during his lifetime was the one contained in chapter 10 of Engels's *Anti-Dühring*.

NOTES

1 See, for example, Moride (1908), Schumpeter (1914: 48; 1954: 238), Bénard (1958), Fox-Genovese (1976), Schicchi (1978), Malle (1979), Rieter (1983) and particularly Meek (1962: 27).

2 See more recently the contributions by Cartelier (1976), Gilibert (1977) and Vaggi (1987).

3 We may note here that in Quesnay's writings there is not only the well known distinction between 'classe productive' and 'classe stérile', but also the distinction between 'travail productif' and 'travail stérile': 'Les cultivateurs . . . partagent le produit de leurs travaux avec le souverain et les propriétaires des terres; *mais il n'y a que les travaux productifs qui puissent se défrayer eux-mêmes, et fournir de plus le surcroît de richesse qui forme le revenu des nations, c'est par ces avantages qu'ils différent essentiellement des travaux stériles dont on paye les frais, et qui ne rapportent rien au-delà des frais*' (Quesnay 1958: 829; in the original the italicized part is capitalized; see also ibid.: 911).

4 There are, however, passages in the writings of major physiocrats which point in the direction of agriculture as a self-contained or vertically integrated sector of the economy. Quesnay's *Dialogue sur les travaux des artisans*, which Marx had excerpted, contains the following statement: 'Ainsi l'origine, le principe de toute

dépense, et de toute richesse, est la fertilité de la terre, dont on ne peut multiplier les produits que par ces produits mêmes. C'est elle qui fournit les avances au cultivateur qui la fertilise, pour la faire produire davantage. *L'artisan n'y peut contribuer que par la formation de quelques instruments nécessaires pour remuer la terre, et qu'au défaut d'artisans, le cultivateur formerait lui-même. Qu'importe qui en soit l'ouvrier . . .*' (Quesnay 1958: 892; emphasis added). Compare this with Marx's statement in Engels's *Anti-Dühring*: 'Finally, recall that during Quesnay's time in France, as more or less everywhere in Europe, the own home industry of the farmer's family supplied by far the greater part of the needs and wants that did not belong to the class of the means of subsistence, and which therefore will be assumed as the obvious accessories [*selbstverständliches Zubehör*] of agriculture' (*MEW* 20: 231).

5 Marx's interpretation of the physiocrats bears a close resemblance to Sraffa's 'corn model' interpretation of Ricardo's early theory of profits. According to Sraffa's interpretation, 'in agriculture the same commodity, namely corn, forms both the capital . . . and the product' (Sraffa 1951: xxxi). Hence, whether or not a surplus is generated in agriculture, as well as the absolute size of that surplus and its size relative to the capital advanced (seed corn and corn wages), can be ascertained 'without any question of valuation' (ibid.). Sraffa himself notes that Ricardo's view 'thus appears to have a point of contact with the Physiocratic doctrine of the "produit net" in so far as the latter is based, as Marx has pointed out, on the "physical" nature of the surplus in agriculture which takes the form of an excess of food produced over the food advanced for production; whereas in manufacturing, where food and raw materials must be bought from agriculture, a surplus can only appear as a result of the sale of the product' (Sraffa 1960: 93). (Sraffa refers to two passages in volumes 1 and 3 of *TSV*.)

6 As Marx pointed out later, it was, however, wrong to set aside the fact that 'the owners of the conditions of labour and the labourers . . . confront each other as owners of commodities, and consequently there is no assumption here of production independent of exchange' (ibid.: 58).

7 It should be noted, however, that Quesnay's article *Hommes*, which contains perhaps the most elaborate account of physiocratic price concepts, was not accessible to Marx. None the less Marx could hardly have overlooked the existence of such concepts, given his intensive and careful study of Daire's *Physiocrates* edition. There are indeed several passages in his writings in which he discusses such concepts; see, for example, *TSV* 1: 46–7, 59, 60; *C* II: 215–16; *C* III: 198.

8 Therefore the view occasionally to be found in the literature that Marx denied that the physiocrats had a theory of value is difficult to sustain; see, for example, Cartelier (1976: 78) and Gilibert (1989: 125). Some authors interpret the physiocrats as advocating a land theory of value, with relative prices proportional to the direct and indirect land requirements in production; see in particular Samuelson (1959).

Francis Seton (1992: 28) has used the distinction between '*cost*-based' and '*use*-based' approaches to the theory of value to classify, among others, the contributions by Marx and the physiocrats, both of which are said to represent different 'monomanias'. While Marx's theory of value is said to represent a 'mono *cost*-fetishistic approach', because it allegedly recognizes only one cost element, labour, the physiocrats' theory is said to represent a 'mono *use*-fetishistic approach', because it allegedly recognizes the usefulness of only one output element, 'grain'. In our view both characterizations are dubious: Marx did not consider labour to be the only cost or input element, nor did the physiocrats consider 'grain' to be the only proceeds or output element.

9 Ironically, Eugen von Böhm-Bawerk in his frontal assault on Marx's analysis after the publication of the third volume of *Capital* accused Marx of having left out of consideration other candidates for the role of the 'common factor': following Marx's line of reasoning, commodities could with the same justice be said to 'exchange in proportion to the quantity of material incorporated in them' (Böhm-Bawerk 1949: 85). The purpose of the suggested material-based theory of value was to ridicule Marx's procedure by pointing out its arbitrariness. However, as we have seen, Marx had taken this option into account and had rejected it. It should be noted that in Böhm-Bawerk's view the source of value was to be sought neither in labour nor in some material input, but in the marginal value in use of commodities. Böhm-Bawerk's criticism of Marx owes much to his former teacher, Karl Knies, who in 1873 had set against Marx's concept of 'abstract labour' that of 'a value in use *in genere*' (cf. Knies 1885: 160). See also Kurz (1995: section 5).

10 See, in particular, *C* II: 397–8; we shall come back to the significance of this passage on p. 203.

11 Prior to this Marx had developed the scheme in a manuscript entitled 'Reproduktion' in May or early June 1863; see *MEGA* II.3.6 (Text): 2,271. See also Appendix B.

12 As in the *Tableau* the concept of an 'industry', 'sector' or 'department' is an analytical one. Yet while in Quesnay the dividing line between the two departments is whether a line of production is 'productive' or not, in Marx the dividing line is whether it produces means of production or means of consumption.

13 At that time Marx also called the variable capital the 'wage fund' (*Fonds des Arbeitslohns*) (ibid.: 364).

14 On the similarities and differences between the conceptions of production as a circular flow in Marx and Quesnay see the appendix by Tsuru in Sweezy (1942).

15 This asymmetrical treatment of the distributive variables distinguishes the analyses of Quesnay and Marx, and also those of the classical economists from Adam Smith to David Ricardo, from later marginalist (or 'neoclassical') analyses which attempt to determine all distributive variables symmetrically in terms of supply and demand in regard to the 'services' of the 'factors of production': labour, land and capital. See on this Kurz and Salvadori (1995: chapters 1, 13, 14).

16 Quesnay was also clear about the importance of technological and organizational improvements in the production process. On Quesnay's contribution to the theory of economic growth see Eltis (1975).

17 In this context it is to be noted that a first formulation of the transformation of values into prices of production is to be found in a 'Digression' on Rodbertus's theory of rent (cf. *TSV* 2: 64–71) which was written in mid-June 1862 (cf. *MEGA* II.3.1 (Apparat): 13), that is, shortly after the 'Digression' on Quesnay's *Tableau*. In December 1862, after he had written the major part of the *TSV* (notebooks VI–XV), Marx produced a draft of a section entitled 'Capital and Profit' which contained the original form of the argument of the first parts of volume III of *Capital*. He then returned to a study of the *Tableau économique* in 1863, from which emerged his schemes of reproduction of volume II of *Capital* (see pp. 196–203 above). Part II of the third volume of *Capital* was drafted shortly afterwards in 1864–5 (cf. *MEGA* II.3.5 (Text): 7^{++}–32^{++}; see also

Oakley 1983: 82–105). It is also known that Marx then revised his earlier draft on the schemes of reproduction. His new findings in the theory of value and distribution are echoed in the introductory paragraph of chapter XX of the second volume of *Capital*: 'It is . . . assumed that products are exchanged at their values . . . The fact that prices diverge from values cannot, however, exert any influence on the movements of the social capital. On the whole, there is the same exchange of the same quantities of products, although the individual capitalists are involved in value-relations no longer proportional to their respective advances and to the quantities of surplus-value produced singly by every one of them' (*C* II: 397). In the manuscript 'Reproduktion' of May or early June 1863 (cf. note 11 above) Marx touched upon the value-price problem. He wrote on the margin of the manuscript, in large letters, 'Profitrate', to indicate that there was a problem waiting to be solved; see *MEGA* II.3.6 (Text): 2,246. This evidence suggests that Marx's work on the schemes of reproduction and on the 'transformation problem' were intimately intertwined and bore joint fruit.

18 Marx's criticism of Ricardo reads: 'He presupposes *a general rate of profit* . . . Instead of *postulating* this *general rate of profit*, Ricardo should rather have examined how far its *existence* is in fact consistent with the determination of value by labour-time, and he would have found that instead of being consistent with it, *prima facie*, it *contradicts* it, and that its existence would therefore have to be explained through a number of intermediary stages, a procedure which is very different from merely including it under the law of value.' Marx continues: 'He would then have gained an altogether different insight into the nature of profit and would not have identified it directly with surplus-value' (*TSV* 2: 174).

19 It was noted above (p. 195) that Turgot's analysis of value and distribution partly anticipated classical political economy. Faccarello (1990: 69–78) has pointed out that especially in one respect Marx's transformation of values into prices of production bears a close resemblance to the analyses of Turgot and his disciples, Condorcet and Roederer. These latter authors started from the physiocratic doctrine that only the agricultural sector of the economy is productive, that is, capable of generating surplus value. At the same time it was clear to them that in competitive conditions a uniform rate of profit on the capital advanced in the different sectors must obtain. Hence there is the idea of the *redistribution* of a *predetermined* aggregate surplus value in proportion to the capital advanced in the various spheres of production. It may be conjectured that Marx got this idea from these authors and that he generalized it to all spheres of production in which surplus labour is performed.

20 This set of data fits well with the 'naturalistic' or 'materialist' points of view of the physiocrats and Marx, since all the exogenous variables referred to in order to determine the endogenous ones can be observed and measured.

21 There is no need to assume simple reproduction in order to be able to 'transform' values into prices of production, as Bortkiewicz (1907) maintained; see on this Garegnani (1960: appendix C).

22 It should be noted that, prior to Marx, Robert Torrens had displayed a clear understanding of the duality relationship, and there is evidence that Marx had benefited from Torrens's work. On the historical origins of the concept of duality see also Kurz and Salvadori (1995: chapter 13). Morishima (1973: 8) has stressed, 'It is indeed a great surprise to find that many of von Neumann's novel ideas were clearly stated in *Capital*.'

23 It also applies, though perhaps in a lesser degree, to the Marx–Engels manuscript *The German Ideology* of 1845–6 and to volumes II and III of *Capital*. On

the other hand, the works that Marx managed to get published during his lifetime, with the exception of his contribution to Engels's *Anti-Dühring*, contain only comparatively little that is of direct relevance to our theme: see the passages referred to below from *Misère de la philosophie* of 1847, from *A Contribution to the Critique of Political Economy* of 1859, and from volume I of *Capital* of 1867.

24 'Political economy . . . was only raised by the Physiocrats to a distinctive science and since then has been treated as such' (*MEW* 3: 397).

25 Marx's excerpts are reproduced in full length in the editor's notes of M. Kuczynski's (German) edition of Quesnay's writings (cf. Quesnay 1971/6).

26 According to Oakley (1983: 36) it is doubtful whether Marx had even begun with the drafting of a publishable manuscript when the book contract was finally cancelled in February 1847; Marx may therefore not have completed his 'thorough examination' of Daire's *Physiocrates* edition either.

27 The *Critique* includes, however, an argument relating to the physiocrats' alleged failure to understand 'the true nature of value' that was not presented again in the *TSV*: 'But for both the Physiocrats and their opponents the crucial issue was not what kind of labour creates *value* but what kind of labour creates *surplus value*. They were thus discussing a complex form of the problem before having solved its elementary form' (*Critique*: 57).

28 Cf. the references on pp. 54–65 of *TSV* 1. Marx had excerpted extensively from Turgot's work in January 1860 (*MEGA* II.3.2 (Apparat): 80). In this context it must also be noted that the version of Turgot's *Réflexions* used by Marx was that of Daire's 1844 re-edition of the *Œuvres de Turgot* (first edited by Dupont), which does not give Turgot's original text of 1766 but contains the alterations that Dupont had introduced into the *Ephémérides* version (cf. the translator's introduction in Turgot [1770] 1971: viii–x). Chapter II of *TSV* 1 contains only four quotations from Daire's volume, three of which are from Quesnay's *Maximes générales* and one of which is from the *Analyse*. For these quotations Marx used 'short excerpts' which he had taken in connection with his study of Turgot's *Réflexions* in early 1860 (cf. *MEGA* II.3.2 (Apparat): 80).

29 This may be taken as an indication that this manuscript was different in character from the others and perhaps not meant to be combined with the other material of the *TSV*.

30 According to the editors of *TSV*, Marx had in all probability written almost the whole of the 'Digression' in April 1862, during his stay in Manchester (cf. *TSV* 1: 484 n. 88). There is, however, some evidence which suggests that the 'Digression' was only written in May 1862, that is, after Marx had returned to London (cf. *MEGA* II.3.2 (Apparat): 13).

31 It is perhaps noteworthy that Marx first labelled the notebook which contains his manuscript 'Heft [notebook] ultimum', and only later relabelled it 'Heft XVI'.

32 In the last phase of his work on the 'Economic manuscripts of 1861–3' Marx started eight separate 'supplementary notebooks' with excerpts ('supplementary notebooks A–H'). The material they contained was used only in the manuscripts of notebooks XXII and XXIII, which Marx wrote from May to July 1863 (*MEGA* II.3.1 (Apparat): 17). The excerpts from the physiocrats are mainly contained in the 'supplementary notebook C'; quotations from some of the articles appear in the 'Addendum to the chapters on the Physiocrats' (*TSV* 1: 378–80).

33 According to M. Kuczynski (1976: 19) it is unclear whether for some reason the excerpts from 1846 were not at Marx's disposal in 1863 or whether there was

any other reason for this repetition. (The excerpts from all the articles are reproduced in the editor's notes of Quesnay 1971/6.)

34 A section on 'Reproduktion' in a manuscript in notebook XXII, written in May or June 1862, contains a first version of Marx's own reproduction schemes (cf. *MEGA* II.3.6 (Text): 2,271–83). This version is identical with the one that Marx included in his letter to Engels of 6 July 1863 (see above, pp. 197–203).

35 According to Marx, Gray's work 'contains a very excellent and compressed résumé of the Physiocratic doctrine' (*TSV* 1: 382).

36 The following account of Marx's discussion of the *Tableau économique* concentrates mainly on the 1862 to 1863 period, because it was then that Marx made productive use of it. Owing to limitations of space we cannot provide a full account of Marx's later discussion of Quesnay's *Tableau* in his contributions dating from 1877. However, occasionally we will take note of some aspects which had troubled Marx during his earlier studies and which he was able to clarify, at least to his own satisfaction, in his later ones.

37 In view of this, Marx's polemic against Dühring in Friedrich Engels's *Herrn Eugen Dühring's Umwälzung der Wissenschaft* (cf. *MEW* 20: 227–37) is somewhat ironic. Engels's opinion that Marx's 'clarification' of the *Tableau* in his contribution to the *Anti-Dühring* could be regarded as the final solution of 'this enigma of the sphinx [*Sphinxrätsel*] which proved unsolvable to modern economics' (*MEW* 20: 15) is questionable. For a succinct account of the interpretative problems of the *Tableau* see Meek (1962: 265–96).

38 While Marx refers to farmer, landlord, labourer and capitalist, what he means are the respective classes, 'of course' (*TSV* 1: 322).

39 The problem arises because Marx had assumed that only *one-fifth* of the total agricultural production does not enter into circulation. He notes this problem again in the 'Addendum' (cf. *TSV* 1: 379). In his contribution to Engels's *Anti-Dühring* Marx writes, 'the money value of the part of the [agricultural] gross produce taken out in advance equals two milliards. This part therefore does not enter into general circulation' (*MEW* 20: 231). Marx apparently only clarified this point in his preliminary work for Engels's *Anti-Dühring* (cf. *MEGA* I.27 (Text): 210–14); in a letter to Engels he blames the Abbé Baudeau's 'Explication du Tableau Économique' for having caused this and other 'misunderstandings' (cf. *MEGA* I.27 (Text): 214).

40 The same criticism is again put forward in the 'Addendum' (cf. *TSV* 1: 379). It is not to be found in Marx's contribution to Engels's *Anti-Dühring*.

41 Denoting with M the amount of money needed in order to circulate n commodities the sum total of prices of which equals

$$Y = \sum_{i=1}^{n} q_i p_i$$

(where q_i denotes the quantity of commodity i and p_i its unit price), given the velocity of circulation of money, U, gives

$$M = \frac{Y}{U}$$

which is a well-known relationship.

42 A first version of Marx's own reproduction schemes is contained in a manuscript entitled 'Reproduktion', drafted in May or June 1863 (cf. *MEGA* II.3.6

(Text): 2,271–83). The scheme developed there is identical with the one that Marx included in his letter to Engels of 6 July 1863 (see above, pp. 197–203).

43 In Marx's contribution to Engels's *Anti-Dühring* of 1878 we read: 'The operating capital expended by the "sterile" class in the course of the entire year (avances annuelles) consists of raw material in the value of one milliard – only raw material, because tools, machinery etc. belong to the products of this class itself. The multifarious roles which such products assume in the operation of the industries themselves, however, are equally none of the Tableau's concern as is the commodity and money circulation that only takes place within this group' (*MEGA* I.27 (Text): 516–17).

44 The relevant passage was omitted in the first two editions of Engels's *Anti-Dühring*; it therefore only appears in the third edition (cf. *MEGA* I.27 (Text): 417–25 and 517).

REFERENCES

Bénard, J. (1958) 'Marx et Quesnay', in F. Quesnay, *François Quesnay et la physiocratie*, Paris: Institut national d'études démographiques (INED), II, 105–30.

Blanqui, A. (1839) *Histoire de l'économie politique en Europe dupuis les anciens jusqu'à nos jours, suivie d'une bibliographie raisonnée des principaux ouvrages d'économie politique*. Brussels.

Böhm-Bawerk, E. von (1949) 'Karl Marx and the close of his system', in P. M. Sweezy (ed.), *Karl Marx and the Close of his System*, New York: Augustus M. Kelley. English translation of 'Zum Abschluß des Marxschen Systems', in O. von Boenigk (ed.), *Staatswissenschaftliche Arbeiten. Festgaben für Karl Knies*, Berlin: Haering, 1896.

Bortkiewicz, L. von (1906–7) 'Wertrechnung und Preisrechnung im Marxschen System', *Archiv für Sozialwissenschaft und Sozialpolitik* 23 (1906): 1–50; 25 (1907): 10–51, 445–88.

—— (1907) 'Zur Berichtigung der grundlegenden theoretischen Konstruktion von Marx im 3. Band des "Kapital" ', *Jahrbücher für Nationalökonomie und Statistik* 34: 319–35.

Cartelier, J. (1976) *Surproduit et reproduction – la formation de l'économie politique classique*, Paris: Maspero.

Daire, E. (ed.) (1846) *Physiocrates*, Paris.

Eltis, W. (1975) François Quesnay: a reinterpretation' 2, 'The theory of economic growth', *Oxford Economic Papers* 27.

Engels, F. (1972) *Herrn Eugen Dührings Umwälzung der Wissenschaft* (*Anti-Dühring*), in *Marx–Engels–Werke* 20, Berlin: Dietz. (Quoted as: *MEW* 20.)

Faccarello, G. (1990) 'Le legs de Turgot: aspects de l'économie politique sensualiste de Condorcet à Roederer', in G. Faccarello and P. Steiner (eds), *La pensée économique pendant la révolution française*, Grenoble: Presses Universitaires de Grenoble.

Fox-Genovese, E. (1976) *The Origins of Physiocracy: Economic Revolution and Social Order in Eighteenth-century France*, Ithaca: Cornell University Press.

Garegnani, P. (1960) *Il capitale nelle teorie della distribuzione*, Milan: Giuffrè.

—— (1987) 'Surplus approach to value and distribution', in J. Eatwell, M. Milgate and P. Newman (eds), *The New Palgrave* 4, London: Macmillan, pp. 560–74.

Gilibert, G. (1977) *Quesnay, la costruzione della 'macchina della prosperità'*, Milan: Etas Libri.

—— (1989) 'François Quesnay (1694–1774)', in J. Starbatty (ed.), *Klassiker des ökonomischen Denkens* 1, Munich: Beck, pp. 114–33.

Gray, J. (1797) *The Essential Principles of the Wealth of Nations, Illustrated, in Opposition to some false Doctrines of Dr. Adam Smith, and Others*, London.

Knies, K. (1885) [1873] *Das Geld. Darlegung der Grundlehren von dem Gelde*. 1st edn. Berlin: Weidmann.

Kuczynski, M. (1976) 'Vorbemerkung zu "Das Naturrecht"', in F. Quesnay (1971/76), *Ökonomische Schriften in zwei Bänden* 2, part 1, Berlin: Akademie Verlag, pp. 3–24.

Kurz, H. D. (1995) 'Marginalism, classicism and socialism in German-speaking countries, 1871–1932', in I. Steedman (ed.), *Socialism and Marginalism, 1870–1930*, London: Routledge.

Kurz, H. D. and Salvadori, N. (1995) *Theory of Production: A Long-period Analysis*, Cambridge: Cambridge University Press.

Malle, S. (1979) 'Marx on Physiocracy', *Rivista Internazionale di Scienze Economiche e Commerciali* 26 (4): 364–86.

Marx, K. (1954) *Capital* I, Moscow: Progress Publishers. English translation of *Das Kapital* I, Hamburg [1867]: Meissner. (Quoted as: *C* I.)

—— (1956) *Capital* II, Moscow: Progress Publishers. English translation of *Das Kapital* II, ed. F. Engels, Hamburg [1885]: Meissner. (Quoted as: *C* II.)

—— (1959a) *Capital* III, Moscow: Progress Publishers. English translation of *Das Kapital* III, ed. F. Engels, Hamburg [1894]: Meissner. (Quoted as: *C* III.)

—— (1959b) *Das Elend der Philosophie*, in *Marx–Engels–Werke* 4, Berlin: Dietz. (Quoted as: *MEW* 4.)

—— (1963) *Theories of Surplus Value*, part 1, Moscow: Progress Publishers. English translation of *Theorien über den Mehrwert*, part 1, Berlin [1956]: Dietz. (Quoted as: *TSV* 1.)

—— (1964) *Economic and Philosophic Manuscripts of 1844*, New York: International Publishers. English translation of *Ökonomisch-philosophische Manuskripte aus dem Jahre 1844*, Berlin [1932]: Dietz. (Quoted as: *EPM 1844*.)

—— (1968) *Theories of Surplus Value*, part 2, Moscow: Progress Publishers. English translation of *Theorien über den Mehrwert*, part 2, Berlin [1959]: Dietz. (Quoted as: *TSV* 2.)

—— (1970) *A Contribution to the Critique of Political Economy*, New York: International Publishers. English translation of *Zur Kritik der Politischen Ökonomie*, Berlin [1964]: Dietz. (Quoted as: *Critique*.)

—— (1971a) *Theories of Surplus Value*, part 3, Moscow: Progress Publishers. English translation of *Theorien über den Mehrwert*, part 3, Berlin [1962]: Dietz. (Quoted as: *TSV* 3.)

—— (1971b) *Das Elend der Philosophie*, in *Marx–Engels–Werke* 4, Berlin: Dietz. (Quoted as: *MEW* 4.)

—— (1974) *Grundrisse der Kritik der Politischen Ökonomie, Rohentwurf 1857–1858*, Frankfurt: Europäische Verlagsanstalt. (Quoted as: *Grundrisse*.)

Marx, K. and Engels, F. (1958) *Die deutsche Ideologie*, in *Marx–Engels–Werke* 3, Berlin: Dietz. (Quoted as: *MEW* 3).

—— (1964) *Briefwechsel zwischen Marx und Engels Januar 1860–September 1864*, in *Marx–Engels–Werke* 30, Berlin: Dietz. (Quoted as: *MEW* 30).

—— (1976) *Karl Marx. Zur Kritik der Politischen Ökonomie (Manuskript 1861–1863), Apparat, Teil 1*, in *Marx–Engels–Gesamtausgabe* (*MEGA*), 2nd section, vol. 3, part 1, Berlin: Dietz. (Quoted as: *MEGA* II.3.1 (Apparat).)

—— (1977) *Karl Marx. Zur Kritik der Politischen Ökonomie (Manuskript 1861–1863),*

Apparat, Teil 2, in *Marx–Engels–Gesamtausgabe* (*MEGA*), 2nd section, vol. 3, part 2, Berlin: Dietz. (Quoted as: *MEGA* II.3.2 (Apparat).)

—— (1980) *Karl Marx. Zur Kritik der Politischen Ökonomie (Manuskript 1861–1863), Text, Teil 5*, in *Marx–Engels–Gesamtausgabe* (*MEGA*), 2nd section, vol. 3, part 5, Berlin: Dietz. (Quoted as: *MEGA* II.3.5 (Text).)

—— (1981) *Exzerpte und Notizen 1843 bis Januar 1845, Apparat*, in *Marx–Engels–Gesamtausgabe* (*MEGA*), 4th section, vol. 2, Berlin: Dietz. (Quoted as: *MEGA* IV.2 (Apparat).)

—— (1982) *Karl Marx. Zur Kritik der Politischen Ökonomie (Manuskript 1861–1863), Text, Teil 6*, in *Marx–Engels–Gesamtausgabe* (*MEGA*), 2nd section, vol. 3, part 6, Berlin: Dietz. (Quoted as: *MEGA* II.3.6 (Text).)

—— (1988a) *Herrn Eugen Dührings Umwälzung der Wissenschaft (Anti-Dühring), Text*, in *Marx–Engels–Gesamtausgabe* (*MEGA*), 1st section, vol. 27, Berlin: Dietz. (Quoted as: *MEGA* I.27 (Text).)

—— (1988b) *Herrn Eugen Dührings Umwälzung der Wissenschaft (Anti-Dühring), Apparat*, in *Marx–Engels–Gesamtausgabe* (*MEGA*), 1st section, vol. 27, Berlin: Dietz. (Quoted as: *MEGA* I.27 (Apparat).)

Meek, R. L. (1962) *The Economics of Physiocracy: Essays and Translations*, Cambridge, Mass.: Harvard University Press.

Mercier de la Rivière, P.-P. (1767) *L'ordre naturel et essentiel des sociétés politiques*, London and Paris.

Moride, P. (1908) *Le produit net des physiocrates et la plus-value de Karl Marx*, Paris: Librairie Nouvelle de Droit et de Jurisprudence.

Morishima, M. (1973) *Marx's Economics: A Dual Theory of Value and Growth*, Cambridge: Cambridge University Press.

Oakley, A. (1983) *The Making of Marx's Critical Theory: A Bibliographical Analysis*, London: Routledge.

—— (1985) *Marx's Critique of Political Economy: Intellectual Sources and Social Evolution* II, *1861–1863*, London: Routledge.

Physiocratie (1767) Publié par Dupont, Leyde, Paris.

Quesnay, F. (1958) *François Quesnay et la Physiocratie*, ed. L. Salleron, Paris: Institut national d'étudés demographiques (INED).

—— (1971/6) *Ökonomische Schriften in zwei Bänden*, trans. and ed. Marguerite Kuczynski, Berlin: Akademie Verlag.

Rieter, H. (1983) 'Zur Rezeption der physiokratischen Kreislaufanalogie in der Wirtschaftswissenschaft', in H. Scherf (ed.), *Bedeutung und Fortwirkung der Physiokraten, Studien zur Entwicklung der ökonomischen Theorie III, Schriften des Vereins für Socialpolitik, Neue Folge*, Bd 115/III, Berlin: Duncker & Humblot.

Samuelson, P. A. (1959) 'A modern treatment of the Ricardian economy: the pricing of goods and of labor and land services', *Quarterly Journal of Economics* 73: 1–35. Reprinted in J. E. Stiglitz (ed.), *The Collected Scientific Papers of Paul A. Samuelson* 1, Cambridge and London: MIT Press, 1966, pp. 373–407.

—— (1974) 'Marx as a mathematical economist: steady state and exponential growth equilibrium', in G. Horwich and P. A. Samuelson (eds), *Trade, Stability and Macroeconomics: Essays in Honor of Lloyd A. Metzler*, New York: Academic Press, pp. 269–307. Reprinted in H. Nagatani and K. Crowley (eds), *The Collected Scientific Papers of Paul A. Samuelson* 4, Cambridge and London: MIT Press, 1977, pp. 231–69.

—— (1982) 'Quesnay's *Tableau Economique* as a theorist would formulate it today', in I. Bradley and M. Howard (eds), *Classical and Marxian Political*

Economy: Essays in Honour of Ronald L. Meek, London and Basingstoke: Macmillan, pp. 45–78.
Schicchi, S. (1978) *Quesnay e Marx*, Catania: Bonanno.
Schmalz, T. A. H. (1826) *Économie politique*, trans. Henri Jouffroy, Paris.
Schumpeter, J. A. (1914) 'Epochen der Dogmen- und Methodengeschichte', in *Grundriss der Sozialökonomik* I, *Wirtschaft und Wirtschaftswissenschaft*, Tübingen: Mohr (Paul Siebeck), pp. 19–124.
—— (1954) *History of Economic Analysis*, London: Allen & Unwin.
Seton, F. (1992) *The Economics of Cost, Use and Value*. Revised and expanded edition of *Cost, Use and Value* (1985), Oxford: Clarendon Press.
Sraffa, P. (1951) 'Introduction' in vol. I of *The Works and Correspondence of David Ricardo*, ed. P. Sraffa with the collaboration of M. H. Dobb, Cambridge: Cambridge University Press.
—— (1960) *Production of Commodities by Means of Commodities: Prelude to a Critique of Economic Theory*, Cambridge: Cambridge University Press.
Sweezy, P. M. (1942) *The Theory of Capitalist Development*, New York: Monthly Review Press.
Tsuru, S. (1942) Appendix 'On reproduction schemes', in P. M. Sweezy, *The Theory of Capitalist Development*, New York: Monthly Review Press, pp. 365–74.
Turgot, A.-R.-J., de l'Aulne (1844) [1766] *Réflexions sur la formation et la distribution des richesses*, in *Œuvres de Turgot*, ed. Eugène Daire, Paris.
—— (1971) [1770] *Reflections on the Formation and the Distribution of Riches*, trans. W. J. Ashley, New York: Augustus M. Kelley.
Vaggi, G. (1987) *The Economics of François Quesnay*, London: Macmillan.

ACKNOWLEDGEMENTS

An earlier version of this chapter was presented at the conference *La Diffusion Internationale de la Physiocratie* held at the École Normale Supérieure de Fontenay/Saint-Cloud, Saint Cloud, France, in September 1993. We should like to thank the participants and particularly José Luis Cardoso, Peter Groenewegen and Gianni Vaggi for helpful discussions. Valuable suggestions and comments were also received from Nick Baigent, Alain Béraud, Alfred Bürgin, Gilbert Faccarello, Pierangelo Garegnani, John King, Antoin Murphy, Heinz Rieter, Neri Salvadori, Paul Samuelson, Ian Steedman and two anonymous referees of the *European Journal of the History of Economic Thought*. It goes without saying that all remaining errors and misconceptions are our responsibility. Translations of sources of which no English version was available are ours.

11

NO RESWITCHING? NO SWITCHING!

Neri Salvadori and Ian Steedman

It has been pointed out often enough (see, for instance, Samuelson 1983: 12) that reswitching cannot occur between techniques both of which have 'equal organic compositions of capital', i.e. price-ratio invariance and, therefore, linear wage–profit frontiers. It has even been proved (Brown and Chaing 1976; see also Brown 1980) that capital aggregation is assured, and an aggregate production function can be built up, if the labour shares in all sectors are equal, i.e. if all relevant techniques have the 'equal organic compositions' property. But Baldone (1984: section 4) observes in the course of an interesting article that, flukes aside, such techniques cannot switch *even once*. The object of the present chapter is to reinforce and to generalize this striking point, the importance of which has not yet received sufficiently widespread recognition and acknowledgement.

MAIN RESULT

Let a single product technique be defined by the pair $(\mathbf{A}, \mathbf{l})$ where $\mathbf{A}$ is the $n \times n$ matrix of inputs and $\mathbf{l}$ is the column n vector of labour inputs. The column vector of labour 'values', $\mathbf{v}$, is then defined by

$$\mathbf{v} = \mathbf{Av} + \mathbf{l}$$

Technique $(\mathbf{A}, \mathbf{l})$ has the 'equal organic compositions' property if and only if

$$\mathbf{l} = R\mathbf{Av} \tag{1}$$

where R is the maximum rate of profit for technique $(\mathbf{A}, \mathbf{l})$. Let there be a second technique $(\mathbf{A} + \Delta\mathbf{A}, \mathbf{l} + \Delta\mathbf{l})$ which also has the 'equal organic compositions' property, and which will be in use at 'high' rates of profit, whilst the technique $(\mathbf{A}, \mathbf{l})$ will be in use at 'low' rates of profit. Then

$$\mathbf{l} + \Delta\mathbf{l} = (R + \Delta R)\,(\mathbf{A} + \Delta\mathbf{A})\,(\mathbf{v} + \Delta\mathbf{v}) \tag{2}$$

where $\Delta R > 0$ (because the second technique is in use at high rates of profit) and $\Delta\mathbf{v} > 0$ (because the second technique is *not* in use at low rates of profit). Now let activity j be common to the two techniques. (It is well known that, in input–output systems, two adjacent techniques will differ in only one process, except for fluke cases: see Bruno *et al.* 1966; Pasinetti 1977: 162). From (1) and (2) we see that

$$(R + \Delta R)\, \mathbf{e}_j^T\, (\mathbf{v} + \Delta\mathbf{v}) = R\mathbf{e}_j^T\mathbf{A}\mathbf{v}$$

or

$$\mathbf{e}_j^T\mathbf{A}\ [(R + \Delta R)\Delta\mathbf{v} + \Delta R\mathbf{v}] = 0 \tag{3}$$

But with $\Delta R > 0$, $\Delta\mathbf{v} > 0$, $\mathbf{v} > 0$, (3) is self-contradictory, unless $\mathbf{e}_j^T\mathbf{A} = \mathbf{0}$. Hence switching – never mind reswitching – is impossible between any two 'equal organic compositions' techniques which have in common even one activity using some produced inputs. Since the general rule is, as just noted, that, in an n commodity economy, adjacent techniques will have $(n - 1)$ processes in common, the fact that *one* common process suffices to rule out switching between 'equal organic compositions' techniques is rather striking.

A DIAGRAMMATIC EXPLANATION

While the above formal argument should be clear, it may be helpful to present a diagrammatic argument as well. This argument is based on that presented by Mainwaring (1984: chapter 7). To each point on any real wage–rate of profit frontier there corresponds a particular set of relative prices of the commodities. Taking those relative prices as fixed, we may draw a hypothetical, linear wage–profit frontier for each process separately. It is clear that these hypothetical frontiers must intersect at the corresponding point on the actual wage–profit frontier. In addition, as Mainwaring has shown (ibid.), the absolute slope of the actual frontier, at the point in question, must lie between the maximum and minimum absolute slopes of the hypothetical frontiers (see Figure 11.1). In the special 'labour theory of value' case, of course, the relative prices are independent of distribution and hence each hypothetical frontier is the same whichever point on the actual frontier one starts from. And so each hypothetical frontier coincides with all the others and with the actual frontier – hence this last is linear also.

Now, let there be a choice between two 'labour theory of value' techniques. At a switch point the two actual frontiers must intersect and imply the same prices. But each actual frontier, as we have just seen, coincides with all its corresponding hypothetical frontiers. Hence if the two techniques *have a process in common*, all the frontiers – actual and hypothetical – coincide. It is thus self-contradictory to assume a switch between two distinct 'labour theory of value' techniques with one or more processes in common.

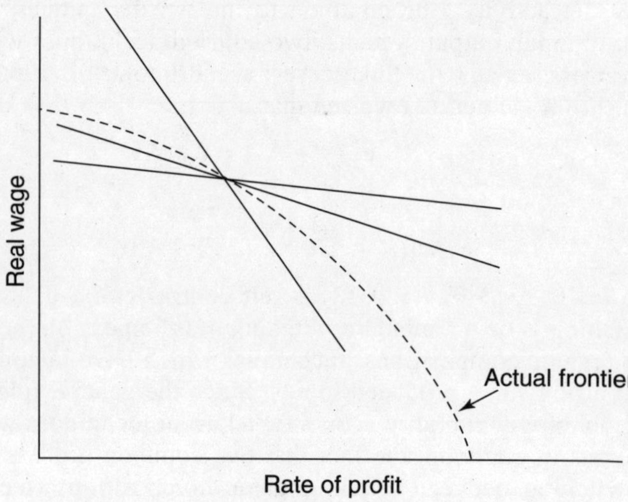

Figure 11.1

Table 11.1

Processes	*Commodity inputs* (1)	(2)	(3)	*Labour*		*Commodity outputs* (1)	(2)	(3)
(1)	α	0	0	1	→	1	0	0
(2)	α	0	0	1	→	0	0	1
(3)	0	β	0	1	→	0	γ	0
(4)	0	β	0	1	→	0	0	γ

SOME APPARENT COUNTER-EXAMPLES

The result of Baldone, reconsidered above, might *appear* to be contradicted by more than one kind of example. The purpose of this section is to consider three such examples, showing in each case the exact way in which it fails genuinely to be a counter-example. The section will conclude with some observations intended to clarify a number of rather subtle points arising in the literature.

Case 1

Technology is described by Table 11.1, where $0 < \beta < \alpha\gamma < \alpha < 1 - \gamma + \beta$; only commodity (3) is consumed.

Let us use commodity (3) as the numeraire, this being the only commodity which is always produced. If $0 \leq r < \bar{r} \equiv [(1 - \gamma)/(\alpha - \beta)] - 1$, then technique (1, 2) is utilized: $p_1 = 1$, $w = 1 - (1 + r)\alpha$. If $\bar{r} < r \leq (\gamma/\beta) - 1$, then technique (3, 4) is utilized: $p_2 = 1$, $w = \gamma - (1 + r)\beta$. Hence, at all relevant rates of profit, the relative prices of the commodities *actually produced* are independent of distribution. In this sense the labour theory of value holds good.

If all three commodities were consumed, then it would become clear that the labour theory of value did not hold: if $0 \leq r < \bar{r}$ then technique (1, 2, 3) is utilized and $p_2 = \{[1 - (1 + r)\alpha]/[\gamma - (1 + r)\beta]\}$; if $\bar{r} < r \leq (1/\alpha) - 1$, then technique (1, 3, 4) would be utilized and $p_1 = \{[\gamma - (1 + r)\beta]/[1 - (1 + r)\alpha]\}$. Moreover, if the numeraire were changed from commodity 3 to be a bundle of all three commodities, then neither section of the wage–profit frontier would be linear.

However, even when only commodity 3 is consumed, this case does *not* provide a counter-example to the main result. That is because there is no process in common between the techniques.

Case 2 (Burmeister 1980)

Commodity $j (j = 1, 2, \ldots, n)$ is produced by an infinite number of processes which can be arranged on the following iso-quant:

$$1 = l_j^{\alpha} a_{1j}^{\alpha_{1j}} \ldots a_{ij}^{\alpha_{ij}} \ldots a_{nj}^{\alpha_{nj}}$$

with

$$\sum_i \alpha_{ij} = 1 - \alpha$$

Let $(\bar{\mathbf{A}}, \mathbf{l})$ be the technique utilized at $r = \bar{r}$, and let $\bar{\mathbf{p}}$ and $\bar{w}$ be its price vector and wage rate for $r = \bar{r}$; then

$$\alpha[\mathbf{I} - \bar{\mathbf{A}}]\bar{\mathbf{p}} = \bar{w}\mathbf{l}$$

which implies that the price vector $\mathbf{p}$ and the wage rate w of technique $(\bar{\mathbf{A}}, \mathbf{l})$ are

$$\mathbf{p} = \bar{\mathbf{p}} \equiv (\bar{w}/\alpha\bar{r})\,(1 + \bar{r} - \alpha)\mathbf{l}$$
$$w = (\bar{w}/\alpha\bar{r})\,[\bar{r} - (1 - \alpha)r]$$

for each $0 \leq r \leq [\bar{r}/(1 - \alpha)]$.

Even if only some of the existing techniques satisfy the 'equal organic composition' property, the labour theory of value holds, since the techniques which do not satisfy that property are dominated everywhere. This does not require anything with respect to switch points; there is no rate of profit at which two alternative techniques are equally viable and hence there is no switch point. This is allowed by the fact that a continuum of techniques exists, i.e. that the set of existing techniques is infinite and uncountable.

Case 3

Let technology be defined by Table 11.2.

Let commodity (1) be the numeraire. If $0 \leq r < (1/5)$, then technique (1, 3) is utilized: $p_2 = 1$, $w = (1/3)(1 - 2r)$; if $(1/5) < r \leq 1$, then technique (2, 4) is utilized: $p_2 = 1$, $w = (1/4)(1 - r)$. If $r = (1/5)$, *all* processes may be operated.

Even if only two existing techniques satisfy the 'equal organic compositions' property, the labour theory of value holds at each admissible rate of profit, since the two techniques which do not satisfy that property – i.e. techniques (1, 4) and (2, 3) – are dominated everywhere. This requires, since the set of available techniques is finite, that at each switch point all processes are changed: in more general cases, with n commodities, $2n$ processes must be operable at each switch point (rather than $n + 1$, as usual)! Such a 'total switch', as it might be called, is at the opposite extreme from the case shown to be normal by Bruno *et al.* and by Pasinetti (see p. 227 above), and is, of course, a complete fluke. The fact that the two techniques have not even one process in common means that their respective sets of price equations are utterly independent of each other; it is thus not surprising that their wage–profit frontiers are not prevented from intersecting. This extreme case is, naturally, not an exception to the 'main result' of pp. 226–7.

In Samuelson's (1962) surrogate production function *no* two techniques had *any* process in common; hence switching between techniques with linear wage–profit frontiers was possible. But his construction did not rely on 'equal organic compositions' alone; it also turned on the 'no common activities' assumption (and on the 'radioactive depreciation' assumption; see Steedman 1979), the former being obtained, as in case 1, by assuming the final utilization of only *one* commodity. Hence the surrogate construction is even more special than has often been thought.

Table 11.2

	Commodity inputs				*Commodity outputs*	
Processes	(1)	(2)	*Labour*		(1)	(2)
(1)	0	2/3	1	→	1	0
(2)	0	1/2	2	→	1	0
(3)	2/3	0	1	→	0	1
(4)	1/2	0	2	→	0	1

The examples of aggregation of production functions provided by Brown and Chaing (1976), Brown (1980) and Burmeister (1980) rely on the *not* unimportant assumption that there is a continuum of techniques, as in case 2. If the set of available techniques is finite, the conditions for aggregation of production functions are much more strict – to avoid common activities – than Brown and Chaing's (1976), Brown's (1980) and Burmeister's (1980) analyses may suggest, and require the condition stated in our comments on case 3.

GENERALIZATIONS

The result of pp. 226-7 can be easily generalized to joint production, if the following (reasonable) definition of 'equal organic compositions' is accepted for the joint production case.

Let **B**, **A** be $n \times m$ matrices (where m may equal n) and let $\mathbf{l}$ be an $n \times 1$ vector, the jth rows of which show the outputs from, the producted inputs to and the homogeneous labour input to the jth production activity operated at rate of profit $\bar{r} > 0$, where the price vector is $\bar{\mathbf{p}} \geq \mathbf{0}$ and the wage rate is $\bar{w} > 0$. It is easily proved that there exists a scalar $\alpha(0 < \alpha < (1/\bar{w}))$ such that

$$\mathbf{Bv} = \mathbf{Av} + \mathbf{l}$$
$$\mathbf{v} = \alpha\bar{\mathbf{p}}$$

if, and only if, for each $0 \leq r \leq R = [\bar{r}/(1 - \bar{w}\alpha)]$, there exists a scalar $w \geq 0$ such that

$$\mathbf{B}\bar{\mathbf{p}} = (1 + r)\mathbf{A}\bar{\mathbf{p}} + w\mathbf{l} \tag{4}$$

If this is so, then we say that 'technique' (**B**, **A**, **l**) has the 'equal organic compositions' property. It is also readily checked that (**B**, **A**, **l**) has the 'equal organic compositions' property if and only if (1) holds, irrespective of whether **B** is or is not a diagonal or even a square matrix. Thus the argument of pp. 226–7 applies again.

An alternative argument would run as follows. Equation (4) holds, for each $0 \leq r \leq R$, if and only if $\mathbf{B}\bar{\mathbf{p}}$, $\mathbf{l}$ and $\mathbf{A}\bar{\mathbf{p}}$ are all proportional to one another. In particular, $\mathbf{B}\bar{\mathbf{p}} = (1 + R)\mathbf{A}\bar{\mathbf{p}}$, where $w = 0$ and where $r = R$. Thus $w\mathbf{l} = (R - r)\mathbf{A}\bar{\mathbf{p}}$ for any 'technique' with fixed relative prices and a linear wage–profit frontier. Suppose now that there are two such 'techniques', square or non-square, and that their frontiers intersect at the switch point ($w^s > 0$, $r^s > 0$). If $\bar{\mathbf{p}}$ must be the *common* price vector at the switch point,

$$w^s\mathbf{l} = (R - r^s)\mathbf{A}\bar{\mathbf{p}}$$

and

$$w^s(\mathbf{l} + \Delta\mathbf{l}) = (R + \Delta R - r^s)(\mathbf{A} + \Delta\mathbf{A})\bar{\mathbf{p}}$$

Hence

$$w^s \Delta \mathbf{l} = (R - r^s)\Delta \mathbf{A}\bar{\mathbf{p}} + \Delta R(\mathbf{A} + \Delta \mathbf{A})\bar{\mathbf{p}}$$

Now let activity j be common to the two systems; it follows that

$$0 = \Delta R \mathbf{e}_j^T \mathbf{A}\bar{\mathbf{p}}$$

Unless $\mathbf{e}_j^T \mathbf{A}\bar{\mathbf{p}} = 0$, this is a contradiction.

The above argument can take account of heterogeneous labour if we set

$$\mathbf{l} = \mathbf{E}\mathbf{u}$$

where **u** is a given vector and **E** is a *matrix* of heterogeneous labour inputs. (This amounts to supposing fixed *relative* wages.)

REFERENCES

Baldone, S. (1984) 'From surrogate to pseudo-production functions', *Cambridge Journal of Economics* 8 (3).

Brown, M. (1980) 'The measurement of capital aggregates: a post reswitching problem', in Usher, D. (ed.), *The Measurement of Capital*, Chicago: University of Chicago Press.

Brown, M. and Chaing, W. W. (1976) 'Capital aggregation in a general equilibrium model of production', *Econometrica* 44.

Bruno, M., Burmeister, E. and Sheshinski, E. (1966) 'The nature and implications of the reswitching of techniques', *Quarterly Journal of Economics* 80.

Burmeister, E. (1980) 'Critical observations on the labour theory of value and Sraffa's Standard commodity', in Klein, L. R., Nerlove, M., and Tsiang, S. C. (eds), *Quantitative Economics and Development: Essays in Memory of Ta-Chung Liu*, New York: Academic Press.

Mainwaring, L. (1984) *Value and Distribution in Capitalist Economies*, Cambridge: Cambridge University Press.

Pasinetti, L. L. (1977) *Lectures on the Theory of Production*, London: Macmillan.

Samuelson, P. A. (1962) 'Parable and realism in capital theory: the surrogate production function', *Review of Economic Studies* 23.

—— (1983) 'Durable capital inputs: conditions for price ratios to be invariant to profit rate changes', *Zeitschrift für Nationalökonomie* 43.

Steedman, I. (1979) 'Fixed capital and the surrogate production function', in Patterson, K. D. and Schott, K. (eds), *The Measurement of Capital: Theory and Practice*, London: Macmillan.

ACKNOWLEDGEMENTS

We should like to thank two referees of the *Cambridge Journal of Economics* for their comments on an earlier version.

Part IV

ON THE CRITIQUE OF NEOCLASSICAL THEORY

12

ON CRITICS AND PROTECTIVE BELTS

Heinz D. Kurz and Neri Salvadori

In *Vom Kriege* (*Of War*), published posthumously in 1832, Carl von Clausewitz maintained that '*the defensive form of leading a war is in itself stronger than the attacking one*' (Clausewitz [1832] 1963: 139; emphasis in the original). He expounded: 'He who is on the attack has only the advantage of the sudden attack, whereas he who is on the defence is able to permanently surprise the enemy in the course of the battle in terms of the strength and forms of his counter-attacks' (ibid.: 141). It hardly needs to be stressed that academic disputes are not military battles and that the critics of a particular theory and its advocates are not warriors attempting to defeat each other by all means, including the extinction of the adversary. Nevertheless, the view appears to be widespread that there are some similarities between intellectual debates and military battles. Otherwise it would be difficult to understand why the former are frequently described in terms of a vocabulary that derives from the realm of the latter. Two examples suffice to illustrate this. Eugen von Böhm-Bawerk in a heated controversy about alternative theories of value and distribution between advocates of the classical cost of production theory on the one hand and advocates of marginal utility theory on the other spoke of the 'showdown between the old and the new doctrine' (Böhm-Bawerk 1892: 321). And John Maynard Keynes coined the formula that 'Ricardo conquered England as completely as the Holy Inquisition conquered Spain' (Keynes 1936: 32).

In this chapter an attempt will be made to reflect upon Clausewitz's claim that defence is easier than attack with regard to a recent debate in economics: the controversy in the theory of capital and interest, also known as the 'Cambridge controversy' (Harcourt 1969). This controversy has been chosen for the following reasons. First, many people can be counted upon to have some knowledge about it. Hence the barriers to entry to a fruitful discussion should not be too large to most contemporary economists. Second, the controversy under consideration involved a major challenge to the long-period version of what is frequently called 'mainstream' or 'neoclassical' economics. It saw a clash of schools, which, in the terminology suggested by Mäki (1996), advocated 'strong substitutes' containing 'rival core claims to nothing but the truth about the ontic core' (see Mäki 1996). As is well known, long-period neoclassical theory explains all prices and quantities, including the distributive variables – the wage rate(s) and the rate of interest (profit) – in terms of 'supply and demand'. Emphasis is on situations characterized by 'free' or 'perfect' competition. Third, the development the controversy took exemplifies in an almost ideal way the different possibilities of reacting to criticism: the strategies of negligence, misrepresentation, elimination, claiming complementarity, vector addition and unification (cf. also Mäki 1996). It displays a whole set of 'protective belts' utilized by the advocates of the theory under attack. Hence the title of our chapter.

The structure of the argument is as follows. The next section gives a simple argument in favour of pluralism in economics. In the following section (pp. 238–43) a typology of possible reactions to criticism is provided and some considerations as to the factors affecting the probability of the criticism being successful are put forward. The fourth section (pp. 243–6) summarizes the criticism levelled at traditional long-period neoclassical theory. In the fifth (pp. 246–56) neoclassical responses will be dealt with. The last section contains some concluding remarks.

IN DEFENCE OF PLURALISM

Max Planck, the famous physicist, is said to have decided not to study economics because he felt it was too difficult for him. The view that economics is an intrinsically difficult subject is also conveyed in the writings of major economists. Notwithstanding this, studying the economic literature one frequently gets the impression that, although the questions posed are extremely intricate, it is simple to find the appropriate answers provided one adopts the right perspective, analytical method, intellectual paradigm. While this attitude is understandable as a device to promote a particular point of view, it lacks conviction. The reason for this is obvious. If many of the questions posed in economics are indeed as difficult as people tend to believe, then there is no reason to presume that there are simple answers. There is even less reason to presume that any of the rival theories available at a given moment of time could provide a full answer to the question under consideration.

Think about an ordinary and at first sight simple-looking economic problem such as what determines the price of a particular commodity at a given moment of time or the average of the actual prices of that commodity over a certain interval of time. Confronted with a question of this kind, the layman would probably come up with a large number of considerations that are pertinent to the question. The economist would presumably add some further considerations, systematize the different factors contemplated, reason about their relative importance and possible interactions, etc. He might point out that the price of a commodity may depend on the prices of other commodities and the prices of primary factors of production; he might take into consideration, for example, the impact of state regulations on price formation, etc. In short, after a few rounds of reflection upon the problem the answer to an allegedly simple question tends to get out of control: a mass of considerations would be accumulated which nobody could oversee any longer, and worse – there would be no end in sight at which the question would actually be settled.

Economic theory is a device to provide an answer to questions of this kind within a fairly short period of time. In order to be able to do so, economic theory has to focus attention on what are considered to be the main factors affecting the phenomenon that is to be explained. This does not mean that there are no other factors, or that those factors as a whole have no impact, because they compensate one another. It only means that they will be set aside in the explanation on the grounds that the impact of these factors is assumed to be negligible. There is no deeper justification for setting aside these factors than the success of the explanation given. Since no theory can take into consideration all factors there is scope for pluralism in economic theory. Theories may be discriminated according to which factors they take into consideration in explaining a certain phenomenon. However, even if two theories were to take into account the same set of factors there would still be scope for pluralism: the importance attributed to each of the factors and their interaction might be conceptualized differently. There is scope for this because the explanation given by each of the theories is of necessity non-exhaustive owing to the neglect of some factors. In both cases discussed it could be argued that the alternative theories are not really alternative but complementary, that is, each of them contributes to a better understanding of the phenomenon under discussion. To seek dominance for one theory over all the others with the possible result that all the rival theories are extinguished amounts to advocating scientific regress. To paraphrase Voltaire: in a subject as difficult as economics a state of doubt may not be very comfortable, but a state of certainty would be ridiculous.

What has just been said does not mean that anything goes (or should go). There are criteria which any kind of theory ought to fulfil. These criteria can only be formal, since any kind of substantive imposition would imply that we do know the answer, which we don't. There appears to be wide, although not unanimous, agreement that an important requirement is that the theory be logically coherent. To refer to the example which will concern us in the following, a theory which puts the 'principle of substitution' in the centre of its explanation of economic phenomena should apply that principle in a logically consistent way. In neoclassical long-period analysis that principle, applied to the sphere of production, is said to imply that an increase in the price of factor of production i, p_i, involves a decrease or at best the constancy of the quantity of that factor used per unit of output, q_i, that is,

$$\frac{(\Delta q_i)}{(\Delta p_i)} \leq 0$$

All propositions of the theory can be traced back to this basic idea. If it is not true in general, the theory appears to be in trouble. The question then is, how the advocates of the theory respond to the demonstration that this idea cannot be sustained in general. The following section prepares the ground for a treatment of that question.

HOW TO DEFEND A THEORY: A TYPOLOGY

Different ways to cope with criticism

The history of our subject shows that there are (at least) the following ways to deal with critics and their criticisms against doctrines or theories that are in high esteem in the scientific community in a given period of time. The critics and their criticism may be (i) ignored, (ii) misrepresented, (iii) played down as non-pertinent, (iv) refuted, (v) absorbed by putting the doctrine or theory on a more general basis or (vi) accepted. In this chapter attention will focus on cases (i)–(v).

Reaction (i): strategy of negligence

For obvious reasons we can only deal with cases in which the criticism put forward is not permanently ignored, but has been ignored for a certain period of time only. To ignore temporarily new findings that run counter to established doctrines is very common indeed and not difficult to explain. It can be traced back either to a lack of understanding of the new findings and their implications for the received doctrines or to ideological commitments on the part of the majority of scholars or academic bodies supervising their research and teaching. While the politico-ideological aspects do seem to play a considerable role in the process of the production and preservation of theories we shall in the discussion in this section set them aside. Hence in the case under consideration it is the speed with which people are able to learn. This speed depends on a variety of factors, including the technical ability of scholars to come to grips with the new results if these are arrived at by using new techniques, for example new mathematical tools, and the demanding character of these which accounts for the fact that several major findings have been ignored for a long time by large parts of the scientific community. What has been ignored at one time can of course be refuted, absorbed or accepted at another time. Here it suffices to emphasize that the mere fact that learning processes are time-consuming activities favours, at least for some time, the survival of existing doctrines that have become obsolete with the discovery of new results.

Reaction (ii): strategy of misrepresentation

When a new theory is put forward, and particularly when it is perceived as a strong substitute for the going dominant theory, then there is the danger that the new theory will be misrepresented by certain advocates of the incumbent theory. The history of our subject offers many illustrations of this. The misrepresentation may or may not be due to a lack of understanding of the alternative. In the case in which it is, the misrepresentation would vanish as the theory is gradually grasped better. The strategy of false representation is often combined with the following one.

Reaction (iii): strategy to play down the new results

Attempts to play down new results and even entire theories that may constitute an alternative to the dominant one(s) are a recurrent phenomenon in the history of our subject. There are essentially two variants of this, one related to the theoretical novelty of the alternative, the other related to its empirical importance. The phenomena which the dominant theory is unable to explain are often played down as cases which, though conceivable, can be ignored because they are said to represent but 'anomalies' or 'perverse cases'. Scepticism is expressed as to the relevance of the alternative. Very often the scepticism is based on a preconception of 'the real world out there'. The novel phenomenon is taken to be empirically unimportant. Hence theories are rejected on grounds of 'relevance', empirical and other. It goes without saying that this is a highly dubious response, since its claimant pretends to be possessed of some prior knowledge of the explanandum which is not available to the scientific community at large.

Reaction (iv): strategy of elimination

The demonstration that a criticism put forward against a theory is ill-founded may contribute to strengthening the 'belief' in the correctness of the theory and can thus be compared in its effects to a successful vaccination of a person. To be able to show that certain propositions are correct and the objections levelled at them are wrong or not pertinent is the best way to give support to a theory. However, economic theories are not rejected only because of slips in the argument. There are also cases in which certain theoretical possibilities which cannot be denied for the simple reason that they can be shown to exist are rejected on the grounds that they can be ruled out empirically. According to this view the theory under attack is a simplified picture of reality that cannot be challenged by 'exceptions' pointed out by the critics. This way of choosing between different theories, or rather of attempting to immunize a theory against its critics, appears to be very common indeed. The accusation of being empirically irrelevant has become a major strategy to silence critics. The success of this strategy presupposes that the theory under attack has proved to be long-lived, i.e. characterized by a high fitness to survive. This fitness to survive seems to be closely related to its capacity to absorb certain criticisms either by providing a more general conceptualization of the theory which allows one to take care of the phenomena referred to in the critique, leaving the basic approach of the theory intact, or by changing that approach without, however, dispensing with major features of the theory. To reject a criticism on empirical grounds implies the adoption of the falsificationist's criterion.

Reaction (v): strategy of vector addition and of unification

The absorption of a criticism in terms of a combination of a new bit of analysis with the received doctrine or of a more general formulation of the theory appears to be the common route taken in the development of a theory. However, one ought to distinguish between effective and spurious absorptions of arguments within a given analytical framework. There are cases in the history of our subject where a new theory has wrongly been conceived as more general than, and thus including as a special case, an earlier or a different theory.

On the (in)effectiveness of criticism(s)

In order to understand why some criticism proved to be effective, whereas some other criticism did not, a few additional considerations should be taken into account. Keynes in his attempt to explain the success of Ricardian economics in England pointed towards a couple of factors that may have played some role.[1] Since the types of factor mentioned are frequently invoked in similar contexts, it is useful to quote Keynes's reasoning in full:

> The completeness of the Ricardian victory is something of a curiosity and a mystery. It must have been due to a complex of suitabilities in the doctrine to the environment into which it was projected. That it reached conclusions quite different from what the ordinary uninstructed person would expect, added, I suppose, to its intellectual prestige. That its teaching, translated into practice, was austere and often unpalatable, lent it virtue. That it was adapted to carry a vast and consistent logical superstructure, gave it beauty. That it could explain much social injustice and apparent cruelty as an inevitable incident in

> the scheme of progress, and the attempt to change such things as likely on the whole to do more harm than good, commended its authority. That it afforded a measure of justification to the free activities of the individual capitalist, attracted to it the support of the dominant social force behind authority.
>
> (Keynes 1936: 32–3)

So much for the success of the doctrine. What about the causes that gradually undermined its authority? Keynes continues:

> But although the doctrine itself has remained unquestioned by orthodox economists up to a late date, its signal failure for purposes of scientific prediction has greatly impaired, in the course of time, the prestige of its practitioners. For professional economists, after Malthus, were apparently unmoved by the lack of correspondence between the results of their theory and the facts of observation; – a discrepancy which the ordinary man had not failed to observe, with the result of his growing unwillingness to accord to economists that measure of respect which he gives to other groups of scientists whose theoretical results are confirmed by observation when they are applied to the facts.
>
> (ibid.: 33)

Hence, in Keynes's view, the ultimate judgement passed on economic theories is whether or not they possess predictive power.

While there is certainly some truth in the view that economic theories which consistently misread 'reality' are in danger of being jettisoned, there is no reason to presume that this will of necessity be the case. The main reason is that it is difficult, even impossible, to falsify a theory. This accounts for the fact that theories, once established, are long-lived. It also helps to explain why new theories normally meet with large difficulties in getting accepted.

As to the problem mentioned last, one aspect deserves to be stressed. There is reason to think that for a criticism to be effective it matters whether it is put forward by someone from within the camp of those who advocate the theory that is being challenged, or whether it is put forward by someone from outside that camp. This may be exemplified in terms of Sraffa's 1926 criticism of partial equilibrium theory on the one hand and Sraffa's 1960 book on the other (Sraffa 1926, 1960). While his article triggered the development of the theory of imperfect (monopolistic) competition, which is still an integral part of standard microeconomics textbooks, that is, was absorbed by mainstream economics, the propositions of his book, though generating an enormous literature, did not filter into mainstream texts. A possible explanation of this asymmetrical reception is that the latter criticism concerned allegedly a 'family quarrel conducted mainly by Cambridge-trained economists' (Newman 1960: 594).

The criticism of Marshallian analysis, on the other hand, was seen to show a way out of the *impasse* which partial analysis had got into. The author of *The Economics of Imperfect Competition*, Joan Robinson, wrote in the introduction of her *Collected Economic Papers*: 'Marshall's *Principles* was the Bible, and we knew little beyond it. . . . Marshall was economics' (Robinson 1951: vii). It is also true that Sraffa's earlier criticism was not fully understood. It was enough for the participants in the debate to believe to have realized Sraffa's message.[2] A completely different story has to be told on pp. 244–6 below with respect to the impact of *Production of Commodities* on mainstream economics. Sraffa's contribution was considered to come from an outsider, with the effect that it was largely ignored by the mainstream.

This suggests that successful criticisms are often those put forward by people who have themselves, at one point, strongly advocated the theory they are now attacking. Only in very rare cases are criticisms coming from the outside accepted. While this appears to be a fair statement, it deserves emphasizing that the willingness, or otherwise, to accept a new result or the criticism of an established theory depends also on whether the scope, method or content of that theory is challenged.

Scope, method and content of theories

Differences in scope generally involve differences in the conceptual framework elaborated in order to answer the questions that define the very scope of an analysis. Differences in scope must not, however, be mistaken for differences in theory; they may simply reflect a strategy of division of labour. Frequently, analyses characterized by different scopes may be integrated into a single, coherent whole that is, or is not, more general than its parts; we may then speak of strategies of vector addition or integration. The basic principles in terms of which the different phenomena are explained may be the same, that is, derived from a single theory. In Mäki's terminology we face strong or weak complements. Similarly with regard to method. Differences in method lead to different perspectives on and analytical treatments of the same phenomenon. These methods may, however, be mutually compatible. In other words, differences in method must not be mistaken for differences in theory. For example, the problem of price may be dealt with from a short-period and a long-period analysis in terms of a single theory, as, for example, is the case with Marshallian theory. It is only content which of necessity involves different theories.

From these considerations it follows that protective belts often prove effective in the case of scope; they are also effective in the case of method, provided there is mutual compatibility. They cannot, as a matter of logic, be effective in the case of content. Yet there is ample evidence that theories survive despite the demonstration that they are flawed. How is this possible? This brings us to our case study: the capital controversy of the 1960s and 1970s.

THE CRITIQUE OF TRADITIONAL NEOCLASSICAL THEORY

The aggregate production function

The macroeconomic version of neoclassical theory was the target of a criticism put forward by Joan Robinson in her 1953 paper 'The production function and the theory of capital' (Robinson 1953), which was the proper beginning of what has become known as the 'Cambridge controversies in the theory of capital' (see Harcourt 1969, 1972). In the course of investigating the meaning of a production function for total output, Joan Robinson set up what Robert Solow (1963) later dubbed a 'pseudo-production function', consisting of the possible positions of equilibrium, corresponding to alternative levels of the rate of profits, given the set of alternative techniques of production. She showed 'that there is no meaning to be given to a "quantity of capital" apart from the rate of profit, so that the contention that the "marginal product of capital" determines the rate of profit is meaningless' (Robinson 1970: 309). In constructing a 'pseudo-production function' she found that over certain ranges of it the technique that becomes eligible at a lower real wage rate (to which corresponds a higher rate of profits) may be less labour-intensive than that chosen at a higher wage rate (to which corresponds a lower rate of profits). This finding contradicted the 'well-behaved production function', the popular workhorse of neoclassical macroeconomic theory, which assumes that a lower real wage rate is always associated with a more labour-intensive technique.

Joan Robinson called this finding a 'perverse relationship' (Robinson 1956: 109–10), a 'curiosum'. Paul Samuelson (1962), in an attempt to counter Joan Robinson's attack on the aggregate production function, claimed that even in cases with heterogeneous capital goods some rationalization can be provided for the validity of simple neoclassical 'parables' which assume that there is a single homogeneous factor called 'capital', the marginal product of which equals the rate of return. Samuelson based his defence of traditional theory in terms of the construction of a 'surrogate production function' in a model which takes into account heterogeneous capital in a very special way: corn is produced with labour and a machine, which is itself produced by labour and the same machine, but for each process to produce corn there is a different machine. In constructing the 'surrogate production function' Samuelson, alas, assumed equal proportions of labour to the machine in both sectors of the economy for each technique (cf. ibid.: 196–7). This implied, however, that the two goods could not sensibly be discriminated in the sense that the price of the machine in terms of corn is not affected by changes in income distribution. By this token the 'real' economy with heterogeneous goods was turned into the 'imaginary' economy with a homogeneous output, i.e. the 'surrogate production function' was nothing more than the infamous aggregate production function. This was shown, among others, by Garegnani (1970). Samuelson (1966) openly admitted that he was wrong and that what he called the 'Ramsey–Clark parable', i.e. the aggregate production function, cannot generally be sustained. In the introduction to her 1953 paper Joan Robinson stressed that 'the production function has been a powerful instrument of miseducation' (Robinson 1953: 81). The economic literature published since shows that, strangely enough, it still is.

'Capital' as a factor of production

The use of the value of capital as a factor of production alongside the factors labour and land which are measured in terms of their own technical units in the production function of single commodities had already been rejected by Knut Wicksell. It implied 'arguing in a circle' (Wicksell [1901] 1934: 149), since capital and the rate of interest enter as a cost in the production of capital goods themselves. Hence the value of the capital goods inserted in the production function depends on the rate of interest and will generally change with it. Following Joan Robinson (1953: 95), the dependence of prices on distribution was discussed under the heading of 'price Wicksell effects'.[3]

However, even though the phenomenon under consideration had been well known since the classical economists and was referred to also by several neoclassical authors, especially Wicksell (e.g. [1901] 1934: 147–51), the earlier authors were not fully aware of the complications involved. In particular, they were of the opinion that with a rise in the rate of profits, *r*, given the system of production, the ratio of prices of any two commodities would stay constant *or* rise *or* fall, throughout the range of variation of *r*. This opinion was closely related to the hypothesis that the capital–labour or capital–output ratios of the different industries could be brought into a ranking that is independent of distribution. Yet, as Sraffa has shown, this is generally not possible, i.e. 'the price of a product . . . may rise or it may fall, or it may even alternate in rising and falling, relative to its means of production' (Sraffa 1960: 15). Therefore, to characterize an industry as 'capital-intensive' or 'labour-intensive' in general makes no sense unless the level of the rate of profits is specified at which this characterization is supposed to apply.

According to Marshall the applications of the principle of substitution 'extend over almost every field of economic inquiry' (1920: 284). This principle forms the very basis of the marginalist theory of value and distribution. Hence any criticism of that theory has to deal with the problem of choice from a set of alternatives contemplated by the principle of substitution. In the Cambridge controversy over the theory of capital emphasis was naturally on the problem of the choice of technique rather than on that of consumer choice.

Reswitching is a situation in which a technique is cost-minimizing at two disconnected ranges of the rate of profits and not so in between those ranges. Samuelson has recognized that 'this phenomenon can be called "perverse" only in the sense that the conventional parables did not prepare us for it' (1966: 578). The implication of the possibility of the reswitching of techniques is that the direction of change of the 'input proportions' cannot be related unambiguously to changes in the so-called 'factor prices'. The central element of the neoclassical explanation of distribution in terms of supply and demand is thus revealed as defective. The demonstration that a fall in the wage rate (i.e. a rise in the rate of profits) may lead to the adoption of the less 'labour-intensive', i.e. more 'capital-intensive' of the two techniques, destroyed, in the minds of the critics of traditional neoclassical theory, the whole basis for the neoclassical view of substitution in production. Moreover, since a fall in the wage rate may cheapen some of the commodities, the production of which at a higher level of the wage rate was characterized by a relatively low 'labour intensity', the substitution among consumption goods contemplated by the traditional theory of consumer demand may result in a higher, as well as a lower, 'labour intensity'. It follows that the principle of substitution in consumption cannot offset the breakdown of the principle of substitution in production. It should be noted, however, that in order for the input use per unit of output to be positively related to the price of the input, reswitching is not needed. Hence the inequality stated on p. 238 cannot generally be taken for granted.

We talk of *reverse capital deepening* when the relationship between the value of capital (*per capita*) and the rate of profits is increasing. The negative implication of reswitching and reverse capital deepening for traditional theory can be illustrated by means of the example of Figure 12.1, in which the value of capital (K) corresponding to the full employment level of labour is plotted against the rate of profits (r). Obviously, if with traditional analysis we conceived the curve KK' as the 'demand curve' for capital, which, together with the corresponding 'supply curve' $K^*K^{*\prime}$, is taken to determine the equilibrium value of the rate of profits, we would have to conclude that this equilibrium, although unique, is unstable.[4] With free competition, conceived, as it is in neoclassical theory, as including the perfect flexibility of the distributive variables, a deviation of r from r^* would lead to the absurd conclusion that one of the two income categories, wages and profits, would disappear. According to the critics of traditional neoclassical theory, this result demonstrates all the more impressively the

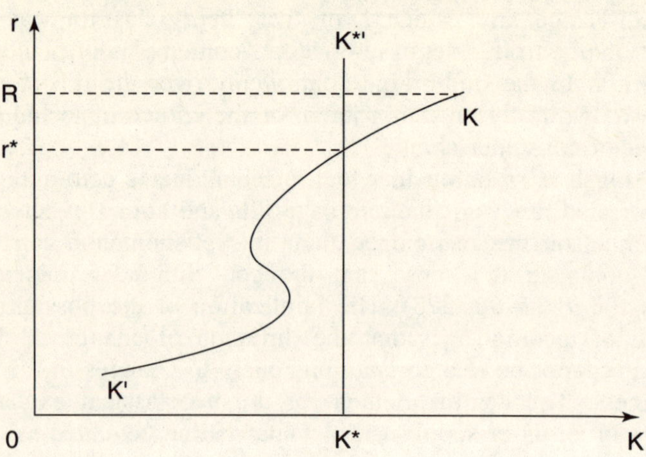

Figure 12.1

failure of the supply and demand approach to the theory of normal distribution, prices and quantities.

NEOCLASSICAL RESPONSES

It is hardly surprising that the protagonists of the supply and demand approach should have shown so much concern when confronted with the critique. In what follows we shall briefly summarize their consecutive responses to the critique. We may distinguish broadly between two types of response: (i) attempts to defend traditional neoclassical theory and (ii) counter-attacks on the alternative theory from which the criticism had been developed. Historically, the answers belonging to the first type generally preceded those belonging to the second.

In defence of traditional neoclassical theory

The very first reaction followed Christian Morgenstern's famous dictum that 'it cannot be what must not be', that is, it amounted to the strategy of elimination. In 1965 David Levhari, a student of Paul Samuelson's, claimed to have demonstrated that reswitching was impossible, i.e. that systems of production can be ordered according to 'degrees of mechanization' (cf. Levhari 1965). This claim was shown to be false by Luigi Pasinetti, who was encouraged to do so by Piero Sraffa (cf. Baranzini and Harcourt 1993: 9), in a paper presented at the First World Congress of the Econometric Society in Rome in 1965. A revised version of Pasinetti's paper was then published in the November 1966 issue of the *Quarterly Journal of Economics* (Pasinetti 1966) together with papers by

Levhari and Samuelson (1966), Morishima (1966), Bruno *et al.* (1966), Garegnani (1966) and Samuelson (1966).[5] Samuelson and Levhari in their joint paper and Samuelson in his 'summing up' paper frankly admitted that the no-reswitching theorem was wrong. Samuelson also gave some numerical examples which illustrated in simple terms why reswitching and capital reversing are possible. See also Burmeister and Turnovsky (1972).[6]

Since the possibility of reswitching and reverse capital deepening could no longer be denied, doubts were raised as to its empirical importance (see, for example, Ferguson 1969). The adopted strategy of negligence consisted of playing down the importance of the new results, thereby insinuating that neoclassical theory was a simplified picture of reality, the basic correctness of which could not be endangered by 'exceptions' of the kind analysed in the capital debate.[7] This sort of reasoning was implicitly dealt with by Sraffa in an oral intervention at the 1958 Corfu conference on the theory of capital. Counterposing the statistician's measure with measurement in theory, which should be able to take into account all possible cases, i.e. be universally applicable, Sraffa emphasized:

> The theoretical measures required absolute precision. . . . The work of J. B. Clark, Böhm-Bawerk and others was intended to produce pure definitions of capital, as required by their theories, not as a guide to actual measurement. If we found contradictions, then these pointed to defects in the theory, and an inability to define measures of capital accurately.
>
> (Cf. Lutz and Hague 1961: 305–6)

Furthermore, it should be clear that attempts to disprove reswitching in terms of wage–profit curves constructed from input–output data for different years (cf. Krelle 1977; Ochoa 1989; see also Petrovič 1991) are fundamentally mistaken. Leaving aside data problems and the conceptual difficulties concerning the required 'translation' of empirical 'facts' into the categories of the analytical framework, the finding that the w–r curves associated with the techniques of 1988 and 1993, for example, do not possess several switchpoints cannot be considered an empirical counterexample to reswitching, since the latter refers to the technical knowledge *at a given moment of time*.[8]

Some authors attempted to preserve the traditional neoclassical theory by simply ruling out reswitching and other 'perverse', i.e. non-conventional, phenomena in terms of sufficiently bold assumptions about available techniques. This route was followed, for example, by Sato (1974). It should come as no surprise that, given these assumptions, the central neoclassical postulate of the inverse relation between the capital–labour ratio and the rate of profits should re-emerge as 'one of the most powerful theorems in economic theory' (Sato 1974: 355). However, in order to be clear about this move it deserves to be stressed that it was motivated, as one author expressly admits, by the fact that 'regular economies' have 'desirable properties' (Burmeister 1980: 124).[9]

Other advocates of the neoclassical approach were conscious of how defective the attempts were to avoid reswitching and capital reversing or to play down their importance using the 'empirical' route. Since the phenomenon was irrefutable it had to be absorbed and shown to be compatible with the more sophisticated versions of the theory, i.e. those at the 'frontier of knowledge' (cf. Hahn 1975: 363). In responses of the second type the criticism of traditional neoclassical theory is therefore generally accepted. Instead of defending what cannot be defended, the alternative classical theory is examined. It is claimed that the latter does not constitute an alternative to the *modern* versions of neoclassical theory, i.e. those based on the notions of temporary or intertemporal equilibrium (strategy of complementarity or of unification). This was argued by Christopher Bliss (1975), Edwin Burmeister (1980) and especially by Frank Hahn (1975, 1982). Their responses can be said to reflect Clausewitz's dictum: 'he who is on the defensive is able to permanently surprise the enemy in the course of the battle in terms of the strength and forms of his counter-attacks'.

'General' vs. 'special' theories

Hahn frankly admitted that the Sraffa-based critique is correct with respect to 'many writers whom we regard as neoclassical who have either made mistakes of reasoning or based themselves on special assumptions which have themselves nothing to do with neoclassical theory' (Hahn 1982: 354). He also expressed the opinion that 'Sraffa's book contains no formal propositions which I consider to be wrong although here and there it contains remarks which I consider to be false' (ibid.: 353). However, the main point of Hahn's argument is a different one: 'I assert the following: there is not a single formal proposition in Sraffa's book which is not also true in a General Equilibrium model constructed on his assumptions' (Hahn 1975: 362; similarly 1982: 353). This has the following implications stressed by Hahn. First, the criticism of traditional neoclassical theory has no bearing upon general equilibrium theory of the Arrow–Debreu variety.[10] Secondly, it is contended that Sraffa's analysis represents but a 'special case' of the latter. Both propositions are ultimately traced back to the fact that in modern general equilibrium theory the distribution of income is determined in terms of arbitrarily given *physical* endowments of agents. Since the endowment of the economy with capital goods is not given a scalar representation, as in traditional theory, the capital critique is said not to be applicable. Moreover, since in general equilibrium there will generally be as many 'own' rates of return as there are different assets in the endowment set, Sraffa's analysis, which revolves around the uniformity of profit rates, is said to be concerned with 'a very special state of the economy' (ibid.: 363).

To qualify the analyses of other schools of thought as special cases of one's own analysis is a time-honoured device in intellectual controversy amongst economists. Keynes, for example, presented his own theory, which allows for persistent unemployment, as the *General Theory*, implying that the conventional full employment theory is a 'special case' (Keynes 1936: 3). Representatives of the 'neoclassical synthesis' in macroeconomics on the other hand maintained that Keynes's analysis lacks generality, because it is based on special assumptions concerning the flexibility of wages, etc. But does this method carry us very far? While there can be no doubt that in some cases it is appropriate, in others it is not. For example, it is well known that a model of a non-Euclidean geometry can be built up within the axioms of Euclidean geometry. Does this entitle us to consider the non-Euclidean geometry a 'special case' of the Euclidean one? Similarly, take a model inspired by Sraffa's analysis in which there are different qualities of land but there is neither capital nor labour. This model is very similar to a neoclassical model in which income distribution is determined by the relative scarcities of the 'factors of production'. Do we have to conclude from this that the neo-classical analysis is a 'special case' of 'classical' analysis?

There is an obvious way to decide whether a particular analysis is, or is not, a special case of the Arrow–Debreu model. If it were, it would start from the *same* set of data but impose special restrictions on this set. The set of data, or exogenous variables, on which modern general equilibrium theory is based is summarized by Hahn in the following definition of what he means by a 'neoclassical theory':

> I shall call a theory neoclassical if (a) an economy is fully described by the preferences and endowments of agents and by the production sets of firms; (b) all agents treat prices parametrically (perfect competition); and (c) all agents are rational and given prices will take that action (or set of actions) from amongst those available to them which is best for them given their preferences. (Firms prefer more profit to less.)
>
> (Hahn 1982: 354)

Attention has to focus on element (a), since the other two elements (regarding competition and rationality) are also to be found in classical analysis, with the concept of 'free competition' replacing that of 'perfect competition'. In element (a) we encounter (i) preferences, (ii) initial endowments (labour powers, lands, capital goods, etc.) and the distribution of property rights among agents, and (iii) technical alternatives. The main difference between neoclassical and classical theory of value and distribution concerns item (ii), that is, the assumption entertained in neoclassical theory of given endowments of capital goods.

Hahn is thus confronted with the task of showing that Sraffa, very much like modern general equilibrium theory, starts from given initial endowments, and in addition, very much like a special case of that theory, presupposes a particular composition of those endowments (see also Garegnani 1990b: 113–15). Yet this cannot be demonstrated, for the simple reason that Sraffa, following the classical approach to the theory of value and distribution, develops his analysis in terms of a *different* set of data, thus putting forward a *different* theory. The difficulty of the task Hahn has set himself can be seen in the way he attempts to tackle it. As to the first aspect of this task, i.e. that of discovering *some* assumption about endowments in Sraffa, Hahn simply *claims* that 'it cannot be part of the doctrine that you are uninterested whether there [are enough commodities in a given year that can be used as means of production] to meet demand' (Hahn 1982: 365). In the immediately following sentence Hahn admits, however, that his claim is contradicted by Sraffa's analysis: 'Yet Mr Sraffa does not consider this matter' (ibid.). Interestingly, this finding does not prompt Hahn to question his 'special case' interpretation. It rather makes him seek to establish its correctness by adopting a different route: instead of providing direct evidence in support of the claim that Sraffa started from given endowments, he looks out for indirect evidence. He believes he has found it in Sraffa's concern with a uniform rate of profits. Clearly, to impose a uniform rate of profits on a general equilibrium system would render it overdetermined. Hence data (i), (ii) or (iii) mentioned above cannot be taken as independent variables. Now it is Hahn's contention that at the basis of Sraffa's price equations there must be a special proportion between the initial endowments, i.e. (ii) is tacitly assumed to be specified accordingly. 'So the neoclassical economist who is always happy to consider interesting special cases sets to work to find a proper equilibrium for Mr Sraffa' (ibid.). Combining the familiar assumptions of general equilibrium theory of given preferences and technical alternatives with the unfamiliar one of a given and uniform rate of profits implies that the composition of the capital stock cannot be taken as independently determined, but must be seen as depending on the givens mentioned: as Hahn emphasizes with regard to the two-commodity illustrations of his argument, 'we must make one of [the two endowments] into an unknown' (ibid.). This concludes Hahn's attempt to demonstrate that the 'special case' interpretation of Sraffa's analysis is correct.

Hahn's interpretation does not stand up to close examination. First, it deserves to be stressed that Sraffa does *not* start from given endowments of capital goods, i.e. produced means of production, in order to determine distribution and normal prices. He rather takes as given *gross outputs* and one of the distributive variables. The quantities of the capital goods available in the system are considered as dependent rather than independent variables. Following the classical economists, he assumes that the capital stocks installed in the different industries are adjusted to these outputs and the given level of the distributive variable, by an appropriate choice of technique, such that these outputs can be produced at minimum cost. The tendency towards normal capital utilization and a uniform rate of profits is taken to be the outcome of the working of competition. Sraffa's is a different theory of value and distribution which manages to meet its objective, i.e. to determine relative prices and the remaining distributive variable(s) in terms of *these* data. Secondly, what Hahn thinks to be an adequate interpretation of Sraffa's analysis is in fact a reiteration of a finding in older neoclassical authors: as has been seen above (pp. 243–6), several representatives of traditional neoclassical theory were aware that in order to be consistent with the notion of a competitive equilibrium the capital endowment could only be given in value terms, with the physical composition to be determined endogenously. Hence, ironically, Hahn attributes to Sraffa what Sraffa had identified as the major difficulty of traditional neoclassical theory, i.e. that the 'quantity of capital' and the distribution of income cannot be ascertained independently of one another.

In what follows two further observations on the 'special case' interpretation will be provided. To claim that the Arrow–Debreu model is general, whereas Sraffa's analysis is special, misses the fact that the former is short-period and the latter is long-period. Thus, in dealing with a 'private ownership economy', Debreu (1959: 39, 78) assumes a *given* number of producers and *given* shares of the profit of the various producers received by consumers. While these assumptions are necessary within the schema of Debreu's short-period theory, there is no room for them in the different schema of Sraffa's analysis.

Duménil and Lévy (1985; see also Dana *et al.* 1989) take intertemporal general equilibrium theory as it is and ask whether it is possible to locate in its formalism the concept of 'natural' prices, or prices of production, and a uniform rate of profits. They show that under certain conditions, over an infinite horizon, prices in the intertemporal model tend toward 'natural' prices as the relative prices progressively stabilize. They conclude:

> What can be conserved in the intertemporal equilibrium is only its asymptotic behaviour position, i.e. *that which coincides with the classical conception of equilibrium*! Therefore, prices of production are not an uninteresting particular case of the neoclassical model. On the contrary, every price described in the neoclassical story which does not correspond to prices of production is totally deprived of any economic significance.
>
> (ibid.: 343, original emphasis)

In their view the tracks of 'natural' prices are clearly discernible in the neoclassical equilibrium model. This undermines, they conclude, the claim that the latter is the general case and the classical long-period theory the special one.[11]

Finally, it should be noted that there is an asymmetry in the way in which Sraffa's analysis is perceived by advocates of general equilibrium theory and the way in which that theory is perceived by advocates of the Sraffian, i.e. 'classical', analysis. From the point of view of the former Sraffa's analysis, though correct, is but a 'special case' of general equilibrium theory. Yet, from the point of view of the latter, general equilibrium theory is not only different from Sraffa's analysis but also difficult to sustain. More particularly, it is argued that temporary and intertemporal theory, not differently from traditional neoclassical theory, cannot avoid the problem of capital. We shall come back to this claim on pp. 253–4.

Temporary and intertemporal equilibrium and the problem of capital

We may conclude this section by way of summarizing what we consider to be the main features of intertemporal and temporary equilibrium models, as far as the problem of capital and interest is concerned. We begin with a discussion of temporary equilibrium.

Temporary equilibrium models are characterized by a seemingly complete evaporation of the concept of capital. Markets exist only for the exchange of commodities at the present date. Supply and demand determine present prices at which individual plans are mutually consistent, given the initial data, which include individual agents' expectations about future prices.[12] Nothing guarantees that these expectations will be realized, so that individual plans will be revised as actual prices are found to differ from what was anticipated. In each single period capital goods cannot be seen differently from natural resources inherited from the preceding period which earn their proprietor a rent if and only if they are scarce. However, while it is true that in these models the concept of capital as a *stock* magnitude has been dispensed with, the concept of capital as a *flow* magnitude is still there. To see this, we have to leave the capital market and turn to the investment–savings market.

Similarly in intertemporal models, in which the problem of capital is also seemingly removed from the scene: the capital goods available at the beginning of the first period have the character of 'primary' factors of production and can thus be treated on a par with scarce natural resources, such as land. The income a capital good yields its owner is again similar to the rent of land. These capital goods, together with the other primary factors, are used to produce consumption goods and new means of production in correspondence with intertemporal preferences of consumers, coping with the ever-present problem of scarcity as well as possible, given the initial endowments and the available technical alternatives. As the offspring of rent-yielding assets the newly produced means of production bear the stamp of their origin and are also rent-yielding factors. Some uneasiness about the treatment of produced means of production and the asymmetric treatment of the past and the present in intertemporal equilibrium models is expressed by Geanakoplos:

> the assumption of a finite number of commodities (and hence of dates) forces upon the model the interpretation of the economic process as a one-way activity of converting given primary resources into consumption goods. If there is universal agreement about when the world will end, there can be no question about the reproduction of the capital stock. In equilibrium it will be run down to zero. . . . One certainly cannot speak about the production of all commodities by commodities (Sraffa, 1960), since at date zero there must be commodities which have not been produced by commodities.
>
> (Geanakoplos 1987: 122)

What can at most be said is that, along the avenue leading from original factor services to consumption goods, intermediate goods will emerge which gradually transmute themselves into final goods. To all appearances, the problem of capital is again successfully circumnavigated.

Yet, as with temporary equilibrium, these appearances are deceptive. As Malinvaud pointed out in his entry 'Intertemporal equilibrium and efficiency' in *The New Palgrave* (cf. Malinvaud 1987), 'it is now realized that the rate of interest is related in a very complex way to the many exogenous determinants of equilibrium and that changes in relative prices, which are associated with changes of interest, may be responsible for paradoxical effects' (ibid.: 960). This admitted, the challenge to intertemporal equilibrium theory posed by these findings is right away played down using the (infamous) 'empirical' route (cf. p. 247 above): 'The significance of these various negative theoretical results should of course [!] not be overstated. While reflecting the basic complexity of the relationship between the full system of discounted prices and its determinants, the results do not prove that "pathological cases" are often empirically relevant' (ibid.: 960).

To see more clearly why the modern versions of neoclassical theory are not immune to the criticism of the traditional neoclassical notion of 'capital' (as summarized on pp. 243–6), a few additional considerations may prove useful. In this context it is worth mentioning that it was particularly Garegnani (most recently 1990a, 1993) who argued that, notwithstanding the fact that capital is resolved into a set of physical factors, the modern versions cannot evade the problem of capital. First, recall that the demand and supply functions for capital, a stock, in the older theories were assumed to operate over time through a sequence of demand functions for gross investment confronted with supply functions for gross savings, i.e. flows. The interest elasticity of these demand functions for investment was seen to reflect the interest elasticity of the demand for capital as a stock. Once this is understood, 'it also becomes clear that the difficulties associated with the demand for "capital" in the traditional long-period versions have to be present also in the contemporary short-period versions of the theory' (Garegnani 1990a: 60). For these short-period versions cannot do without (gross) investment and (gross) saving functions, i.e. functions which refer to 'capital' in its 'free' form. In equilibrium investment equals savings, i.e. the aggregate demand for the outputs of means of production equals the aggregate supply. However, there is no guarantee that the equilibrium is stable. With reswitching and capital reversing there is no reason to presume that with a fall (rise) in the effective rate of interest investment demand will increase (decrease). In short, the presence of these phenomena would be reflected in a multiplicity of equilibria, one or several of which would be unstable. However, as was argued on pp. 245–6 with regard to 'perversely' shaped, i.e. upward-sloping, factor-demand functions, this possibility would call into question the validity of the entire economic analysis in terms of demand and supply.[13]

The above considerations should have made clear the following. First, there is no presumption that the neoclassical theories of intertemporal or temporary equilibrium are 'general' whereas the classical theory is 'special'. The truth is that these theories are *different*: while the former are short-period, the latter is long-period. Secondly, although in the modern neoclassical theories there is no single 'quantity of capital' representing the endowment of the economy with produced means of production, the problem of capital is not avoided: it reappears in the investment–savings market and is reflected in the instability of equilibrium. Finally, the modern versions of the demand and supply approach are beset with several methodological and conceptual difficulties which raise serious doubts about their usefulness.

CONCLUDING REMARKS

This chapter has illustrated Clausewitz's dictum that 'defence is easier than attack' in terms of the capital controversy of the 1960s and 1970s. It has been shown that if a dominant theory is challenged by a strong substitute, its advocates will try to defend that theory by producing protective belts or engaging in counter-attacks. While in that controversy it was conclusively shown that the view long-period neoclassical theory takes of the relationship between input use (per unit of output) and the price of the input cannot generally be sustained, surprisingly that view has not been jettisoned. This chapter attempts to contribute to an explanation of this in terms of a detailed account of the different aspects of the debate. The disquieting fact remains that in economics propositions that have been proved wrong are still used by many of its practitioners.

NOTES

1 It goes without saying that Keynes's account of the situation in the time after Ricardo's death up to the 1930s is grossly exaggerated. Even 'Say's law' was not as widely accepted, and correspondingly some sort of 'principle of effective demand' rejected, as Keynes insinuated.

2 Interestingly, Joan Robinson dedicated a copy of her *Economics of Imperfect Competition* to Sraffa with the words 'To the Piero of 1933 from a disciple of the Sraffa of 1926'.

3 See, for example, Bhaduri (1966), Samuelson (1966), Harcourt (1972: 39–45) and Bliss (1975: 114–17). From the point of view of the history of economic thought this terminology is unfortunate, since the first author ever to analyse in some depth the influence of distribution on relative prices was Ricardo (see, in particular, Ricardo [1817] 1951: 30–43).

4 It goes without saying that Figure 12.1 is constructed on the implicit assumption that the numeraire is the consumption unit (that is, a given vector of consumption goods), so that the supply of capital, as forgone consumption, is a vertical straight line. (This implies also that we assumed that commodities are always consumed in given proportions, an assumption which permeates large parts of steady-state capital theory.) A change in the numeraire may, of course, change the shape of the two curves, *but* it cannot change their relative shape: if the former cuts the latter from above (below) in terms of one numeraire, it does so also in terms of any other numeraire. That is, a change in the numeraire does not change the stability properties of the system.

5 The numerical counter-example, provided by Pasinetti in 1965 did not meet all the assumptions underlying Levhari's argument, whereas the one published in 1966 did.

6 Some authors claimed that there is an analogy between reswitching and the long-known possibility of the existence of multiple internal rates of return. They remarked, quoting the Bible, 'there is no new thing under the sun' (Bruno *et al.* 1966: 553). However, whereas the phenomenon of multiple internal rates of return is a discovery within the *partial* framework of microeconomic theory of investment, reswitching presupposes a *general* framework. On multiple internal rates of return see especially Irving Fisher (1930). Interestingly, there are passages in Fisher which indicate that he was aware that prices may vary, possibly in a complex way, with variations in the rate of interest. He contended, however, that this complication is 'more intricate than important' (ibid.: 170–1).

7 Occasionally, reswitching was compared with the 'Giffen good' case in consumer theory (cf. Hicks 1965: 154; Stiglitz 1974). On the fallacy of this analogy see Garegnani 1990a: 72).

8 More recently there have been attempts to define and then assess the 'probability' of reswitching (or capital reversing) in a given analytical framework; see on this D'Ippolito (1987, 1989) and Mainwaring and Steedman (1993). These attempts are not to be confounded with the applied works referred to above.

9 A 'regular economy' is defined as one for which the 'real Wicksell effect' is always negative (cf. Burmeister 1980: 101), where a 'real Wicksell effect' gives the change in the value of capital due to the fact that steady-state capital stocks vary with the rate of profits. That is, the value of capital is taken to be inversely related to the rate of profits. The notion of a 'regular economy' is also called 'a necessary and sufficient condition to preclude paradoxical behavior' (ibid.: 119). 'Such economies exhibit behavior that insome important qualitative respects is

similar to that of the standard one-sector model', which in turn is said to be tentatively acceptable, 'on the basis of empirical evidence' (ibid.: 101).

10 In another place Hahn admitted that he himself 'every so often slipped into the aggregate version of the neo-classical model' (Hahn 1972: 8).

11 Comparing the classical notion of gravitation of market prices to 'natural' prices and the asymptotic behaviour of prices in intertemporal equilibrium theory, Duménil and Lévy contended that the latter could at most be considered 'an uninteresting particular case of the classical convergence process' (1985: 343 n.).

12 A weakness of the theories of temporary equilibrium concerns the necessarily arbitrary choice of hypotheses about individual price expectations. Indeed, as Burmeister stressed, 'all too often "nearly anything can happen" is the only possible unqualified conclusion' (Burmeister 1980: 213). Moreover, the stability properties of this kind of equilibrium are unclear, since small perturbations caused by accidental factors may entail changes in expectations, which define that very equilibrium.

13 The above considerations also show the futility of Solow's attempt, inspired by Fisher (1930), to avoid the problem of capital in terms of the concept of the 'social rate of return' which gives the ratio of the present value of the additional stream of future income generated by investment and that investment; see Solow (1963, 1967). For a criticism of that concept see Pasinetti (1969).

REFERENCES

Baranzini, M. and Harcourt, G. C. (1993) 'Introduction', in M. Baranzini and G. C. Harcourt (eds), *The Dynamics of the Wealth of Nations: Growth, Distribution and Structural Change. Essays in Honour of Luigi Pasinetti*, New York: St Martin's Press, pp. 1–42.

Bhaduri, A. (1966) 'The concept of the marginal productivity of capital and the Wicksell effect', *Oxford Economic Papers* 18: 284–8.

Bliss, C. J. (1975) *Capital Theory and the Distribution of Income*, Amsterdam: North-Holland.

Böhm-Bawerk, E. von (1892) 'Wert, Kosten und Grenznutzen', *Jahrbücher für Nationalökonomie und Statistik*, 3rd series 3: 321–67.

Bruno, M., Burmeister, E. and Sheshinski, E. (1966) 'The nature and implications of the reswitching of techniques', *Quarterly Journal of Economics* 80: 526–53.

Burmeister, E. (1980) *Capital Theory and Dynamics*, Cambridge: Cambridge University Press.

Burmeister, E. and Turnovsky, S. J. (1972) 'Capital deepening response in an economy with heterogeneous capital goods', *American Economic Review* 65: 842–53.

Clausewitz, C. von (1963) *Vom Kriege*, first published in 1832, in *Rowohlts Klassiker der Literatur und Wissenschaft* 12, Munich: Rowohlt.

Dana, R. A., Florenzano, M., Le Van, C. and Lévy, D. (1989) 'Asymptotic properties of a Leontief economy', *Journal of Economic Dynamics and Control* 13: 553–68.

Debreu, G. (1959) *Theory of Value: an Axiomatic Analysis of Economic Equilibrium*, New York: Wiley.

D'Ippolito, G. (1987) 'Probabilità di perverso comportamento del capitale al variare del saggio dei profitti: il modello embrionale a due settori', *Note Economiche* 2: 5–37.

—— (1989) 'Delimitazione dell'area dei casi di comportamento perverso del capitale in un punto di mutamento della tecnica', in L. L. Pasinetti (ed.), *Aspetti controversi della teoria del valore*, Bologna: Il Mulino, pp. 191–7.

Duménil, G. and Lévy, D. (1985) 'The classicals and the neo-classicals: a rejoinder to Frank Hahn', *Cambridge Journal of Economics* 9: 327–45.

Ferguson, C. E. (1969) *The Neo-classical Theory of Production and Distribution*, Cambridge: Cambridge University Press.

Fisher, I. (1930) *The Theory of Interest*, New York: Macmillan.

Garegnani, P. (1966) 'Switching of techniques', *Quarterly Journal of Economics* 80: 554–67.

—— (1970) 'Heterogeneous capital, the production function and the theory of distribution', *Review of Economic Studies* 37: 407–36.

—— (1990a) 'Quantity of capital', in J. Eatwell, M. Milgate and P. Newman (eds), *Capital Theory*, London: Macmillan, pp. 1–78.

—— (1990b) 'Sraffa: classical versus marginalist analysis', in K. Bharadwaj and B. Schefold (eds), *Essays on Piero Sraffa: Critical Perspectives on the Revival of Classical Theory*, London: Unwin Hyman, reprinted by Routledge, pp. 112–41.

—— (1993) Sraffa Lecture (mimeo).

Geanakoplos, J. (1987) 'Arrow–Debreu model of general equilibrium', in J. Eatwell, M. Milgate and P. Newman (eds), *The New Palgrave* 1, London: Macmillan, pp. 116–24.

Hahn, F. H. (1972) *The Share of Wages in the National Income: an Enquiry into the Theory of Distribution*, London: Weidenfeld & Nicolson.

—— (1975) 'Revival of political economy: the wrong issues and the wrong argument', *Economic Record* 51: 360–64.

—— (1982) 'The neo-Ricardians', *Cambridge Journal of Economics* 6: 353–74.

Harcourt, G. C. (1969) 'Some Cambridge controversies in the theory of capital', *Journal of Economic Literature* 7: 369–405.

—— (1972) *Some Cambridge Controversies in the Theory of Capital*, Cambridge: Cambridge University Press.

Harrod, R. F. (1961), 'Production of commodities', *Economic Journal* 71: 783–7.

Hicks, J. R. (1965) *Capital and Growth*, Oxford: Clarendon Press.

Jevons, W. S. (1871) *The Theory of Political Economy*, London: Macmillan.

Keynes, J. M. (1936) *The General Theory of Employment, Interest and Money*, London: Macmillan.

Krelle, W. (1977) 'Basic facts in capital theory: some lessons from the controversy in capital theory', *Révue d'Economie Politique* 87: 282–329.

Levhari, D. (1965) 'A nonsubstitution theorem and switching of techniques', *Quarterly Journal of Economics* 79: 98–105.

Levhari, D. and Samuelson, P. A. (1966) 'The nonswitching theorem is false', *Quarterly Journal of Economics* 80: 518–19.

Lutz, F. A. and Hague, D. C. (eds) (1961) *The Theory of Capital*, London: Macmillan.

Mäki, U. (1996) 'The one world and the many theories', in A. Salanti and E. Screpanti (eds), *Pluralism in Economics: New Perspectives in History and Methodology*, Aldershot: Edward Elgar, pp. 37–47.

Mainwaring, L. and Steedman, I. (1993) 'On the Probability of Reswitching and Capital Reversing in a Two-sector Sraffian Model', Manchester (mimeo).

Malinvaud, E. (1987) 'Intertemporal equilibrium and efficiency', in J. Eatwell, M. Milgate and P. Newman (eds), *The New Palgrave* 2, London: Macmillan, pp. 958–62.

Marshall, A. (1920) *Principles of Economics*, 1st edn 1890, 8th edn 1920. Reprint, London: Macmillan, 1977.

Morishima, M. (1966) 'Refutation of the nonswitching theorem', *Quarterly Journal of Economics* 80: 520–25.

Newman, P. (1960) 'The erosion of Marshall's theory of value', *Quarterly Journal of Economics* 74: 587–600.

Ochoa, E. M. (1989) 'Values, prices and wage profit curves in the US economy', *Cambridge Journal of Economics* 13: 413–29.

Pasinetti, L. L. (1966) 'Changes in the rate of profit and switches of techniques', *Quarterly Journal of Economics* 80: 503–17.

—— (1969) 'Switches of techniques and the "rate of return" in capital theory', *Economic Journal* 79: 508–31.

Petrovič, P. (1991) 'Shape of a wage–profit curve: some methodology and empirical evidence', *Metroeconomica* 42: 93–112.

Ricardo, D. (1951) *On the Principles of Political Economy and Taxation* (1st edn 1817), ed. P. Sraffa with the collaboration of M. H. Dobb, Cambridge: Cambridge University Press.

Robinson, J. V. (1951) *Collected Economic Papers*, Oxford: Blackwell.

—— (1953) 'The production function and the theory of capital', *Review of Economic Studies* 21: 81–106.

—— (1956) *The Accumulation of Capital*, London: Macmillan.

—— (1970) 'Capital theory up to date', *Canadian Journal of Economics* 3: 309–17.

Samuelson, P. A. (1962) 'Parable and realism in capital theory: the surrogate production function', *Review of Economic Studies* 29: 193–206.

—— (1966) 'A summing-up', *Quarterly Journal of Economics* 80: 568–83.

Sato, K. (1974) 'The neo-classical postulate and the technology frontier in capital theory', *Quarterly Journal of Economics* 88: 353–84.

Solow, R. M. (1963) *Capital Theory and the Rate of Return*, Amsterdam: North-Holland.

—— (1967) 'The interest rate and the transition between techniques', in C. H. Feinstein (ed.), *Socialism, Capitalism and Economic Growth: Essays presented to Maurice Dobb*, Cambridge: Cambridge University Press, pp. 30–9.

Sraffa, P. (1926) 'The laws of returns under competitive conditions', *Economic Journal* 36: 535–50.

—— (1960) *Production of Commodities by Means of Commodities: Prelude to a Critique of Economic Theory*, Cambridge: Cambridge University Press.

—— (1962) 'Production of commodities: a comment', *Economic Journal* 72: 477–9.

Stiglitz, J. E. (1974) 'The Cambridge controversy in the theory of capital: a view from New Haven. A review article', *Journal of Political Economy* 82: 893–903.

Wicksell, K. (1901) *Föreläsingar i Nationalekonomi* I, Lund: Berlingska Boktrycheriet. English translation in Wicksell (1934).

—— (1934) *Lectures on Political Economy* I, London: Routledge. Translation of Wicksell (1901) by E. Classen, ed. Lionel Robbins.

13

'PRODUCTIVITY CURVES' IN *THE ACCUMULATION OF CAPITAL*

Neri Salvadori

> Two types of diagram have been used in this discussion. In Sraffa's diagram . . . a family of curves shows each technique at all rates of profit. In the other, a family of curves ('productivity curves') shows all techniques at each rate of profit, with the corresponding values of capital in terms of output.
>
> (Robinson and Naqvi 1967: 582–3)

In *The Accumulation of Capital* Joan Robinson (1956) developed a description of technology in terms of 'productivity curves'. After the publication of *Production of Commodities by Means of Commodities* by Piero Sraffa (1960), Joan Robinson seemed to abandon that description of technology. However she still maintained its use in 1967 – in a paper written with Naqvi where some productivity curves were drawn side-by-side with other diagrams, but not really used (see the epigraph to this chapter, above) – and continued to use, for a number of years, a relationship between output per man and capital per man[1] that she called the 'pseudo-production function'. This relationship, in fact, can be obtained both from Sraffa's construction and from the Robinsonian productivity curves (see below). Finally, 'in 1974' Joan Robinson 'took the pseudo production function in pieces again' (Robinson 1980b: 138; see also 1980c: 133).[2]

In the four years between the publication of *The Accumulation of Capital* and that of *Production of Commodities by Means of Commodities* no mathematical formalization of the Robinsonian productivity curves was put forward. In the years afterwards the lack of interest by Joan Robinson herself certainly did not invite a job like that. This is a pity for at least one reason: the description of technology in terms of productivity curves is much more workable for economists with a neoclassical background and an interest in macroeconomics. This fact becomes especially relevant now that growth theory is again fashionable with endogenous growth. This is the reason why in this chapter I shall try to present a formalized version of the Robinsonian 'productivity curves'.

A 'productivity curve' is a sort of production function built upon the assumption that the rate of profit is kept constant. This assumption allows one to measure capital in terms of the consumption good correctly (consumption is assumed to be proportional to a given basket of commodities). Of course, a productivity curve has interest only at the point(s) of the function where the slope equals the given rate of profit. Because this analysis can be performed for each feasible rate of profit, the wage rate–profit rate relationship, the capital–profit rate relationship, and the output–profit rate relationship can be determined.

The present chapter can also be read as a comment on the first part of an appendix to *The Accumulation of Capital* called 'Diagrams' (1956: 411–23). Each of the following sections starts with references to this appendix which are useful for grasping the relevant concepts as stated by Joan Robinson. These concepts are then analysed with the help of the mathematical tools that have been considered appropriate. The relevant concepts mentioned are those of a 'productivity curve', a 'family of productivity curves' and a 'pseudo-production function'. Joan Robinson (1956) considered the growth rate as given and I will follow her in doing so in this chapter. Only in the appendix will I consider the growth rate as a(n independent) variable. This is done in order to stimulate possible uses of the Robinsonian 'productivity curves' outside the growth theory supported by Joan Robinson herself.

A PRODUCTIVITY CURVE

At the very beginning of the 'Diagrams' appendix we are informed that the diagrams to be dealt with illustrate what can be expressed 'in two dimensions' and therefore all relations 'can be illustrated in terms of comparisons of static positions' (Robinson 1956: 411). Then Joan Robinson adds:

> For this purpose we imagine that we are comparing positions in each of which the stock of capital goods is being maintained, item by item, and the flow of output is being consumed. . . . Output consists of commodities produced in fixed proportions, and is measured in units of a composite commodity consisting of a representative sample of production.
>
> (ibid.: 411)

Here there is a small problem. In these circumstances the problem of accumulation cannot be taken into consideration unless the 'capital goods' consist of the same 'composite commodity' as the product. In order to avoid this problem, in this chapter it will be assumed that *consumption* 'consists of commodities' *consumed* 'in fixed proportions', whereas output will consist of units of the same 'sample of consumption' only if the growth rate equals zero. If, on the contrary, the growth rate is positive, the output will be measured in *value*, the 'sample of consumption' being the numeraire. The first diagram considered in the 'Diagrams' appendix (1956: 412, Fig. 1) is 'adapted' from a diagram used by Wicksell. 'The vertical axis represents output per annum measured in units of the composite commodity. The horizontal axis represents stocks of capital goods measured in terms of the labour time required to produce them, reckoned at a given notional rate of interest' (ibid.: 411). The measure of capital suggested by Joan Robinson implies that the numeraire consists of labour. Since it is convenient to measure the values of commodities in terms of the same numeraire, in this chapter capital will be measured in terms of the 'sample of consumption' as well as the product.[3] The amount of labour is assumed to be unity, so that the vertical axis represents output per man and the horizontal axis represents the capital(−labour)[4] ratio. In Figure 13.1, OJ (J = A, B, C, D) is the output per man when all workers are employed with technique υ ($\upsilon = \alpha, \beta, \gamma, \delta$) and O$j$ ($j = b, c$) is the value of capital per man when all workers are employed with technique υ ($\upsilon = \beta, \gamma$). All these quantities are measured assuming that a given rate of profit and a given growth rate hold.

> Between Oc and Ob lie stocks of capital goods with a rising proportion of Beta outfits to Gamma outfits, so that CB represents the difference in output per man due to using Beta rather than Gamma technique, and cb represents the increase in the . . . capital ratio involved by that difference. The curve $\delta\gamma\beta\alpha$ is a *productivity curve* showing the relation between output and the . . . capital ratio.
>
> (ibid.: 411–12)

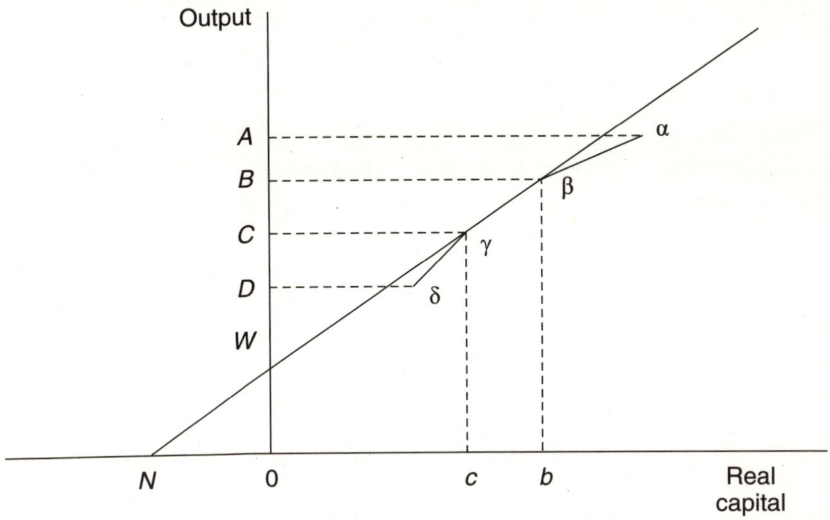

Figure 13.1

To formalize the concept of the productivity curve as introduced and used by Joan Robinson some preliminaries are needed. Let us first assume that there are n commodities. For each commodity i there is at least one process $(\mathbf{a}, \mathbf{e}_i, l)$ that is able to produce it: the n vector $\mathbf{a}$ is the material input vector, the ith unit n vector $\mathbf{e}_i$ is the output vector, and the scalar l is the labour input. A collection of n processes, each producing a different commodity, is called a *technique* and is described by the triplet $(\mathbf{A}, \mathbf{I}, \mathbf{l})$, where $\mathbf{A}$ is the material input matrix, the identity matrix $\mathbf{I}$ is the output matrix, and $\mathbf{l}$ is the labour input vector. (In the following, matrix $\mathbf{I}$ will be dropped when no doubt could arise.)

If technique $(\mathbf{A}, \mathbf{l})$ holds, commodities are consumed in proportion to vector $\mathbf{d} \geq \mathbf{0}$, the growth rate equals $g \geq 0$, and one unit of labour is employed, then the intensity vector, $\mathbf{x}$, and the consumption per man, c, must be such that:

$$\mathbf{x}^T = c\mathbf{d}^T + (1 + g)\mathbf{x}^T\mathbf{A}$$
$$\mathbf{x}^T\mathbf{l} = 1$$

If technique $(\mathbf{A}, \mathbf{l})$ holds, the rate of profit equals $r \geq 0$, and the numeraire consists of the 'sample of consumption' $\mathbf{d}$, then the price vector, $\mathbf{p}$, and the wage rate, w, must be such that:

$$\mathbf{p} = (1 + r)\mathbf{A}\mathbf{p} + w\mathbf{l}$$
$$\mathbf{d}^T\mathbf{p} = 1$$

Hence at the growth rate, g, and at the rate of profit, r, the output per man, y, and the capital ratio, k, relative to technique $(\mathbf{A}, \mathbf{l})$ are:

$$y = \mathbf{x}^T(\mathbf{I}-\mathbf{A})\mathbf{p} = w + r\mathbf{x}^T\mathbf{A}\mathbf{p} = c + g\mathbf{x}^T\mathbf{A}\mathbf{p}$$
$$k = \mathbf{x}^T\mathbf{A}\mathbf{p}$$

If there are several techniques, there is a pair (k, y) for each of them and all these k's and y's can be plotted in a diagram such as that provided by Joan Robinson because all k's (and all y's) are expressed in the same unit of measure, the 'sample of consumption'. In this way we get a set of points in the (k, y) plane. Appropriate assumptions may make this set dense. Let us first assume that, if $(\mathbf{A}, \mathbf{l})$ is a technique, then $(\mathbf{B}, \mathbf{m})$ is also a technique provided that $\mathbf{B} \geqq \mathbf{A}$ and $\mathbf{m} \geqq \mathbf{l}$. The interpretation of this assumption is that waste is always possible. Of course, technique $(\mathbf{B}, \mathbf{m})$ is an inferior technique with respect to $(\mathbf{A}, \mathbf{l})$; nevertheless it is a technique. Secondly, let us assume that, if $(\mathbf{A}_i, \mathbf{l}_i)$ and $(\mathbf{A}_j, \mathbf{l}_j)$ are techniques, then $(\lambda\mathbf{A}_i + (1 - \lambda)\mathbf{A}_j, \lambda\mathbf{l}_i + (1 - \lambda)\mathbf{l}_j)$ is also a technique, provided that $0 \leq \lambda \leq 1$. That is, returns to scale are constant and it is possible to combine several techniques. The productivity curve relative to the rate of profit r (and the growth rate g) can now be defined as the function

$$y = f_r(k) \tag{1}$$

which is obtained by choosing for each k the maximum y such that (k, y) is the pair of the capital ratio and the output per man for a technique at the rate of profit r (and growth rate g).

Is it always possible to construct a productivity curve? Certainly not. If the rate of profit is too high there is no technique that would give non-negative prices at that rate of profit, and therefore no productivity curve can be built up at that rate of profit. However, it is possible to prove that, if the rate of profit is not too high, the corresponding productivity curve can be constructed. In order to simplify the exposition, let us assume that all commodities are *basic* (in the sense of Sraffa 1960) in all techniques. As is well known, for each technique there is a maximum rate of profit, i.e. a rate of profit corresponding to a zero wage rate and positive prices. Moreover, for each positive rate of profit smaller than that, the wage rate and the prices relative to that technique are positive, whereas for each rate of profit larger than that, either the wage rate or some price relative to that technique is negative, some other prices being positive. Let R be the maximum of all these 'maximum rates of profit', i.e. R is a rate of profit corresponding to which no technique has both a positive wage rate and positive prices and at least one technique has both a zero wage rate and positive prices. It can be

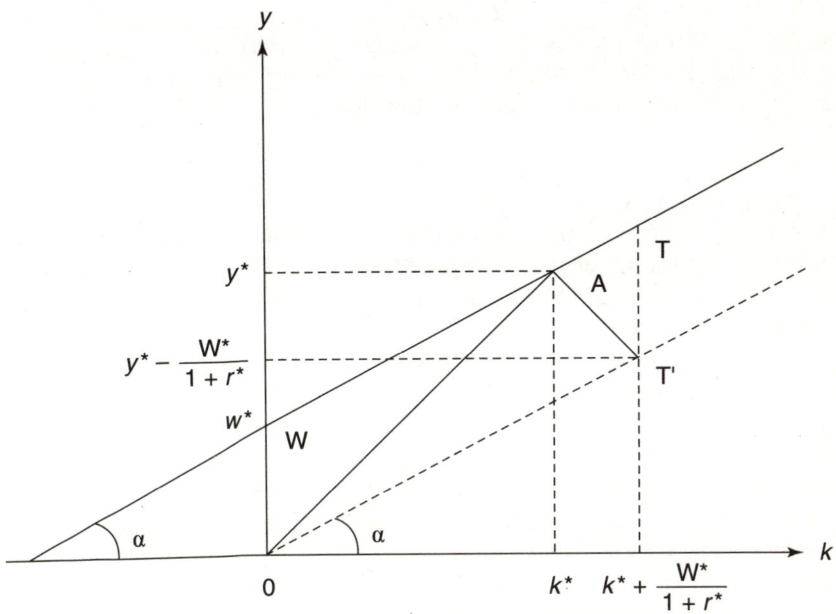

Figure 13.2

shown that, if $g \leq r^* \leq R$, the productivity curve corresponding to r^* can be constructed.

Let r^* be not smaller than g but smaller than R. We know that a cost-minimizing technique at the rate of profit r^* $(\mathbf{A}^*, \mathbf{l}^*)$ is a technique that gives rise to a wage rate w^* such that no other technique allows a wage rate higher than w^* for $r = r^*$. This technique determines also the pair of capital ratio and output per man (k^*, y^*) as depicted in Figure 13.2, where $r^* = tg\ \alpha^*$. The property of w^* just mentioned implies that all pairs (k, y) relative to the available techniques must be either on the straight line WT or under it. As a consequence, the maximum problem that is involved in determining the productivity curve always has a solution, except for those k's that cannot be associated with any technique at the rate of profit r^*.

In order to show that the productivity curve is defined for $0 \leq k \leq k^*$, let us consider the technique $(\mathbf{A}^*, (1 + t)\mathbf{l}^*)$, $t > 0$. This is an inferior technique because it is obtained from technique $(\mathbf{A}^*, \mathbf{l}^*)$ by wasting a portion of labour for each unit of labour performed (workers 'twiddle their thumbs', so to speak, for a portion of their work time). The capital ratio and the output per man associated with this technique at rate of profit r^* are $(1 + t)^{-1}k^*$ and $(1 + t)^{-1}y^*$, respectively. This is enough to assert that the productivity curve is defined for $0 \leq k \leq k^*$ and in this range it is not only not above the segment WA but also not below the segment OA. Similarly, let us consider the inferior technique $(\mathbf{A}^* + t\mathbf{l}^*\mathbf{d}^T, \mathbf{l}^*)$, $0 < t \leq (1 + r^*)^{-1}w^*$. (If $t > (1 + r)^{-1}w^*$, the wage rate is negative.) The capital ratio and the output per man associated with this technique at rate of profit r^* are $k^* + t$ and $y^* - t$, respectively. This is enough to assert that the productivity curve is defined for $k^* \leq k \leq k^* + (1 + r^*)^{-1}w^*$, and in this range it is not only not above the segment AT but also not below the segment AT′. We know enough to maintain that there is a $K > k^*$ such that the productivity curve is defined for $0 \leq k \leq K$ and it is concave and increasing on the left at $k = k^*$.

Let us now consider all the other relevant techniques. The corresponding pairs (k, y) are neither above the straight line WT nor under the straight line OT′ because at the rate of profit r^* these techniques give rise to wage rates that are not larger than w^* and not smaller than 0. If there are other cost-minimizing techniques, the corresponding pairs (k, y) are on the straight line WT, and the segments of the straight line WT joining two pairs (k, y) associated with two distinct cost-minimizing techniques are segments of the productivity curve because each point of this segment can be associated with a technique obtained by combining two cost-minimizing techniques. This is so because cost-minimizing techniques have the same wage rate and the same price vector.

In general it is not true that, if (k_i, y_i) and (k_j, y_j) are two pairs associated with two distinct techniques, then the straight-line segment joining the two points consists of pairs (k, y) that can be associated with combined techniques. This difficulty does not allow us to use a well known procedure that ensures that production functions relative to one-commodity economies are continuous, concave and not decreasing if returns to scale are constant. However, as has been shown, these properties hold at the points of the productivity curve that are on the straight line WT. Moreover, as will be shown in what follows, what happens at all other points is irrelevant in a static analysis. Then, in the following it will be assumed that there is a $K_r^* \geq k^*$ such that function (1) is defined, continuous, non-decreasing and concave for $0 \leq k \leq K_r^*$, where k^* is the larger capital ratio associated with a cost-minimizing technique. Hence, if function (1) is twice differentiable, then

$$f_r'(k) \geq 0, \quad f_r''(k) \leq 0 \quad 0 \leq k \leq K_r^*$$

If these assumptions hold, then the cost-minimizing techniques on the productivity curve are those and only those that have the property[5]

$$f_r'(k) = r$$

In the limiting case in which $r^* = R$, the straight lines WT and OT′ coincide because $w^* = 0$. As a consequence, the productivity curve is $f_R(k) = Rk$, $0 \leq k \leq k^* = K_R^*$, which is increasing, differentiable and such that $f_R'(k) = R > 0, f_R''(k) = 0$. The *technically* inferior techniques in which there is a waste of labour are also cost-minimizing because the wage rate equals zero.

A FAMILY OF PRODUCTIVITY CURVES

In the 'Diagrams' appendix Joan Robinson proceeds to compare positions with different rates of profit:

> The [consumption per man] corresponding to each technique is the same irrespective of the [rate of profit], and the outfits of capital goods required for each technique are the same from an engineering point of view. . . . The productivity curve therefore has to be redrawn for each rate of profit to exhibit the difference in the . . . capital ratio due to a different element of interest in the cost . . . of a given outfit of capital goods.
>
> (Robinson 1956: 413)

Figure 13.3, which is Figure 2 of the 'Diagrams' appendix, represents three productivity curves depicted as $\delta_i\gamma_i\beta_i\alpha_i$ (i = 1, 2, 3). 'The thick line represents all the positions of static equilibrium which are possible in the given technical conditions' (ibid.: 413–14) with a range of rates of profit. If the rate of profit is that relative to the slope of segment $\delta_3\gamma_3$, then two techniques, δ and γ, are cost-minimizing. If the rate of profit is lower, but higher than that relative to the slope of segment $\gamma_2\beta_2$, then one technique, γ,

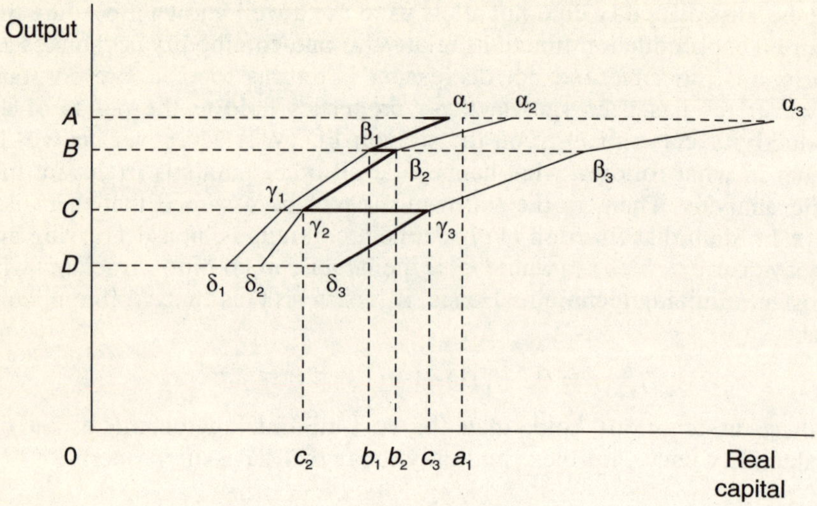

Figure 13.3

is cost-minimizing, and the change in prices related to changes in the rate of profit implies a relationship between k and y that is a straight-line segment with a slope equal to the growth rate. (In Figure 13.3 the growth rate is zero.) This is so because of the choice of the numeraire, which guarantees that consumption per man is unchanged for a given technique. If the rate of profit is that relative to the slope of segment $\gamma_2\beta_2$, then again two techniques, γ and β, are cost-minimizing. And so on.[6]

From the results presented in the previous section, we get that the function

$$y = F(k, r) := f_r(k) \tag{2}$$

is defined for $g \leq r \leq R$ and $0 \leq k \leq K(r) := K_r^*$. Function (2) is called a 'family of productivity curves' (at the given growth rate g). Let us assume that $F(k, r)$ is continuous and twice continuously differentiable; moreover

$$\frac{\partial F}{\partial k} \geq 0, \quad \frac{\partial^2 F}{\partial k^2} \leq 0$$

A simple argument will determine the relationship between the derivatives of the family of productivity curves. Let $\alpha := (\mathbf{A}, \mathbf{l})$ be a technique and let

$$k_\alpha(r) = \mathbf{x}_\alpha^T \mathbf{A} \mathbf{p}_\alpha(r) \tag{3.1}$$

$$y_\alpha(r) = \mathbf{x}_\alpha^T (\mathbf{I} - \mathbf{A}) \mathbf{p}_\alpha(r) = c_\alpha + g k_\alpha(r) = w_\alpha(r) + r k_\alpha(r) \tag{3.2}$$

where $\mathbf{x}_\alpha$ and c_α are the intensity vector and the consumption per man of technique $(\mathbf{A}, \mathbf{l})$ (at growth rate g) and $\mathbf{p}_\alpha(r)$ and $w_\alpha(r)$ are the price vector and the wage rate of technique (**A**, **l**) at rate of profit r. Let (k^*, r^*, y^*) be a point on the family of productivity curves such that $k^* = k_\alpha(r^*)$ and $y^* = y_\alpha(r^*)$, i.e. $y_\alpha(r^*) = F(k_\alpha(r^*), r^*)$.

Finally, consider the function

$$z(r) := F(k_\alpha(r), r) - y_\alpha(r)$$

In the range in which function $z(r)$ is defined it is non-negative because of the definition of the family of productivity curves. Since $z(r^*) = 0$, if $r^* < R$, the function $z(r)$ has an internal minimum at $r = r^*$. Since function $k_\alpha(r)$ is differentiable, and since function $F(k, r)$ has been assumed to be so, then, at (k^*, r^*),

$$\frac{\partial F}{\partial k} k'_\alpha(r) + \frac{\partial F}{\partial r} - y'_\alpha(r) = 0$$

Thus

$$\frac{\partial F}{\partial r} = \left(g - \frac{\partial F}{\partial k}\right) k'_\alpha(r) \tag{4}$$

since $y'_\alpha(r) = gk'_\alpha(r)$. Let us add that, for $k = k^*$ and $r = r^*$,

$$\text{if } \frac{\partial F}{\partial k} = r, \text{ then } \frac{\partial F}{\partial r} < k \tag{5}$$

since $w'_\alpha(r) < 0$ and, because of (3.2), $w'_\alpha(r) = (g - r)k'_\alpha(r) - k_\alpha(r)$.

If capital and product consist of the same commodity, then $k'_\alpha(r) = 0$ for each α and each r and, as a consequence, all the productivity curves of the family are identical to each other and the derivatives of any order of function $F(k, r)$ with respect to r equal zero.

As has been shown in the previous section, costs are minimized when

$$\frac{\partial F}{\partial k} = r \tag{6}$$

Equation (6) defines implicitly a relationship between k and r. This relationship is a correspondence because it is possible that, for some pair (k, r) in which equation (6) is satisfied, it is also true that

$$\frac{\partial^2 F}{\partial k^2} = 0 \tag{7}$$

This is the case in which two techniques are simultaneously cost-minimizing. If (k^*, r^*) is a pair satisfying equation (6) but not equality (7), then there is a neighbourhood of (k^*, r^*) in which equality (7) does not hold; in that neighbourhood the relationship between k and r is a differentiable function, and

$$\frac{\mathrm{d}k}{\mathrm{d}r} = \frac{1 - \dfrac{\partial^2 F}{\partial k \partial r}}{\dfrac{\partial^2 F}{\partial k^2}} \tag{8}$$

Equations (2) and (6) also define implicitly a relationship between y and r. This relationship too is a correspondence. If (y^*, r^*) is a pair for which there is a k^* such that y^*, r^* and k^* satisfy equations (2) and (6) but not equality (7), then there is a neighbourhood of (y^*, r^*) in which the relationship between y and r is a differentiable function and

$$\frac{\mathrm{d}y}{\mathrm{d}r} = \frac{\partial F}{\partial r} + r\frac{\mathrm{d}k}{\mathrm{d}r} = \frac{\partial F}{\partial r} + r\frac{1 - \dfrac{\partial^2 F}{\partial k \partial r}}{\dfrac{\partial^2 F}{\partial k^2}} \tag{9}$$

Finally, since

$$w = F(k, r) - rk \tag{10}$$

equations (6) and (10) define w as a function of r for $0 \leq r \leq R$. Moreover (see statement (5))

$$\frac{\mathrm{d}w}{\mathrm{d}r} = \frac{\partial F}{\partial r} - k + \left[\frac{\partial F}{\partial k} - r\right]\frac{\mathrm{d}k}{\mathrm{d}r} = \frac{\partial F}{\partial r} - k < 0$$

A PSEUDO-PRODUCTION FUNCTION

The 'thick line' in Figure 13.3 is called 'real-capital ratio curve' (p. 414) in the 'Diagrams', but it will be called here 'pseudo-production function', which is the name Joan Robinson (1979: 82, 1980b: 136, 1978b: 103) said she had borrowed from Solow (1963) and which she used in later publications.[7] A few pages of the 'Diagrams' are then utilized to move from the measurement of capital in terms of labour to measurement in terms of the product and to introduce a continuum of techniques so that both the productivity curves and the pseudo-production function can 'be drawn as smooth continuous curves' (1956: 416). Finally Joan Robinson illustrates, with the help of two figures (Fig. 5 on p. 417 and Fig. 6 on p. 418, which are here Figures 13.4 and 13.5 respectively), 'a "perverse" relationship in which a lower rate of profit corresponds to a less mechanised technique' (ibid.: 418). This 'perversity' is recognized in Figure 13.4 as a 'reswitching' of techniques. This possibility was to become famous shortly after the publication of *The Accumulation of Capital*. Technique β, in fact, is cost-minimizing for two disconnected ranges of the rate of profit, technique γ being cost-minimizing in the range in between. Therefore, either in the first switch or in the second, 'a lower rate of profit corresponds to a less mechanised technique'. Joan Robinson adds that with 'discontinuities

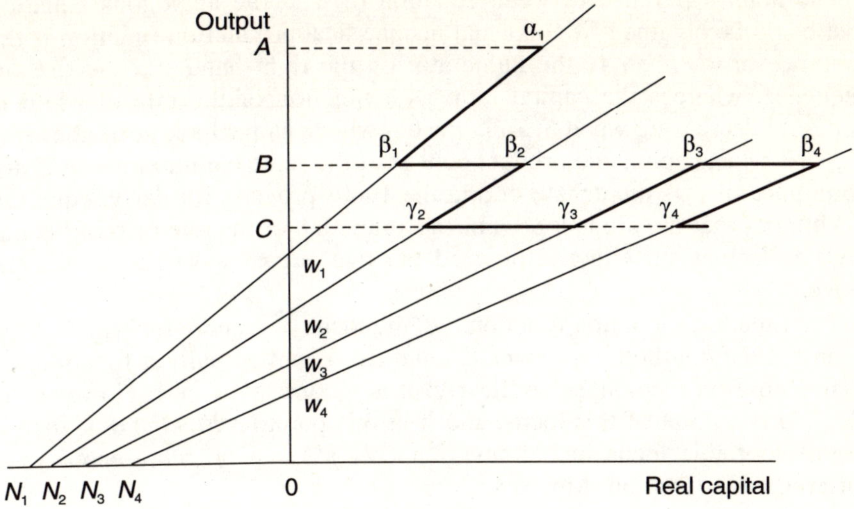

Figure 13.4

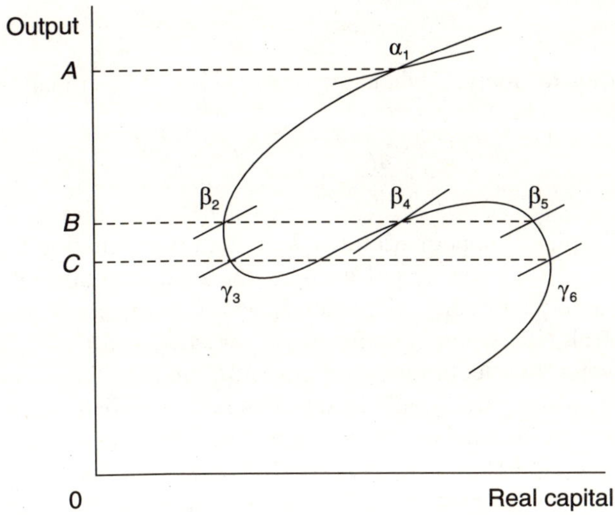

Figure 13.5

smoothed out the [pseudo-production function] would appear as in [Figure 13.5]' (ibid.: 418). As is well known, these 'perversities' were at the centre of the capital controversy during the 1960s. (A classical and almost complete account of the controversy has been provided by Harcourt 1972; see also Harcourt 1986, 1992; Kurz and Salvadori 1995: chapter 14.)

The main difference between equation (8) and the analogous equation that could be obtained from a usual neoclassical production function is the presence of $\partial^2 F/\partial k \partial r$ in the numerator on the right-hand side. As a consequence, whereas the capital ratio as a function of the rate of profit is certainly decreasing when $\partial^2 F/\partial k \partial r = 0$ – which, as we have seen above, is the case when capital and product consist of the same commodity – it is not so in general – as the debate during the 1960s proved. Similarly, equation (9) implies that the product per man as a function of the rate of profit is not always decreasing, either. Nor need the two curves have the same sign slope.

The pseudo-production function, i.e. the locus of k and y for which there is an r satisfying both equations (2) and (6), is not actually a function, as Joan Robinson recognized so clearly: it is a correspondence. However, if (k^*, y^*) is a point of this locus, and if at this point $(\partial^2 F/\partial k \partial r) \neq 1$, then a segment of this locus including point (k^*, y^*) can be represented as a differentiable function. Moreover,

$$\frac{\mathrm{d}y}{\mathrm{d}k} = r + \frac{\partial F}{\partial r} \; \frac{\dfrac{\partial^2 F}{\partial k^2}}{1 - \dfrac{\partial^2 F}{\partial k \partial r}} \tag{11}$$

It is interesting to analyse when $\mathrm{d}y/\mathrm{d}k = r$. This is obviously the case when either

$$\frac{\partial F}{\partial r} = 0 \tag{12}$$

or equation (7) holds. From equation (4) we obtain that equation (12) holds (i) when $k'_\alpha(r) = 0$ for each α and each r, i.e. when capital and product consist of the same commodity; (ii) when $k'_\alpha(r) = 0$ at the point considered, but not in general; (iii) when equation (6) is satisfied and $r = g$. Equation (7) holds (iv) when two techniques are cost-minimizing. These four cases are well known to the participants in the reswitching debate. Case (i) has been investigated by Samuelson (1962), Bhaduri (1969) and mainly Garegnani (1970); see also Robinson (1978b: 105) and Harcourt (1972: 131–54). Case (ii) is Ng's counter-example (see Harcourt 1972: 149–50). Case (iii) is related to the 'golden rule of accumulation': Bhaduri (1966) maintained that it was proved by von Weizsäcker (with no reference); Harcourt (1972: 149) referred to Koopmans (1965), Pearce (1962), Bhaduri (1966), Nell (1970) and Harcourt (1970), and maintained that the formulation presented by himself is due to Laing (with no reference); see also Robinson (1962). Case (iv) has been investigated by Solow (1967, 1970), whose interpretation of this result has been criticized by Pasinetti (1969, 1970); see also Robinson (1978a) and Harcourt (1972: 109–11, 157–69).

Finally, it is interesting to study when $\mathrm{d}y/\mathrm{d}k = g$. From equations (4) and (11) we obtain that this is the case when

$$(r - g)\left[1 - k'_\alpha(r)\,\frac{\dfrac{\partial^2 F}{\partial k^2}}{1 - \dfrac{\partial^2 F}{\partial k \partial r}}\right] = 0 \qquad (13)$$

Equation (13) holds when either $(r - g) = 0$, as in case (iii) above, or $\mathrm{d}k/\mathrm{d}r = k'_\alpha(r)$ – see equation (8). The latter condition holds on each segment of the pseudo-production function where only one technique is cost-minimizing.

The 'Diagrams' appendix goes on to deal with technical progress, the introduction of land and the value of invested capital. But we will not follow Joan Robinson in these analyses, since they are beyond the scope of this chapter.

APPENDIX

At the beginning of this chapter it was mentioned that the construction suggested by Joan Robinson might be useful to evaluate some recent contributions to growth theory known as 'endogenous growth'. But in order to do so comparisons of positions with different growth rates must be allowed. This necessitates taking more explicitly into consideration that productivity curves depend not only on the rate of profit but also on the growth rate. As a consequence, equation (1) becomes

$$y = f_{rg}(k)$$

equation (2) becomes

$$y = F(k, r, g)$$

equations (3.1–2) become

$$k_\alpha(r, g) = \mathbf{x}^T_\alpha(g)\mathbf{A}\mathbf{p}_\alpha(r)$$

$$\mathbf{y}_\alpha(r, g) = \mathbf{x}^T_\alpha(g)[\mathbf{I} - \mathbf{A}]\mathbf{p}_\alpha(r) = c_\alpha(g) + gk_\alpha(r, g) = w_\alpha(r) + rk_\alpha(r, g)$$

where $\mathbf{x}_\alpha(g)$ and $c_\alpha(g)$ are the intensity vector and the consumption per man of technique $(\mathbf{A}, \mathbf{l})$ at growth rate g. If (k^*, r^*, g^*, y^*) is a point on the family of productivity curves such that $k^* = k_\alpha(r^*, g^*)$ and $y^* = y_\alpha(r^*, g^*)$, i.e. $y_\alpha(r^*, g^*) = F(k_\alpha(r^*, g^*), r^*, g^*)$, the function

$$z(r, g) := F(k_\alpha(r, g), r, g) - y_\alpha(r, g)$$

has an internal minimum at the point (r^*, g^*). Since function $k(r, g)$ is differentiable, and if also function $F(k, r, g)$ is assumed to be so, then, at (k^*, r^*, g^*),

$$\frac{\partial F}{\partial k}\frac{\partial k_\alpha}{\partial r} + \frac{\partial F}{\partial r} - \frac{\partial y_\alpha}{\partial r} = 0$$

$$\frac{\partial F}{\partial k}\frac{\partial k_\alpha}{\partial g} + \frac{\partial F}{\partial g} - \frac{\partial y_\alpha}{\partial g} = 0$$

Thus

$$\frac{\partial F}{\partial r} = \left(g - \frac{\partial F}{\partial k}\right)\frac{\partial k_\alpha}{\partial r}$$

$$\frac{\partial F}{\partial g} = \left(r - \frac{\partial F}{\partial k}\right)\frac{\partial k_\alpha}{\partial g}$$

since $\partial y_\alpha/\partial r = g\, \partial k_\alpha/\partial r$ and $\partial y_\alpha/\partial g = r\, \partial k_\alpha/\partial g$. Hence $\partial F/\partial g$ equals zero in equilibrium.

NOTES

1 The expressions output or capital 'per unit of labour' or '*per capita*' would perhaps be more appropriate in modern literature, which prefers non-sexist expressions. Here, however, I have preferred to use expressions closer to those used by Joan Robinson in 1956 in order to avoid complications with quotations.

2 The quotation continues as follows: 'Obviously, stocks of equipment appropriate to different techniques cannot co-exist both in time and space. It should never have been drawn in a plane diagram in the first place. Different techniques are not isolated from each other on "islands". They succeed each other through time as new discoveries and inventions become operational. Normally, a new technique is *superior* to the one in use and does not have to wait for a change in the rate of profit to be installed' (Robinson 1980b: 138). In the present chapter the productivity curves are not utilized to study the procession of innovations. They are utilized as a description of a given set of techniques and a tool to determine the cost-minimizing technique(s) within this set. Hence this (self) criticism by Joan Robinson does not apply.

3 The measurement of capital in terms of the 'product' is also used by Joan Robinson herself (1956: 417 and Fig. 4 on p. 416) and by Pasinetti (1958) in an early note on Robinson's contribution.

4 The expression used by Joan Robinson is 'real-capital ratio'. The word 'real' is used because of the numeraire chosen for the capital goods, and is therefore dropped here. The word 'ratio' is connected with the fact that this variable measures the capital per unit of labour. I refrain myself from calling it 'capital–labour ratio' in the body of the chapter and I use the expression 'capital ratio', which is closer to that used by Joan Robinson.

5 If $f_r(k)$ is not continuously differentiable, the property in the text can be stated as $[f_r'(k)]^- \leq r \leq [f_r'(k)]^+$.

6 In Figure 13.3, to each increase in the ratio of profit with no switch of technique there corresponds an increase in the capital ratio k. This is so since Figure 13.3 is nothing else than Fig. 2 of the 'Diagrams' appendix, the capital ratio is measured

in terms of labour and, therefore, an increase in the rate of profit determines an increase in all prices. With the measurement of the capital ratio used in this chapter this fact does not need to hold. I am indebted to Enrico Bellino for this comment.

7 In 1977 Joan Robinson argued (see also Robinson 1978a: 92–3, 1978b: 103–4, 1979: 78–9, 1980c: 119–21): 'The pseudo-production function consists of the specification of a set of mutually non-inferior techniques, each requiring a particular stock of means of production per man employed. Each is eligible for at least one rate of profit, and none is superior to the rest at every rate of profit. When the techniques are listed in order of the flow per man employed of a homogeneous net output, it can be seen that a higher output is not necessarily associated with "more capital", that a technique that is eligible at a higher rate of profit may require a larger value of capital at the corresponding prices, and that the same technique may be eligible at widely different rates of profit' (Robinson 1980a: 21). This is exactly the way in which the pseudo-production function can be obtained from the Sraffa framework: just draw on the same (k, y) space all the values for k and y that (a) are relative to techniques that are cost-minimizing for some rate of profit and (b) are calculated at the rate of profit at which the appropriate technique is cost minimizing.

REFERENCES

Bhaduri, A. (1966) 'The concept of the marginal productivity of capital and the Wicksell effect', *Oxford Economic Papers* 18: 284–8.

—— (1969) 'On the significance of recent controversies on capital theory: a Marxian view', *Economic Journal* 79: 532–9.

Garegnani, P. (1970) 'Heterogeneous capital, the production function and the theory of distribution', *Review of Economic Studies* 37: 407–36.

Harcourt, G. C. (1970) 'G. C. Harcourt's reply to Nell', *Journal of Economic Literature* 7: 44–5.

—— (1972) *Some Cambridge Controversies in the Theory of Capital*, Cambridge: Cambridge University Press.

—— (1986) *Controversies in Political Economy: Selected Essays of G. C. Harcourt*, ed. O. F. Hamouda, Brighton: Wheatsheaf.

—— (1992) *On Political Economists and Modern Political Economy: Selected Essays of G. C. Harcourt*, ed. C. Sardoni, London: Routledge.

Harris, D. J. (1973) 'Capital, distribution, and the aggregate production function', *American Economic Review* 63: 100–13.

Koopmans, T. C. (1965) 'On the concept of optimal economic growth', in Pontificiae Academiae Scientiarum, *Scripta Varia*, Amsterdam: North-Holland.

Kurz, H. D. and Salvadori, N. (1995) *Theory of Production*, Cambridge: Cambridge University Press.

Nell, E. J. (1970) 'A note on Cambridge controversies in capital theory', *Journal of Economic Literature* 7: 41–4.

Pasinetti, L. L. (1958) 'Il recente modello di sviluppo di J. Robinson e la teoria neoclassica del capitale: alcune osservazioni', *Rivista Internazionale di Scienze Sociali* 66: 429–44.

—— (1969) 'Switches of techniques and the "rate of return" in capital theory', *Economic Journal* 79: 508–31.

—— (1970) 'Again on capital theory and Solow's "rate of return"', *Economic Journal* 80: 428–31.

Pearce, I. F. (1962) 'The end of the golden age in Solovia: a further fable for growthmen hoping to be "one up" on Oiko', *American Economic Review* 52: 1088–97.

Robinson, J. V. (1956) *The Accumulation of Capital*, London: Macmillan.

—— (1962) *Essays in the Theory of Economic Growth*, London: Macmillan.

—— (1978a) [1964] 'Pre-Keynesian theory after Keynes', in *Contributions to Modern Economics*, Oxford: Blackwell.

—— (1978b) [1970] 'Capital theory up-to-date', in *Contributions to Modern Economics*, Oxford: Blackwell.

—— (1979) [1975] 'The unimportance of reswitching', in *Collected Economic Papers* V, Oxford: Blackwell.

—— (1980a) [1977] 'What are the questions?' in *Further Contributions to Modern Economics*, Oxford: Blackwell.

—— (1980b) [1979] 'Misunderstandings in the theory of production' in *Further Contributions to Modern Economics*, Oxford: Blackwell.

—— (1980c) *Further Contributions to Modern Economics*, Oxford: Blackwell.

Robinson, J. V. and Naqvi, K. A. (1967) 'The badly behaved production function', *Quarterly Journal of Economics* 81: 579–91.

Samuelson, P. A. (1962) 'Parable and realism in capital theory: the surrogate production function', *Review of Economic Studies* 29: 193–206.

Solow, R. (1963) 'Heterogeneous capital and smooth production functions: an experimental study', *Econometrica* 31: 623–45.

—— (1967) 'The interest rate and transition between techniques', in C. H. Feinstein (ed.), *Socialism, Capitalism and Economic Growth: Essays presented to Maurice Dobb*, Cambridge: Cambridge University Press, pp. 30–9.

—— (1970) 'On the rate of return: reply to Pasinetti', *Economic Journal* 80: 423–8.

Sraffa, P. (1960) *Production of Commodities by Means of Commodities*, Cambridge: Cambridge University Press.

ACKNOWLEDGEMENTS

This chapter utilizes much of the material produced in preparing my Laurea dissertation, defended at the University of Naples in 1976. At the time I was not able to recognize that my 'family of production functions depending on the parameter *r*' was nothing less than the 'family of productivity curves' introduced by Joan Robinson. This became clear to me only a few years later when I read a paper by Don Harris (1973). This is perhaps the place to express my gratitude to Bruno Jossa and Augusto Graziani. The former was my supervisor in the preparation of my Laurea thesis. Suggestions and advice from both of them have been forthcoming ever since. My dissertation was also read, as far as I remember, by Pierangelo Garegnani, Giorgio Lunghini, Marco Lippi, Massimo Marrelli and Ian Steedman. I thank them all, as well as Enrico Bellino, Heinz Kurz and the editors of *The Economics of Joan Robinson* (1996), C. Marcuzzo, L. L. Pasinetti and A. Roncaglia, in whose volume this chapter first appeared, and who commented on a draft. The figures from the 'Diagrams' appendix to *The Accumulation of Capital* by Joan Robinson are reproduced here by permission of the publishers, Macmillan

Ltd. I should like to thank Macmillan for having granted free permission to use the figures. Financial support from the Italian Ministry of University and Scientific Research (MURST) and the Italian National Research Council (CNR) is also gratefully acknowledged.

NAME INDEX

Aghion, P. 86
Allen, R. G. D. 119–20
Arrow, K. J. 14, 25, 28, 32, 48–9, 83, 90, 248–51

Baldone, S. 18, 226, 228
Baranzini, M. 175, 246
Barone, E. 119
Barro, R. J. 67, 75
Barton, J. 169
Baudeau, N. Abbé de 215, 221
Baumol, W. J. 41, 50–1
Becker, G. S. 86
Bellino, E. 260–1
Bénard, J. 216
Bhaduri, A. 255, 270
Bharadwaj, K. 10, 117–18
Bidard, Ch. 56, 147
Blanqui, A. 209
Blaug, M. 64, 144, 173
Bliss, C. J. 248, 255
Bloomfield. A. I. 57, 59
Böhm-Bawerk, E. von 6–7, 177, 218, 235, 247
Borland, J. 86
Bortkiewicz, L. von 18, 34, 40–1, 47–8, 50, 204, 206, 219
Brody, A. 48, 56
Broome, J. 145
Brown, M. 226, 231
Bruno, M. 227, 230, 247, 255
Burgstaller, A. 17
Burmeister, E. 18, 145, 227, 229–31, 247–8, 255–6

Campanelli, G. 51
Cannan, E. 179
Cantillon, R. 34
Caravale, G. 179
Carneiro, D. 145
Cartelier, J. 217
Carver, T. N. 120
Casarosa, C. 149, 179
Cassel, G. 25–8, 32–3, 45–7, 49–50
Chaing, W. W. 226, 231
Chakravarty, S. 25, 51
Champernowne, D. 31, 33, 49, 52
Charasoff, G. von 18, 34–6, 40, 47, 50, 206
Chipman, J. S. 48
Clark, J. B. 6, 244, 247
Clausewitz, C. von 235, 248, 254
Condorcet, M. J. A. N. Caritat de 219
Cournot, A. A. 49
Craver, E. 48

D'Agata, A. 89, 147, 172
D'Ippolito, G. 255
Daire, E. 208–10, 215–16, 219–20
Dana, R. A. 251
Debreu, G. 14, 50, 248–9, 251
Dmitriev, V. K. 18, 34, 49–50, 206
Dobb, M. H. 148, 176
Dore, M. 25, 50, 51
Dorfman, R. 25, 49
Dupont de Nemours, P. S. 208, 220
Duffner, H. 50
Dühring. E. 211, 221
Duménil, G. 251, 255

Eatwell, J. 117, 145
Edgeworth, F. Y. 118
Egidi, M. 50
Ekelund, R. B. 64
Eltis, W. 218

Engels, F. 187, 198, 207–8, 210–1, 215–16, 219–22

Faccarello, G. 56, 219
Ferguson, C. E. 247
Fisher, I. 255–6
Flaschel, P. 138, 145, 147
Florenzano, M. 251
Fox-Genovese, E. 216
Franklin, J. 157
Freni, G. 122, 172
Frobenius, G. 41, 51, 137

Gale, D. 51
Garegnani, P. 18–19, 56, 118–19, 122, 144, 147, 205, 219, 244, 247, 250, 253–5, 270, 261
Geanakoplos, J. 253
Gehrke, Ch. 18, 56, 65, 89
Georgescu-Roegen, N. 90
Gibb, J. W. 49
Gilibert, G. 50–1, 56, 216–17
Goldfeld, S. M. 41, 50–1
Goodwin, R. M. 25, 33, 51
Gram, H. 95, 175
Gray, J. 210, 221
Graziani, A. 261
Grossman, G. M. 67

Hague, D. C. 29, 32–3, 247
Hahn, F. H. 248–51, 255
Harcourt, G. C. 56, 87, 117, 122, 147, 175, 235, 243, 246, 255–6, 270
Harris, D. 261
Harrod, R. F. 66, 142–3
Hayek, F. A. von 13–4
Hebert, R. F. 64
Helpman, E. 67
Henderson, J. P. 51
Hicks, J. R. 11, 13, 113, 142–3, 158, 166, 179, 255
Hollander, S. 57, 59–60, 176, 178–9, 182, 184
Howitt, P. 86
Huth, T. 50

Jevons, W. S. 6, 66
Jones, L. E. 75, 78
Jossa, B. 147, 261

Kaldor, N. 29–33, 49, 51, 66, 70, 73, 118
Kalmbach, P. 56
Keynes, J. M. 66, 104–5, 116–19, 148, 150, 167, 235, 240–1, 249, 255
King, R. G. 75–6, 78–9, 81
Knies, K. 218
Knight, F. H. 86
Koopmans, T. C. 49, 90, 270
Krause, U. 56
Krelle, W. 247
Kuczynski, M. 208, 211, 220
Kurz, H. D. 14, 18–19, 25, 38, 49–50, 63–4, 75, 86–7, 89, 97, 122, 137, 143, 145, 151, 160, 172–3, 181, 184, 206, 218–19, 256, 261

Laing, N. F. 270
Le Van, C. 251
Leijonhufvud, A. 48
Leontief, W. 15, 18, 35, 41, 50, 51, 206
Leske, K. W. 208
Levhari, D. 246–7, 255
Lévy, D. 251, 255
Lindahl, E. 13–4
Lippi, M. 261
Lucas, R. E. 17, 67, 75, 79–83, 87
Lunghini, G. 261
Lutz, F. A. 29, 32–3, 247

McCulloch, J. R. 126–8, 130–1, 144, 151
McKenzie L. W. 25
Mainwaring, L. 227, 255
Mäki, U. 235–6, 242
Malinvaud, E. 253
Malle, S. 216
Malthus, T. R. 70, 119, 125, 128–9, 133, 150, 152, 164, 177, 179–80, 241
Maneschi, A. 103, 117–8
Manuelli, R. 75, 78
Marcuzzo, C. 124, 261
Marrelli, M. 261
Marschak, J. 48
Marshall, A. 6–7, 19, 32, 41, 51, 103–5, 107, 112–19, 176, 182, 242, 244
Marx, K. H. 6, 33–4, 39–40, 42, 66, 119, 137, 143, 148–50, 166, 187–222
Medio, A. 145
Meek, R. L. 216
Menger, C. 66
Menger, K. 27–9, 32, 36, 48
Mercier de la Rivière, P.-P. 209

Mill, J. 128
Mill, J. S. 62, 119, 150
Mirabeau, V. R. Marquis de 194
Mises, L. von 7
Miyao, T. 146
Mongiovi, G. 56
Montani, G. 172
Morishima, M. 33, 148–53, 155, 158–73, 176, 182, 184, 247
Moride, P. 216
Murphy, K. M. 86
Myint, H. 57, 62–3

Naqvi, K. A. 255, 259
Negishi, T. 57, 173
Nell, E. J. 270
Neumann, J. von 15–16, 18, 25–34, 36–8, 40–1, 45–52, 66, 95, 158, 173, 206, 207
Newman, P. 51, 241
Ng, Y. K. 270
Nuti, D. M. 49–50

O'Brien, D. 64
Oakley, A. 207–8, 210, 219–20
Ochoa, E. M. 247
Okishio, N. 51
Ong, N.-P. 143
Ostwald, W. 49

Panico, C. 114, 119–20, 147
Pasinetti, L. L. 149–50, 152–3, 155, 158, 161, 163–4, 172–3, 175, 227, 230, 246, 255–6, 259, 261, 270
Peach, T. 176–84
Pearce, I. F. 270
Perron, O. 51, 137
Petrovič, P. 247
Petty, W. 8, 34, 125
Pigou, A. C. 120
Porta, P. L. 56
Proudhon, P. J. 211
Punzo, L. F. 28, 51, 56

Quadrio-Curzio, A. 172
Quesnay, F. 8, 34, 187–8, 194–5, 197–8, 201–3, 206, 208–11, 213–21

Ramsey, F. 244
Rebelo, S. 75–81
Remak, R. 18, 27, 40–8, 51–2
Ricardo, D. 3–4, 6, 8–9, 15, 33–4, 37–9, 47, 49, 59, 66–7, 69–72, 85–6, 104–5, 116–19, 123–33, 138, 140–5, 148–53, 158–62, 164–73, 176–84, 188–90, 203–4, 206, 217–18, 255
Rieter, H. 216
Robbins, L. 57
Robinson, J. V. 19, 113–14, 116, 173, 242–4, 255, 259–73
Rodbertus, K. J. 210
Rodriguez-Clare, A. 86
Roederer, P.-L. 219
Romer, P. M. 67, 75, 83–4
Roncaglia, A. 117–18, 122, 145, 147, 261
Rosselli, A. 124

Sala-i-Martin, X. 67, 75
Salvadori, N. 14, 18–19, 25, 49, 56, 75, 86–7, 89, 94–5, 97, 120, 137, 143, 145, 147, 151, 160, 172–3, 181, 206, 218–19, 259
Samuelson, P. A. 16–17, 25, 32, 49–50, 56, 60, 90, 95, 119–20, 144–5, 149, 166, 172, 175, 217, 226, 230, 243–7, 255, 270
Sato, K. 247
Say, J. B. 59, 63, 66, 148–51, 166–7, 170–2, 182, 255
Seton, F. 217
Schefold, B. 49, 56, 119–20, 138, 147
Schicchi, S. 216
Schlesinger, K. 28, 47–8
Schmalz, T. A. H. 209, 211, 216
Schumpeter, J. A. 150, 216
Schwarz, H. A. 41
Sheshinski, E. 227, 230, 247, 255
Smith, A. 3, 5, 8, 15, 18, 34, 37–9, 47, 50, 57–64, 66–9, 73, 86–7, 104, 125, 164, 178, 180, 183, 188–90, 196, 203–4, 208, 218
Solow, R. M. 17, 25, 29, 49, 66, 78, 243, 256, 270
Sraffa, P. 15, 18–19, 25, 31, 37, 50–1, 85, 95, 103–20, 123–4, 127–8, 130, 132–3, 134–43, 145–6, 148–50, 153–5, 158–63, 172–3, 176–84, 206, 217, 241–2, 244, 246–53, 255, 259, 263
Steedman, I. 5, 18, 32, 50, 56, 95, 122, 143, 147, 172–3, 175, 230, 255, 261
Stigler, G. J. 64
Stiglitz, J. E. 255

Sylos Labini, P. 116, 118
Sweezy, P. M. 218

Talamo, O. 117, 118–19
Taylor, L. 145
Torrens, R. 4, 34, 47, 49, 128, 144, 159, 219
Tozer, J. E. 39–40
Trower, H. 127
Tsuru, S. 218
Turgot, A. R. J. 190–5, 209, 219–20
Turnovsky, S. J. 247

Ulam, S. 41
Uzawa, H. 79

Vaggi, G. 216
Varri, P. 50
Viner, J. 57, 107, 120

Wald, A. 28, 47, 48
Walras, L. 6, 9–10, 25–7, 29, 32–3, 37, 45, 51, 66, 148–50, 160, 182
Weintraub, E. R. 25, 28, 48, 51
Weizsäcker, C. Ch. 94, 270
Whewell, W. 39, 40, 47, 51
Wicksell, K. 6, 12–4, 29, 32, 50, 150, 244, 255, 261
Wicksteed, P. H. 110–1, 117
Wittgenstein, L. 1
Wittmann, W. 41–2, 45
Woods, J. E. 145

Yang, X. 86
Young, A. 69, 73

Zauberman, A. 49
Zazzaro, A. 89
Zeuthen, F. 50

SUBJECT INDEX

absolute cost 57
absolute value 125, 127–8, 131, 151
aggregate production function 13, 152–3, 155–8, 172, 226, 231, 243–4
agricultural theory of the rate of profits 34, 177–8, 191

backstop technology 69, 72–3

capital, adjusted in long period 6, 8, 49, 68, 251
capital aggregation 226, 231
capital controversy 13, 87, 235–6, 243–54, 269; reswitching of techniques 13, 154, 226–7, 245–8, 254–5, 268, 270; reverse capital deepening 13, 245, 247–8, 254–5
capital reversing *see* capital controversy, reverse capital deepening
capital, human and physical 17–18, 68, 75, 77–82, 85, 87
capitalism and socialism 42–5
ceteris paribus *see* partial equilibrium
change in the proportions in which factors are employed 103, 108, 110, 112; *see also* returns, decreasing
change in the scale of production 103, 108, 112; *see also* returns, increasing
choice of technique 13, 15, 38–40, 46–7, 154, 245
circular flow 26, 33–4, 47, 50, 56, 207
competition 3, 11, 17, 26, 37–9, 49, 69, 80, 105–6, 112, 115, 117, 119, 144, 177, 181, 198, 203–4, 217, 236, 241–2, 245, 249, 251, 255
content of a theory *see* method vs. content of a theory *and* set of data defining the content of a theory
corn model 133, 138, 145, 177–82
criticism (different ways to cope with); strategy of elimination 236, 239, 246; strategy of misrepresentation 236, 239; strategy of negligence 236, 238, 247; strategy of playing down the new results 239, 248; strategy of unification 236, 240, 242, 248

demand and supply 10–3, 17, 26–8, 31–2, 41, 51, 85–6, 108, 144, 171, 182–4, 236, 245–6, 252–4
depreciation 76, 158–9, 168, 172, 202, 230
distribution and relative prices 13, 32, 123, 126, 129, 134, 137–46, 153, 161, 163, 173, 181, 244, 253, 255, 266
division of labour 3, 57, 59, 68–9, 73, 86, 192, 242; *see also* returns, increasing
duality 34, 36, 47–8, 207, 219
dynamic theory 2–7, 13–14, 18

economies of scale *see* returns, increasing
effective demand 44, 66, 180, 201, 222, 255
effectual demand 5
endogeneous growth theory 17, 32, 66–87, 259, 271
exchangeable value 126–8, 131, 151
excess demand 86, 170–1
excess supply 28, 37, 50, 58, 61, 63, 170–1
exchangeable value 126–31, 151
externality 73, 78–80, 84, 112–20

feudalism 194–5, 208
firm 73, 83, 103–7, 112–20
fixed capital 29, 33, 67, 94, 104, 126, 130, 143, 150, 158–9, 167–73, 190, 204–5, 215
foreign trade 18, 57–64, 149, 151, 164–6, 172
full employment of labour 12, 47, 66–7, 144, 149, 167, 245, 249

general glut of commodities 59, 167, 180
given quantities (in Sraffa) 103–7, 113–17, 153
gravitation 3–5, 18, 66, 179, 255

horizon (finite or infinite) 14, 17, 251

inequalities in the analysis of cost-minimizing techniques 28, 34, 36, 38–40, 47–8, 50
instantaneous production 151–2, 172
interspatial and intertemporal comparisons (in Ricardo) 123–6, 128, 133, 161, 181–2
intertemporal equilibrium 2, 13–14, 17, 83, 248, 251–5
invariable measure of value 123–8, 132–3, 138, 140–5, 151, 160–1, 173, 181

joint production 15–16, 18, 25, 37, 40, 46, 58, 60–4, 90, 159, 231

labour theory of value 9, 18, 36, 60, 133, 143, 145, 162, 176, 180, 188, 191–6, 202–5, 227, 229, 230
labour power 190–4, 213
learning by doing 83
long-period method 2–7, 13, 18, 180

machinery 6, 37–9, 150–1, 165–73, 177, 180, 191, 198, 201, 222
Malthusian law of population 70, 164
market (actual) values 3–7, 18, 86, 164, 179, 183, 255
material-based theory of value 188, 191–6, 205, 217
mercantilism 58–9, 62–3, 208, 216
method vs. content of a theory 2–7, 14, 28, 38, 242

natural (normal) values 3–9, 13, 45, 47, 68, 86, 129, 151, 163–7, 172, 179, 181, 183, 198, 204, 246, 250–1, 255
natural resources 4, 6, 8–10, 14–15, 29, 37, 45, 47, 50, 68, 71, 153, 183, 252
neo-classical economics 1–2, 6–7, 9–19, 26–8, 31–3, 37, 48–9, 66–8, 85–6, 218, 236, 243–56
Neumann, von, growth model 15–16, 25–52, 95
non-substitution theorem 16–19, 77, 79–81, 87, 90–4
numeraire 11, 124–32, 136–46, 151–2, 159–63, 172–3, 262, 266, 272

organic composition of capital 202, 226–31

partial equilibrium 117–19, 241
period of production 4, 11, 29, 33, 46, 132, 150–2, 158, 168, 172
physiocracy 187–221
pluralism 236–7
prices of production 4, 8, 183, 189, 198, 203–6, 210, 251
productive and unproductive labour 190, 192, 194, 197, 201, 208, 216, 218
productivity curves 19, 74, 259–74
protective belts 235–6, 238–42, 254
pseudo-production function 243, 259–60, 268–71, 273
public good 79, 83

quantity of capital 10–11, 32, 46, 66, 136, 243, 251, 254

rate of profit as determined by technology and profit maximization alone 76–7, 79–81, 84–5, 87
rent theory 10, 37, 150, 152–8, 172
reswitching of techniques *see* capital controversy, reswitching of techniques
returns 103–20; constant 15–16, 29, 69, 78–83, 87, 90, 105, 108, 114, 117–20, 145, 262, 265; decreasing 69, 71, 73, 75, 77, 84, 107–8, 110–13, 119, 153–4, 178–9, 183; increasing 57, 68–9, 73–4, 83–5, 107, 112, 114; variable 103–4, 107–8, 112–14, 116–17

reverse capital deepening *see* capital controversy, reverse capital deepening
rule of free goods 28, 30, 34, 36–7, 40, 47, 50, 60–1, 63, 91

Say's law 59, 63, 66, 148–51, 166–7, 170–2, 176–7, 179–80, 222, 255
schemes of reproduction 119, 188, 196–203, 219, 221–2
set of data defining the content of a theory 2, 7–10, 15–16, 31, 67–9, 181, 202–4, 206, 249–52
social surplus 8, 192, 195, 197, 203, 207
sphere of circulation and sphere of production 192, 197, 202, 204, 206, 214
Standard commodity 15, 104, 123–4, 132–43, 144–6, 149, 160–3, 173, 181–2
Standard system 50, 133, 136–8, 141, 145–6, 160, 162–3
standard of value *see* numeraire
static method 4, 7, 13–4, 118, 183, 265
stationary state 7, 16, 49, 70–1, 94, 164, 167, 173, 179
steady state 16–17, 28, 46, 76, 78, 83–5
substitutability 11, 13, 27, 29, 73, 90, 171, 245
superposed prices 41–3, 47, 51
surplus 49, 85, 134, 137, 162, 168, 182, 189–95, 202–3
surplus product 70, 143, 167–8, 188–95, 202, 204, 206, 217
surplus-labour 195, 202
surplus-value 36, 190, 192, 194–5, 197, 201, 202, 204, 206–7, 209, 213, 219–20
surrogate production function 230, 243–4

Tableau Économique 8, 34, 187–8, 191, 196–8, 201–4, 206, 208–11, 213–16, 218, 221–2
technological change 4, 51, 71, 83, 133, 142–4, 203
technology producing labour 18, 74, 82–3, 85
temporary equilibrium 2, 13–14, 248, 252–4, 256
Turnpike theorem 16–17, 49

unemployment 43, 150, 166, 170–1, 249
Uruguay round 64
use-value 60, 190–4, 196, 198, 218

vent for surplus 18, 57–64

Walras-Cassel model 25–7, 32–3, 45
Wicksell effects 244, 255